Rome

Anthony Pereira and Nick Skidmore

Mitchell Beazley

THE AMERICAN EXPRESS ® TRAVEL GUIDES

Published by Mitchell Beazley International Ltd, Michelin House, 81 Fulham Road, London SW3 6RB

Edited, designed and produced by Castle House Press, Llantrisant, Mid Glamorgan CF7 8EU, Wales

First published 1983 as *The American Express Pocket Guide to Rome*. Second edition 1986, reprinted 1988. Third edition 1990. This edition, revised and updated, published 1992.

A cataloguing-in-publication record for this book is available from the British Library.

ISBN 1 85732 923 6

The editor, authors and publisher thank Dottore Elvio Costanzo of the Rome Provincial Tourist Board (EPT), the London office of the Italian State Tourist Board, Marina Engel and Sylvia Hughes-Williams for their assistance during the preparation of this edition.

FOR THE SERIES:
General Editor:
   David Townsend Jones
Map Editor: David Haslam
Indexer: Hilary Bird
Cover design:
   Roger Walton Studio

FOR THIS EDITION:
Edited on desktop by:
   Sharon Charity
Art editor: Eileen Townsend Jones
Illustrators: Jeremy Ford
   (David Lewis Artists), Illustrated
   Arts, Oxford Illustrators Ltd,
   Sylvia Hughes-Williams,
   David Evans
Gazetteer: Sharon Charity
Cover photo: Tony Stone Worldwide

FOR MITCHELL BEAZLEY:
Art Director: Tim Foster
Managing Editor: Alison Starling
Production: Sarah Schuman

PRODUCTION CREDITS:
Maps by Lovell Johns, Oxford, England
Metropolitana map by TCS, Aldershot, England
Typeset in Garamond and News Gothic
Desktop layout in Ventura Publisher
Linotronic output by Tradespools Limited, Frome, England
Printed and bound in Great Britain by HarperCollins Manufacturing, Glasgow

Contents

Culture, history and background

Basic information

Planning and walks

Sights and places of interest

Where to stay

Eating and drinking

Nightlife and entertainment

Shopping

Recreation

Excursions

Words and phrases

Maps

How to use this book

Few rules and pointers are needed to understand how this travel guide works. Your enjoyment and efficiency in reading and using it will be enhanced if you note the following remarks.

HOW TO FIND WHAT YOU WANT

- For the general organization of the book, see CONTENTS, on the pages preceding this one.
- Wherever appropriate, chapters and sections are arranged alphabetically, with headings appearing in **CAPITALS.**
- Often these headings are followed by location and practical information printed in *italics*.
- As you turn the pages, you will find subject headers, similar to those used in telephone directories, printed in CAPITALS in the top corner of each page.
- If you still cannot find it, look in the comprehensive and exhaustively cross-referenced INDEX at the back of the book.
- Following the index, a LIST OF STREET NAMES provides map references for all roads and streets mentioned in the book that are located within the area covered by the main city maps.

CROSS-REFERENCES

These are printed in SMALL CAPITALS, referring you to other sections or alphabetical entries in the book. Care has been taken to ensure that such cross-references are self-explanatory. Often, page references are also given, although their excessive use would be intrusive and ugly.

FLOORS

We use the European convention in this book: "ground floor" means the floor at ground level (called by Americans the "first floor").

KEY TO AREA MAP SYMBOLS

■	Place of Interest	——	Minor Road
▨	Built-up Area	══SS4══	Road Number
▨	Park	- - -	Ferry
═O═	Autostrada (with access point)	════	Railway
═ ═	Autostrada (under construction)	✈	Airport
		✦	Airfield
═══	Main Road / 4-Lane Highway	⌂	Abbey, Monastery
		∴	Ancient Site, Ruin
▬▬	Other Main Road	ℜ	Good Beach
——	Secondary Road	**16**	Adjoining Page No.

KEY TO SYMBOLS

☎	Telephone	ⓜ	MasterCard/Eurocard
Tx	Telex	VISA	Visa
Fx	Facsimile (fax)	🚗	Secure garage
★	Recommended sight	🏠	Quiet hotel
☆	Worth a visit	⬥	Elevator
❀	Good value (in its class)	♿	Facilities for disabled
i	Tourist information		people
⬅	Parking	⬜	TV in each room
🏛	Building of architectural	☎	Telephone in each room
	interest	🐕	Dogs not allowed
†	Church or cathedral	❀	Garden
🔲	Free entrance	⬳	Outstanding views
🔳	Entrance fee payable	🎾	Tennis
▪	Entrance expensive	⛱	Sauna
📷	Photography forbidden	👥	Conference facilities
✗	Guided tour	♈	Bar
▪	Cafeteria	⬛	Refrigerator in room
✴	Special interest for children	⬏	Restaurant
🐦	Hotel	⬤	Simple (restaurant)
■	Simple (hotel)	⬢	Luxury (restaurant)
🏨	Luxury (hotel)	🍴	A la carte available
⬜	Cheap	▪	Set (fixed-price) menu
▨	Inexpensive		available
▨	Moderately priced	≣	Good for wines
▨	Expensive	🚗	Open-air dining
▨	Very expensive	⬤	Disco dancing
⊞	Air conditioning	♫	Live music
AE	American Express	▶	Nightclub
◉	Diners Club	⬛	Revue

PRICE CATEGORIES

These are denoted by the symbols ⬜ (cheap), ▨ (inexpensive), ▨ (moderately priced), ▨ (expensive) and ▨ (very expensive). For **hotels** and **restaurants** they correspond approximately to the following actual local prices, which give a guideline **at the time of printing**. Naturally, prices tend to rise, but, with a few exceptions, hotels and restaurants will remain in the same price category.

Price categories	Corresponding to approximate prices	
	for **hotels**	for **restaurants**
	double room with bath and breakfast (single not much cheaper)	*meal for one with service, tax and house wine*
▨ very expensive	over ₺400,000	over ₺150,000
▨ expensive	₺250,000-400,000	₺100,000-150,000
▨ moderately priced	₺175,000-250,000	₺75,000-100,000
▨ inexpensive	₺100,000-175,000	₺50,000-75,000
⬜ cheap	under ₺100,000	under ₺50,000

About the authors

The late **Anthony Pereira**, who died in 1982 just before publication of the first edition of this guide, was a travel writer with profound knowledge of Italy. His other publications included guides to Sicily, Naples, Pompeii and Southern Italy. Contributors to the original edition included **Burton Anderson**, **Diana Grant** and **Helen Langdon**.

This fourth edition has been extensively revised and updated by **Nick Skidmore**, an independent TV producer who lived for two years in Italy as a freelance journalist and writer.

Important contributions were also made throughout this edition by **Andrea Carlino**, who lives in Rome. He is the author of a forthcoming book on Renaissance science to be published by Einaudi for the University of San Marino.

A message from the series editor

In redesigning *American Express Rome* we aimed to make this revised and updated edition simple and instinctive to use, like all its sister volumes in our new, larger paperback format.

The hallmarks of the relaunched series are clear, classic typography, confidence in fine travel writing for its own sake, and trust in our readers' innate intelligence to find their way around the books without heavy-handed signposting by editors.

Readers with anything less than 20:20 vision will doubtless also enjoy the larger, clearer type, and may even dispense with the mythical magnifying glasses we never issued free with the old pocket book series.

Updating author **Nick Skidmore**, together with contributing author **Andrea Carlino** and editor **Sharon Charity**, have made enormous efforts to ensure that this edition is as accurate and up to date as possible at the moment it goes to press. But time and change are forever the enemies, and in between editions we appreciate it when you, our readers, keep us informed of changes that you discover.

As ever, I am indebted to all readers who wrote during the preparation of this book. Please remember that your feedback is extremely important to our efforts to tailor the series to the very distinctive tastes and requirements of our sophisticated international readership.

Send your comments to me at Mitchell Beazley International Ltd, Michelin House, 81 Fulham Road, London SW3 6RB; or, in the US, c/o American Express Travel Guides, Prentice Hall Travel, 15 Columbus Circle, New York, NY 10023.

David Townsend Jones

Rome

The eternal city: 2,000 years of change

The name of Rome will always hold an irresistible fascination for the traveler. The influence of the city that grew from the farms and villages perched on seven insignificant hills has reached farther than even its greatest emperor could have dared imagine. Countries and continents undreamed of by Augustus owe their language and their laws, their calendar and their faith to Rome.

The continuity of the city as a seat of power under the papacy and as capital of modern Italy has ensured the survival of many of its great monuments. The Pantheon, triumphal arches and columns stand today much as they did on the day of their completion, although most of the temples, stadiums and baths are now in ruins, and countless treasures still lie buried beneath later construction.

The area to which most tourists are drawn is the heart of old Rome, across the river from St Peter's. Here the rich complexity of 2,000 years of decay and renewal can bewilder even the best informed of sightseers. On entering Piazza Navona, do you see the original form of Domitian's racetrack, or a magnificent open-air gallery of Baroque sculpture, or simply a convenient pedestrian mall with inviting café tables at which to rest your aching feet?

With such dazzling riches to choose from it is best to be selective in your goals. Devout pilgrims will make straight for Piazza San Pietro, but the less pious visitor with a casual interest in architecture and the growth of Christianity must choose between 280 churches within the Aurelian Walls, and miles of catacombs without. Of particular historical significance are the mosaics and frescoes of the very early churches and basilicas. But if your taste is for the Baroque, the city abounds in fine examples by Bernini and Borromini. For many people, however, it is a Romanesque church such as Santa Maria in Cosmedin, with its humble brick and tile exterior and simple campanile, which most eloquently evokes the spirit of Rome.

Compared with the grandiose monuments of other ages, the scale of Romanesque architecture is reassuringly human. This is no accident, for in the late Middle Ages Rome's fortunes were at their lowest ebb. As the popes' powers fluctuated in never-ending quarrels with the Holy Roman Emperors, the population dwindled from one million to as little as 30,000. A fraction of the land enclosed by the original walls was built upon. Sheep and cattle grazed on the Capitol and in the Forum, while the Colosseum and other monuments served as quarries for local builders.

In the 15th century, when the popes returned from Avignon after the Great Schism, Rome began to expand once more. Julius II, more Renaissance man than prelate, brought in by his military exploits sufficient revenue to rebuild the city. He ordered the destruction of the old St Peter's and commissioned Bramante to design its replacement. When Michelangelo and Raphael were summoned to the court, Rome became once more the greatest artistic center in the world.

However, it was not long before the Church had to withstand the most potent challenge ever directed at its authority, as the tide of Protestantism swept across Catholic Europe. Papal finances were also hard hit by the sacking of Rome by the Emperor Charles V. Fortunately for the city, the zeal of the Counter-Reformation was employed not only in the imposition of orthodoxy but also in erecting even more spectacular churches to the glory of the orthodox God. The astute tax reforms of Sixtus V provided subsequent popes with seemingly bottomless purses. Commissions poured forth, the lion's share falling into the hands of Gianlorenzo Bernini.

After the flourishing of the Baroque, two centuries passed before the city experienced any vigorous renewal. In 1870 the pope was forced to cede his temporal dominions to the House of Savoy, and Rome became capital of a united Italy. A vast building program was undertaken to house the ministries of the new kingdom. The centralization of government continued under Mussolini, and Rome today remains a mecca for civil servants, rivaling even Brussels in her bureaucracy.

The population of the city now exceeds three million. In the postwar years building laws were openly flouted and whole streets sprang up, unmarked on any official map. Over this chaos presides the Comune di Roma, the city council. Seated in traditional splendor in Michelangelo's Palazzo Senatorio on the Capitol, the councilors devise well-meaning laws that prove impossible to enforce. The city's debts are legendary, and the lack of essential amenities causes grave concern. A few drops of Tiber water can be fatal, due to the untreated sewage that flows into the river. Yet, by a typically Roman paradox, the city's magnificent ornamental drinking fountains provide only pure spring water brought by aqueducts from distant hills.

Years of subjection to the Church have made the Romans outspokenly anticlerical and anti-authoritarian, yet they seem resigned to the fact that things will never change. Visitors disturbed by what they read of terrorism and kidnappings have little to fear: the majority of Romans are far too easy-going to engage in violent political activism. A more likely threat is posed by handbag snatchers on motorcycles and scooters. Italian traffic is another hazard, but drivers are quick-witted and usually manage to avoid pedestrians except, curiously, on statutory crossings.

Belated attempts have recently been made to save Rome from the automobile by building an extension of the Metropolitana to the east of the city and a much-needed train service to Fiumicino Airport. The historical centre is closed to private cars for most of the day to protect people and monuments from the danger of fumes.

Public and private sponsorship have provided much-needed financial support for restorations, archeological excavations and urban projects that concern historic areas of the city. But Rome, in which almost every stone is a significant piece of history, is a difficult and demanding city to run, and the notoriously languid pace of Italian bureaucracy sometimes makes such efforts more arduous than they need be. So, although Trajan's forum has at last been reopened to the public after major restoration, the elaborate plans to excavate the rest of Via dei Fori Imperiali and turn the whole area into a huge archeological park have never quite come to fruition.

The afternoon is a privileged time when tourists have Rome to themselves. Find yourself a peaceful shaded spot on the Aventine or Palatine and look out across the great gray domes that seem to hover protectively above the crooked red-tiled roofs. As the city slumbers in the hazy sunshine, you can sense its eternal quality. Forget about the traffic that threatens to destroy its foundations. Forget about the museums, churches and palazzi closed for years in endless restoration. Forget about the absurd bureaucracy, which seems to exist purposely to ensure that nothing ever gets done. Rome has lived through perils far greater than these and yet has always survived.

The extraordinary beauty of the eternal city still glitters, seemingly imperishable and sneering at the passage of time. It is impossible to resist her charm. Rome, in spite of its defects, is still a wonderful stage on which the history of human civilization is permanently displayed. The show is a delight to the mind as well as to the senses.

Si fueris Romae, Romano vivito more;
Si fueris alibi, vivito sicut ibi.
When in Rome, live as the Romans do; when elsewhere, live as
they live elsewhere.
(St Ambrose's advice to St Augustine)

Culture, history and background

Landmarks in Rome's history

ORIGINS AND KINGDOM

753BC: Legendary date of the foundation of Rome by the brothers Romulus and Remus. The story of the city's origin is probably fictitious. According to archeological evidence Rome was a simple farming community until about **600BC**, but tradition has it that Romulus was the first of seven kings of Rome.

715-509: The Sabine kings Numa Pompilius, Tullus Hostilius and Ancus Martius left little mark, although Numa Pompilius was the legendary founder of Roman religious customs. Under Tarquinius Priscus (**616-578BC**), the first of the Etruscan kings, Rome began its transformation from an agricultural settlement into a city of great monumental architecture. The Forum was drained, the sewerage system begun and the foundations laid for a great temple on the Capitoline Hill.

The next king, Servius Tullius, built the first wall around Rome. He was succeeded by the tyrant Tarquinius Superbus ("The Proud"), who reduced the role of the Senate and concentrated judicial power in his own hands. He completed the sewerage system and the three-fold temple on the Capitoline Hill, dedicated to Jupiter, Juno and Minerva, though always known as the Temple of Jupiter Optimus Maximus.

REPUBLIC

509: Tarquinius was driven out and a Republic was established. **390**: The Gauls raided Italy and sacked Rome. This was the first of many invasions of the city, which it somehow always managed to survive.

264-241: First Punic War (against the North African state of Carthage). Rome's struggles with Carthage were related by the historian Livy, in the 1stC BC. They were decisive in promoting Rome's growth to an international power. **214-201**: Second Punic War. The Carthaginian leader Hannibal crossed the Alps and threatened but did not vanquish Rome. The Roman general Scipio Africanus was an almost equally charismatic military leader. The war ended in the defeat of Carthage. **149-146**: The Third Punic War brought about the destruction of Carthage by Rome.

81-79: Rule of the dictator Sulla, the first Roman general to use his troops against political opponents. His example was followed by later politicians, including Julius Caesar. **58-49**: Caesar's campaign in Gaul. **55-54**: Caesar's invasion of Britain. **49**: Caesar crossed the Rubicon with his army and made himself master of Italy, effectively ending the Republic. **44**: Caesar assassinated in the Senate.

EMPIRE

27BC-AD14: Octavian, Caesar's great-nephew, became the first Roman emperor, taking the name of Augustus. He began an extensive building program, boasting that he "found Rome brick and left it marble". His reign was a golden age of Roman culture. Writers of the Augustan Age included Virgil, Horace, Ovid and Livy.

54-68: Reign of Nero, who was held responsible for the great fire of **64** and was said to have "fiddled while Rome burned." He blamed the disaster on the Christians, and initiated their persecution, but it gave him the opportunity to build a magnificent palace, known as the Golden House, over a huge area of devastation stretching all the way from the Palatine to the Esquiline and Coelian Hills.

79-81: The reign of Titus included the destruction of the Temple at Jerusalem; his subsequent triumph is recorded on the Arch of Titus in the Roman Forum. In **80** another great fire in Rome destroyed the Temple of Jupiter Optimus Maximus (rebuilt in **82**).

98-117: Trajan's reign saw important military campaigns that extended the frontier of the empire beyond the Danube. These triumphs are recorded on Trajan's Column in the Forum of Trajan. By the end of his reign, Roman territory stretched east from Spain to the Caspian Sea and south from Britain to North Africa.

117-138: Hadrian was a very different emperor from his predecessor. He spent most of his time traveling through the empire, spreading the civilizing influence of Rome.

161-180: The philosopher-emperor Marcus Aurelius was at the same time a notable general and an exceptionally cultured ruler. He is known for his *Meditations,* a book of reflections on life, imbued with his Stoic philosophy. During the reign of Marcus Aurelius, Rome experienced the first heavy barbarian attacks on her frontiers. He died at Vienna while campaigning against the Danube tribes.

180-286: During the century following the death of Marcus Aurelius, Rome was continually at war with barbarian tribes in many parts of the empire. It was also a time of political instability. A series of emperors came and went with great rapidity as one military coup succeeded another. The rulers of these years included the bloodthirsty and depraved Commodus and the equally brutal Caracalla.

286: Diocletian divided the empire into East and West, making himself ruler of the Eastern Empire and Maximian ruler of the West. **306-337**: Reign of Constantine the Great, the first Christian emperor. He brought both parts of the empire under his own rule, legalized Christianity in **313** and moved his capital to Byzantium, which he re-named Constantinople. Under his reign the first churches and basilicas began to be constructed in Rome.

337-476: These years marked the final decline and collapse of the Western Empire. On the death of Theodosius in **395** the two halves of the empire were again divided, never again to be joined. In Rome, chaos and unrest reigned as the army vainly tried to defend her frontiers. In **410** the Visigoths under Alaric captured and looted the city. In **455** it was the turn of the Vandals to plunder Rome. Finally, in **476** the German chieftain

Odoacer deposed the last emperor, Romulus Augustulus, and made himself master of the Italian peninsula.

DARK AND MIDDLE AGES

493: Odoacer was defeated by Theodoric, King of the Ostrogoths. **552**: The Ostrogoths were finally defeated, and Rome for a time became part of the Eastern Empire. **568**: The Lombards, another Germanic tribe, invaded Italy. By **593** they were threatening Rome itself.

590-604: The papacy of Gregory the Great, distinguished by sensitive handling of the Lombards, marked the beginning of effective papal intervention in the world of politics.

754-756: Stephen III appealed to the Franks for help against the Lombards. The Frankish king Pepin the Short defeated the Lombards and gave part of central Italy to the pope. **774**: Pepin's son Charlemagne defeated the Lombards again, winning control of Italy for the Franks and securing the power of the popes. **800**: Charlemagne was crowned Holy Roman Emperor.

9thC: Gradual disintegration of the Carolingian empire. Rome was torn by struggles between rival princes. Powerful families vied for the papacy. **962**: The Saxon king Otto I became Holy Roman Emperor. Popes now claimed the right to crown emperors, and emperors in turn claimed the right to confirm the election of popes.

1084: Robert Guiscard and his Norman troops expelled the Emperor Henry IV from Rome and subjected the city to ruthless sacking. **1144-55**: Commune set up in Rome by Arnold of Brescia, in defiance of both pope and emperor. **1198-1216**: Under Innocent III, the papacy gained the upper hand against the emperors. **1241**: A year of even greater strife than usual between the papal and Imperial parties. The Mausoleum of Augustus was virtually destroyed.

RENAISSANCE TO MODERN TIMES

1308: The papacy was transferred to Avignon, in France, and although there was a brief return in 1378, the popes were not to be firmly re-established in Rome until 1417. In the meantime the city lost its importance as a focus of affairs. **1347**: Cola di Rienzo led a popular rebellion against the nobility and established a democratic republic. He was murdered in **1354**.

1378-1417: The years of the Great Schism in the Church, when Europe was divided in its support for rival claimants to the papacy. **1417-31**: The papacy of Martin V ended the discord, and Rome's cultural life gradually began to revive. **1447-55**: Papacy of Nicholas V, known for his chapel frescoed by Fra Angelico. He also contributed generally to the reconstruction of the city. **1471-84**: Sixtus IV built the Sistine Chapel as his private place of worship and brought in a group of the best Tuscan and Umbrian artists to decorate the walls.

1492-1503: Reign of Alexander VI, Rodrigo Borgia. Securing the office by bribery, he proceeded to indulge in the most flagrant nepotism, making his bloodthirsty son, Cesare, a cardinal. **1503-13**: Julius II, not much more admirable as a man than Alexander VI, is held in greater respect by posterity for having commissioned Michelangelo to paint the ceiling of the Sistine Chapel, Raphael to decorate the Stanze, and Bramante to build the new St Peter's. **1513-21**: Leo X continued the artistic initiative of his predecessor. Seldom had Rome's future seemed more secure, although the first rumblings of Lutheranism were heard. **1527**: German and Spanish troops raided Rome, destroying buildings and stealing many of the city's treasures.

1534-49: Paul III, the first Counter-Reformation pope, licensed the Jesuit Order and convened the Council of Trent (1545). He inspired another, though less intense, period of artistic ferment, approving Michelangelo's *Last Judgment*. **1585-90**: Sixtus V began to plan the urban development of Rome.

1623-44: Urban VIII's reign as pope saw the great period of the Baroque in Rome, presided over by the sculptor, painter and architect Bernini. The city was now the undisputed artistic capital of Europe. **1644**: With the commencement of Innocent X's papacy, the Pamphili replaced the Barberini as the ruling dynasty in Rome. **1656**: Construction of Piazza San Pietro, Bernini's supreme piece of townscape architecture, began.

1700-21: Under the papacy of Clement XI, Rome's prestige declined, and the 18thC was a period of relative insignificance.

1798: Rome was attacked by the French army and Revolutionary forces occupied the city. **1809**: Napoleon annexed the Papal States and took Pius VII into captivity. **1814**: Pius VII was freed, and the Papal States were restored to the Vatican.

1848-49: Mazzini and Garibaldi began the revolution *(Risorgimento)* that was to lead to the unification of Italy and the final secularization of most of the papal territories. A republic was briefly established in Rome. **1861**: The whole of Italy, apart from Rome, was unified under Victor Emmanuel II of Sardinia and Savoy. **1870**: Rome was added to the Kingdom of Italy and became its capital. The political power of the popes was henceforth confined to the Vatican.

1922: Mussolini's march on Rome and seizure of power marked the beginning of the Fascist government of Italy. The Lateran Pact was signed between Italy and the Vatican State. **1943-44**: Fascism was brought to an end, with the liberation of Rome by the Allies. **1946**: Establishment of the Italian Republic.

1958-63: The papacy of John XXIII brought new life to the Catholic Church. **1962-65**: The Second Vatican Council introduced many reforms. **1978**: Following the untimely and controversial death of John Paul I, a Polish Cardinal, Karol Wojtyla, became John Paul II, the first non-Italian pope since 1523.

Who's who

A list of the famous whose names are linked with Rome would be endless. The following is a personal selection of notable figures associated with ancient and modern Rome, many of whom are mentioned in this book.

Agnes, St *(died 304)*
A young Roman girl who consecrated herself to God and was martyred during Diocletian's persecutions.

Alexander VI (Rodrigo Borgia) *(1431-1503)*
The most corrupt and worldly of all the Renaissance popes, Alexander disposed of his enemies by poisoning them.

Algardi, Alessandro *(c.1598-1654)*
Bolognese sculptor who represented a graver, more Classical style than his extrovert rival, Bernini.

Angelico, Fra (Giovanni da Fiesole) *(c.1387 or c.1400-55)*
Dominican friar who frescoed the Chapel of Nicholas V (in the VATICAN MUSEUMS), but worked mainly in Florence.

Augustus, Caius Octavianus *(63BC-AD14)*
Julius Caesar's great-nephew and designated successor, Augustus enjoyed a long, peaceful and illustrious reign after defeating his former ally, Mark Anthony, at Actium in 31BC.

Barocci, Federico *(c.1535-1612)*
His highly emotional paintings looked forward to the Baroque.

Bernini, Gianlorenzo *(1598-1680)*
As both sculptor and architect, a tremendously influential figure of the Baroque. His energy and invention and, above all, his joy in life, were apparently boundless.

Boniface VIII (Benedetto Caetani) *(pope 1294-1301)*
The great villain of Dante's *Inferno,* he used his office to advance the fortunes of his family against the Colonna.

Borromini, Francesco *(1599-1667)*
With his contemporary, Bernini, he virtually created the Roman Baroque style in architecture, but for sheer novelty and daring his ideas were unparalleled.

Bramante, Donato *(1444-1514)*
A fundamental figure of the High Renaissance, Bramante exerted great influence through his designs for ST PETER'S.

Caesar, Caius Julius *(c.101-44BC)*
Roman general and writer who documented his military exploits in Gaul and Britain in *De Bello Gallico.* Having returned to defeat his great rival Pompey at the battle of Pharsalus (48BC), he became sole ruler, but was soon afterwards assassinated.

Caligula, Caesar Germanicus *(12-41)*
Roman emperor who manifested various mental disorders in the course of his short reign. Remembered for his appalling cruelty, Caligula attempted to transform the imperial throne into an absolute monarchy.

Canova, Antonio *(1757-1822)*
Neoclassical sculptor, best known for his study of *Pauline Borghese,* Napoleon's sister, in the BORGHESE GALLERY.

Caracalla (Marcus Aurelius Severus Antoninus) *(186-217)*
An unpopular emperor who murdered his brother and co-ruler, Geta. His nickname derives from the Gaulish coat he wore.

Caravaggio, Michelangelo Merisi da *(1573-1610)*
The violent realism of his paintings was as controversial as his life. After murdering a man in a brawl, he was forced to flee the city and died before a pardon could be obtained.

Carracci, Annibale *(1560-1609)*
Less flamboyant than his rival, Caravaggio, Carracci exerted a decisive influence on 17thC Classical painting.

Catullus, Caius Valerius *(84-54BC)*
One of the great love poets of all time, whose lyrics are often addressed to his beloved Lesbia.

Cavallini, Pietro *(active 1273-1308)*
Artist whose mosaics and frescoes provided a Classical link between antiquity and the Renaissance.

Cecilia, St *(died 3rd or 4thC)*
Her legend centers around the church of SANTA CECILIA IN TRASTEVERE, where her body was rediscovered in 1599.

Cellini, Benvenuto *(1500-71)*
Florentine sculptor and goldsmith, whose *Autobiography* contains a fascinating account of the Sack of Rome in 1527.

Cicero, Marcus Tullius *(106-43BC)*
Orator, philosopher and prominent political figure of Republican Rome.

Clement VII (Giulio de' Medici) *(1478-1534)*
During the Sack of Rome in 1527, Clement was forced to take refuge in the CASTEL SANT' ANGELO — a humiliation from which he never recovered. His dealings with Henry VIII of England led to the triumph of English Protestantism.

Constantine the Great *(c.274-337)*
Following his victory over Maxentius at the Milvian Bridge (312), Constantine became sole ruler in the West, and the first Christian emperor.

Cortona, Pietro Berrettini da *(1596-1669)*
Almost equally distinguished as architect and painter, he is the third great creator of the Roman Baroque after Bernini and Borromini.

Cosmati *(active 12th to 14thC)*
This name was originally given to a single family of Roman marble workers — one of whom bore the Christian name Cosmatus — and thence to all artists working in this medium, notably the Vassalletti family.

Diocletian, Caius Aurelius Valerius *(245-313)*
A notable builder, as the great BATHS OF DIOCLETIAN demonstrate, but mainly remembered as a persecutor of Christianity.

Domitian (Titus Flavius Domitianus) *(51-96)*
Despotic emperor who feared assassination and was duly murdered.

Frances of Rome, St *(1384-1440)*
A Roman matron who devoted her life to charitable works.

Garibaldi, Giuseppe *(1807-82)*
Soldier and patriot who, with Mazzini and Cavour, was responsible for the unification of Italy. Earlier, he defended Rome from French attack on the JANICULUM HILL (1849).

Giulio Romano *(1492 or 1499-1546)*
Pupil of Raphael who helped to develop the Mannerist style in both architecture and painting.

Gregory I, St (the Great) *(c.540-604)*
One of the four Doctors of the Church, and the pope who sent St Augustine to England.

Hadrian *(76-138)*
An exceptionally cultivated although sometimes ruthless emperor, best known as the builder of the PANTHEON.

Horace (Quintus Horatius Flaccus) *(65-8BC)*
Perhaps the greatest of the Roman lyric poets, Horace wrote odes inspired by the beauty of nature and by the philosophy of *Carpe diem* ("Pluck the day" or "Live life to the full").

Innocent X (Giovanni Battista Pamphili) *(1574-1655)*
Although nominally responsible for the redevelopment of PIAZZA NAVONA into a Baroque showpiece, Innocent was a weak pope, dominated by his sister-in-law, Olimpia Maidalchini.

John XXIII (Angelo Giuseppe Roncalli) *(1881-1963)*
His untiring work to promote Christian unity included the setting up of the Second Vatican Council in 1962.

John Paul II (Karol Wojtyla) *(born 1920)*
The first non-Italian pope for more than 450 years, he has traveled more widely and spoken out more strongly on issues of human rights than any previous pontiff.

Julius II (Giuliano della Rovere) *(1443-1513)*
The archetypal Renaissance pope, Julius was a great warrior as well as a great churchman, and patron of both Michelangelo and Raphael. He began the rebuilding of ST PETER'S.

Leo X (Giovanni de' Medici) *(1475-1521)*
Outstanding patron of learning and the arts, he created and sold new offices to finance his grandiose schemes.

Lucretius (Titus Lucretius Carus) *(99-55BC)*
Author of *De Rerum Natura,* a long poem expounding the principles of Epicurean philosophy.

Maderno, Carlo *(1556-1629)*
The first major architect of the Roman Baroque.

Marcus Aurelius Antoninus *(121-180)*
An able general and emperor of high principles and great culture, best remembered for his *Meditations.*

Michelangelo Buonarroti *(1475-1564)*
Painter, sculptor, architect and poet, he was the archetypal genius. His powerful representations of the human figure have never been equaled.

Moravia, Alberto *(1907-1990)*
Pen name of Alberto Pincherle, the Roman novelist whose work has been dubbed Neo-Realism.
Mussolini, Benito *(1883-1945)*
Fascist dictator of Italy from 1922-43, he significantly altered Rome's appearance by driving major roads through its historic quarters.
Nero, Claudius Caesar *(37-68)*
An emperor as monstrous as is popularly supposed. He murdered his mother and his first wife, persecuted Christians, and was held responsible for the great fire of Rome in 64.
Nerva, Marcus Cocceius *(c.30-98)*
Benevolent but feeble emperor, whose reign brought greater freedom after the tyranny of Domitian.
Ovid (Publius Ovidius Naso) *(43BC-AD18)*
Roman poet, chiefly remembered for his *Metamorphoses,* relating the transformations of the gods in Classical legend. His treatise on love, the *Ars Amatoria,* was considered obscene and may have been one cause of his banishment to the Black Sea by Augustus.
Palestrina, Giovanni Pierluigi da *(1525-94)*
Composer of sacred choral music. His lovely *Missa Papae Marcelli* inspired a legend that he had heard angels singing.
Paschal I, St *(817-24)*
Early medieval pope who founded a number of churches in Rome and had himself depicted in the mosaics therein.
Paul, St *(died c.67)*
Paul was beheaded at Aquae Salviae (now Tre Fontane), and buried on the spot where SAN PAOLO FUORI LE MURA now stands. Tre Fontane takes its name from the tradition that Paul's severed head bounced upon the ground three times, causing three fountains to spring up.
Paul III (Alessandro Farnese) *(1468-1549)*
An enlightened patron of the arts, he was also the first Counter-Reformation pope.
Peter, St *(died c.64 or 67)*
The apostle, whose role as Bishop of Rome made him the first pope, was martyred under Nero. SAN PIETRO IN MONTORIO is said to mark the place of his crucifixion.
Philip Neri, St *(1515-95)*
Sometimes called the second apostle of Rome, he founded the Congregation of the Oratorians and built the CHIESA NUOVA.
Pinturicchio, Bernardino *(c.1454-1513)*
Artist who frescoed the Borgia Apartments (VATICAN MUSEUMS). He was greatly influenced by Perugino.
Piranesi, Giovanni Battista *(1720-78)*
Architect turned etcher, he recorded ancient and modern Rome in a series of etchings known as the *Vedute.* These were widely circulated and were considered to be highly influential in the development of the Neoclassical style.
Pliny the Elder *(23-79),* **Pliny the Younger** *(62-113)*
Author of a monumental scientific work, the *Historiae Naturalis,* Pliny

the Elder died while investigating the eruption of Vesuvius. The *Letters* of his nephew, Pliny the Younger, give a marvelously sharp insight into everyday Roman life.

Raphael (Raffaello Sanzio) *(1483-1520)*
With Leonardo da Vinci and Michelangelo he was one of the three great creators of the High Renaissance. Because of his early death, his promise as an architect was never really fulfilled and his greatest works are the frescoes of the so-called Raphael Stanze in the VATICAN MUSEUMS.

Rienzo, Cola di *(1313-54)*
Popular hero and short-lived tribune, he was greatly admired by Petrarch and inspired Wagner's unfinished opera, *Rienzi*.

Sansovino, Andrea *(c.1467-1529)*
Florentine sculptor whose fascination with the antique brought about a new style in funerary monuments.

Sixtus IV (Francesco della Rovere) *(1414-84)*
By bringing great artists to Rome to decorate the so-called Sistine Chapel, this pope set a trend of great importance.

Tacitus, Caius Cornelius *(c.56-120)*
Historian and brilliant stylist, whose *Annals* provided vivid accounts of Roman politics in the 1stC AD.

Trajan *(c.53-117)*
A great soldier and prolific builder, Trajan was also a wise and benevolent administrator.

Urban VIII (Maffeo Barberini) *(1568-1644)*
His reign as pope was a period of tremendous artistic activity, with Bernini in supreme command.

Valadier, Giuseppe *(1762-1839)*
Architect and town-planner, responsible for the dramatic arrangement of PIAZZA DEL POPOLO.

Vasari, Giorgio *(1511-74)*
Painter, architect and author of the *Vite dei Più Eccellenti Architetti, Pittori, et Scultori*.

Vassalletto See COSMATI (above).

Vespasian (Titus Flavius Vespasianus) *(9-79)*
A shadowy figure whose greatest achievement was to prevent the dissolution of the Empire after Nero's death.

Victor Emanuel II *(1820-78)*
Proclaimed first King of Italy in 1861, he did not acquire Rome until 1870. He is buried in the PANTHEON.

Vignola (Jacopo Barozzi) *(1507-73)*
Important late Renaissance architect who built the GESÚ, one of the most powerful symbols of the Counter-Reformation.

Virgil (Publius Vergilius Maro) *(70-19BC)*
Epic poet, author of the *Eclogues* and *Georgics,* and of the *Aeneid*. The latter tells the story of the wanderings of Aeneas, proto-founder of Rome, after the Fall of Troy.

Chronology of Roman emperors

In the later Empire, succession was more often disputed than not. Even in its first 200 years, assassinations interrupted the Julio-Claudian (27BC-AD68), Flavian (69-96) and Antonine (including Trajan and Hadrian, 98-192) dynasties.

Augustus 27BC-AD14
Tiberius 14-37
Caligula 37-41
Claudius 41-54
Nero 54-68
Galba 68-69
Otho 69
Vitellius 69
Vespasian 69-79
Titus 79-81
Domitian 81-96
Nerva 96-98
Trajan 98-117
Hadrian 117-138
Antoninus Pius 138-161
Marcus Aurelius 161-180
Commodus 180-192
Pertinax 193
Didius Julianus 193
Septimius Severus
  193-211
Caracalla 198-217
Geta 211-212
Macrinus 217-218
Heliogabalus 218-222
Alexander Severus
  222-235
Maximinus the Thracian
  235-238

Gordian I 238
Gordian II 238
Pupienus 238
Balbinus 238
Gordian III 238-244
Philip the Arabian
  244-249
Decius 249-251
Gallus 251-253
Aemilian 253
Valerian 253-260
Gallienus 253-268
Claudius II 268-270
Quintillus 270
Aurelian 270-275
Tacitus 275-276
Florian 276
Probus 276-282
Carus 282-283
Numerianus 283-284
Carinus 283-285
Diocletian 284-305
Maximian 286-305
Constantius I 305-306
Galerius 305-311
Flavius Severus 306-307
Maxentius 306-312
Constantine the Great
  306-337

Licinius 308-323
Maximinus Daia
  309-313
Constantine II 337-340
Constans 337-350
Constantius II 337-361
Magnentius 350-353
Julian the Apostate
  361-363
Jovian 363-364
Valentinian I 364-375
Valens 364-378
Gratian 365-383
Valentinian II 375-392
Theodosius 379-395
Honorius 395-423
John 423-425
Valentinian III 425-455
Petronius Maximus 455
Avitus 455-456
Majorian 457-461
Libius Severus
  461-465
Anthemius 467-472
Olybrius 472
Glycerius 473-474
Julius Nepos 474-475
Romulus Augustulus
  475-476

Chronology of popes

The dates of the early pontificates cannot be authenticated, and the distinction between pope and antipope was often decided many years later, sometimes rather arbitrarily.

St Peter martyred 64 or
  67
St Linus 67-76(?)
St Cletus 76-88(?)
St Clement I 88-97(?)
St Evaristus 97-105(?)
St Alexander I 105-115(?)
St Sixtus I 115-125(?)

St Telesphorus
  125-136(?)
St Hyginus 136-140(?)
St Pius I 140-155(?)
St Anicetus 155-166(?)
St Soter 166-175(?)
St Eleutherius 175-189
St Victor I 189-199

St Zephryrinus 199-217
St Calixtus I 217-222
St Urban I 222-230
St Pontian 230-235
St Anterus 235-236
St Fabian 236-250
St Cornelius 251-253
St Lucius I 253-254

St Stephen I 254-257
St Sixtus II 257-258
St Dionysius 259-268
St Felix I 269-274
St Eutychian 275-283
St Caius 283-296
St Marcellinus 296-304
St Marcellus I 308-309
St Eusebius 309-310
St Melchiades 311-314
St Sylvester I 314-335
St Marcus 335-336
St Julius I 337-352
St Liberius 352-366
St Felix II 355-365
St Damasus I 365-384
St Siricius 384-399
St Anastasius I 399-401
St Innocent I 401-417
St Zosimus 417-418
St Boniface I 418-422
St Celestine I 422-432
St Sixtus III 432-440
St Leo I (the Great)
    440-461
St Hilarius 461-468
St Simplicius 468-483
St Felix III 483-492
St Gelasius I 492-496
St Anastasius II 496-498
St Symmachus 498-514
St Hormisdas 514-523
St John I 523-526
St Felix IV 526-530
Boniface II 530-532
John II 533-535
St Agapetus I 535-536
St Silverius 536-537
Vigilius 537-555
Pelagius I 556-561
John III 561-574
Benedict I 575-579
Pelagius II 579-590
St Gregory I (the great)
    590-604
Sabinian 604-606
Boniface III 607
St Boniface IV 608-615
St Deodatus I 615-618
Boniface V 619-625
Honorius I 625-638
Severinus 640
John IV 640-642
Theodore I 642-649

St Martin I 649-655
St Eugenius I 654-657
St Vitalianus 657-672
Deodatus II 672-676
Donus I 676-678
St Agatho 678-681
St Leo II 682-683
St Benedict II 684-685
John V 685-686
Conon 686-687
St Sergius I 687-701
John VI 701-705
John VII 705-707
Sisinnius 708
Constantine I 708-715
St Gregory II 715-731
St Gregory III 731-741
St Zacharias 741-752
Stephen II 752
Stephen III 752-757
St Paul I 757-767
Constantine II 767-768
Philip 768
Stephen IV 768-772
Adrian I 772-795
St Leo III 795-816
St Stephen V 816-817
St Paschal I 817-824
Eugenius II 824-827
Valentinus 827
Gregory IV 827-844
Sergius II 844-847
St Leo IV 847-855
Benedict III 855-858
St Nicholas I 858-867
Adrian II 867-872
John VIII 872-882
Marinus I 882-884
St Adrian II 884-885
Stephen VI 885-891
Formosus 891-896
Boniface VI 896
Stephen VII 896-897
Romanus 897
Theodore II 897
John IX 898-900
Benedict IV 900-903
Leo V 903
Sergius III 904-911
Anastasius III 911-913
Landonius 913-914
John X 914-929
Leo VI 928
Stephen VIII 929-931

John XI 931-935
Leo VII 936-939
Stephen IX 939-942
Marinus II 942-946
Agapetus II 946-955
John XII 955-964
Leo VIII 963-965
Benedict V 964-966
John XIII 965-972
Benedict VI 973-974
Benedict VII 974-983
Boniface VII 974, 984-985
John XIV 983-984
John XV 985-996
Gregory V 996-999
John XVI 997-998
Sylvester II 999-1003
John XVII 1003
John XVIII 1004-09
Sergius IV 1009-12
Benedict VIII 1012-24
John XIX 1024-32
Benedict IX 1032-48
Sylvester III 1045
Gregory VI 1045-46
Clement II 1046-47
Damasus II 1048
St Leo IX 1049-54
Victor II 1055-57
Stephen X 1057-58
Benedict X 1058-59
Nicholas II 1059-61
Alexander II 1061-73
St Gregory VII 1073-85
Victor III 1086-87
Urban II 1088-99
Paschal II 1099-1118
Gelasius II 1118-19
Calixtus II 1119-24
Honorius II 1124-30
Innocent II 1130-43
Celestine II 1143-44
Lucius II 1144-45
Eugenius III 1145-53
Anastasius IV 1153-54
Adrian IV 1154-59
Alexander III 1159-81
Lucius III 1181-85
Urban III 1185-87
Gregory VIII 1187
Clement III 1187-91
Celestine III 1191-98
Innocent III 1198-1216
Honorius III 1216-27

Gregory IX 1227-41
Celestine IV 1241
Innocent IV 1243-54
Alexander IV 1254-61
Urban IV 1261-64
Clement IV 1265-68
Gregory X 1271-76
Innocent V 1276
Adrian V 1276
John XXI 1276-77
Nicholas III 1277-80
Martin IV 1281-85
Honorius IV 1285-87
Nicholas IV 1288-92
St Celestine V 1294-96
Boniface VIII 1294-1303
Benedict XI 1303-04
Clement V 1305-14
John XXII 1316-34
Benedict XII 1334-42
Clement VI 1342-52
Innocent VI 1352-62
Urban V 1362-70
Gregory XI 1370-78
Urban VI 1378-89
Boniface IX 1389-1404
Innocent VII 1404-06
Gregory XII 1406-17
Martin V 1417-31

Eugenius IV 1431-47
Nicholas V 1447-55
Calixtus III 1455-58
Pius II 1458-64
Paul II 1464-71
Sixtus IV 1471-84
Innocent VIII 1484-92
Alexander VI 1492-1503
Pius III 1503
Julius II 1503-13
Leo X 1513-21
Adrian VI 1522-23
Clement VII 1523-34
Paul III 1534-49
Julius III 1550-55
Marcellus II 1555
Paul IV 1555-59
Pius IV 1559-65
St Pius V 1566-72
Gregory XIII 1572-85
Sixtus V 1585-90
Urban VII 1590
Gregory XIV 1590-91
Innocent IX 1591
Clement VIII 1592-1605
Leo XI 1605
Paul V 1605-21
Gregory XV 1621-23
Urban VIII 1623-44

Innocent X 1644-55
Alexander VII 1655-67
Clement IX 1667-69
Clement X 1670-76
Innocent XI 1676-89
Alexander VIII 1689-91
Innocent XII 1691-1700
Clement XI 1700-21
Innocent XIII 1721-24
Benedict XIII 1724-30
Clement XII 1730-40
Benedict XIV 1740-58
Clement XIII 1758-69
Clement XIV 1769-74
Pius VI 1775-99
Pius VII 1800-23
Leo XII 1823-29
Pius VIII 1829-30
Gregory XVI 1831-46
Pius IX 1846-78
Leo XIII 1878-1903
St Pius X 1903-14
Benedict XV 1914-22
Pius XI 1922-39
Pius XII 1939-58
John XXIII 1958-63
Paul VI 1963-78
John Paul I 1978
John Paul II 1978-

Rome's architecture

The architecture of ancient Rome, like its painting and sculpture, was inspired in the first place by that of **Greece**. However, far from being the inferior imitation that it has sometimes, unfairly, been seen as, Roman architecture displays a number of its own original and inventive styles. The ravages of time are only too apparent in the state of preservation of some monuments, and it can be hard to visualize the original appearance of a great temple on the basis of a few remaining columns. However, the ruins of ancient Rome still provoke astonishment and admiration. The **Roman Forum**, to give just one example, is endlessly fascinating, and provides a rich seam of inspiration for the historian or the archeologist as much as for the lover of architecture.

Typical of Rome's surviving antique monuments are her columns and triumphal arches. **Trajan's Column** (in the FORUM OF TRAJAN) and the **Column of Marcus Aurelius** are impressive monuments to military and Imperial achievement that were not much imitated, while the **Arches of Titus and Septimius Severus** (both in the ROMAN FORUM) and the **Arch of Constantine** have had an appropriately monumental influence on the history of European architecture. Both are notable for their simple but perfectly balanced proportions and for their exquisite sculptural reliefs.

Arch of Constantine

The more practical side of ancient Roman architecture can be seen in what remains of the public buildings. Structures such as the **Colosseum** and **Theater of Marcellus** demonstrate the sheer scale of achievement, while the great **Baths of Caracalla** and **Baths of Diocletian** give some idea of the complexity of planning as well. The same impression is gained on a visit to **Hadrian's Villa** at Tivoli (see ROME ENVIRONS), where ingenious ground-plans and vaulting systems abound. Even the quasi-domestic buildings on the PALATINE HILL were remarkably inventive.

But if one building has to stand for all that is best in Classical Roman architecture, it must surely be the **Pantheon**, whether for the timeless

The Pantheon

nobility of its majestic portico or for the exhilarating lightness of its domed interior. The Pantheon survived the ravages of the Middle Ages by being converted into a Christian church, while the **Mausoleum of Hadrian** was assured of continuity by its transformation into the military edifice now known as the **Castel Sant' Angelo**. Most other ancient buildings were not so fortunate. Temples were destroyed for their fine marble columns, which went into the building of the new Christian basilicas. But the attitude to the past remained respectful in terms of artistic if not moral values. With their processions of columns and rich mosaics, the early basilicas — **old St Peter's**, **San Paolo fuori le Mura**, **Santa Maria Maggiore** and **San Giovanni in Laterano** — reflected the grandeur and assurance of the Classical tradition.

But Roman **medieval architecture** can also be delicate and intimate. There are exquisite little centrally-planned buildings like **Santa Costanza** and the **Lateran Baptistry**, and smaller aisled churches such as **Santa Sabina** and **Santa Maria in Cosmedin** (pictured on page 135), where arcades replace the previously standard colonnades.

This innovation apart, the basic basilican style hardly changed from the 4thC to beyond the millennium, so that a church like **San Clemente** (1108) is later than it perhaps at first appears. This impression is reinforced by the knowledge that there was relatively little new building in Rome in the later Middle Ages, and that the city was all but untouched by Gothic influences. The church of **Santa Maria sopra Minerva** is the sole exception, a strange link between two pseudo-Classical traditions.

The **Renaissance** came relatively late to Rome, even though it was essentially a revival of Classical forms. The two most distinguished early Renaissance buildings, **Palazzo Venezia** and **Palazzo della Cancelleria**, are of doubtful authorship, although the courtyard of the latter is sometimes attributed to **Bramante**. This architect's grand plans for the new **St Peter's** were vastly important, while his **Tempietto** outside **San Pietro in Montorio** epitomizes the High Renaissance ideals of Classical fidelity and proportional perfection (see illustration on page 146).

After Bramante's death, **Michelangelo** came to be the decisive force in the rebuilding of **St Peter's**. The marvelous **dome**, with garlands and paired columns round the base, is basically his invention, although it was completed by Giacomo della Porta. Otherwise his major architectural work in Rome involved the reorganization of the Capitol into **Piazza del Campidoglio**, where his use of a colossal order — giant pilasters reaching up through two stories — looks forward to the Baroque.

Palace building continued unabated through the 16thC, ranging from the grandly massive **Palazzo Farnese** (pictured on page 105), begun by **Antonio da Sangallo** and completed by Michelangelo, to the ornate **Palazzo Spada**, and the highly original **Palazzo Massimo alle Colonne** by **Peruzzi**. This was also the golden age of the **villa**, perhaps best expressed in the **Villa Giulia**, that gloriously fanciful creation built for Julius II by **Vignola**, **Ammannati** and **Vasari**.

Villa Giulia

Vignola was also the architect of the **Gesù** (pictured overleaf), which was the prototype of Counter-Reformation churches throughout Europe. The wide nave and barrel vault made it ideal, both spatially and acoustically,

The Gesù

for preaching purposes. But **della Porta's** gracefully voluted facade was even more frequently copied.

The first major architect of the Roman **Baroque** was **Carlo Maderno**. He was responsible for the extension of the nave of **St Peter's** and for its somewhat disappointing facade, but he also began **Palazzo Barberini** (now the GALLERIA NAZIONALE D'ARTE ANTICA) and designed the splendidly rhythmic facade of **Santa Susanna**. Although he was perhaps not an architect of the very first rank, the dignity of his style looks forward to **Bernini**, the most talented and wide-ranging artist of the period. Looking at a church like **Sant' Andrea al Quirinale**, for all its fine qualities, we may wonder what all the excitement is about. But Bernini was much more than the sum of the individual buildings with which he was involved: he was a man who changed the whole appearance of a great city. The fountains of Rome, the statues of the **Ponte Sant' Angelo**, the appearance of **Piazza Navona**, are all products of Bernini's extraordinary imagination, while the spread of his influence is incalculable.

His great rival **Borromini** had a very different kind of personality, both tortured and introspective, but as an architect he was perhaps even more talented. Churches such as **Sant' Ivo** and **San Carlo alle Quattro Fontane** or the facade of the **Oratory of the Filippini** (part of the

ORATORY COMPLEX) might tempt us to dismiss him as a gifted but small-scale eccentric, but the restraint and assurance of his refurbishing of the interior of **San Giovanni in Laterano** show that he was also able to work on a grander scale.

Least well known of the great Baroque triumvirate is **Pietro da Cortona**, whose masterpiece, the church of **Santi Luca e Martina**, is a centrally planned building of great strength and charm that seems to look back to the High Renaissance. His other great work is the facade of **Santa Maria della Pace** (pictured on page 138), distinctive for its semicircular, colonnaded porch.

Oratory of the Filippini

These are the great figures of the Baroque in Rome, but there are many other important works whose creators are generally forgotten. The **Spanish Steps** and **Trevi fountain** (the latter illustrated on page 154) are both well-known 18thC Roman landmarks, characteristically public in conception. If the courtyard personifies the Renaissance sensibility, then the **piazza** sums up the Baroque. The theatrical tradition inaugurated by Bernini in his oval-colonnaded **Piazza San Pietro** continued into the 19thC with Valadier's imaginative treatment of **Piazza del Popolo**.

Piazza San Pietro

Although **Neoclassicism** was born in Rome, and despite its international significance, it made little impression on the fabric of the city itself. It is symptomatic that **Piranesi**, the greatest architectural visionary of the period, executed only one trivial commission in Rome, the **Piazza dei Cavalieri di Malta** on the AVENTINE HILL. For the rest, he was engaged in retrospection, recording in etchings the city's architectural heritage.

The **19thC** was even less memorable in terms of new architecture. Despite a vigorous building program to house the new bureaucracy of a united Italy, only one edifice has come to represent the rather pompous excesses of the age, the much-ridiculed **Monument to Victor Emmanuel II** (pictured on page 98). By contrast, **modern architecture** has left the city's skyline mercifully clear. Mussolini was more concerned with knocking buildings down to build impressive new roads such as **Via dei Fori Imperiali** and **Via della Conciliazione**. The dream architecture for a better tomorrow was left for **EUR** (see ROME ENVIRONS), which stands apart both geographically and culturally, very much a Fascist period piece.

Stazione Termini

Although there are impressive postwar buildings in Rome, such as the pioneering **Stazione Termini** complex, the 20thC has yet to produce a design to compete with the ubiquitous glories of the past.

Glossary of architecture and art

Aedicule   Niche framed by columns

Ambo   Early form of pulpit

Architrave   Supporting beam above a column

Archivolt   Continuous molding around a door or window

Atrium   Central room or court of pre-Christian house; forecourt of early Christian church

Baldacchino   Canopy, usually over altar, throne, etc.

Basilica   Rectangular Roman civic hall; early Christian church of similar structure

Bottega   Artist's workshop

Campanile   Bell tower

Camposanto   Cemetery

Caryatid   Carved female figure used as column

Chiaroscuro   (Heightened) light and shade effects in painting

Ciborium   Altar canopy; casket for the Host

Crossing   Space in church at intersection of chancel, nave and transepts

Diptych   Work of art on two hinged panels

Ex-voto   Work of art offered in fulfilment of a vow

Fresco   Technique of painting onto wet plaster on a wall

Graffiti   Designs scratched into glaze to reveal base color

Herm   Sculpted male nude or bust on tapered pillar

Intarsia   Inlay of wood

Loggia   Gallery or balcony open on at least one side

Lunette   Semicircular surface or panel, often painted or carved

Misericord   Ledge or bracket projecting from pew or stall

Ogival   Of a double-curved line, both concave and convex

Piano nobile   Main floor of house, usually raised

Pieve   Parish church

Pietà   Representation of the Virgin lamenting over the dead Christ

Pietradura   Mosaic of semiprecious stone

Predella   One or more small paintings attached to the bottom of an altarpiece

Putto   Plump, naked child, often winged, in works of art

Scagliola   Plaster-work polished to resemble marble

Sinopia   Preparatory drawing made beneath a fresco

Stucco   Light, reinforced plaster

Tondo   Circular painting or sculpture

Transept   Transverse arms of a cruciform church

Tribune   Raised area of gallery in a church; the apse of a basilica

Triptych   Work of art on three hinged panels

Painting and sculpture

In the 6thC, despite raids and sacks and changes of ruler, Rome still possessed most of the statuary and painting she had accumulated in almost unbelievable quantities during the **Imperial** period. But with the end of the enlightened stewardship of the Ostrogoth Cassiodorus, the metropolis quickly collapsed, her economy disintegrated, and her gardens, palaces and temples merged into a vast, unkempt parkland. A few pieces, such as the bronze boy known as the *Spinario* (now in the CAPITOLINE MUSEUMS), were gathered outside the Lateran Palace for the disquieted amazement of pilgrims.

The VATICAN MUSEUMS and Museo Nazionale Romano in the BATHS OF DIOCLETIAN give some idea of the quantities of marble statues once in Rome. To these should be added all those now dispersed in collections around Europe, and for every surviving large marble statue one should probably count a lost lifesize bronze or silver one. Most Imperial Roman art derives from the Hellenistic tradition, although the naturalistic portrait bust and various forms of propaganda art (as expressed in the triumphal arches or ARA PACIS AUGUSTAE) are peculiarly Roman obsessions. The ancient Romans were also prolific painters and decorators. The evidence at Pompeii (see EXCURSIONS) or in the now-dank corridors of NERO'S GOLDEN HOUSE shows that even the back rooms of palaces and patrician houses were painted — and mosaic floors were as pervasive then as carpets are today.

In the **Middle Ages**, the dominant influence came to be Byzantine, although Roman art of this period preserves a kind of rigid Classicism that gives it an identity of its own. A typical example is the mosaic work in SANTA PRASSEDE, built by Paschal I in the 9thC and demonstrating the continuing activity, if also the limited resources, of the early medieval popes. By the late 13thC Rome was a leading art center, with Pietro Cavallini showing an increased mastery of composition in the frescoes of SANTA CECILIA IN TRASTEVERE, and the sculptor Arnolfo di Cambio making similar advances toward realism in *St Peter Enthroned*, now in ST PETER'S. A little later, Giotto painted the *Stefaneschi Altarpiece* for old St Peter's (now in the Pinacoteca of the VATICAN MUSEUMS). But in 1308 Clement V was removed to Avignon, and what Petrarch termed the Babylonian Captivity of the popes transformed Rome into a gloomy backwater for more than a century.

A great deal of **Early Renaissance** art in the city has been lost, but some sculpture survives in Filarete's bronze doors for old St Peter's and Antonio Pollaiolo's tombs for Sixtus IV and Innocent VIII (all now in ST PETER'S). In painting, Fra Angelico's work can still be seen in the frescoes of the Chapel of Nicholas V in the VATICAN MUSEUMS. Here, too, the Sistine Chapel contains frescoes by Botticelli, Ghirlandaio and Perugino — a superb team effort, united both visually and thematically by a richness of incident and profusion of gold. A little later, Filippino Lippi frescoed the Carafa Chapel in SANTA MARIA SOPRA MINERVA and Pinturicchio decorated the Borgia Apartments (now part of the VATICAN MUSEUMS). Pinturicchio also did important work in SANTA MARIA D'ARACOELI and SANTA MARIA DEL POPOLO. This last church also contains two splendid tombs by Andrea Sansovino, which are the first real signs of a new Classicism in sculpture.

Meanwhile Michelangelo and Raphael were making their marks on the city. From the ST PETER'S *Pietà* and Sistine ceiling through the fragmentary tomb of Julius II (in SAN PIETRO IN VINCOLI), the *Redeemer* (in SANTA MARIA SOPRA MINERVA) and the *Last Judgment,* Michelangelo towers over half a century of Roman art. Less uncompromising but equally influential, Raphael is best known for his frescoes in the papal apartments now known as the Raphael Stanze (in the VATICAN MUSEUMS), in the VILLA FARNESINA and SANTA MARIA DELLA PACE, and for a number of altarpieces now in the BORGHESE GALLERY and the Pinacoteca of the VATICAN MUSEUMS.

The years between Raphael's untimely death (1520) and the Sack of Rome (1527) saw many of the most talented painters in Italy at work in Rome. Disappointingly little survives by Giulio Romano, Perin del Vaga, Parmigianino and Rosso Fiorentino, but they were pioneers of a new, sometimes restless and contorted style call **Mannerism**. After the Sack, they fled the city, and their ideas spread with them. Rome remained one of the centers of the new style, and artists such as Pellegrino Tibaldi and Francesco Salviati were leading exponents. Painting continued to thrive, but sculpture was less successful, possibly inhibited by the overpowering figure of Michelangelo.

As the 16thC drew to a close, even the painters were beginning to look weary, and the inspiration had to come from an eccentric outsider from Urbino. In the boldness and coloristic exuberance of his work in the CHIESA NUOVA, Federico Barocci heralds the excitements of the **Baroque**.

At the forefront of this new movement was the notorious Caravaggio, whose paintings in the Borghese collection (now the BORGHESE GALLERY), SAN LUIGI DEI FRANCESI and SANTA MARIA DEL POPOLO earned both praise and censure for their earthy realism and compacted drama. His equally important rival, Annibale Carracci, was in many respects a more traditional and Classical figure. Carracci's magnificent frescoes in PALAZZO FARNESE are no longer accessible, but his powers as a landscape painter can be seen in the Galleria Doria Pamphili in PALAZZO DORIA.

In the next generation, Bernini brought the Baroque to a grand climax in a fluent, virtuoso style most enjoyable in his statues for Cardinal Borghese, now in the BORGHESE GALLERY, and most spectacular in his dramatic showpiece for the Cornaro Chapel of SANTA MARIA DELLA VITTORIA and scenic visions for the interior of ST PETER'S.

The Baroque was also of course the great age of the illusionistic ceiling painting, as demonstrated by the spectacular, floating fantasies of Pietro da Cortona in Palazzo Barberini (now the GALLERIA NAZIONALE D'ARTE ANTICA), of Giovanni Battista Gaulli in the GESÙ and of Padre Andrea Pozzo in SANT' IGNAZIO.

Although the **Neoclassical** style was born in Rome, and Piranesi's etchings and Canova's sculpture (in the BORGHESE GALLERY and ST PETER'S) were influential, the artists responsible for the new movement were mainly English, French and German. From this time onward, Rome was an artistic mecca of international appeal, largely bereft of the inward motivation inspired by such earlier giants as Michelangelo, Raphael and Bernini. Even the significant contributions of the 20thC **Futurist** and **Metaphysical** painters (in the GALLERIA NAZIONALE D'ARTE MODERNA) tend to be overlooked in a city enfolding two millennia of artistic treasures.

Roman mythology

As Rome grew from a small town on the fringe of Etruria to become the capital of the Mediterranean, she adapted and expanded her culture according to new ideas arriving from **Greece** and elsewhere. Her official religion, chiefly concerned with the aversion of unfavorable omens, remained hidebound; but in art and literature local deities were matched with foreign ones and increasingly took on new identities. By the time of Augustus, poets such as Ovid and Tibullus were zestfully narrating the loves of fully naturalized Greek gods.

In the **Christian era** these pagan gods were permitted to survive in the guise of allegorical figures or astrological symbols. Ovid's *Metamorphoses*, a mock-epic catalog of the love affairs of the Olympians, was allowed to circulate widely in the Middle Ages because its spicy tales were supposed to enclose cryptic moral meanings. The gods retained their astrological significance into the Renaissance, playing their part in the increasingly recondite allegories devised by the new humanists.

During the austere years of the **Counter-Reformation**, the gods were briefly banished, but with the new confidence of the **Baroque** they returned to attain a splendor and power reconcilable with a passionate Catholicism. A different kind of allegory, where Christian virtues mingled with pagan deities, was invented.

In the 18thC, the enlightenment lost patience with these effete reflections of an unreal antiquity, and **Neoclassical** writers and artists drew their inspiration from Roman history rather than Roman myth, from deeds rather than symbols.

APOLLO

Son of Jupiter and **Leto**, and brother of Diana, Apollo did not feature among the early Roman gods and was taken over entirely from Greek

religion. He was the god of prophecy, healing, music, the arts and philosophy, and is represented as a handsome, clean-shaven young man, often carrying a bow (with which he shot plague arrows) and wearing a laurel wreath. Early on he also acquired an identification with the sun and with the name **Phoebus** ("bright one"). In Roman copies of Greek statues of him — most famous is the *Apollo Belvedere* (pictured left) in the VATICAN MUSEUMS — he appears as the paragon of male beauty.

Apollo is shown as the god of music, leading the Muses on Mount Parnassus, on one of the walls of Raphael's Stanza della Segnatura, also in the VATICAN MUSEUMS. In allegorical contexts he represents reason and inspiration of a good kind — and perhaps this is intended in one of the small, fake-mosaic episodes on the ceiling of the same room, where the god flays the satyr **Marsyas**, the long-eared embodiment of lust and carnality. Apollo nevertheless had several love affairs, notably with the nymph **Daphne**. The couple are brought to life with the full force of Baroque realism in a group by Bernini in the BORGHESE GALLERY.

BACCHUS (*Greek Dionysos*)

The god of wine, and so the very opposite of Apollo, Bacchus stood not simply for drunkenness but for general lack of control and absence of reason and morality. He, too, is represented as a beardless, handsome young man, but is more effeminate than Apollo and is usually shown lounging with a cup in hand, his hair wreathed with vine leaves. He is commonly accompanied by his intoxicated entourage, consisting of satyrs with goat-legs, semi-draped and frenzied women known as *maenads,* and an extremely drunk old man called Silenus who is usually shown falling off the back of a donkey.

The *Triumph of Bacchus*, in which the god is depicted in a chariot drawn by leopards, is represented on numerous sarcophagi. One of its most famous versions is by Annibale Carracci on the ceiling of the gallery of the PALAZZO FARNESE. Here, he shares his triumph with **Ariadne**, the nymph he found on the Greek island of Naxos.

CUPID (*Greek Eros*)

The god of falling in love, Cupid was generally perceived in Greek and Roman art as a handsome adolescent, although by the time of the Renaissance he was more usually represented as a prepubertal *putto.* He is still an adolescent, however, in Raphael's depiction of the story of Cupid's love for **Psyche**, the decorative theme of the loggia in the VILLA FARNESINA.

Otherwise the Renaissance Cupid is a chubby infant, shooting golden arrows from his bow to pierce his victims' hearts. He wears a blindfold to signify the blind and irrational nature of passion, but nevertheless appears as a cheerful, happy force. Cupids scampering and fluttering through paintings generally express the well-being of nature — as in Raphael's *Galatea*, also in the VILLA FARNESINA.

DIANA (*Greek Artemis*)

Daughter of Leto, sister of Apollo, Diana was the goddess of wild places and animals, a personification of the moon and a symbol of chastity. She is typically shown clad in a tunic as a huntress, bearing bow, arrows and quiver, and is best known for her zealous protection of her own virginity. When discovered bathing by the hunter Actaeon, Diana took her revenge by turning him into a stag, to be destroyed by his own hounds — a favorite theme in Renaissance art, demonstrating the moral that lust turns man into a wild beast.

The goddess also punished overweening pride, however, and when **Niobe** rashly boasted that her own children were as beautiful as those of Leto, Diana and her brother shot Niobe and all her children with arrows. There is a magnificent representation of the dying *Daughter of Niobe*, a 5thC BC Greek statue, in the Museo Nazionale Romano in the BATHS OF DIOCLETIAN.

JUNO (*Greek Hera*)

Wife of Jupiter and the prototype of all good wives. She was an important goddess in the early Roman cult, being one of the triad to whom
the Capitol was dedicated in the first year of the Republic. Her chief
role in myth was to act vindictively against the nymphs her husband
seduced, and the resulting children. She is usually shown accompanied
by a peacock.

JUPITER (*Greek Zeus*)

The god of the sky (hence one attribute, his eagle), the
god of lightning (hence his thunderbolt) and the ruler of
gods and humanity (whence his customary enthrone-

ment). His Temple of Jupiter Optimus
Maximus ("best and greatest") on the
Capitol was the center of the state religion. The so-called *Jupiter of Otricoli*
in the VATICAN MUSEUMS, a copy of a
4thC BC original, shows his appropriate grandeur and majesty.

Identified with the Greek Zeus,
Jupiter took on a rather more frivolous
aspect. This is the god whom Ovid
shows in his *Metamorphoses* transfor-
ming himself — for a succession of
extra-marital purposes — into a swan
with **Leda**, a shower of gold with
Danae, a fellow-nymph with **Callisto**,
and lightning with **Semele**. All made
good subjects for bedroom pictures and
even for more public works of art.

MARS (*Greek Ares*)

The armed god of war, the father of **Romulus**, founder of Rome. The
Greek Ares was a bloodthirsty warrior, universally disliked, but Mars
had greater dignity. His cult was of great importance to the Roman
state, and the Temple of Mars Ultor, Mars the Avenger, in the FORUM OF
AUGUSTUS, was one of several temples dedicated to him.

In the Renaissance, Homer's story of Mars being trapped in a net with
Venus by her husband **Vulcan**, god of metalworking, became a favorite
subject, though with varying meanings (see **Venus**).

MERCURY (*Greek Hermes*)

One of the most diverse of the gods. His two prime roles were as
Jupiter's messenger and as the guide of the souls of the dead to the
Underworld; but he was also the patron of commerce, travel, elo-
quence, good sense and thieving. He, too, is represented as a beardless
young man, but wears a helmet and winged sandals and carries a
curved sword and a *caduceus* (a wand with two serpents entwined
about it, symbolizing his arcane wisdom and power to reconcile op-
posing parties by oratory).

Although the story of Mercury stealing Apollo's cattle is not uncom-
mon — it occurs, for instance, in a painting by Claude in the Galleria

Doria Pamphili (PALAZZO DORIA) — in post-medieval art the god usually represents prudence and sound judgment.

MINERVA (*Greek Athene*)

The Roman patroness of arts and crafts who later became identified with the Greek goddess of war and wisdom. She is always shown with helmet, spear and breast-plate, and a shield bearing the severed head of the snake-haired **Medusa**. In Post-Classical art, she appears as the defender of righteousness and is seen protecting the pope from the horrors of heresy in Pietro da Cortona's ceiling fresco in the Palazzo Barberini (GALLERIA NAZIONALE D'ARTE ANTICA).

NEPTUNE (*Greek Poseidon*)

The god of the sea. He is typically represented as a heroic figure, with windswept locks and beard, wielding a trident. In later art, he acquired no moral force, and merely represents his element (including fresh water). Riding a large shell drawn by sea horses, he towers over Nicolò Salvi's TREVI FOUNTAIN.

VENUS (*Greek Aphrodite*)

An obscure Roman goddess of gardens until she became associated with the Greek goddess of love. Several Roman copies of high quality show her as seductively as the Greeks intended. Most celebrated of these is the copy of Praxiteles' *Cnidian Venus* in the VATICAN MUSEUMS, a figure famed for her sensual yet serene beauty. The birth of the goddess from the sea, later a popular Renaissance theme, is shown on the 5thC BC Ludovisi Throne in the Museo Nazionale Romano in the BATHS OF DIOCLETIAN.

Venus took on a particular importance in the 1stC AD as the mother of **Aeneas**, the proto-founder of Rome, from whom the Julian emperors claimed descent. The myth was promulgated by Virgil's *Aeneid*, which inspired the frescoes by Pietro da Cortona in the PALAZZO PAMPHILI.

In post-Classical art Venus could stand for any variety of love, and her complex nature is thought to be the subject of Titian's *Sacred and Profane Love* in the BORGHESE GALLERY. A commoner theme, Venus' love affair with Mars (see **Mars**), can be interpreted either as civilization softening barbarism or as wicked adultery.

Basic information

Before you go

DOCUMENTS REQUIRED

For citizens of the US and British Commonwealth, a **passport** is the only document required for visits not exceeding three months; for citizens of the EC a **Visitor Card** will suffice. For longer visits, and for most other nationals, a **visa** must be obtained in advance in the country of departure. **Vaccination certificates** are not normally required, but if you are traveling from the Middle East, Far East, South America or Africa, you should check when buying your ticket.

To drive a car in Italy, you must carry a valid national **driver's license** accompanied by a translation (obtainable from **CIT**, **ACI** or the Italian Tourist Office in the country of origin). If you intend bringing your car into the country, you must carry the **vehicle registration document** (logbook) and an **international green card** or other valid insurance, and display a **national identity sticker**.

TRAVEL AND MEDICAL INSURANCE

It is advisable to travel with an insurance policy that covers loss of deposits paid to airlines, hotels and tour operators, and the cost of dealing with emergency requirements, such as special tickets home and extra nights in a hotel.

Travelers from EC countries are entitled to all free health services, but should still take out insurance to cover emergency expenses incurred for medical reasons. All other nationals should take out comprehensive travel and medical insurance. Travelers from the US should always consult their own insurance company for advice when going abroad.

UK nationals entitled to full UK benefits should obtain **form E111** from the DSS before leaving. If medical aid is required, present the form to the nearest **USL (Unità Sanitaria Locale)** office (see the publication *Rete di Roma)*, which will issue a certificate confirming your right to treatment.

For US citizens the **IAMAT** (International Association for Medical Assistance to Travelers) is worth joining, and membership is free. It has member hospitals and clinics throughout the world, including several in Rome and in other parts of Italy, and has a list of English-speaking doctors who will call, for a fee. It also provides information on health risks overseas. For further information, and a directory of doctors and hospitals, write to **IAMAT** headquarters in the US or in Europe *(417, Center Street, Lewiston, NY 14092, USA or 57 Voirets, 1212 Grand-Lancy, Genève, Switzerland)*.

MONEY

The monetary unit is the lira (plural lire £). There are coins for 50, 100, 200 and 500 lire, and notes for 1,000, 2,000, 5,000, 10,000, 50,000 and 100,000 lire. There are no restrictions on other currencies or travelers checks taken into the country, but if you intend exporting more than 1 million lire's worth of any currency exceeding the money that you have imported, you should complete **form V2** at customs on entry.

Travelers checks issued by all major companies are widely recognized. Make sure you read the instructions included with your travelers checks. It is important to note separately the serial numbers of your checks and the telephone number to call in case of loss. Specialist travelers check companies such as **American Express** provide extensive local refund facilities through their own offices or agents.

European visitors who hold a **Eurocheque Encashment Card** can cash personal checks in most banks. The principal **charge and credit cards** accepted are American Express, Diners Club, MasterCard/Eurocard and Visa.

American Express also has a **MoneyGram** ® money transfer service that makes it possible to wire money worldwide in just minutes, from any American Express Travel Service Office. This service is available to all customers and is not limited to American Express Card members. See USEFUL ADDRESSES on page 45.

CUSTOMS

The completion of the European Single Market takes place at the end of 1992. Under the Single Market arrangements due from January 1, 1993, travelers between EC countries need only make a declaration to Customs for prohibited or restricted goods. Limits on duty- and tax-paid goods purchased within the EC will end after 1992, although there will be certain higher limits on tobacco goods and alcoholic drinks, designed to prevent unfair commercial exploitation of the new arrangements.

These new higher limits will be: **Tobacco** — 800 cigarettes *plus* 400 cigarillos *plus* 200 cigars *plus* 1kg tobacco; **Alcohol** — 10 liters of liquor (spirits) *or* 20 liters fortified wine *plus* 90 liters wine (not more than 60 percent sparkling) *plus* 110 liters beer.

Limits that apply within the EC until the end of 1992 only are widely publicized in duty-free shops and at ports, airports and international crossing-points. All allowances apply to travelers aged 17 and over.

The EC decision is that duty- and tax-free shopping will continue until July 1999 based on what is referred to as a "vendor control system." What this appears to mean is that no duty or tax will be charged within the appropriate stores, but prices charged for goods on sale will be up to the store management. Our best advice is: be on your guard.

Travelers from countries outside the EC will still have to declare any goods in excess of the Customs allowances. If you are in any doubt at all, inquire before you depart.

When leaving Italy, you may export up to 1 million lire's worth of goods. The export of works of art is restricted and an application must be made to the Export Department of the Italian Ministry of Education.

When passing through customs, it is important that you have dated receipts for any valuable items you are carrying, such as cameras or watches, or there is a possibility that you will be charged duty on them.

ITALIAN TOURIST OFFICES

UK Italian State Tourist Office (ENIT), 1, Princes St., London W1R 8AY ☎(071) 408 1254

USA Italian Government Travel Office (ENIT), 630, 5th Ave., Suite 1565, New York, NY 10111 ☎(212) 245 4822

There are also offices in **Chicago** (☎ *(312) 644 0990);* **San Francisco** (☎ *(415) 392 6206)* and **Toronto** (☎ *(416) 363 1348).*

GETTING THERE

By air: Leonardo da Vinci Airport (Fiumicino), 36km (22 miles) SW of Rome, serves both international and domestic flights. Some domestic and international charter flights arrive at Ciampino, 16km (10 miles) SE of the city.

By train: International and most national trains arrive at Stazione Termini, Piazza dei Cinquecento, situated in the center of Rome *(map 6 H8).*

By bus: International buses also stop at Piazza dei Cinquecento.

By car: The country's main N-S and E-W highways *(autostrade),* which run from Florence to Naples and from l'Aquila to Civitavecchia, connect with the city via a huge 4-lane beltway (ring road), called the *raccordo anulare.*

CLIMATE

Although the climate is generally mild and pleasant, Rome is best visited in spring or fall. Winters are usually moderate, but January and February can sometimes be freezing cold and wet. Even the Romans avoid the city in July and August if they possibly can; temperatures reach as high as 35°C (95°F).

CLOTHES

Lightweight clothing is the obvious choice for summer; a warm coat, gloves and umbrella are all essential in winter. Remember to take comfortable shoes for sightseeing and foot-slogging around cobbled streets. Short skirts and bare arms are not acceptable in churches. Romans have a reputation for stylish dressing, but they maintain this with a degree of informality. Ties are generally unnecessary, and evening dress is rarely worn.

GENERAL DELIVERY (POSTE RESTANTE)

Letters marked **Fermo Posta** and addressed to **Palazzo delle Poste, Piazza San Silvestro, 00186** *(map 5 G6)* will be held for collection. You will need to show your passport and pay a small fee to claim your mail. **American Express** provides a short-term general delivery service for clients at **Piazza di Spagna 38, 00187** *(map 5 G6).*

Getting around

FROM THE AIRPORTS TO THE CITY

A speedy **rail link** now connects **Fiumicino** with the **south** of the city. Trains leave every $\frac{1}{2}$-hour, and the trip from Fiumicino to **Stazione Ostiense** *(map 8L6)* takes 35 minutes. The government has spent a considerable amount of money improving facilities at Stazione Ostiense, which has become the city's main air terminal. From here, you can take the Metropolitana to underground stations across the city. The entrance to the Metropolitana is 150 yards away from Ostiense station. The rail link also serves **Stazione Trastevere** *(map 7L4)*.

Buses and taxis are also available, just at the exit of the rail station. **Ciampino** is linked to Stazione Termini by suburban bus and train lines; but it is cheaper to take the **ACOTRAL** bus from the airport entrance and join the Metropolitana Line A at **Subangusta**.

Metered **taxis** are available from both airports (allow 30 minutes from Fiumicino, 20 minutes from Ciampino), but a supplement is payable from Fiumicino. **Self-drive cars** may be rented at both airports.

PUBLIC TRANSPORTATION

The best way of getting around the city is by **bus**. **Bus stops** are marked *Fermata*. Most buses now run without a conductor, and tickets for these must be bought from tobacconists or ATAC offices. You enter the bus by the rear door and place a ticket in the machine, and leave the bus by the middle door. **Trams** are still in use on some routes. Bus services to the environs of Rome are run by **ACOTRAL**, whose information office is located in Via Ostiense 131 *(☎ 5915551)*.

The **subway system (Metropolitana)** has only two lines, but they link stations in many of the key tourist locations and most itineraries can be planned around them. Stations are denoted by the white letter **M** in a black circle in our maps on pages 168-177.

There is a flat fare for the Metropolitana, buses and trams. The **Romapass Tourist Pass** (available from travel agents and some ATAC offices) is valid for three days on public transportation and also gives free admittance to public museums. Maps showing bus, tram and Metropolitana routes are available from the ATAC office outside Stazione Termini.

For property lost on buses or trams, apply to the main **ATAC** office *(Via Volturno 65 ☎ 46951, map 6G8)*.

TAXIS

Taxis may be picked up at taxi stands, or summoned by telephone for a small extra fee. See the annotated maps in *Rete di Roma* (available in most bars with phones) for lists of local taxi stands. Supplements are payable for luggage, and also for service at night, on Sunday and on public holidays.

GETTING AROUND BY CAR

Driving in Rome has little to recommend it. Parking is hard to find; the Romans' fast and aggressive tactics and the congested conditions have been aggravated by the closure of many streets to traffic. If you do use a car, remember to yield at intersections to vehicles coming from your right. A **speed limit** of 50kph (30mph) applies, but is often ignored by local drivers. The largest city parking lot is under the Villa Borghese.

Tourists who bring cars into Italy are entitled to **gasoline coupons** and **highway vouchers**. UK visitors can buy these through the AA and RAC. Visitors who have rented a car elsewhere in Europe can obtain them in the country in which the car is rented. They can also be bought at Italian frontier points from the Italian Automobile Club (ACI) — but not within Italy. They can be refunded only through the issuing office. Passport and car log book must be presented.

For more information contact **ACI** (*Via Cristoforo Colombo 261, 00144* ☎ *514971, and at Via Marsala 8, 00185* ☎ *49981* ☎ *610686, map 10 H9);* it gives free assistance to members of affiliated clubs, such as the AAA, AA and RAC. AAA members should obtain the pamphlet *Offices to Serve You Abroad* (from the AAA).

RENTING A CAR
Cars may be rented at Fiumicino and Ciampino airports or at a number of offices in the city (see Yellow Pages), or reserved in advance through travel agents. Rates generally include breakdown service and basic insurance, but it is advisable to inquire. Most firms require a deposit equal to the estimated total cost of rental (payable by charge or credit card) and set a minimum age limit of 21. You must also have held a driver's license for at least one year.

GETTING AROUND ON FOOT
Pedestrians have the right of way at pedestrian crossings, and at traffic lights when a green lighted sign reads *Avanti*. (Stop when you see a red lighted sign saying *Alt*). But it must be noted that Italian drivers often fail to yield at pedestrian crossings and have a habit of jumping traffic lights.

RAILWAY SERVICES
Italian State Railways offer a wide choice of services at reasonable prices. The information office at Stazione Termini is open 7am-10.40pm (☎ *47751*).
Inter City (IC): Fast trains running between main Italian cities. A supplementary ticket is necessary and seat reservation is sometimes obligatory.
Pendolino: 1st-class-only trains that offer special services to travelers; they are faster than the usual ICs.
Euro City (EC): Fast trains running between major Italian cities and European countries. A supplementary ticket is necessary and seat reservation is obligatory.
Espresso: Long-distance express trains stopping only at main stations, with both 1st- and 2nd-class cars.
Diretto: Trains stopping at most stations; both classes.
Locale: 2nd-class-only trains stopping at all stations.

DOMESTIC AIRLINES

Distances involved in N-S travel make flying a sensible option. Major cities are served by **Alitalia**, smaller centers by its subsidiary **ATI** *(Via Bissolati 13* ☎ *5456 for both airlines)* and Sardinia by **Alisarda** *(Via Salandra 36* ☎ *460032).* Domestic flights serve both airports.

OTHER TRANSPORTATION

To rent a **scooter**, you must be more than 21 years old and will need to present your passport and driver's license. Rent from **Scoot-a-long** *(Via Cavour 302* ☎ *6780206, map 9 I7),* **Scooters for Rent** *(Via della Purificazione 66* ☎ *465485, map 9 I7)* or **Saint Peter Rent** *(Via di Porta Castello 43* ☎ *6875714, map 4 G4).* Bicycles can be rented from **R. Collalti** *(Via del Pellegrino 81* ☎ *6541084, map 5 H4-5).*

Horsedrawn carriages may be rented in Piazza di Spagna, Via Veneto and Piazza San Pietro, and at the Trevi Fountain, Colosseum and Stazione Termini. They are expensive: you are advised to determine the fee in advance.

On-the-spot information

PUBLIC HOLIDAYS

January 1; Easter Monday; Liberation Day, April 25; Labor Day *(Festa del Lavoro),* May 1; Assumption of the Virgin *(Ferragosto),* August 15; All Saints Day *(Ognissanti),* November 1; Conception of the Virgin Mary *(Festa della Madonna Immacolata),* December 8; December 25 and 26.

TIME ZONES

Italy is 6 hours ahead of Eastern Standard Time and from 7-9 hours ahead of the other time zones in the US. It is one hour ahead of GMT in winter and 2 hours ahead in summer.

BANKS AND CURRENCY EXCHANGE

Banks are open Monday to Friday 8.30am-1.20pm and 3-4pm. **Personal checks** may be cashed by Eurocheque Encashment Card holders. **Travelers checks** can also be cashed at hotels, but the rate is usually less favorable. **Foreign exchanges** *(cambio)* are open during normal office hours. **American Express** *(Piazza di Spagna 38* ☎ *67641 or 722801* Tx *614335)* also has an exchange desk.

If you arrive in Rome outside normal banking hours without local currency, and you can't find a *cambio,* there is now an **automatic exchange machine** at Credito Romagnolo, Via Veneto 76 *(map 6 G7),* which accepts banknotes of major currencies.

SHOPPING HOURS

Shops are normally open 9am-1pm and 3.30-7.30pm. In summer they reopen at 4pm and close at 8pm. Few shops are open on Sunday. From

September to April most food stores are closed on Thursday afternoons and non-food stores are closed on Monday mornings; from May to September many shops are closed on Saturday afternoons.

RUSH HOURS
Every daylight hour is a rush hour in the city center, but congestion peaks between 8-9.30am and 5-8pm.

POST AND TELEPHONE SERVICES
You can buy **stamps** at some tobacconists (marked **T** outside), but fewer and fewer find it worth the trouble to stock them. It is often safer to head straight for a post office. **Mail boxes** are red. The **main post office** (*Palazzo delle Poste, map 5 G6*) is at Piazza San Silvestro, open Monday to Friday 8am-9pm and Saturday 8am-noon. The branch at Stazione Termini keeps the same hours. All other post offices close Monday to Friday 2pm, Saturday noon.

The **Vatican City** operates a highly efficient postal service, with its own distinctive stamps. In winter these may be bought from post offices on either side of Piazza San Pietro and in summer from a mobile post office parked in the square, open daily 8.30am-7pm except Saturday, when it closes an hour earlier. **Vatican mail boxes** are blue.

Continuing improvements to the Rome **telephone system** mean that numbers are liable to change.

To operate a **public telephone**, you must have 100-, 200- or 500-lire coins or a **telephone card** (5,000- and 10,000-lire). These are sold by tobacconists, bars and some newsstands. Direct calls inside Italy (dialing **0**) and to other countries (dialing **00**) may be made from public, private and hotel telephones or from **SIP offices** at Piazza San Silvestro or Stazione Termini. To send **international telegrams**, you should either call **Italcable** (☎ *47701*) or go to a post office.

PUBLIC LAVATORIES
They are scarce in Rome. Most small bars offer rudimentary facilities. More expensive establishments may display a saucer to recoup a small service charge. Look for the familiar symbols, or signs for *Signori* (Men) and *Signore* (Women).

ELECTRIC CURRENT
Current is 220V AC. The standard two-pin round-pronged plugs or adaptors can be purchased in most countries.

LAWS AND REGULATIONS
Strictly speaking, you should register with the police within three days of entering Italy. At hotels, you hand over your passport on checking in and the procedure is taken care of for you. In Rome, call the **Police Information Office** for details (☎ *4686 ext. 2858*).

Never leave your vehicle registration book or rental agreement in your car. If the car is stolen or towed away, the police will not co-operate unless you can prove your right to drive the car.

The wearing of seatbelts is now compulsory. Although widely ignored in the helter-skelter of traffic within the city, once on the *autostrade* even Italian drivers belt-up.

Laws against jaywalking and topless sunbathing are rarely enforced. A warning is much more likely than a fine.

CUSTOMS AND ETIQUETTE

Romans tend to be less excitable than other southern Italians, although they do their fair share of gesticulating and occasionally give way to histrionics. Manners are typical of capital city dwellers: courteous but reserved. Young Roman men pursue foreign girls by age-old tradition. Such attentions are generally playful and easily ignored.

When visiting churches where a service is in progress, try to create as little disturbance as possible or you may cause offense.

TIPPING

A 15-percent service charge is generally added to hotel and restaurant bills, but waiters expect a small tip in addition. You should tip taxi drivers 10 percent. Theater and cinema ushers expect a tip for showing you to your seat, and it is customary to leave a few coins on the counter when buying a drink at a bar. You should be more generous to sacristans or custodians who do you a special favor by opening up parts of churches or museums that are normally closed to the public.

DISABLED TRAVELERS

Rome has limited facilities for the disabled, but staff in airports, museums and other public buildings are ready and willing to give assistance. Rest rooms that accommodate wheelchairs are available at **Fiumicino** and **Ciampino** airports, **Stazione Termini** (adjacent to platform 1), **Termini** and **EUR Metropolitana stations**, **Museo Nazionale Romano**, and on the s side of **Piazza San Pietro**. The last has a few steps to negotiate, but an attendant will assist with wheelchairs. Most restaurants are happy to accept wheelchairs, provided they have advance notice.

For suitable accommodations and information, American visitors should consult *Access to the World: a Travel Guide for the Handicapped,* which can be obtained from **Facts on File Inc.,** *(460 Park Ave., New York, NY 10016).* For further information and details of tour operators specializing in tours for handicapped people, write to the **Travel Information Service**, Moss Rehabilitation Hospital *(12th St. and Tabor Rd., Philadelphia, Pa. 19141)* or to **Mobility International USA** *(PO Box 3551, Eugene, Or. 97403).*

British visitors should consult *Holidays for Disabled People,* published by **RADAR** *(25 Mortimer Street, London W1N 8AB ☎ (071) 637-5400).* A useful guide can be obtained, which is based on the personal experiences of disabled travelers in Rome and Florence, from **Project Phoenix Trust** by sending a check for £2.25, including postage, to secretary Mrs V. Saunders *(68 Rochfords, Coffee Hall, Milton Keynes MK6 5DJ ☎ (0908) 678038).*

LOCAL AND FOREIGN PUBLICATIONS

The *Daily American* and the *International Daily News* are published locally and give the main international and local news stories. The *International Herald Tribune* is available on the day of issue, as are most other major European newspapers. *This Week in Rome,* which is published monthly in both English and Italian, has listings of events, entertainments, hotels, restaurants and shops, as does *Un Ospite di Roma,* bi-lingual and bi-monthly, available free at many hotels or at **Via Monte della Farina 19** (☎ *6569641, map 4I5),* while *Il Messaggero* and *La Repubblica,* both published in Italian, have comprehensive lists of local movies and plays.

The telephone directory *Rete di Roma,* available by some public telephones, gives detailed, local information in map form.

PAPAL AUDIENCES

General papal audiences are usually held on Wednesday at 11am. In winter, they are in the Audience Hall or in St Peter's itself; in early summer, they are in Piazza San Pietro; and in late summer, they are at the Pope's hill-top residence at Castel Gandolfo. For tickets, apply to **Prefettura della Casa Pontificia** *(Città del Vaticano, 00120* ☎ *6982),* giving not more than one month's and not less than two days' notice. State the nationality and number of people in your party and the proposed date.

On Christmas Day and Easter Sunday, at noon, the Pope gives a blessing from the balcony of St Peter's. Every Sunday when in residence he makes a brief appearance at his study window in the Apostolic Palace, to say a few prayers.

Useful addresses

TOURIST INFORMATION

American Express Travel Service *(Piazza di Spagna 38* ☎ *67641 or 722801* [Tx] *614335, map 5 G6)* is a valuable source of information for any traveler in need of help, advice or emergency services.

Rome Provincial Tourist Board (EPT — Ente Provinciale per il Turismo) *(Via Parigi 11* ☎ *4881851, map 6 G8).* Other branches of EPT are at Fiumicino Airport, Stazione Termini, and the autostrada service areas at Salaria Ovest (when arriving from Florence) and Frascati Est (when arriving from Naples).

MAIN POST OFFICE

Palazzo delle Poste   Piazza San Silvestro 00186
☎ 6771, map **5** G6

TELEPHONE SERVICES

News   ☎ 190
Time   ☎ 161

Emergency information

EMERGENCY SERVICES
For **Police**, **Ambulance** or **Fire** ☎113 (Call free from any telephone).

HOSPITALS WITH EMERGENCY DEPARTMENTS
Policlinico Umberto 1   Viale del Policlinico ☎49971, map **6**G9
Policlinico Gemelli   Largo Gemelli 8 ☎30151
San Giacomo   Via Canova 29 ☎67261, map **5**G5
San Giovanni   Via Amba Aradam ☎77051, map **10**J8
Santo Spirito   Lungotevere in Sassia ☎6838901, map **4**H4

OTHER MEDICAL EMERGENCIES
Consult the telephone directory Yellow Pages to find a doctor or dentist. For private hospital treatment or consultation, contact **Salvator Mundi International Hospital** (*Viale delle Mura Gianicolensi 66/67* ☎ *586041*).

LATE-NIGHT AND ALL-NIGHT PHARMACIES
Pharmacies operate a late-night roster. For those currently open, look for a notice in the door/window of the nearest pharmacy. Alternatively ☎**1921**. The following remain open all night:
Arenula   Via Arenula 73 ☎6543278, map **4**I5
Internazionale   Piazza Barberini 49 ☎4825456, map **6**G7
Tre Madonne   Via Bertoloni 5 ☎8073423, map **6**D7
Cola di Rienzo   Via Cola di Rienzo 213 ☎3721816, map **3-4**G3-4

HELP LINES
Local police (Carabinieri)   ☎212121
Police headquarters (Questura)   ☎4686
 Samaritans   ☎6789227, 7.30-10.30pm.

Weather in Rome   ☎1911
Road report   ☎194
Alarm call service   ☎114
ACI   ☎116

TOUR OPERATORS
American Express   Piazza di Spagna 38 ☎67641 or 722801
🆃🆇614335, map **5**G6
Appian Line   Via Barberini 109 ☎4884151 🆃🆇610193, map **6**G7
Carrani Viaggi   Via Torino 124 ☎4742501, map **6**G7
CIT   Piazza della Repubblica 68 ☎47941 🆃🆇610434, map **6**G-H8

AUTOMOBILE ACCIDENTS
- Call the police immediately.
- Do not admit liability or incriminate yourself.
- Ask any witness(es) to stay and give a statement.
- Exchange names, addresses, car details and insurance companies' names and addresses with other driver(s).
- Remain to give your statement to the police.
- Report the accident to your insurance company.

CAR BREAKDOWNS
- Put on hazard warning lights and place a warning triangle 50m (55 yards) behind the car.
- ☎116 and give operator your location, car registration and make. The ACI will bring assistance.

LOST PASSPORT
Contact the police, then your consulate (see page 48).

LOST TRAVELERS CHECKS
You should notify the local police immediately, then follow the instructions provided with your travelers checks, or contact the issuing company's nearest office. If you are stranded with no money, contact your consulate or American Express (☎ *67641/ 722801*).

EMERGENCY PHRASES
Help! *Aiuto!*
There has been an accident. *C'è stato un incidente.*
Where is the nearest telephone/hospital? *Dov'è il telefono/l'ospedale più vicino?*
Call a doctor/ambulance. *Chiamate un dottore/un' ambulanza.*
Call the police. *Chiamate la polizia.*

MAJOR LIBRARIES
American Library   Via Vittorio Veneto 119a ☎46742481,map **6**G7
Biblioteca Nazionale Centrale   Viale Castro Pretorio 105 ☎4989
English Library   British Council, Via Quattro Fontane 20 ☎4756641, map **6**H7
French Library   Centro di Cultura Francese, Piazza Campitelli 3 ☎6789291, map **8**I6

MAJOR PLACES OF WORSHIP
Roman Catholic confessions are heard, in most of the major European languages, in the four great basilicas: **St Peter's**, **San Giovanni in**

Laterano, **San Paolo fuori le Mura** and **Santa Maria Maggiore**; also in the **Gesù**, **Santa Maria sopra Minerva**, **Santa Sabina**, **Sant' Anselmo** and **Sant' Ignazio**. Mass is celebrated daily in the basilicas and principal churches, High Mass with music on Sunday. Roman Catholic churches associated with the English-speaking community are:

Saint Patrick's   Via Boncompagni 31 (Irish) ☎4885716, map **6**G7
San Silvestro   Piazza San Silvestro (British) ☎6797775, map **5**G-H6
Santa Susanna   Via XX Settembre 14 (American) ☎4827510, map **6**G7-8

OTHER PLACES OF WORSHIP

Adventist   Lungotevere Michelangelo 7 ☎3211207, map **5**F4-5
American Episcopal: St Paul's   Via Napoli 58 ☎4883339, map **6**H7
Anglican: All Saints   Via del Babuino 153 ☎6794357, map **5**F-G6
Baptist   Via della Lungharetta 124 ☎5813888, map **8**J5
Islamic Centre   Via della Moschea ☎8082167, map **6**D7
Jewish Synagogue   Lungotevere dei Cenci 9 ☎6864648, map **8**I5
Lutheran   Via Sicilia 72 ☎4817519, map **6**F7
Methodist   Via Firenze 38 ☎4814811, map **6**H7
Presbyterian: St Andrew's   Via XX Settembre 7 ☎4827627, map **6**G7-8
Russian Orthodox   Via Palestro 71 ☎4450729, map **6**G9

EMBASSIES AND CONSULATES

Australia   Via Alessandria 215 ☎832721, map **6**F8
Canada   Via G.B. de Rossi 27 ☎8415341
Ireland   Largo del Nazzareno 3 ☎6782541, map **5**G-H6
New Zealand   Via Zara 28 ☎4402928
United Kingdom   Via XX Settembre 80A ☎4825441, map **6**G7-8
United States   Via Vittorio Veneto 119A ☎46741, map **6**G7

Planning
and walks

When to go

Roman weather is surprisingly fickle, and summer and winter temperatures can be more extreme than most people imagine. Spring and fall are the most temperate seasons, but they also attract more tourists. At these times, major sights tend to become overcrowded and accommodations are scarce.

SPRING
This is usually mild and dry, with plenty of sunshine, although good weather cannot be guaranteed. Easter week brings pilgrims and tourists flooding in from all over the world, determined to catch a glimpse of the Pope on the balcony of St Peter's and to join in the Christian celebrations all over the city. Other major springtime attractions are the international horse show, held in the VILLA BORGHESE, and the international tennis championships at the Foro Italico. (See CALENDAR OF EVENTS.)

For all these reasons, spring is the height of the Roman tourist season, and museums and galleries can be uncomfortably crowded, and restaurants and hotels perhaps just a little too busy. During Easter week in particular, hotels and *pensioni* are packed to overflowing and it is essential to make reservations well in advance.

SUMMER
This time of year is invariably hot, with temperatures in July and August reaching 35°C (95°F). Now it is the scorching heat rather than the crowds that may deter you from sightseeing, particularly in the case of open-air sights such as the ROMAN FORUM and PALATINE HILL.

In other respects, heat is not the problem it used to be, for many hotels, shops and restaurants are now fully air conditioned, giving you the best of both worlds. In fact, to know the city without its searing summer is to miss a vital ingredient: sitting under a shady umbrella in the sweltering heat of the midday sun, sipping an ice-cold drink; or dining *al fresco* in the warm, balmy evening air; or taking in an opera at midnight in the BATHS OF CARACALLA, under a cooler, starlit sky. These are all part of the unforgettable Roman experience.

June is the best of the summer months, followed by July. In August, the city virtually closes down and many movie theaters, shops and restaurants go out of action.

Orientation map

51

FALL
This is perhaps the best season. The city is alive and busy, but is spared a tourist invasion of springtime proportions. The days draw in quickly, but are usually fine and very warm. The only drawback is the occasional bad weather, which, when it arrives, persists for days on end. Yet, of all the months of the year, October is probably the most reliable for consistently good weather.

WINTER
Perhaps the most unpredictable season of all, but there are numerous compensations. Daytime temperatures may be freezing cold, or so mild that a coat is unnecessary out of doors. As a general but not infallible rule, cold, wet weather is more likely after mid-January. Nighttime temperatures are invariably cold, but with central heating provided by nearly all hotels and *pensioni,* this is no problem. Many restaurants and hotels light log fires in the evenings, a friendly gesture that is typical of the seasonally relaxed attitude of managers and waiters. Theater and opera flourish around this time of year, and the famous sights such as the VATICAN MUSEUMS and ST PETER'S are relatively uncrowded.

Calendar of events

See also PUBLIC HOLIDAYS on page 42 and SPORTS on pages 235-7.

JANUARY
‡ New Year's Day: **candlelit processional Te Deum** in the Catacombs of Priscilla to mark the martyrdom of the early Christians. ‡ Jan 5: carnival in Piazza Navona on last day of **children's market** (see ROME FOR CHILDREN). Continues until dawn the following day. ‡ Jan 17: **Festa di Sant' Antonio Abate**. Special service where animals are blessed, at Sant' Eusebio all' Esquilino. ‡ Jan 18: **Festa della Cattedra di San Pietro**. Celebration of the authority of the apostle. ‡ Jan 21: **Festa di Sant' Agnese**. Two lambs are blessed and shorn, and their wool later used for palliums, at Sant' Agnese fuori le Mura. ‡ Jan-June: **flat races and steeplechases** at Ippodromo delle Capanelle racecourse (see SPORTS).

FEBRUARY
‡ The weeks leading up to Lent: **Carnival**, once actively celebrated all over the city, is now barely observed. Children indulge in occasional high-spirited antics, throwing flour and water or water-filled balloons. Smaller children dress up for a parade on Via Cola di Rienzo and Via Nazionale. (See local press for details.)

MARCH
‡ Mar 9: **Festa di Santa Francesca Romana**. Blessing of cars at Piazzale del Colosseo near the church of Santa Francesca Romana (more

correctly known as Santa Maria Nova) in the Roman Forum. ‡ Mar 19: **Festa di San Giuseppe**. The statue of the saint is decorated with colored lamps, stalls sell *frittelle* (fritters), and there are sporting events and concerts. The Festival is held in the Trionfale Quarter, N of the Vatican.

APRIL
‡ **Festa della Primavera**. The Spanish Steps are decked out with colorful banks of flowering azaleas, and choral and orchestral concerts are held in Trinità dei Monti. ‡ Holy Week: special events include **pilgrimage to Scala Santa** near San Giovanni in Laterano. ‡ Good Friday: the Pope leads the **Procession of the Cross** at 9pm in the candlelit Colosseum. ‡ Easter Sunday: at noon, the Pope gives his **blessing** from the balcony of St Peter's. ‡ Easter Monday: **Pasquetta**. Traditional day for the first picnic of the year. ‡ Apr 21: **anniversary of the birth of Rome**, in Piazza del Campidoglio. Celebrated with flags and pageantry. ‡ Apr or May: **international water polo championships**.

MAY
‡ **Open-air art exhibition** in Via Margutta. ‡ May 1: **Festa del Lavoro**. Public holiday. ‡ First ten days in May: **Il Concorso Ippico Internazionale** (International Horse Show). Held at Piazza di Siena in Villa Borghese. ‡ May 6: **swearing in of the new guard** at the Vatican on the anniversary of the Sacking of Rome in 1527. ‡ Mid-May: **antiques fair** in Via dei Coronari. ‡ Last weekend in May: **Carosello Storico**. Mounted military parade at Piazza di Siena in Villa Borghese. ‡ Whit Sunday: **Festa della Madonna del Divino Amore**. Pilgrimage of penitence to the Sanctuary of the Madonna, Castel di Leva, 15km (9 miles) s of Rome. ‡ Last week in May: **Campianato Internazionale di Tennis** (International Tennis Championships) at Foro Italico. ‡ May and June: **Rose Show**. Held at Via di Valle Murcia on the Aventine Hill. ‡ May and June: **Fiera di Roma** (International Trade Fair), held at exhibition grounds on Via Cristoforo Colombo.

JUNE
‡ **Flower festival** at Genzano, 20km (12 miles) s of Rome. A huge section of the main street is carpeted with flower petals, composed into artistic arrangements by local people. ‡ First Sunday in June: **Festa della Repubblica**. Military parade centering on Via dei Fori Imperiali. Shops close. ‡ Early June to end of Sept: **Son et Lumière** in Roman Forum and at Tivoli (see EXCURSIONS). ‡ June 23-24: **Festa di San Giovanni**. Held at Piazza di Porta San Giovanni. Large quantities of snails and sucking pig consumed. ‡ June 29: **Festa di San Pietro**. The most important Roman religious festival, celebrated with solemn rites in St Peter's. ‡ June-Aug: **Estate Romano** (Roman Summer) organized by the City Council. Open-air events — concerts, movies, dances, etc. ‡ June-Aug: **Concerts** in the Basilica of Maxentius in the Roman Forum.

· JULY

‡ **Tevere Expo**. Booths and stalls along the banks of the Tiber display arts and crafts, foods and wines of the Italian regions. Folk music and firework displays provide nighttime entertainment. ‡ July 4: **picnic organized by American community**. Stalls, hamburgers and evening fireworks display. Buses leave from American Embassy *(Via Vittorio Veneto 119a* ☎ *46741)*. ‡ Last two weeks in July: **Festa de Noantri**. Processions, entertainments and other festivities in the old quarters of Trastevere. Genuine Roman feasting, with abundant food and wine laid on. ‡ July and Aug: **open-air opera** in Baths of Caracalla, **concerts** at Villa Ada, **theater** at Ostia Antica (see NIGHTLIFE AND ENTERTAINMENT and EXCURSIONS).

AUGUST

‡ **Open-air movie festival** outside one of the famous monuments of ancient Rome (see NIGHTLIFE and local press for details). ‡ Aug 1: **Festa delle Catene**. The relics of St Peter's captivity go on display in the church of San Pietro in Vincoli. ‡ Aug 5: **Festa della Madonna della Neve**. Held at Santa Maria Maggiore to commemorate the miraculous fall of snow associated with the building of the church. White flower petals flutter down during the service. ‡ Aug 15: **Ferragosto**. Important midsummer holiday. Shops and most restaurants are closed.

SEPTEMBER

‡ **Open-air exhibition** in the Via Margutta. ‡ Early Sept: **Sagra dell' Uva**. A harvest festival in the Basilica of Maxentius in the Roman Forum. Grapes are sold at knock-down prices, and entertainment is provided by musicians dressed in folk costume. ‡ Last week of Sept and first week of Oct: **Crafts show** in Via dell' Orso, near Piazza Navona. ‡ Sept-Nov: **flat races and steeplechases** are held at Ippodromo delle Capannelle racecourse. ‡ Sept-May: **soccer** on Sunday afternoons at Stadio Olimpico.

OCTOBER

‡ Oct-Apr: **chamber music recitals** at Eliseo theater (see page 213 in NIGHTLIFE AND ENTERTAINMENT).

NOVEMBER

‡ Nov 22: **Festa di Santa Cecilia**. Held at the church of Santa Cecilia in Trastevere. Also a ceremony in the Catacombs of St Calixtus where St Cecilia was buried. ‡ Nov-June: **main opera season** at Teatro dell' Opera (see NIGHTLIFE AND ENTERTAINMENT).

DECEMBER

‡ Dec 8: **Festa della Madonna Immacolata** in Piazza di Spagna. Floral tributes are left at the column of the Madonna by papal and government envoys, and firemen climb a ladder to lay a wreath on the statue's head. From time to time the Pope himself drives through the city. ‡ Mid-Dec: **children's market** begins in Piazza Navona (see

JANUARY). ‡ Dec 20-Jan 10: many churches such as Santa Maria d'Aracoeli display beautiful **nativity scenes**, and a **collection of antique cribs** is on show in Via Giulia. ‡ Dec 24: **Midnight Mass** at Santa Maria Maggiore, with veneration of the wood and metal relics of the holy crib. Masses at Santa Maria d'Aracoeli and Sant' Anselmo (on the Aventine Hill) also recommended. ‡ Dec 25: at noon, the Pope gives his **blessing** from the balcony of St Peter's. ‡ Dec 31: **New Year's Eve**. Traditional food and wine to accompany the usual revelries are *panettone,* a yeasty kind of fruit cake, and *spumante,* a sweet sparkling wine. Midnight is greeted by joyful explosions, as every Roman launches fireworks at his neighbors.

Where to go

Several attempts have been made to organize the city's development during its 2,000-year history, but, not surprisingly, the overall pattern is haphazard. Rome does not belong to any one period. It is several cities within a city, and there is no homogeneous or instantly recognizable architectural style as in, for example, Paris or Florence. For most people, the layered richness of the city's texture is the essence of its appeal, the lack of order a major part of its charm.

The original city was built on the celebrated **seven hills** to the E of the Tiber, and soon afterwards encircled by the **Servian Wall** (4thC BC). With the exception of the **Aventine Hill**, the hills have lost their prominence through centuries of landfill and erosion, but fragments of the Servian Wall survive.

The later **Aurelian Wall** (3rdC AD) took in a much larger area, briefly crossing the Tiber to include the district known as **Trastevere**. Despite its great age, the Aurelian Wall is still very much in evidence and, even more remarkably, it still defines the city center. With the exception of the **Borgo** and **Vatican City** lying to the W of the Tiber, areas outside the Wall are strictly suburban.

Because much of the ancient city is occupied by ruins and therefore uninhabited, the focal point of Rome has shifted gradually N, swinging from W to E and back again over the centuries. In the main fold of the Tiber are the predominantly medieval and Renaissance quarters, respectively to the N and S of **Corso Vittorio Emanuele**. These labels can only be applied loosely, however, for each quarter of the city is a medley of ancient, medieval and Renaissance buildings, with a lavish overlay of Baroque.

Development in the 18thC was minimal, but in the 19thC a smart commercial area was established over on the E of the city, between **Piazza Barberini** and **Piazza della Repubblica**, and prestigious residential development continued N and E. Of all the districts to have achieved prominence over the ages, this easterly area, in which **Stazione Termini** is the main landmark, is the only one subsequently to have suffered a sharp decline.

In the early 20thC the spotlight moved to **Via Veneto**, birthplace of *La Dolce Vita* and erstwhile rich man's playground. Although most of the city's luxury hotels remain clustered around this elegant boulevard, it too has lost much of its tone.

Emphasis has shifted back to **Piazza di Spagna**, now surrounded by fashionable hotels and stores, and to the N of the **Villa Borghese**, where aristocratic villas and chic nightclubs nestle discreetly among the quiet, tree-lined enclaves of suburban Parioli.

Back in the city center, the gentrified Bohemian charms of the **medieval** and **Renaissance quarters** ensure their continuing popularity with tourists, and they are a lot safer than the equally arty district of **Trastevere**, a rough area worth visiting for its fine restaurants and local color, but not recommended for staying in nor for strolling around in after dark.

North of Trastevere and the pine-covered slopes of the **Janiculum Hill** is the **Vatican City**, the smallest state in the world, yet guardian of many of its greatest treasures and the home of the Roman Catholic Church. For many people, these twin attractions make the Vatican the focal point of any visit, and accommodations are plentiful in the residential areas surrounding the City, particularly in the **Borgo**, the medieval quarter leading up to the **Castel Sant' Angelo**.

ORIENTATION

Listed below are the major areas of interest, with some of the more important sights located within them.

MEDIEVAL QUARTER *(map 4 H5)*. One of the most attractive areas in the whole of Rome, centering around PIAZZA NAVONA and the PANTHEON. It is also known as the CAMPUS MARTIUS, referring to its ancient role as an open plain for sports and military exercises, but is now a maze of narrow medieval streets and alleys, rich in Renaissance churches and palaces, and best explored on foot. (See WALKS.) To the N are the ARA PACIS AUGUSTAE and the ruins of the MAUSOLEUM OF AUGUSTUS.

MONTE MARIO *(maps 1 D2 & 11 C3)*. A recently developed, prestigious residential area on the NW outskirts of the city, with fine easterly views from outside the Villa Madama (begun by Raphael but closed to the public) and the Cavalieri Hilton hotel.

PARIOLI *(map 2 D6)* The most select of all the residential quarters, enclosed by the parklands of the VILLA BORGHESE to the S, and by Villa Ada and Villa Glori to the N. Not surprisingly, it boasts superlatives in all directions, from the city's finest hotels to its most exclusive nightclubs.

PIAZZA DELLA REPUBBLICA *(map 6 G7-H8)*. An area within easy reach of the central rail station (Stazione Termini) and other public transportation, including airport buses. It is also conveniently placed for the GALLERIA NAZIONALE D'ARTE ANTICA, the BATHS OF DIOCLETIAN (incorporating the Museo Nazionale Romano) and SANTA MARIA MAGGIORE. The district long ago lost any pretence of being fashionable, but it's well served by accommodations, and some good hotels remain.

PIAZZA DI SPAGNA *(map 5 G6)*. Since the 17thC, a popular and picturesque tourist center. Keats stayed in the house now known as the KEATS-SHELLEY MEMORIAL, overlooking the SPANISH STEPS. Above the Steps are some fine hotels with outstanding views; below, a crisscross of narrow, cobbled streets contain the city's smartest shops and most elegant cafés.

PRATI *(map 3F3)*. More and more tourists are venturing into this quiet, middle-class suburb N of the VATICAN CITY and CASTEL SANT' ANGELO, where several hotels and restaurants of quality have sprung up in recent years. Via Cola di Rienzo is an alternative to the shops around Piazza di Spagna, and fine-quality men's and women's clothes, leather goods and shoes can be found here. The flower market in the Trionfale Quarter to the W is well worth visiting.

RENAISSANCE QUARTER *(map 8I5)*. A particularly delightful part of the old city, S of Corso Vittorio Emanuele, with a predominantly Renaissance flavor that emanates above all from the magnificent PALAZZO FARNESE. The Via Giulia is an elegant backwater with a scattering of antique stores, modern art galleries and smart hotels.

TRASTEVERE *(map 7J4-8J5)*. The inhabitants of Trastevere claim to be of purer Roman stock than their neighbors across the river. Their mixed ancestry (Roman, Greek and Jewish) makes this unlikely, but they are certainly a breed apart and speak their own dialect. The area has recovered from the acute poverty it suffered in the 19thC, but is still seedy in parts, and street caution is more advisable here than elsewhere in the city. During the day the ancient churches of SANTA MARIA IN TRASTEVERE and SANTA CECILIA IN TRASTEVERE are worth a visit, while at night all kinds of entertainments abound.

VATICAN CITY *(map 3G-H2-3)*. Much of this miniature but immensely influential state is occupied by the basilica of ST PETER'S and the VATICAN MUSEUMS. The museums, housed in a vast palace complex, contain some of the greatest art collections in the world. Beyond the E boundary of PIAZZA SAN PIETRO is the BORGO, a predominantly medieval quarter which has some fine Renaissance palaces. It is cut through by VIA DELLA CONCIL-IAZIONE, Mussolini's grand processional route from the CASTEL SANT' ANGELO.

VIA VENETO *(map 6F-G7)*. Once the haunt of the international jet-set, it still has the greatest concentration of luxury hotels (see WHERE TO STAY). Those at the top of the street have fine views over the VILLA BORGHESE and are reasonably close to the BORGHESE GALLERY. The Via Veneto is brightly lit and busy after dark, with much of the city's nightlife located in the surrounding streets.

ORGANIZING YOUR TIME
If you are paying only a fleeting visit to the city, it is important to plan your time carefully. Here is a suggested sightseeing program for a three-day visit.

DAY 1
- Begin in PIAZZA DI SPAGNA. Take a bus to PIAZZA DEL POPOLO and climb the slopes of the PINCIO to enjoy the view over the city. Visit SANTA MARIA DEL POPOLO for its art treasures.
- Walk down the Corso to PIAZZA COLONNA. Make your way to the church of SANT' IGNAZIO to see a superb Baroque ceiling painting.

Continue through the medieval streets to the PANTHEON and PIAZZA NAVONA, a good place to have lunch.

- In the afternoon, cross the Corso Vittorio to admire the fine Renaissance facades of the PALAZZO DELLA CANCELLERIA and PALAZZO FARNESE. Returning to the Corso Vittorio, walk past SANT' ANDREA DELLA VALLE, and stop at the GESÙ for more Baroque illusionism.
- Walk down Via di Aracoeli and climb the steps up to PIAZZA DEL CAMPIDOGLIO. Briefly visit the CAPITOLINE MUSEUMS and nearby church of SANTA MARIA D'ARACOELI.
- Finish your tour at the MONUMENT TO VICTOR EMMANUEL II in Piazza Venezia.

DAY 2

- Begin at the CASTEL SANT' ANGELO or proceed straight to ST PETER'S, taking in the magnificent view from the battlements or dome of one or the other.
- Take a bus to Ponte Mazzini, then proceed on foot to the VILLA FARNESINA to see Raphael's frescoes. From here, walk on to Trastevere to see the mosaics of SANTA MARIA IN TRASTEVERE (arrive before 12.30pm or the church will be closed) and to have lunch.
- Spend the afternoon in the VATICAN MUSEUMS, concentrating on the Pio-Clementine Museum (Octagonal Court), Raphael Stanze, Sistine Chapel and Pinacoteca.
- In the late evening, visit the floodlit TREVI FOUNTAIN on the other side of the river.

DAY 3

- Begin with SANTA MARIA MAGGIORE. From here, proceed to Piazza Vittorio Emanuele to see the open-air market.
- Take the Metropolitana to San Giovanni for a tour of SAN GIOVANNI IN LATERANO, including the Baptistry and Scala Santa.
- Take a bus to the COLOSSEUM and walk N to NERO'S GOLDEN HOUSE or to SAN PIETRO IN VINCOLI (for Michelangelo's fragmentary Tomb of Julius II).
- If the weather permits, take a picnic to the PALATINE HILL and spend the afternoon in the ROMAN FORUM, ending with the FORUM OF TRAJAN (for Trajan's Column) and TRAJAN'S MARKETS.
- Alternatively, take the Metropolitana to Barberini, have lunch in the Via Veneto and spend the afternoon shopping around Via del Corso.

Walks in Rome

A thorough appreciation of major sites such as the ROMAN FORUM or the PALATINE HILL naturally entails a great deal of walking, but there you will find your goals spread out clearly before you. However, it is an intrepid visitor who marches unforearmed into the historic center of the city. Hence these four proposed itineraries, which all start in the heart of old Rome. The last two walks share common maps.

WALK 1: AROUND CORSO VITTORIO EMANUELE
See maps 4&5 and map on page 60. Allow $1\frac{1}{2}$ -2hrs.

This walk is best undertaken in the late afternoon. As well as providing some magnificent views, it should help you locate many of the major Renaissance and Baroque monuments that abound on either side of Corso Vittorio Emanuele, the wide thoroughfare that was driven, rather insensitively, through the papal city at the end of the last century, to proclaim the advent of the Royal House of Savoy.

Starting out from the steps of the PANTHEON facing the **obelisk** in Piazza della Rotonda, take the narrow Salita de' Crescenzi to your left. This leads to PALAZZO MADAMA, a Medici palace, now the upper house of the Italian parliament. Turn left, right and right again to reach the front of the building. Across the Corso del Rinascimento, the tiny Corsia Agonale will bring you out into the majestic open space of PIAZZA NAVONA. Every Christmas and New Year a children's fair is held here, and a fairground atmosphere persists all year round. The focal point is Bernini's inspired flight of fancy, the FOUNTAIN OF THE FOUR RIVERS, designed, so legend has it, to mock Borromini's church of SANT' AGNESE IN AGONE behind it.

If you can bear to move on from the sublime proportions of the square and the air of excitement around you, leave by the street directly opposite your point of entry, Via di Sant' Agnese. At the first intersection look up at the decoration on the 15thC **Torre Millina**. Continue onto Via di Tor Millina and, turning right, you will find on your left one of the most beautiful and lively cafés in Rome, the **Bar della Pace**. Via della Pace is dominated by the astonishing Baroque facade of SANTA MARIA DELLA PACE. Following the w side of the church, the tiny Vicolo della Pace opens into a square, Largo Febo. On the right is SANTA MARIA DELL' ANIMA, since the Renaissance the traditional church of Germans in Rome.

This attractive square leads off into Piazza di Tor Sanguigna, where you turn almost immediately left into **Via dei Coronari**, an original Renaissance street, which is agreeably straight after your meandering course so far. Browse among the curiosities displayed in its fascinating antique stores set in imposing 16thC palaces, until you reach the wide Piazza San Salvatore in Lauro on your right. Past the Neoclassical facade of the church on the right of the square is a tiny **grotto fountain** with a carved head, perhaps a lion, so worn as to be unrecognizable. You then pass down the minute, cobbled Vicolo dei Marchegiani to the embankment wall, where wooden steps to your left lead up to Lungotevere.

Ideally the sun should now be setting, for you will be greeted by two of Rome's most picturesque views: the extravagant sculpted angels

Castel Sant'Angelo

WALK 1

N

V. Acciaioli

V. d. Coronari
Pza. d. Tor Sanguigna
Corsia Agonale

S. Maria
d. Pace

Tevere (Tiber)

Lungotevere

Corso d. Rinascimento
Salita d. Crescenzi
Pza. d. Rotonda
V. S. Eustachio

Pza. S.
Salv. in
Lauro

Ponte
Principe
Amedeo

S.M. dell'
Anima

Pal.
Madama

V. d. Pace

Chiesa
Nuova

S. Agnese
in Agona

S. Ivo

Teatro
Valle

Pantheon

S. Giov.
d. Fiorentini

S. Eustachio

Pza. S. Eustachio

Pal. Sacchetti

V. d.
Cartari

S. Filippo
Neri

Oratory
of Filippini

Pal. d.
Cancelleria

V. d. Teatro Valle
Pza. S. Andrea della Valle

S. Andrea della Valle

Pal. Massimo
alle Colonne

| 0 | 250 | 500 m |
| 0 | 250 | 500 yds |

standing sentry on the PONTE SANT' ANGELO, with the CASTEL SANT' ANGELO beyond, and farther to the w, the dome of SAINT PETER'S seen through the hanging branches of the plane trees that line the banks of the Tiber. As you follow the river around to the w, St Peter's disappears from view at the point where Corso Vittorio meets Ponte Vittorio Emanuele. Here, beyond the cumbrous modern bridge, if the water is low, you may glimpse the sparse remains of the ancient **Ponte de Nerone**.

At the next bridge, the more graceful Ponte Principe Amedeo, leave Lungotevere up Via Acciaioli. At the first corner stands the church of **San Giovanni dei Fiorentini**. The church was originally the work of architects Jacopo Sansovino and Antonio da Sangallo, commissioned by Leo X. However, the apse and the strangely elongated dome were added a century later by Carlo Maderno. Turn right onto **Via Giulia**, a Renaissance street with the rare virtue of straightness. Planned by Bramante and opened at the beginning of the 16thC by Julius II, its graceful *palazzi* (**Palazzo Sacchetti**, at #66, is a good example) are redolent of the elegance of Renaissance Rome. Continue for some 250 meters (300 yards), when on your left you will see the ruined church of **San Filippo Neri**, dedicated to St Philip Neri, who is often called the second apostle of Rome.

Cross the demolished area around the church to the narrow Via de' Cartari, which comes out onto Corso Vittorio opposite the ornate facades of the **Oratory of the Filippini** and the CHIESA NUOVA, both part of the splendid complex built to house St Philip's religious community. The street will now be coming to life, as Romans take to the sidewalks in search of an evening's entertainment.

Turn right and stroll along with the crowd, taking care not to miss the massive PALAZZO DELLA CANCELLERIA on your right. Cross over to admire the curving colonnade of PALAZZO MASSIMO ALLE COLONNE, then turn left into Piazza Sant' Andrea della Valle. From the central fountain look back across Corso Vittorio at the splendid dome (the second largest in Rome) of the church of SANT' ANDREA DELLA VALLE. Continue diagonally across the square and, passing to the right of the Fascist-style National Insurance Offices, you come to Via del Teatro Valle. The theater itself is on the left-hand side of the street. It has a fine 19thC colonnade, but you may be more taken by the sight of the dome of Borromini's SANT' IVO rising above it.

Arriving at Piazza Sant' Eustachio you will be puzzled by the extreme popularity of its bar (also called **Sant' Eustachio**). Romans drive here from miles around, not to admire the Romanesque bell tower of the church, but to drink the coffee, which, they swear, is superior to any other in the city. Via Sant' Eustachio up the side of the church takes you past two ancient truncated pillars, the sole remains of **Nero's Baths**, then one right turn brings you back to the Pantheon and Piazza della Rotonda.

WALK 2: AROUND VIA DEL CORSO AND PIAZZA DI SPAGNA

*See map **5** and map on page 62. Allow 2-2½ hrs.*

This elegant quarter of aristocratic *palazzi,* dating from the 17th and 18thC, has always attracted foreign visitors, especially artists and writers. The Romantics who came to Rome for its moss-grown ruins sensibly chose this most civilized part of the city to live in. It was here that Goethe's long career found new direction and Keats's short life expired.

Setting off once more from the PANTHEON, perhaps an hour before sunset, bear half right across Piazza della Rotonda to Via degli Orfani. This leads to Piazza Capranica, where typical Roman opportunism has converted an early Renaissance palace into a movie theater. Walk round **Santa Maria in Aquiro**, the Baroque church to your right, turn left at the end of the lane and you will see the Egyptian **obelisk** brought to Rome by Augustus to act as a sundial in the CAMPUS MARTIUS. The grand facade behind it is Bernini's PALAZZO DI MONTECITORIO, seat of the lower house of the Italian parliament since 1871. Go round the building to the right by way of Via dell' Impresa. You will notice that it has been considerably extended with another (modern) facade in Piazza del Parlamento.

Turning right out of the square, you strike the busy Via del Corso. Nearly 1.5km (1 mile) in length, it is so called because the Romans used to race horses down it, until this became too hazardous for pedestrians. Turn left and walk up the Corso for a block, then turn right into Via della Vite. You are entering one of the smartest shopping areas in the world: the streets here are often laid with red carpet on special sale days at the

WALK 2

N

Trinità dei Monti
Pza. d. Spagna
Spanish Steps
V. Borgognona
Keats-Shelley Memorial
V. Condotti
Pal. d. Spagna
V. d.
V. Bocca di Leone
Corso
V. Frattina
V. d. Propaganda
Pal. Propaganda Fide
V. d. Gambero
V. d. Vite
S. Andrea delle Fratte
V. d. Bufalo
V. S. Andrea delle Fratte
V. Poli
Tritone
Pza. d. Parlamento
V. d. Impresa
V. d.
Pal. d. Montecitorio
Pal. Chigi
V. Poli
Pza. Colonna
S. M. in Aquiro
Trevi Fountain
Pza. Capranica
V. d. Orfani
V. d. Muratte
Pza. Pietra
V. d. Burro
S. Ignazio di Loyola
Pza. d. Rotonda
V. d. Seminario
Pantheon

0   250   500m
0   250   500yds

antique stores. Go first left at Via del Gambero, right at Via Frattina, then left into Via Bocca di Leone. Most of the *palazzi* have now been converted into shops and hotels, but gateways remain through which are glimpsed beautiful courtyards, proclaiming a more stately, leisured way of life.

Shortly after crossing Via Borgognona, note on your left a most unusual sarcophagus-shaped **fountain**. On reaching **Via Condotti**, the smartest street of all, turn right. Ahead of you is PIAZZA DI SPAGNA with the fabled SPANISH STEPS rising in the background. If you can resist the Gucci handbags and Bulgari jewelry on the right, cross to the historic **Caffè Greco**, the resort of artists, painters and musicians for more than 200 years. Unfortunately the appeal of the Spanish Steps is now considerably over-subscribed. As you ascend them you could be in San Francisco circa 1968, but once you reach the top and look back down Via Condotti from TRINITÀ DEI MONTI, your sense of history and place is restored. Below, to your left, is the house where Keats died, which is now known as the KEATS-SHELLEY MEMORIAL.

When you go back down the steps, turn left toward the **Palazzo di Spagna**, the early 17thC residence of the Spanish Ambassador to the Vatican. In front of it stands a 19thC **column** commemorating the dogma of the Immaculate Virgin. Pass to the right of the **Palazzo de Propaganda Fide**. The building was designed by Borromini, but the facade facing the square was built by Bernini. The Via di Propaganda leads to a small piazza, with the church of Sant' Andrea delle Fratte on the left.

Go straight ahead down Via Sant' Andrea delle Fratte, right at Via del Bufalo, then left into Via Poli. This street crosses Via del Tritone and leads down to Rome's most famous feat of combined sculpture and plumbing, the TREVI FOUNTAIN, which makes a wonderful spectacle when floodlit at night.

Via delle Muratte to the right of the fountain leads back to the Corso. Turn right and cross over when you see the COLUMN OF MARCUS AURELIUS in PIAZZA COLONNA. Turning left out of the piazza, you soon come to **Piazza Pietra**, where the columns of an ancient temple have been skillfully used in the construction of an elegant 17thC facade. The building is now the **Stock Exchange**. Cross the square, pass through Via de' Burro and you will find a square with typical 18thC buildings facing a sumptuous Baroque church, **Sant'Ignazio di Loyola**, by Carlo Maderno. Via del Seminario, on your right, will take you back to Piazza della Rotonda and your starting-point at the Pantheon.

WALK 3: TRASTEVERE AND ISOLA TIBERINA
See maps **7&8** and map on page 64. Allow 3hrs.

Although Trastevere is rapidly being taken over by expatriate artists, its irreverent working-class character has not yet been suppressed. Romans still love it and go there for an exciting night out, much as Parisians visit the Left Bank. This walk, however, is more suitable for the morning, when there will be less activity on the streets to distract you.

Leaving the S end of PIAZZA NAVONA, take Via Cuccagna, which leads down the side of **Palazzo Braschi**, home of the ROME MUSEUM. Across Corso Vittorio, the PALAZZO PICCOLA FARNESINA houses a much smaller museum of ancient sculpture. Down to the left of it, Via dei Baullari takes you to the broad market square of PIAZZA CAMPO DEI FIORI. The **statue** in the center is of the 16thC philosopher, Giordano Bruno, who was burned at the stake for heresy on this very spot. Radical opinion in Italy has adopted Bruno as one of its greatest martyrs and the scene of his execution as the appropriate place at which to voice dissent.

Via dei Baullari continues a little way beyond Campo dei Fiori, bringing you to Piazza Farnese, where the imposing Renaissance dignity of PALAZZO FARNESE rivals the finest *palazzi* of Florence. The fleurs-de-lis in its magnificent cornice indicate its Florentine past rather than its present function as the French Embassy.

Turn left in front of the palace and go along Vicolo dei Venti to the tiny **Piazza della Quercia**. The ancient oak tree and unpretentious restaurant give this square an almost rustic flavor. Go straight ahead through Piazza Capo di Ferro past PALAZZO SPADA, with its splendid courtyard leading to the art gallery, until you reach Piazza dei Pellegrini, named after the church of the Trinità dei Pellegrini. As you turn right down Via dei Pettinari to **Ponte Sisto** (named after its builder, Pope Sixtus IV), spare a thought for the poor Trasteverini who used to trudge up this hill carrying their valuables to the pawnbroker at Piazza Monte di Pietà.

Once across the bridge with its distinctive **lamp standards**, you enter Trastevere through Piazza Trilussa. Beside the grand **fountain** stands a **bust of the poet Trilussa** (died 1954), whose witty, vulgar ballads, which were written in a phonetic transcription of the local Trastevere dialect, epitomize the devil-may-care attitude characteristic of the poor of Rome.

Toward the back of the square, on the left, is Vicolo del Cinque, a typical narrow Trastevere street. When you come to a small piazza, bear left past the church of Sant' Egidio. Ahead of you is the apse of SANTA MARIA IN TRASTEVERE. Turn left at Via della Paglia and you will come out into the piazza in front of the church. If there is room on the steps of the fountain, sit down to admire the golden mosaics on the facade and the characteristic Romanesque campanile.

Keeping to the left of the piazza, go down Via della Lungaretta, a long, dark, cobbled street that eventually crosses the top of Viale Trastevere at the bustling intersection of Piazza Sonnino. On your right is **San Crisogono**, a church dating from the 5thC. Cross over to the row of bars and movie theaters, go right, then take the second left, Via dei Genovesi. Past Via della Luce you find **San Giovanni dei Genovesi** on your right. The church itself was rebuilt in the 19thC, but through the entrance to the left of it you can visit the exquisite 15thC cloisters. The brightly colored octagonal marble pillars are set in a garden of almost tropical luxuriance.

At the next intersection you will see to your right the impressive campanile of SANTA CECILIA IN TRASTEVERE. You approach the church through a vast gateway and a pleasant formal garden, before reaching the fine medieval portico. Take note of any concerts being performed at the church. They are usually of high quality, as is only fitting in the church of the patron saint of music.

Returning to Via dei Genovesi, cross straight over it and continue until you come to the largely medieval **Piazza in Piscinula**. On the other side of the square, steps lead up to Lungotevere opposite the ISOLA TIBERINA. As you cross Ponte Cestio, beyond the tower of SAN BARTOLOMEO to your right, there stands one solitary arch of a broken bridge, known simply as the **Ponte Rotto**. The views from the island are magnificent, both back across Trastevere to the JANICULUM HILL and s toward the AVENTINE HILL.

On the far side of the island the short hump-backed **Ponte Fabricio** is, after Ponte Milvio, the oldest bridge still in use. It dates from 62BC. The weather-beaten lumps of marble on the parapet are in fact four-sided **heads of Janus**. Let these be your signal to turn back, and retrace your steps over the island to one of Trastevere's many restaurants and enjoy a well-deserved lunch.

WALK 4: BEHIND THE CAPITOL TO THE AVENTINE
*See maps **7&8** and map opposite. Allow $2\frac{1}{2}$ -$3\frac{1}{2}$ hrs.*
If you can stand the Roman sun, try this walk on a summer's afternoon, when the shimmering heat and stillness make Rome seem a completely different city. On the tranquil heights of the AVENTINE HILL the distant noise of traffic may even be drowned by that of cicadas.

Starting off once again from the PANTHEON, turn right and go down the side of the building along Via della Minerva. At the piazza of the same name you will see the plain Renaissance facade of SANTA MARIA SOPRA MINERVA, with Bernini's delightful *Elephant Supporting an Obelisk* in front of it. Walk straight ahead down Via dei Cestari until you reach LARGO ARGENTINA with its sunken area containing the remains of four **Republican temples**, which only came to light during demolition in the 1920s.

Passing to the left of the excavations down Via San Nicola de' Cesarini, you may observe that those who stand most to benefit from this work of conservation are the stray cats that have made their homes in the ruins.

At the reconstructed **medieval tower** on the corner, cross Via Florida into Via Paganica. This leads to Piazza Mattei and its celebrated TORTOISE FOUNTAIN. Originally this enchanting composition consisted simply of the slender youths with their dolphins; the tortoises were an inspired after-thought. Go left along Via de' Funari, then right down Via Sant' Angelo in Pescheria.

To your right you are looking toward the old GHETTO, where Jews were forced to live in desperately overcrowded conditions until as late as the 19thC. On your left you come to the church of **Sant' Angelo in Pescheria**, so-called because this area was once the home of the city's fish market. In front of the church stand the fascinating ruins of the PORTICO OF OCTAVIA, dating from the 2ndC BC.

Via del Portico d'Ottavia leads down to the river opposite the ISOLA TIBERINA, with the THEATER OF MARCELLUS and Palazzo Orsini on the left and the Synagogue on the right. Turning left past the Theater of Marcellus, across the large Piazza di Monte Savello, you mount some steps and turn right into Via Petroselli (formerly Via del Teatro di Marcello).

The church of **San Nicola in Carcere** on the right is a typical hybrid construction, consisting of a ruined Roman temple, a medieval tower and many later additions and subtractions. Past the large modern Public Records Office, which stands on the site of the docks of ancient Rome, is the **Casa dei Crescenzi**, once the home of one of the city's most powerful families and another striking example of medieval recycling of Classical remains.

Toward the river at the bottom of Via Petroselli, you cannot fail to notice the two small temples, both extraordinarily well-preserved, known wrongly but irrevocably as the TEMPLE OF FORTUNA VIRILIS and the TEMPLE OF VESTA. A slight detour up to your left is strongly recommended to examine the curious multiple 4thC **Arch of Janus**. Then turn your attention to the soaring seven-storied bell tower of SANTA MARIA IN COS-MEDIN, which dominates **Piazza Bocca della Verità**. The famous stone carving that gives the piazza its name can be seen inside the portico of the church.

Walking up to the right of the church brings you to Via del Circo Massimo. The CIRCUS MAXIMUS itself, although the outlines are beautifully restored, seems sad and empty without the 250,000 spectators it used to accommodate, and somewhat threatened by the perilous-looking ruins at the back of the PALATINE HILL. At the wide Piazzale Ugo la Malfa, turn right just before the statue of the great 19thC Republican, **Giuseppe Mazzini**. This street, Via di Valle Murcia, leads up to Via di Santa Sabina and the top of the AVENTINE HILL. Here, a small park of pine and orange trees called **Parco Savello** (Romans refer to it as *Giardino degli aranci*), opens onto one of the most striking views of Rome. On the other side of the Tiber is the imposing **Ospizio di San Michele** and Trastevere. You can also see the JANICULUM HILL on the right, and VILLA MEDICI and TRINITÀ DEI MONTI on the left. The park is dominated by the solemn grandeur of

SANTA SABINA, which looks out over Trastevere. The vast, echoing interior of the church is an ideal place to cool off after your climb.

The ornately-walled piazza at the end of the road, **Piazza dei Cavalieri di Malta**, designed by Piranesi, is named after the Knights of Malta, who own this highly desirable corner of Rome. Their priory is through the impressive entrance to the right, and if you look through the keyhole of the door you will see SAINT PETER'S in the distance framed by trees.

When quiet contemplation among cypresses and pines begins to pall and once more you crave the hurly-burly of the modern city, retrace your steps down Via di Santa Sabina, but then go right along Via del Circo Massimo. This brings you to the Metropolitana and a good selection of bus and tram routes to take you back to the present day.

SIGHTS CLASSIFIED BY TYPE

ARCHES AND COLUMNS
Arch of Constantine 🏛
Arch of Septimius Severus
Arch of Titus
Column of Marcus Aurelius
Trajan's Column ★
BATHS
Baths of Caracalla 🏛 ✻
Baths of Diocletian 🏛
CASTLES AND TOWERS
Castel Sant' Angelo ★ 🏛
Torre delle Milizie
CATACOMBS AND CEMETERIES
Catacombs of Domitilla ★
Catacombs of Priscilla
Catacombs of St Calixtus ★
Catacombs of St Sebastian ★
Pre-Constantinian Necropolis
Protestant Cemetery
Vatican Grottoes
CHURCHES AND BASILICAS
Chiesa Nuova (Santa Maria in Vallicella)
Gesù 🏛
Pantheon ★ 🏛
Sant' Agnese in Agone 🏛
Sant' Agnese fuori le Mura 🏛
Sant' Agostino 🏛
Sant' Andrea al Quirinale 🏛
Sant' Andrea della Valle 🏛
Santi Apostoli 🏛
San Bartolomeo 🏛
San Carlo ai Catinari 🏛
San Carlo alle Quattro Fontane 🏛
Santa Cecilia in Trastevere 🏛
San Clemente 🏛
Santi Cosma e Damiano 🏛
Santa Costanza 🏛
Santa Croce in Gerusalemme 🏛
San Giovanni in Laterano 🏛
Santi Giovanni e Paolo 🏛
San Gregorio Magno 🏛
Sant' Ignazio 🏛
Sant' Ivo 🏛
San Lorenzo fuori le Mura 🏛
Santi Luca e Martina 🏛
San Luigi dei Francesi 🏛
San Marco 🏛
Santa Maria degli Angeli
Santa Maria dell' Anima 🏛
Santa Maria Antiqua
Santa Maria d' Aracoeli 🏛
Santa Maria in Cosmedin 🏛
Santa Maria in Domnica (Santa Maria della Navicella) 🏛
Santa Maria Maggiore 🏛
Santa Maria sopra Minerva 🏛
Santa Maria Nova (Santa Francesca Romana)
Santa Maria della Pace 🏛
Santa Maria del Popolo 🏛
Santa Maria in Trastevere 🏛
Santa Maria della Vittoria 🏛
San Paolo fuori le Mura 🏛
St Peter's ★ 🏛
San Pietro in Carcere
San Pietro in Montorio 🏛
San Pietro in Vincoli 🏛
Santa Prassede 🏛
Santa Pudenziana 🏛
Santi Quattro Coronati 🏛
San Saba 🏛
Santa Sabina 🏛
Santo Stefano Rotondo 🏛
Santa Susanna 🏛
San Teodoro 🏛
Trinità dei Monti 🏛
FORUMS AND MARKETS
Forum of Augustus 🏛
Forum Boarium
Forum of Caesar 🏛
Forum of Nerva
Forum of Trajan 🏛
Forum of Vespasian
Roman Forum ★ 🏛
Trajan's Markets 🏛
FOUNTAINS
Barcaccia Fountain
Fountain of the Bees
Fountain of the Four Rivers ★
Four Fountains
Moor Fountain
Moses Fountain
Naiads' Fountain
Paola Fountain
Tortoise Fountain
Trevi Fountain ★
Triton Fountain
GALLERIES
Borghese Gallery ★ 🏛 ✻
Galleria Colonna
Galleria Doria Pamphili
Galleria Nazionale d' Arte Antica ★ 🏛

Galleria Nazionale d' Arte
  Moderna ♣
Galleria Spada
Pinacoteca Capitolina
Pinacoteca Vaticana
GATEWAYS
Porta Maggiore ⛪
Porta Pia
Porta Portese ⛪
Porta San Pancrazio
Porta San Paolo ⛪
Porta San Sebastiano ⛪
HILLS AND OTHER DISTRICTS
Aventine Hill ⬳
Borgo
Campus Martius
Capitoline Hill ⬳
Coelian Hill
Esquiline Hill
Ghetto
Isola Tiberina
Janiculum Hill ⬳ ♣
Largo Argentina
Ludovisi Quarter
Palatine Hill ⛪
Quirinal Hill
Vatican City
HISTORIC HOUSES
Casa dei Cavalieri di Rodi
Keats-Shelley Memorial
Nero's Golden House
MAUSOLEUMS AND MONUMENTS
Ara Pacis Augustae ★
Mausoleum of Augustus ⛪
Mausoleum of Hadrian
Monument to Victor
  Emmanuel II
Pyramid of Caius Cestius ⛪
MUSEUMS
Barracco Museum
Capitoline Museums ‡
Museo Nazionale Romano
Museo Nazionale di Villa Giulia ‡
Museo di Palazzo Venezia
Rome Museum
Vatican Museums ★ ‡
PALACES AND VILLAS
Lateran Palace ⛪
Oratory Complex ⛪
Palazzo Barberini ⛪
Palazzo Borghese ⛪
Palazzo Braschi
Palazzo della Cancelleria ⛪
Palazzo Chigi ⛪

Palazzo Colonna ⛪
Palazzo Corsini ⛪
Palazzo Doria ⛪
Palazzo Farnese ⛪
Palazzo Madama ⛪
Palazzo Massimo alle Colonne ⛪
Palazzo di Montecitorio ⛪
Palazzo Orsini
Palazzo Pamphili ⛪
Palazzo Piccola Farnesina ⛪
Palazzo del Quirinale ⛪
Palazzo Senatorio
Palazzo Spada ⛪
Palazzo Venezia ⛪
Villa Farnesina ⛪
Villa Giulia ⛪
Villa Medici ⛪
PARKS AND GARDENS
Pincio ⬳
Villa Borghese ♣
Villa Giulia ⛪
Villa Medici ⛪
PIAZZAS
Piazza Bocca della Verità ⛪
Piazza del Campidoglio ⛪
Piazza Campo dei Fiori
Piazza Colonna
Piazza della Minerva
Piazza Navona ★ ♣
Piazza del Popolo
Piazza del Quirinale ⬳
Piazza San Pietro ★
Piazza di Spagna
ROADS, DRAINS AND BRIDGES
Cloaca Maxima
Ponte Sant' Angelo ★
Via della Conciliazione
STADIUMS
Circus Maximus
Piazza Navona ★ ♣
TEMPLES AND PORTICOES
Pantheon ★ ⛪
Portico of Octavia ⛪
Tempietto ⛪
Temple of Fortuna Virilis ⛪
Temple of Venus and Rome ⛪
Temple of Vesta ⛪
THEATERS AND AUDITORIUMS
Colosseum ★ ⛪ ♣
Theater of Marcellus ⛪

‡ indicates a museum with a
significant collection of Etruscan
artifacts.

Sights and places of interest

Introduction

The sheer size and range of Rome's artistic heritage can prove bewildering to a first-time visitor. With more than two thousand years of art and architecture at your disposal — ranging from Classical through Early Christian and medieval to Renaissance and Baroque — some specialization is inevitable and indeed desirable. Once you have taken in the major sights such as the Roman Forum and St Peter's, it is wise to concentrate on just one historical period.

The lack of chronological organization in many museums and galleries can also be confusing. This is often a vestige of the private nature of the original collection. Poor cataloguing, erratic opening times and inexplicable closures are also typical, but all these are minor aggravations when set against the quality of the collections themselves.

USEFUL TO KNOW
Church opening times vary hugely, but are roughly 7.30am-12.30pm, 3-6.30pm. In summer, the afternoon times run about one hour later. Entrance to many of the major state-owned archeological sites and museums is free on the first and third Saturday and the second and fourth Sunday of each month. Works of art in churches are generally covered during the week before Easter Sunday, as a sign of mourning.

HOW TO USE THIS SECTION
In the following pages, Rome's sights are arranged alphabetically, using English or Italian names according to common English-speaking usage. The sights are classified by category on pages 68-69.

Look for the ★ symbol against the most important sights and ▥ for buildings of great architectural interest. Places of special interest for children ✿ and with outstanding views ◁€ are also indicated. For a full explanation of symbols, see page 7. If you only know the name of a museum, say, in English, and cannot find it in the following A-Z, try looking it up in the INDEX. Some lesser sights do not have their own entries but are included within other entries: look these up in the index too.

Bold type is generally employed to indicate outstanding buildings or other highlights. Occasionally it is used to single out an important but now-vanished building or monument. Entries given without addresses and opening times are described more fully elsewhere: check the **cross-references**, which are in SMALL CAPITALS.

Rome's sights A-Z

ARA PACIS AUGUSTAE (Altar of Augustan Peace) ★
Via di Ripetta ☎67102071. Map 4G5 🚌 *Open Tues-Sat 9am-1.30pm; Sun 9am-1pm; also (Apr-Oct) Tues, Thurs, Sat 4.30-8pm. Closed Mon.*

Reflecting the cypresses around the nearby MAUSOLEUM OF AUGUSTUS, great panes of plate-glass surround one of the most interesting monuments in Rome. The Altar of Augustan Peace was built by decree of the Roman Senate, to honor Augustus and celebrate the peace that followed his victories in Spain and Gaul. The main structure is of Carrara marble, and the quality of the carving is of the highest order.

The white marble altar itself is very plain, but the carved screen surrounding it is richly decorated. The screen reliefs are divided into two levels: the upper one consists mainly of figures, the lower one of intricately woven floral patterns and acanthus leaves. The relief at the E end, showing the earth goddess Tellus with a swan, cow and lamb, is a particularly fine composition. Part of the upper level of decoration is a **processional frieze** of exceptional interest: it shows a number of important people at the consecration ceremony on July 4, 13BC, and includes a life-sized portrait of Augustus. You can also see lictors with their rods, four priestly figures with strange headdresses, the Pontifex Maximus, Augustus' wife Livia, his daughter Julia, his niece Antonia and three children — one of them usually identified as the future Emperor Claudius.

The discovery and reclamation of the Ara Pacis is a remarkable story. Several blocks of the altar were found in 1568 during excavations for the Palazzo Fiano, and were cut up and distributed to purchasers. One of them eventually passed to the Louvre and another to the VATICAN MUSEUMS. Further attempts to salvage the remains proved abortive until 1937, when engineers working with a team of archeologists froze the underground spring waters, enabling the palace above to be underpinned and the remains of the altar and screen to be extricated. Several museums both in Italy and outside then cooperated by returning either the original fragments or facsimiles, making possible the exciting task of reconstruction of the Ara Pacis.

ARCH OF CONSTANTINE (Arco di Costantino) 🏛
Piazza del Colosseo. Map 9J7. Metropolitana: Colosseo.

One of the last great monuments of ancient Rome, the Arch of Constantine (see illustration on page 26) was erected by the Senate in 315 to commemorate the Emperor's victory at the Milvian Bridge. The best of its reliefs were taken from earlier monuments to Trajan, Hadrian and Marcus Aurelius, no-tably the fine reliefs of battle scenes high up inside the central arch that show Trajan battling against the Dacians, and the eight rectangular reliefs let into the attic, which originated in a monument to Marcus Aurelius.

The inferior quality of 4thC Roman sculpture is evident in the low-reliefs at the base of the columns, and in the friezes featuring Constantine above the arches.

ARCH OF SEPTIMIUS SEVERUS An enormously influential triumphal arch, built in the 3rdC to celebrate the first ten years of the Emperor's rule and to honor his military victories. It stands at the w end of the ROMAN FORUM.

ARCH OF TITUS The oldest surviving triumphal arch in the city stands resplendent at the E end of the ROMAN FORUM. Its simple but noble proportions and superb high-reliefs make it one of the greatest monuments of ancient Rome.

AURELIAN WALL (Mura Aureliane) ▥
The greater part of the impressive wall erected by Aurelian and Probus between 272 and 279 remains visible today, mostly in good condition. Taking in the Seven Hills, and massively buttressed, it makes an indelible impression. The aim of the wall was to keep out the Alemanni, whom Aurelian had defeated. The wall was 19km (12 miles) in circumference and had 18 main gates and 381 towers.

The best places to see it are at PORTA SAN SEBASTIANO and along Via Campania to the E of Porta Pinciana.

AVENTINE HILL (Aventino)
Map 8J6 ◀€ *Metropolitana: Circo Massimo.*
The Aventine rises S of the PALATINE HILL, and from the Parco di Sant' Alessio affords a marvelous view over the Tiber toward Trastevere and SAINT PETER'S. Here, high on the hill, are the churches of SANTA SABINA, Sant' Alessio and Sant' Anselmo. The delightful 18thC **Piazza dei Cavalieri di Malta** was designed by Piranesi and is famed for its spectacular view of St Peter's. If you look through the keyhole of the door leading to the priory of the Knights of Malta, you can see the basilica framed by trees.

BARCACCIA FOUNTAIN (Fontana della Barcaccia) ★
Piazza di Spagna. Map 5G6. Metropolitana: Spagna.
Commissioned by Urban VIII in 1627, this fountain is generally considered to be the work of Pietro Bernini, although some authorities believe it is by his much more famous son, Gianlorenzo. Here, at the foot of the SPANISH STEPS, you can still sit and watch the world go by, even if it is often impossible to hear the tranquil waters of the fountain above the noise of traffic.

The design ingeniously takes advantage of the low water pressure in the Acqua Vergine aqueduct and represents a sinking boat with water spilling fitfully from both prow and stern. Legend has it that the fountain marks the spot where a boat was once stranded when the Tiber overflowed its banks.

BARRACCO MUSEUM A small collection of Classical, Egyptian and Western Asiatic sculpture, assembled by Baron Barracco and chiefly notable for its Greek pieces. It is now housed in the PALAZZO PICCOLA FARNESINA.

BATHS OF CARACALLA (Terme di Caracalla) 🏛 ★

Piazzale Numa Pompilio ☎*5758626. Map* **9**K7 🚌 ♦ *Open 9am-3pm.*
Metropolitana: Circo Massimo.

Begun by Caracalla in 212 and completed by Heliogabalus and Alexander Severus, these vast baths are still impressive in their ruined state. It takes a considerable effort of imagination, however, to visualize the original splendor of the architecture and decoration. They were perhaps the most luxurious baths ever built in Rome. There was a gymnasium, a stadium, Greek and Latin libraries, a picture gallery, leisure gardens, and room for 1,600 bathers. The assembly rooms and precincts were faced with marble of many colors and were adorned with a magnificent collection of sculpture.

Traces of the once extensive floor mosaics remain, and enough is left of the shattered vaults to make a superb stage setting for open-air operas (see NIGHTLIFE AND ENTERTAINMENT).

BATHS OF DIOCLETIAN (Terme di Diocleziano) 🏛 ★

Piazza della Repubblica. Map **6**G8. *Metropolitana: Repubblica.*

A prominent feature of Piazza della Repubblica is the gaunt, weather-worn mass of brick, almost in a state of ruin, that looms up on the NE side. Part of the remains of the great Baths of Diocletian, it now contains the church of Santa Maria degli Angeli.

The Baths were begun by the Emperor Maximian in 298 on his return from Africa, and completed by Diocletian in 305-306. They were the largest of all the bath complexes, and could accommodate 3,000 people. The basic elements, as of all baths, were the *Calidarium* (hot), the *Tepidarium* (warm) and the *Frigidarium* (cold), but there were also exercise areas, shaded walks, outdoor pools, and even libraries.

Enough remains of the original buildings to convey a sense of their monumental scale and complexity: they once covered an area of 13 hectares (32 acres). The massive bare brick walls were once faced with marble, and the Baths were as luxurious as they were extensive.

The church of **Santa Maria degli Angeli** is one of Michelangelo's least characteristic works. He was commissioned to effect the conversion by Pius IV, and did so with due respect for the ancient Classical structure, using the huge central hall of the Baths as the nave of the new Carthusian church. When Vanvitelli was brought in to refurbish the interior in the 18thC, he altered the orientation so that the nave became an exceptionally wide transept. The ground plan was now wider than it was long, despite the construction of an apse that cut into the wall of the *Frigidarium,* and, with the addition of Vanvitelli's Baroque decorations, much of the force of Michelangelo's conception was lost. The entrance to the church, in Piazza della Repubblica, is all that remains of the *Calidarium.*

Inside the vestibule, or former *Tepidarium,* is the church's only memorable work of art, an imposing statue of St Bruno, founder of the Carthusian order, by Houdon (1766). Clement XIV said the only reason why this statue did not talk was that it was observing the monastic rule of silence. In the left transept, the vast interior is explained by a series of plans and drawings, showing the Baths' original appearance.

barely visible or disappeared

partly or wholly visible

0   50   100m

0   50   100yds

Museo Nazionale Romano ☆

Piazza dei Cinquecento ☎*460856* 🔲 🔲 🗶 *Open Tues-Sat 9am-2pm; Sun 9am-1pm. Closed Mon. Metropolitana: Repubblica or Termini.*

This museum was founded in 1889, to house all the antique works of art of high artistic merit discovered within the city of Rome. In 1906 the State bought the celebrated collection of the Ludovisi family, and this has now been incorporated, although it has been closed to the public during the extensive renovation of the museum and new excavation of the baths. The superb **Ludovisi Throne** (☆) is sometimes on display, in the **Small Cloister** of the old Carthusian monastery that was founded on this spot. It is an original Greek work of the 5thC BC, found in the Villa Ludovisi in 1887. The relief sculpture is dominated by the *Birth of Aphrodite* on the front, but it is the figure of the naked flute girl on the side that charms us with its simplicity.

Apart from the Ludovisi Throne, the most important sculptures in the museum are to be found in a sequence of nine rooms situated off the **Great Cloister**. Room III is of particular interest. It contains the *Daughter of Niobe,* possibly a Greek original dating from 460-430BC; two Greek bronzes of exceptional quality (a young man leaning on a lance, and a weary and probably defeated boxer, signed by Apollonios); and a superb copy of the *Discobolos,* or discus-thrower, by Myron. Room VI is filled with a great variety of Roman portraits, including a magnificent statue of *Augustus as Pontifex Maximus.*

On the first floor of this building is a collection of frescoes, stuccoes and mosaics found mostly in Rome, all fine examples of early Classical decoration; the charming **landscape frescoes** (★) from the House of Livia are particularly beautiful.

BORGHESE GALLERY (Galleria Borghese) ▥ ★
Via Pinciana ☎ *858577. Map* **6F7** ▨ *✗ Open 9am-2pm.*

Designed by Giovanni Vasanzio (Jan Van Santen) between 1613-15, this handsome building was erected for Cardinal Scipione Borghese, nephew of Paul V, patron of Bernini and the greatest collector of his day. It is correctly called the *Casino Borghese,* meaning summer or pleasure house, for it was never intended to be lived in. It is surrounded by the park and gardens, which are now open to the public, of the VILLA BORGHESE, with the Zoo at its northern limits. Inside the gallery there is a collection of sculpture and painting second only to that of the VATICAN MUSEUMS. Sculpture is located mainly on the ground floor.

In 1985 subsidence of the building caused the closure of the gallery, and although it has reopened, access can be restricted.

Entering through the portico, you find yourself in the **Salone**, a large room with a richly painted ceiling. It contains antique sculptures, and on the **pavement** there are some good 3rdC Roman mosaics of gladiators fighting, and hunting scenes. In the near right-hand corner is the entrance to **Room I**. Here is one of the most famous pieces in the whole collection, the reclining figure of *Pauline Borghese* (★), Napoleon's sister. She married Camillo Borghese in 1803, and Antonio Canova's revealing statue of her dates from 1804. Canova is often branded a chill exponent of the Neoclassical style, but this representation of Pauline as Venus is full of life and warmth. Legend relates that Camillo kept it behind locked doors, and only showed it to his intimate friends.

The centerpiece of **Room II** is Bernini's marvelous *David* (★), commissioned by Scipione Borghese (1623-24). It is an astonishing display of virtuosity, the intensity of expression and vitality of movement showing the absolute command of the sculptor over his material. The face is said to be a self-portrait of the young sculptor, and Scipione is alleged to have held the mirror for his young protégé.

In **Room III** Bernini again dominates with his group of *Apollo and Daphne* (1622-25), possibly his masterpiece (★). The story of Apollo's love for the nymph Daphne, of her flight from him and metamorphosis into a laurel tree, is hardly the most obvious of choices for the subject of a sculptural group. But Bernini actually seems to relish the difficulty of his task, and chooses the most dramatic moment possible. Daphne's thighs transformed into bark, and fingers changed into leafy tendrils, tell the beautiful young god that he is just too late, and the poignancy and grace of the moment is perfectly caught.

Room IV is a large hall, with superb 17thC decorations. The marble floor is paved in a beautiful geometric design, there are low-relief carvings high on the walls, and the ceiling is frescoed. Around the walls are busts of Roman emperors in marble and porphyry, and some splendid vases, while in the center there is another great Bernini sculpture, the *Rape of Proserpine* (★). It is an early work (1621-22) and yet again shows the artist's enormous technical skill. The hard shiny surfaces of the muscular King of the Underworld contrast wonderfully with the soft texture of Proserpine's body, as his fierce grip digs into her flesh. At his feet, the grim three-headed Cerberus, guardian of the entrance to the Underworld, bays menacingly.

Room V is a small room with some good sculptures, of which the most interesting is a copy of Phidias' *Athene Parthenos*. **Room VI** contains two further works by Bernini, *Aeneas, Anchises and Ascanius Fleeing from the Sack of Troy,* an early piece in which he collaborated with his father Pietro, and *Truth Unveiled by Time,* a much later work (c. 1652) of which only the figure of Truth was ever completed. The group remained in the sculptor's possession until his death, and provoked the quip that the only place in Rome where one could be sure of finding truth was in Cavaliere Bernini's house. Neither of these works is as captivating as the other Bernini pieces here, but by any other standard they are very fine indeed.

The next two rooms feature Classical sculpture. The *Youth on a Dolphin* in **Room VII** and *Dancing Faun* in **Room VIII** are both Roman copies of Greek originals.

To reach the first floor it is necessary to return to Room IV and climb the spiral staircase. The main attraction of **Room IX** is Raphael's famous *Deposition* (★) (1507). It was executed for Atalanta Baglione in memory of her murdered son, and kept in the church of San Francesco al Prato in Perugia until 1608, when it was obtained by the Borghese. Other note-worthy pictures in this room are the *Portraits of a Man* and *Portrait of a Woman with a Unicorn* by Raphael, a *Crucifixion with Sts Jerome and Christopher* by Pinturicchio, and a *Madonna and Child with St John the Baptist* by Lorenzo di Credi.

The last subject is repeated by Andrea del Sarto in **Room X**, where other outstanding works are *Venus and Cupid* (★) by Cranach and *The Baptism* (★) by Bronzino. Also in this room is the *Head of a Young Girl,* a beautiful early 16thC drawing by the Master of the Pala Sforzesca. **Room XI** contains Savoldo's *Tobias and the Angel,* and two paintings by Lorenzo Lotto: one is a portrait of a man dressed in black whose hand rests on a tiny ivory skull, the other a *Madonna and Child with Two Saints.* The only picture of real distinction in **Room XII** is Domenichino's *Sibyl* (★), also known as *Music.*

Passing through the unremarkable Room XIII, you reach **Room XIV**, frescoed by Lanfranco and the centerpiece of the whole gallery. It contains Bernini's extraordinarily precocious *Jupiter Suckled by the Goat Amalthea* (1615), as well as his two busts of *Scipione Borghese* (★). The reason for the duplication is that Bernini was just finishing the first when a crack appeared in the marble over one eyebrow. In feverish haste he completed another in two weeks. Also here is his terra-cotta model for a marble statue of *Louis XIV*, which survives only in a mutilated and transformed state in Versailles. Among the paintings, the Caravaggios (★) take pride of place. The finest are the early *Boy with a Basket of Fruit* and the so-called *Sick Bacchus*, both remarkable for the realistic treatment of fruit and leaves, the *David and Goliath*, in which Goliath, like Bacchus, is reputed to be a self-portrait, and the *Madonna dei Palafrenieri*, in which Caravaggio's realism brings an obscure dogma to life. (The serpent the Madonna crushes underfoot is a symbol of heresy.) Another picture of interest is Domenichino's *Diana with her Nymphs* (1618). This was commissioned by Cardinal Aldobrandini, but so enchanted Scipione Borghese that he seized it from the artist's studio.

Room XV contains Rubens' powerful *Deposition* (1605), Barocci's version of the Aeneas story depicted by Bernini downstairs, and three portraits ascribed to Bernini, two of which are said to be self-portraits. **Room XVI** is memorable for its collection of pictures by Jacopo Bassano, the best of which are the earthy *Nativity* and *Last Supper*. Leaving the undistinguished Rooms XVII and XVIII, move on to **Room XIX** where Correggio's *Danae* (★) dominates. The seductive grace of the painting of flesh and hair in this picture has perhaps never been equaled; nor has the sense of enjoyment. Other major pictures in this room are the group by Dosso Dossi, of which the finest is of the enchantress *Melissa*. The ceiling was frescoed by the Neoclassical Scottish painter Gavin Hamilton.

Room XX, the last in the gallery, contains Titian's early masterpiece *Sacred and Profane Love* (★), so familiar from reproductions. This is just one of the wonderful Venetian works in this room, which include the brilliant *Portrait of a Man* by Antonello da Messina, a tender late *Madonna and Child* by Giovanni Bellini, Veronese's *St John the Baptist Preaching*, and, perhaps best of all the later Titians, although in a sadly deteriorated condition, *Venus Blindfolding Cupid* (★).

The lack of order in the arrangement of the collection can be confusing, but the quality is never in doubt and more than one visit is required to do it justice. It is not a bad idea to break your tour by stepping out onto the balcony at the front of the house. Here you can pause to enjoy the natural beauty of the park before returning refreshed to the works of art inside.

BORGO

Map 3G3.

The Borgo is the district immediately E of SAINT PETER'S, a part of Rome that is well worth exploring. Typically medieval streets run to the N and S of VIA DELLA CONCILIAZIONE, alongside two handsome Renaissance palaces, **Palazzo Torlonia** and **Palazzo dei Penitenzieri**. The second is now mostly converted into the Hotel Columbus (see WHERE TO STAY).

Off the Borgo Santo Spirito lies the vast complex of the **Ospedale Santo Spirito**. The original hospital was founded by Innocent III in 1198 and rebuilt in the late 15thC. The Palazzo del Commendatore or Director's House dates from 1567 and, with its vast central courtyard, is a building of exceptional charm. Breaking the skyline to the right, the Romanesque bell tower of **Santo Spirito in Sassia** (founded in 726) completes a uniquely Roman setting.

CAMPO DEI FIORI Literally translated as "field of the flowers," this historic site is also known as PIAZZA CAMPO DEI FIORI. In the 16th and 17thC it was the scene of public executions, but it is now better known for its attractive fruit and flower market.

CAMPUS MARTIUS (Campo Marzio)
Map 5G-H5.
This is the area now bounded by the Tiber on one side and the Via del Corso on the other. In ancient times it was a wide open plain, used for military exercises and sporting pastimes such as ball games, gymnastics and horse racing. However, the splendid tract of flat land was too much of a temptation for Augustus' friend and collaborator, Marcus Agrippa. This energetic builder laid out an entirely new monumental quarter, with landscaped gardens and an artificial lake. Among several notable monuments were the Baths of Agrippa, the Basilica of Neptune and the original Pantheon. The whole area was devastated by fire in AD80, and practically all records were lost. However, we do know that Agrippa's Pantheon was built in marble from Carrara, and that some of the columns were decorated with caryatid figures by the Athenian sculptor Diogenes. (Hadrian later replaced this building with a new PANTHEON.) In the Middle Ages, the population of Rome was concentrated here, in Trastevere and in the BORGO.

CAPITOLINE HILL (Campidoglio)
Piazza del Campidoglio. Map 8I6 ◁₠
This was the most famous of the seven hills of Rome, serving as both fortress and sanctuary of the ancient city. It rose to two distinct heights. At the N summit *(Arx)* was the citadel, together with the Temple of Juno Moneta (near which was the site of the early mint). At the S summit *(Capitolium)* stood the Capitol itself: the Temple of Jupiter Optimus Maximus Capitolinus. This was where the newly elected consuls took their vows, and where victorious generals came in procession to offer thanks to the gods. It was the heart of Roman religious life, and was several times rebuilt after the destruction by fire of the earliest temple of the Etruscan kings.

Today the **Palazzo Senatorio** is the official seat of the municipality, but the Capitol is not the political center of the city any more. After years of neglect in the Middle Ages, the whole area was transformed by Michelangelo into the majestic showpiece it is today (see PIAZZA DEL CAMPIDOGLIO).

> It was at Rome, on the fifteenth of October, 1764, as I sat musing amidst the ruins of the Capitol, while the barefoot friars were singing vespers in the Temple of Jupiter, that the idea of writing the decline and fall of the city first started to my mind.
> (Edward Gibbon, *Autobiography*)

CAPITOLINE MUSEUMS (Musei Capitolini)
Piazza del Campidoglio ☎6782862. *Map 8|6* 🚾 *Open Tues-Sat 9am-1.30pm, and 5-8pm on Tues and Sat only; Sun 9am-1pm. Closed Mon.*

Founded in 1471 by Sixtus IV, expanded by Pius V and opened to the public by Clement XII, the Capitoline Museums hold one of the world's most ancient collections. Its two buildings, the Palazzo Nuovo and Palazzo dei Conservatori, face each other across the open space of Michelangelo's PIAZZA DEL CAMPIDOGLIO, and together contain an impressive array of works of art, and in particular, an outstanding collection of antiquities.

The **Palazzo Nuovo** on the NE of the piazza houses several great masterpieces of Classical statuary, such as the *Capitoline Venus* (★), an excellent Roman copy of a Hellenistic original, the *Dying Gaul* (★), another excellent copy, of which the character and poignancy are typical of the 3rdC BC Pergamene School, and the *Marble Faun,* which inspired Nathaniel Hawthorne's book of the same title. Equally fascinating is the **Room of the Emperors**: it is no longer thought that all the 65 busts represent famous Romans, but they are nevertheless an unrivaled portrait gallery, full of life and personality.

The **Palazzo dei Conservatori** on the SW of the piazza contains more Classical pieces. The most remarkable among them are the *Spinario* (★), a bronze of a boy removing a thorn from his foot (1stC BC); the *Capitoline Wolf* (★), an ancient Etruscan bronze dating from the end of the 6thC BC, to which Romulus and Remus were added in the 15thC; and the *Esquiline Venus* (★), a Roman adaptation of a Greek idea, and an outstandingly graceful female nude.

In the same building, the **Pinacoteca Capitolina** contains a number of distinguished paintings. In Room 2, the *Baptism of Christ* by Titian is an early work (c. 1510), remarkable for the beautiful landscape and splendid portrait of the donor. Rubens' typically rich and vigorous version of *Romulus and Remus Suckled by the She-wolf* is in Room 3, close to the wonderfully sensitive *Double Portrait of the Painters Lucas and Cornelius de Wael* (★) by his pupil Van Dyck (1625-26). In the **Cini Gallery**, which houses a collection of porcelain, there is a *St John the Baptist* by Caravaggio. This is almost identical with the painting in the Galleria Doria Pamphili (see PALAZZO DORIA), but this is probably the original version. It is certainly the finer of the two.

The *Rape of the Sabines* in **The Hall of Hercules** is one of several important narrative paintings by Pietro da Cortona, a characteristically dramatic treatment of antique fable. Finally, dominating the room to which it gives its name, there is Guercino's huge altarpiece of the *Burial and Reception into Heaven of St Petronilla* (★), which was painted for SAINT PETER'S.

CASA DEI CAVALIERI DI RODI This house was built into the ruins of the FORUM OF AUGUSTUS in the 12thC, as the Priorate of the order of Knights of St John of Jerusalem (also known as the Knights of Rhodes or of Malta). It was restored in the 15thC and contains important fragments and sculpture preserved from the Forum.

CASTEL SANT' ANGELO 🏛 ★
Lungotevere Castello ☎6875036. *Map* 4G4 🚻 💷 ♿ ◀€ *Open Tues-Sat 9am-2pm; Sun 9am-1pm; Mon 2-6.30pm.*

This famous monument has had an unusually long and varied history. The original structure was begun in 130 by the Emperor Hadrian, as a tomb for himself and his family, and completed in 139, a year after his death, by his successor Antoninus Pius. It has survived remarkably well, first by being converted into a fortress and then by being used successively as prison, barracks and museum.

The Mausoleum of Hadrian was a cylindrical structure of travertine and peperino, faced with marble and set on a high, square platform. Like the earlier MAUSOLEUM OF AUGUSTUS, it was almost certainly based on Etruscan models. Above the drum, a tumulus planted with rings of cypresses was surmounted by a gigantic pedestal. This in turn supported a dramatic group in gilded bronze, showing Hadrian driving a chariot, in the guise of the sun god Apollo. Hadrian, his wife, and his adopted son were all buried here, as were all the emperors until Septimius Severus. Inside the building, a spiral ramp, still in use, led to the Imperial tomb, where urns containing the ashes of successive emperors and their families were kept.

In a commanding strategic position overlooking the wide sweep of the Tiber, the mausoleum was invested with military importance as early as 271, when Aurelian used it as a bridgehead in his defensive walls, thus protecting the approaches to the city from the critical NW direction. In the years following the collapse of Roman power, the mausoleum became the Citadel of Rome. In 590 St Gregory the Great was crossing the Pons Aelius at the head of a procession on its way to St Peter's, to pray for the ending of a terrible plague, when he saw a vision of an angel high above the citadel. The angel was in the act of sheathing its sword, signifying the end of the pestilence. A chapel was forthwith built on the spot where the angel had been seen, and the fortress was renamed after it.

The Castel Sant' Angelo gained additional importance with the creation of the Leonine City in 847, when Leo IV walled in the area of the BORGO as well as the Vatican and converted the fortress into a citadel-residence. He was the first of several popes who felt the need to reside here from time to time, in the interests of security. A covered way to the Vatican was completed by Alexander VI (1492-1503). When Clement VII took refuge here from the troops of the Emperor Charles V during the appalling Sack of Rome in 1527, the defense was assisted by Benvenuto Cellini, who boasted about his exploits in his *Autobiography.* Under Paul III (1534-49) the interior was decorated, and it was at this time that a marble angel by Raffaello da Montelupo (1544) was placed at the summit of the fortress. It is now in the Cortile di Onore (see page 82) and its crowning position is occupied by a bronze angel dating from the 18thC.

For many years during the Renaissance, the Castel was used as a political prison, and horrific accounts have been recorded of its tortures and executions. It was occupied by French troops between 1849-70, and thereafter used as a barracks. Only in 1901 was the initiative taken to restore it, and by 1933 it was ready to open as a museum. The Castel Sant'

THIRD FLOOR

A Loggia of Paul III
B Gallery of Pius IV
C Loggia of Julius II
D Room of the Mausoleum of Hadrian
E Room of the Festoons
F Sala della Biblioteca
G Room of the Secret Archives
H Sala Paolina
I Camera del Perseo
J Camera di Amore e Psiche

SECOND FLOOR

K Rooms of Clement VII
L Prison Cells
M Court of Alexander VI
N Armory
O Hall of Justice
P Cortile di Onore
Q To Historical Prisons
R Prison cells
S Hall of Apollo
T Court of Leo X
U Chapel of Leo X

FIRST FLOOR

V Grain stores
W Oil stores
X Hadrian's funerary chamber
Y Staircase of Alexander VI
Z Historical Prisons
‡ Ramp (entrance from ground floor)

N

Angelo is famous to opera lovers as the scene of the last act of Puccini's *Tosca* — after the murder of her lover Cavaradossi, held prisoner here, Tosca takes her own life by throwing herself off the battlements of the fortress.

The museum is vast and, including the Papal Apartments, covers four floors. It is predominantly military in character, but there are also valuable collections of paintings, antique furniture, and tapestries. Entering by the same door as to the original tomb, you mount the **ramp** leading to **Hadrian's funerary chamber**. The passage is in a superb state of preservation, and includes some of the original black and white mosaic decoration. Where the ramp ends, the gently graded **Staircase of Alexander VI** begins: it cuts diametrically across the great central mass of the building, passing over the funerary chamber. The staircase was once connected to the central mass by a drawbridge, giving complete security to the inner part of the citadel. Now a bridge designed by Valadier spans the gap.

A turn to the left brings you onto the second floor and the **Cortile di Onore** or Court of the Angel, an enchanting courtyard adorned with neat pyramids of marble and stone cannon balls. The major object of interest here is Raffaello da Montelupo's **marble angel**. Leading off the courtyard to the w are rooms housing a large collection of arms dating from the earliest times up to the Middle Ages. At the s end of the courtyard is the **Chapel of Leo X**, designed by Michelangelo. It is kept locked, but you can admire the fine facade of what is perhaps Michelangelo's least-known work. An open stairway leads to the Papal Apartments above.

A door on the E of the courtyard leads into the **Rooms of Clement VII**. The larger of the two rooms contains a splendid stuccoed chimney piece, and the Aldobrandini Pope's arms on the ceiling. Beyond, the **Hall of Justice** contains Perin del Vaga's fresco of *The Angel of Justice*. The hall is in the heart of the building, and dates from Classical times. The next room, the **Hall of Apollo**, is handsomely decorated with grotesques, frescoed for Paul III in 1547. Beyond are two small private rooms lavishly decorated with pictures, including a triptych by Taddeo Gaddi.

A passage leads from here into the large **Court of Alexander VI**, also known as the Court of the Well, on account of the beautiful well-head decorated with the Borgia arms of Alexander VI, or as the Court of the Oil, because of the vast amounts of oil once stored below. On the E side are rooms once used as prison cells, in one of which Benvenuto Cellini was incarcerated.

A doorway on the s side of the courtyard leads to the Historical Prisons (now closed). Among the many notable people confined there were Alessandro Farnese (later Paul III), Beatrice Cenci, Cardinal Carafa and Cagliostro.

At the N end of the courtyard, stairs lead up to the **Loggia of Paul III** on the third floor. This was designed by Raffaello da Montelupo and Antonio da Sangallo the Younger. It leads out onto the open **Gallery of Pius IV**, which surrounds the entire building. From this vantage point there are marvelous views over the Tiber and across the city on one side, and toward the Vatican Hill and Monte Mario on the other. The **Loggia**

of Julius II on the s side was designed by Bramante and faces the PONTE SANT' ANGELO. There is an attractive bar nearby where you can sit down and relax.

From the Loggia of Julius II, a few steps lead up to the **Papal Apartments**. Designed for Paul III (see above), these were only intended to be used in an emergency. The first room, the **Sala Paolina**, is the most splendid, with frescoes by Perin del Vaga and Pellegrino Tibaldi and stuccoes by Girolamo Siciolante da Sermoneta and Baccio da Montelupo. It is a triumph of *trompe l'oeil* decoration.

Next door, in the **Camera del Perseo**, the myth of Perseus is illustrated in a beautiful frieze. This room is exquisitely furnished in Renaissance style, as is the adjoining **Camera di Amore e Psiche**, with its frieze by Perin del Vaga. Both rooms contain a number of pictures, including works by Paris Bordone and Sebastiano del Piombo.

A frescoed corridor leads from the Sala Paolina to the **Sala della Biblioteca**, a magnificent library decorated with frescoes by Luzzi, stuccoes by Girolamo Siciolante da Sermoneta, and a marble fireplace by Raffaello da Montelupo. Next door is the **Room of the Mausoleum of Hadrian**, so called after the frieze by Luzzi. Among several paintings here, Dosso Dossi's *Bacchanal* and Lorenzo Lotto's *St Jerome* are outstanding. Next door, and leading down to three smaller chambers, is the **Room of the Festoons**, named after the motifs of its decoration.

Returning to the Sala della Biblioteca, you can gain access to the **Room of the Secret Archives**, once used as a treasure-house for the papal jewels, gold and precious relics. The walnut cupboards were used to store the papal archives. A narrow staircase built into the solid mass of the ancient structure leads up, past more rooms containing memorabilia, to the **terrace** at the summit of the citadel. All around there are magnificent views, especially toward SAINT PETER'S.

CATACOMBS OF DOMITILLA (Catacombe di Domitilla) ★

Via delle Sette Chiese ☎5110342. Map 12D4 ▧ ✦ ✗ compulsory. Open Wed-Mon 8.30am-noon, 2.30-5pm. Closed Tues. Bus 218 from Piazza San Giovanni in Laterano.

These catacombs are less frequently visited than the better known CATACOMBS OF SAINT CALIXTUS and CATACOMBS OF SAINT SEBASTIAN, but they are only a short distance away from them and have two distinct advantages. They are far less crowded, and have a beautiful and spacious garden where you can relax in the shade after a guided tour.

The Domitilla who gave her name to these catacombs was a Flavian who converted to Christianity, a relative of Vespasian and Domitian. Her land was later used as a burial place for many thousands of Christians. The basilica that was erected here between 390-395 was dedicated to the martyrs Achilleus and Nereus and built on the site of their tomb. According to one account they were Roman soldiers, but another version describes them as servants of Domitilla. The church was destroyed in an earthquake centuries ago but has been reconstructed, and there are many fascinating fragments of the original fabric to be seen, including some antique columns with fine capitals.

From the basilica, a priest will guide you through the labyrinthine galleries of the cemetery. Historically, there has been controversy about the identity of Domitilla, but the theory that she was a Flavian is now generally accepted. It seems that her family constructed a hypogeum or underground tomb, from which the 17km (11 miles) of catacombs on four levels developed. They are the largest in Rome, and contain many early Christian paintings and inscriptions, including one of the earliest representations of *Christ as the Good Shepherd*.

CATACOMBS OF PRISCILLA (Catacombe di Priscilla)
Via Salaria 430. Ring bell at convent door ☎8380408. Map 12C4 ▨ ▨ ⊀ compulsory. Open Tues-Sun 8.30am-noon, 2.30-5pm. Closed Mon. Bus 56 from Piazza Barberini, or 57 or 319 from Stazione Termini.

Founded by the Christian branch of a Senatorial family, these catacombs are among the most ancient in Rome, and well worth the slight inconvenience of reaching them. Guided tours are provided by Benedictine nuns. There are two levels to the catacombs, but the tour is conducted only on the upper one, which is the more ancient.

Of particular interest is a *cubiculum* or small chapel containing the oldest known painting of the Madonna and Child, *The Virgin and Child with Isaiah* (★), dating from the second half of the 2ndC. Beside this is *The Good Shepherd with Two Sheep*. Both are examples of the unusual technique of stucco combined with painting.

Passing through long galleries lined with many burial niches or *loculi* cut into the rock one above the other, you reach the **Greek Chapel**, so called because of the Greek inscriptions on the wall. Among the 2ndC frescoes, note *The Breaking of the Bread at the Last Supper,* which is one of the earliest representations of this scene.

CATACOMBS OF SAINT CALIXTUS (Catacombe di San Callisto) ★
Via Appia Antica ☎5136725. Map 12D4 ▨ ▨ ⊀ compulsory. Open Thurs-Tues 8.30am-noon, 2.30-5pm. Closed Wed. Bus 118 from Colosseo.

Like other Roman catacombs, these probably started as private burial chambers and were only gradually enlarged, so that what you see today took about 300 years to reach its present vast size. The catacombs are excavated on four levels, but the official tour is normally restricted to the second level. The maze of dark narrow galleries is lit and ventilated by shafts placed at wide intervals.

The burial niches or *loculi* are cut into the rock one above the other on either side of the passageways. Usually there are only five or six *loculi* in a tier, but in one dramatically deep gallery there are at least 12 on either side. Occasionally, chapels have been carved out of the rock to form *cubicula,* where all the members of a family could be buried together. One of the most interesting places is the **Crypt of the Popes**. Larger than the normal *cubicula,* it is decorated with beautiful spiral columns along the side walls. Here, with Greek inscriptions over their tombs, lie the remains of St Pontian (died 235), St Anterus (died 236), St Fabian (died 250), St Lucius I (died 254) and St Eutychian (died 284), some of whom were martyred.

Your guide will point out interesting examples of *graffiti,* including signs and symbols proclaiming the Christian faith. Most of the inscriptions are in Greek and are often of extreme simplicity; sometimes there is just a symbolic drawing scratched in the wet plaster that sealed the tomb — an anchor, dove or fish — or perhaps some sign with the same meaning.

The **Cubiculum of St Cecilia** is where the body of the saint was buried after her martyrdom in 230. Her grave was discovered by Pope Paschal I in 821 and her remains transferred to the church of SANTA CECILIA IN TRASTEVERE, where they lie under the main altar. The *cubiculum* is superbly decorated with **frescoes** of the *Raising of Lazarus* and the *Miracle of the Loaves and Fishes.*

A copy of Maderno's famous statue of St Cecilia can be seen in a recess (the original is in the church in Trastevere).

CATACOMBS OF SAINT SEBASTIAN (Catacombe di San Sebastiano) ★
Via Appia Antica ☎ 7887035. Map 12D4 ⬛ ✗ compulsory. Open Fri-Wed 8.30am-noon, 2.30-5pm. Closed Thurs. Bus 118 from Colosseo.

These are the only catacombs in Rome that have always been accessible, and they have suffered as a result. A pagan cemetery occupied the site in the 1stC, and in the following century three tombs were excavated here. In the 3rdC, the owner of the burial ground became a Christian and the excavation of the catacombs began.

The catacombs are on four levels, but not all of these are included in the guided tour. The finest relics are the **2ndC tombs**, one of which belonged to a certain Claudius Hermes. Here you can see well-preserved stuccoes of fine quality, incorporating circular motifs, flowers, shells, acanthus leaves and vines.

Nearby, a staircase leads up to the **triclia** where funeral banquets took place. The walls are inscribed with *graffiti* invoking Sts Peter and Paul. These references are explained by the strong probability that the apostles' bodies were brought here from their previous resting places (the sepulcher in SAINT PETER'S and the site of SAN PAOLO FUORI LE MURA), and hidden during Valerian's persecutions of 258. It is believed that they remained here for 40 years. Certainly, the first church built on this spot was originally dedicated to the two apostles, and only much later to St Sebastian, who was buried here at the end of the 3rdC. St Sebastian was an officer in the Imperial household who was sentenced to be shot to death by arrows, during one of Diocletian's persecutions.

Above the catacombs stands the **Church of San Sebastiano**. It was rebuilt by Flaminio Ponzio in 1612, and contains a recumbent statue of St Sebastian by Antonio Giorgetti. In the **crypt** beneath the church, where the guided tour usually begins, is a bust of the saint attributed to Bernini.

CHIESA NUOVA †
Corso Vittorio Emanuele. Map 4H4.

More correctly known as Santa Maria in Vallicella, the present church replaced an earlier one on the same site, and consequently became known as the New Church. Gregory XIII donated the original church to St Philip Neri in 1575 in recognition of the Oratory he had founded and work began on the new one immediately. The architects were Giovanni Matteo di Città di Castello and Martino Longhi the Elder, while the facade is the work of Fausto Rughesi. The Chiesa Nuova was consecrated in 1599, four years after the death of St Philip, whose expressed desire for a plain and modest building was wilfully ignored by his followers.

In 1647, when the ORATORY COMPLEX was almost completed, Pietro da Cortona began a scheme of decoration in the church that eventually covered the nave vault, dome and apse with splendid frescoes. These are in large part responsible for the Chiesa Nuova's opulent appearance.

But there are other fine paintings to be seen, notably the **high altarpiece**, and two flanking pictures of saints by Rubens, which were painted on slate to counteract the reflections of the light. Also very lovely are Barocci's *Visitation* and *Presentation,* located respectively in the fourth chapel of the left aisle and in the left transept.

St Philip Neri was a Florentine, but he spent 60 years in Rome, and has been called the second apostle of Rome. His cheerful temperament particularly appealed to young people, and such was his influence that many young men were persuaded to abandon a life of luxury to join him in charitable works. St Philip was not just a good man: he had the rarer gift of inspiring good in other people.

CIRCUS MAXIMUS (Circo Massimo)
Via del Circo Massimo. Map 9J6. Metropolitana: Circo Massimo.
The Romans had a passion for horse-racing, and the Circus Maximus was their grandest stadium. Expanded and rebuilt many times, the Circus housed hundreds of thousands of spectators. The circuit itself was more than 1,000m (1,090 yards) long. Arcades on the outside of the Circus contained shops and taverns to meet the needs of thirsty or disappointed punters. The races were mainly two- and four-horse chariot contests, but there were also spectacles such as triumphs, when victorious soldiers returned to Rome from their military campaigns abroad. Today the long wall or *spina* that ran along the middle of the stadium is a grassy strip marked by a solitary cypress at one end. The whole area is open public ground — a better fate than when it was the site of a gasworks.

CLOACA MAXIMA (Cloaca Massima)
Lungotevere Aventino. Map 9J6.
This remarkable drainage system was designed in ancient times to drain the valleys between the Capitoline, Palatine and Esquiline Hills, and largely because of it the land was made ready for the major building program in the ROMAN FORUM. To this day the drain still discharges into the Tiber just s of the Ponte Palatino.

COELIAN HILL (Celio)
Map 9J7.
The most southern of the seven hills of Rome is named after an Etruscan nobleman, Coelius Vibenna, who is thought to have settled here

after helping Romulus to defeat Tatius, the Sabine king. Robert Guiscard caused widespread devastation in 1084, in his vicious incursion to assist his ally Gregory VII, and the area is still far less populated than other parts of central Rome. It contains three exceptionally interesting churches, SANTO STEFANO ROTONDO, SANTI GIOVANNI E PAOLO and SANTA MARIA IN DOMNICA.

COLOSSEUM (Colosseo) ★

Piazza del Colosseo ☎ 7004621. Map 9I7 ◫ (ground floor) ◫ (upper stories) ▣ ✿ ◁ᴇ Open Thurs-Tues 9am-4pm; Wed 9am-1pm. Metropolitana: Colosseo.

Paintings and photographs cannot prepare you for a first sight of the Colosseum: the sheer size and majesty of this, the greatest monument of ancient Rome, come as a surprise. Yet, despite its stupendous bulk, the building is beautifully balanced. The unknown architect avoided any hint of monotony by subtle use of spatial harmony and variation of architectural orders. At night, floodlighting emphasizes this harmony. The deep arcades are lit by an amber glow, and powerful white arc-lamps illuminate the three orders — Doric, Ionic and Corinthian — and the high attic story with its graceful pilasters.

Major restoration work means that the upper levels are once again closed to the public. This is unfortunate, as from above it is possible to see the complex system whereby wild animals, scenery and other material were supplied for the great displays, contests and aquatic shows that took place. At this point, some reflections on the somber history of these ruins are inevitable. It is hard not to visualize the gaping arena resurfaced and spread with sand, the slaughtered animals and humans dragged away, the roars of the crowd packed on the tiers of marble seats.

Many explanations have been ventured as to how the Romans came to degenerate so far as to find pleasure in the baiting and killing of elephants, lions and other wild beasts, in gladiatorial combats, and in the slaughter of Christians and criminals. In the early 2ndC AD, the satirist Juvenal accused the populace of having sold its power for "bread and circuses" (in other words, free food and entertainment), and some educated Romans were undoubtedly repelled by these gory spectacles.

The higher levels of the Colosseum give marvelous views across the city, especially in the direction of the ROMAN FORUM. Note the ARCH OF

CONSTANTINE, the columns and apse of the TEMPLE OF VENUS AND ROME, the soaring Romanesque tower of **Santa Francesca Romana** behind, and the beautifully proportioned **Arch of Titus**.

Vespasian conceived the idea of building the amphitheater in an area that had been earlier expropriated for NERO'S GOLDEN HOUSE, but it was unfinished at his death in 79 and was inaugurated by his son Titus. Domitian completed the building from 81-96. Vespasian, Titus and Domitian were members of the Flavian dynasty, and the building was originally called the *Amphitheatrum Flavium*. By the 7thC, however, it was known by its present name, first recorded in the famous prophecy of the Venerable Bede:

> "While the Coliseum stands, Rome shall stand; when the
> Coliseum falls, Rome shall fall; when Rome falls,
> the world shall fall."

Whether this name was acquired because of the size of the building, or because of the colossal gilded bronze statue of Nero nearby, is unclear.

The building of the amphitheater was an amazing technical feat. After draining an artificial lake, the engineers laid down a ring of *pozzalana* (concrete made with volcanic sand) 7.5m (25ft) thick. The size and weight of the building, which could seat 50,000 people, posed a considerable problem. This was solved by constructing a series of circular walls of tufa (volcanic stone) and a system of barrel vaults that supported the terraced seating and corridors behind.

COLUMN OF MARCUS AURELIUS (Colonna di Marco Aurelio)
Piazza Colonna. Map 5H6.

This column was erected in 180-196 to commemorate the Emperor's victories over the Sarmathians, the Quadi and the Marcomanni. The reliefs of the spiraling narrative are inferior to those of Trajan's Column (see FORUM OF TRAJAN), on which they are modeled, but are interesting for the vivid picture they give of the military practices, life and costumes of the times. The crowning statue of Marcus Aurelius was replaced by one of *St Paul* in 1588.

The architect Domenico Fontana also restored the base at this time, and wrongly attributed the original dedication of the column to Antoninus Pius, Marcus Aurelius' uncle. Even now, it is often called the Antonine Column.

ESQUILINE HILL (Esquilino)
Map 10I8. Metropolitana: Cavour or Colosseo.

The hill has two main summits, the **Oppius** and the **Cispius.** On the former were built NERO'S GOLDEN HOUSE and the Baths of Trajan. A large area is now taken up by the **Parco Oppio**, a public park. To the N, the Cispius is dominated by the great basilica of SANTA MARIA MAGGIORE.

FORUM, THE   This was the political, religious and commercial center of Republican Rome. It is also known as the ROMAN FORUM, to distinguish it from the later IMPERIAL FORUMS.

FORUM OF AUGUSTUS (Foro di Augusto)
Via dei Fori Imperiali. Map 9I6. Metropolitana: Colosseo.
The retaining walls that for 2,000 years have helped prevent the Sa-
burra, the area above the Forum of Augustus, from sliding down the
hillside have been reinforced and shored up. It is therefore impossible
to visit the site from the usual entrance in Piazza del Grillo, but in any
case the full extent of the ruined Forum of Augustus is best seen from
Via dei Fori Imperiali. From there one can still admire the three up-
standing columns of the **Temple of Mars Ultor**, Mars the Avenger.
Augustus vowed to build this temple after his defeat of Brutus and
Cassius at the Battle of Philippi in 42BC, but it was still not complete at
the inauguration of the forum in 2BC. Flanked and fronted by graceful
Corinthian columns, it can be regarded as the culmination of the em-
peror's whole building program, epitomizing the grand ideals of the
Augustan Age.

Forum of Nerva (Foro di Nerva)
The Forum of Nerva, sometimes called the Forum Transitorium in
Classical times because it led into the FORUM OF VESPASIAN, now lies
beneath modern streets and buildings to the E of the Forum of Augustus. Two impressive Corinthian columns remain visible, with a relief
of Minerva between them, at the edge of Via dei Fori Imperiali. The
Temple of Minerva, which originally dominated this forum, was demolished in 1606 — an act of vandalism perpetrated by Paul V, in
order to obtain marble for the construction of the PAOLA FOUNTAIN on
the Janiculum Hill.

Casa dei Cavalieri di Rodi (House of the Knights of Rhodes)
This building, on the w of the Forum of Augustus, is the ancient seat of
the Priorate of the order of Knights of St John of Jerusalem (also known
as the Knights of Rhodes or of Malta). It was built over a Classical
structure at the end of the 12thC and restored in the 15thC. The overall
appearance is of an elegant Renaissance building, with lofty, well-proportioned rooms decorated and furnished in the style of the period.
Several interesting pictures relate to the history of the Order. There is a
splendid view across the forums from the loggia.

From the columned atrium, which dates from the time of Augustus,
you reach the **Antiquarium of the Forum of Augustus**. This contains
sculpture and fragments of great interest, notably a fine head of *Jupiter*
and some exceptionally beautiful carved capitals.

FORUM BOARIUM (Foro Boario)
Map 9I6.
A large but no longer precisely definable area between the Via di San
Teodoro and the THEATER OF MARCELLUS is where, in the earliest days
after the foundation of Rome, the Forum Boarium or cattle market was
situated. Nearer the river, the Forum Olitorium or fruit and vegetable
market became established, and the whole area was soon studded with
temples and public buildings. The remains of a Republican temple can
be seen incorporated into the wall of the church of **San Nicola in
Carcere**.

Two other survivors are the TEMPLE OF VESTA and TEMPLE OF FORTUNA VIRILIS (second half of the 2ndC BC), which stand in the gardens opposite SANTA MARIA IN COSMEDIN.

FORUM OF CAESAR (Foro di Cesare)
Via dei Fori Imperiali. Map 9|6.

Only about a third of the site of this great forum is open to view, the rest lying hidden beneath modern roads. It was originally in the shape of an elongated rectangle, lined by porticoes. Before the Battle of Pharsalus, Julius Caesar vowed that if he defeated Pompey he would build a temple to Venus. The goddess was supposed to have been the mother of Aeneas, hence the name **Temple of Venus Genetrix** (46BC). This stood at the NW end of the Forum and was famous for its sculptures of Venus, Caesar and Cleopatra and for its superlative collection of Greek paintings.

Three fragmented columns, re-erected on the site, are almost all that remains of this noble treasure-house. Stripped of their sumptuous marble facing, they convey little idea of the vast and splendidly ornate Corinthian portico that once dominated the forum.

FORUM OF NERVA   This lies to the E of the FORUM OF AUGUSTUS, its ruins now largely concealed by modern streets and buildings.

FORUM OF TRAJAN (Foro Traiano)
Via dei Fori Imperiali. Map 9|6.

Extensive restoration work has recently been completed and the Forum of Trajan can now be reached from the lower level of TRAJAN'S MARKETS, but the site can also be viewed from above.

It is not easy to visualize the magnificence of Trajan's Forum, for what is left — a sunken area strewn with fractured marble architraves and columns — gives little clue to its original appearance. At the time of its construction and for centuries afterwards it was regarded as one of the architectural wonders of the world. The eastern emperor Constantius II, visiting Rome in 356, pronounced it unequaled in splendor, and references in the 6thC biography of Gregory the Great demonstrate that it was still in good repair at that time.

Designed by the renowned Greek architect Apollodorus of Damascus, it was built between 107 and 113. The complex consisted of a spacious **Forum**, and to the W of this the vast **Basilica Ulpia** (as large as SAN PAOLO FUORI LE MURA), a double-aisled building with an apse at each end. Beyond this soared **Trajan's Column**, flanked on either side by the famous **Greek and Latin Libraries**. Finally, at the extreme NW end, rose the **Temple of Trajan**, one of the finest in Rome.

The reason why it is impossible today to see the whole extent of the ruined site is because of the major landscaping and roadworks that were initiated by Mussolini in 1932. The construction of **Via dei Fori Imperiali** was part of his grandiose plan to open up key areas of Rome for great state processions and parades. It cuts across and hides several of the ruins of the Imperial forums.

In the past there have been tentative plans to undo Mussolini's handiwork, reopening major portions of Trajan's Forum to view. But it is hard to see how the Roman authorities would cope with the traffic problems resulting from the closure of this major road.

To the NE of the sunken area you can see the hemicycle of TRAJAN'S MARKETS, built around the now-vanished semicircular portico; but all that remains standing of the forum itself are some broken columns, belonging to the Basilica Ulpia, and Trajan's Column.

Trajan's Column (★) was so solidly constructed that it has remained remarkably unchanged from the time of its dedication to the Emperor in 113. It celebrated his defeat of the Dacians — the ancient inhabitants of modern Romania — and consists of a frieze of some 2,500 figures, which wind their way up the 38m-tall (125-foot) column. It is the quality of the carving of these low-reliefs, and above all their historical interest, that make this one of the most fascinating monuments in Rome. It is a remarkable record of the military events of Trajan's campaign, a mine of information about weapons, uniforms, fortresses and siege operations. Originally the reliefs were painted in brilliant colors or gold, and this must have made it easier to pick out details with the naked eye. Inside, a spiral staircase (closed to the public) leads to the top of the column, which was once crowned by a statue of Trajan but is now surmounted by the figure of *St Peter* (1587).

FORUM OF VESPASIAN (Foro di Vespasiano)
Via dei Fori Imperiali. Map 9I6. Metropolitana: Colosseo.
Known as the Forum of Peace in ancient times, it was built from 71-75, following Vespasian's war against the Jews. Excavations have brought to light a shrine, some fallen columns, and the remains of a pavement. A large part of the building materials were spoils of the war. Most of the remains lie buried under the Via dei Fori Imperiali and connecting modern roads. By far the most interesting surviving part is the church of SANTI COSMA E DAMIANO, formed by the conversion of one of the halls of the forum. To the N is the early 13thC **Torre dei Conti**, built by Innocent III (Lotario dei Conti di Segni). The tower was severely damaged by an earthquake in 1348, and only the lower section survives.

FOUNTAIN OF THE BEES (Fontana delle Api)
Piazza Barberini. Map 5G6. Metropolitana: Barberini.
This small fountain, on the N side of Piazza Barberini at the corner of Via Veneto, is one of Bernini's most delightful creations. It was constructed in 1644 to honor the 21st anniversary of Urban VIII's accession to the pontificate. Water splashes into a scallop shell, where Barberini bees, alluding to the Pope's family, are seen taking a drink.

FOUNTAIN OF THE FOUR RIVERS (Fontana dei Fiumi)
Piazza Navona. Map 6G7.
Bernini's power to surprise, his love of theatrical effect, are epitomized in this, the most famous of his many fountains. It was commissioned by Innocent X in 1648, as part of a plan to make the approach to the

PALAZZO PAMPHILI more impressive. Bernini incorporated an obelisk into the design, to create a monument sufficiently striking to stand out in the center of the unusually long piazza. The reclining figures personify the four rivers, Nile, Ganges, Danube and Plate. These in turn symbolize the four known quarters of the world, Africa, Asia, Europe and America. Nile is shown covering his face, an allusion to the river's unknown source.

Popular belief interprets his gesture differently. It is said that Bernini intended to cast a slur on his rival Borromini's nearby SANT' AGNESE IN AGONE, by representing Nile cowering in fear at its imminent collapse. Likewise, Plate is said to be holding up his hand in a gesture of defense against the same facade. The church was in fact built some years after the fountain, and Borromini was only partly responsible for its design.

FOUR FOUNTAINS   See QUATTRO FONTANE.

GALLERIA COLONNA   This gallery was designed in the late 17thC to display the private collection of the Colonna family. It is part of the PALAZZO COLONNA and contains many outstanding works.

GALLERIA DORIA PAMPHILI   The finest patrician art collection in Rome, with a number of important paintings and sculptures. It was assembled by the Doria family from the 16thC and is part of the PALAZZO DORIA.

GALLERIA NAZIONALE D'ARTE ANTICA (National Gallery of Early Art) ★
Via delle Quattro Fontane ☎ *4814591. Map 6G7* 🔁 ✗ *Open Mon-Sat 9.15am-2pm; Sun 9.15am-1pm. Metropolitana: Barberini.*
The **Palazzo Barberini** is an imposing Baroque building begun in 1625 by Carlo Maderno and completed by Bernini in 1633. The eccentric top-floor windows on either side of the arcaded center are the work of Borromini. The palace houses the earlier part of the National Art Collection — hence the somewhat misleading *antica* in the name of the gallery.

The pictures are not always to be found in the same rooms from year to year, so it is perhaps best to describe the most interesting in a roughly chronological order. The 15thC Florentines are represented by a triptych of the *Ascension, Pentecost, and Last Judgment* by Fra Angelico, and by two works by Filippo Lippi: these are the *Tarquinia Madonna* (1437) and an *Annunciation with Donors,* the one memorable for the ugliness of the Child, the other for the beauty of the Mother. Piero di Cosimo's *Mary Magdalen,* a bright, superbly finished picture, shows a great love of detail in the treatment of hands and the book the Magdalen is reading. Following these come two pictures by Lorenzo Lotto, a *Portrait of a Young Man* and the *Mystic Marriage of St Catherine with Saints* (1524).

The ceiling of Room VII is decorated with a frescoed *Allegory of Divine Wisdom* by Andrea Sacchi, the great representative of 17thC Classicism in Rome. Close by is Raphael's *Fornarina* (★), said to be a portrait of the baker's daughter who was his mistress, and by far the most famous picture in the collection.

Farther on are El Greco's remarkable *Nativity* and *Baptism of Christ,* with their spectacular lighting effects, and Tintoretto's *Christ and the Woman Taken in Adultery* (c.1546). Then come Quentin Massy's *Portrait of Erasmus,* painted for Thomas More, a masterly study of dignity and composure, and Holbein's *Henry VIII.* The latter dates from about 1540, and shows him dressed in regal splendor for his marriage to Anne of Cleves.

Pietro da Cortona's masterpiece, the frescoed *Allegory of Divine Providence* (★), decorates the ceiling of the Salone, the main room of the palace. Painted between 1638-39, it is a glorification of the Barberini family and of Urban VIII, who was pope at the time. The Barberini bees are clearly visible in the center of the design. The sheer exuberance of the invention may seem excessive to some, but there can be few paintings that convey the virtuosity of the Baroque so forcefully.

In addition to the glories of Palazzo Barberini, the 17th and 18thC paintings at the PALAZZO CORSINI at Via della Lungara 10 also come under the aegis of the Galleria Nazionale d'Arte Antica.

GALLERIA NAZIONALE D'ARTE MODERNA (National Gallery of Modern Art)
Viale delle Belle Arti 131 ☎ *3224151. Map 5E6* ▥ ▣ *Open Tues-Sat 9am-2pm; Wed-Fri 3-7.30pm; Sun 9am-1pm. Closed Mon.*

Modern Italian art tends to be overshadowed by the achievements of earlier ages. As a result, despite occupying a commanding position at the top of the VILLA BORGHESE, this gallery does not get the attention it deserves.

The vast collection of 19thC works includes many uninspiring efforts by worthy academicians, so not all the rooms are of equal interest, although the cool romanticism of Francesco Hayez (Room IV) and brilliant coloring of the Italian Impressionists, or *Macchiaioli,* in Room VIII are worth investigating.

The most celebrated of the modern Italian painters represented are the Futurist Umberto Boccioni and the metaphysical Giorgio de' Chirico. There are also works by major 20thC foreign painters and sculptors, including Max Ernst, Henry Moore and Jackson Pollock.

The 20thC section is undergoing complete redecoration and reorganization at present and is therefore closed, and only a few works from the collection are on show in the large central hall. When the section reopens, the gallery should be rejuvenated.

GALLERIA SPADA
Piazza Capo di Ferro 13 ☎ *6861158. Map 5I5* ▥ *Open 9am-1.30pm.*
A small but select family collection of Titian, Guido Reni, Andrea del Sarto and other 17thC artists, in the PALAZZO SPADA.

GESÙ 血 † ★
Corso Vittorio Emanuele. Map 9I6.
This impressive Jesuit church was built between 1568 and 1575 and became a model for Counter-Reformation churches all over Europe. The facade by Giacomo della Porta and interior by Vignola were

equally influential (see illustration on page 28). The decoration of the interior is exceptionally rich, with sumptuous details in colored marble and lapis lazuli.

The major work of art is Giovanni Battista Gaulli's superb fresco of the *Triumph of the Name of Jesus* on the vault of the nave, which dates from about a century after the completion of the church. Gaulli, also called Baciccia, was a colleague of Bernini and his exuberant style is very similar, albeit on a two-dimensional level. The other great attraction of the interior is the **Chapel of St Ignatius Loyola** by Andrea Pozzo (1696-1700), irresistibly excessive in its opulence.

GHETTO

Lungotevere dei Cenci. Map 8|5.

In 1556, during the pontificate of Paul IV, the Jews of Rome were confined to a very restricted area s of the Via del Portico d'Ottavia. They were forbidden to own land or practice in one of the professions, and these and other restrictions added to their poverty and misery, as did the overcrowding. Relief of a sort came only after 1870. It is in this area, on the banks of the Tiber, that the **Synagogue** (1904) is situated.

IMPERIAL FORUMS   Toward the end of the Republic, it became clear that the ROMAN FORUM was no longer able to accommodate the administrative and commercial life of the city. Julius Caesar acquired land to the N of the forum for a new complex that became known as the FORUM OF CAESAR. His great-nephew Octavian, later the Emperor Augustus, continued the expansion N, with the FORUM OF AUGUSTUS. The next Imperial forum was built by Vespasian and called the Forum of Peace, although it is now known as the FORUM OF VESPASIAN. Later emperors added the Forum of Nerva (of which the scant remains can be viewed from the FORUM OF AUGUSTUS or from Via dei Fori Imperiali) and the FORUM OF TRAJAN, largest and most splendid of the Imperial forums. See the plan opposite.

ISOLA TIBERINA (Tiber Island)

Map 4|5.

The Tiber Island is situated mid-stream in the bend of the river as it sweeps past Trastevere on the right and the Cenci district on the left. It is joined to either bank by two ancient bridges, one of which — **Ponte Fabricio** (★), opposite the THEATER OF MARCELLUS — is in a marvelous state of preservation considering it was built in 62BC. Crossing to the island from this side, you will see looming up on the left the severe lines of the medieval **Torre dei Caetani**, and on the right the bulky mass of the modern **Hospital of the Fatebenefratelli**, which literally translated means the "Do-good-brothers." The road leads into a small piazza, one of the most secluded and delightful spots in Rome, where the roar of traffic from either embankment is muffled by the old buildings and the sizeable church of SAN BARTOLOMEO.

The Tiber Island's association with medicine and healing is very ancient. It is likely that the church of San Bartolomeo was built on the site of the Temple of Aesculapius, the God of Healing. The temple was

barely visible or disappeared

partly or wholly visible

```
0        50      100m
0        50      100yds
```

1 Temple of Trajan
2 Santa Maria di Loreto
3 Latin Library
4 Trajan's Column
5 Santissimo Nome di Maria
6 Greek Library
7 Basilica Ulpia
8 Monument to Victor Emmanuel II
9 Santa Maria d'Aracoeli
10 Trajan's Markets
11 Torre delle Milizie

12 Temple of Venus Genetrix
13 Santi Luca e Martina
14 Arch of Trajan
15 Casa dei Cavalieri di Rodi
16 Curia
17 Temple of Mars Ultor
18 Basilica Aemilia
19 Temple of Minerva
20 Temple of Antoninus and Faustina
21 Torre dei Conti
22 Santi Cosma e Damiano

erected here after a serpent sacred to the god was brought to Rome from Epidaurus, reputedly bringing the great plague of 291BC to an end. The serpent chose the island for its dwelling-place, and hence caused it to be consecrated to healing. In the Middle Ages, the faithful would spend the night under the church portico, hoping to be cured.

To reach Trastevere from the island you cross the Ponte Cestio, first built in 46BC and restored, using original material, in the 19thC.

JANICULUM HILL (Gianicolo)
Map 313 ◄€ ♣
Set back from the W bank of the Tiber, the Janiculum rises to a height of 82m (270ft) at PORTA SAN PANCRAZIO. From here, and especially from the path leading past Gallori's imposing **Garibaldi Monument** (1895), there is a superb view across the river toward the old city in the E. Immediately below are the wooded slopes of the **Gianicolo park** (see ROME FOR CHILDREN). The Janiculum takes its name from the god Janus, who in ancient times was believed to have founded a city here. It is not, however, one of the original Seven Hills of Rome.

KEATS-SHELLEY MEMORIAL
Piazza di Spagna ☎6784235. Map **5G6** ☒ Open Mon-Fri 9am-1pm,
2.30-5.30pm (June-Sept 3.30-6pm). Closed Sat; Sun; one week in Aug.
Metropolitana: Spagna.
In the house overlooking the SPANISH STEPS from the S are rooms once used by the poet John Keats and his friend Joseph Severn. These now form a working library for students of Keats and Shelley, who both died in Italy. Leaving behind the hectic bustle of Piazza di Spagna, you climb the stairs to be greeted by a curator who will ask you to sign a visitors' book. Keats died here in 1821, aged 25, and during his last months he must have derived some pleasure from the animated scenes that were enacted under his bedroom window. A death-mask on display is a sad reminder of how high talent was cut short in its prime by tuberculosis. Keats is buried in the PROTESTANT CEMETERY.

LARGO ARGENTINA (Largo di Torre Argentina) ★
Map **8I5.**
This open space is named after the **Torre Argentina**, the handsome house with a loggia in the adjoining Via del Sudaria. The house was built in 1503 by Bishop Burckhardt of Strasbourg (then in the diocese of Argenturatum, from which the name derives), incorporating a tower already there.

For many centuries the Largo Argentina was densely overbuilt and it was not until 1926-30 that the houses on it were cleared to reveal four **Republican Temples**, among the earliest examples remaining in the city. They are well below the present street level and can be viewed from the railings above. Although the remains are sparse, you can see the clear outline of three temples and part of a fourth (not fully excavated).

In spite of the care and attention given to these excavations by scholars and archeologists, surprisingly little is known about the temples — not even to which gods they were dedicated. Viewing them from the W, **temple D** on the left dates from around 200BC and **temple C** next to it is one or two centuries earlier. Next in line, **temple B** is the latest of the four. It is circular, with steep front steps. A few of the columns have been re-erected, but give little idea of the 18 magnificent travertine columns that once stood here, their Corinthian capitals luxuriously carved out of marble. **Temple A**, on the extreme right, was probably built in the 3rdC BC. A few standing columns remain, and the site now includes the ruins of a medieval church.

On the W side of the Largo is the 18thC facade of the **Teatro Argentina**, home of the Teatro di Roma theater company. It was here that Rossini's *Barber of Seville* was booed at its first performance in 1816.

LATERAN PALACE (Palazzo del Laterano)
*Piazza San Giovanni in Laterano. Map **10**J9. Metropolitana: San Giovanni.*
The original Lateran palace was the official residence of the popes until 1309, when they moved to Avignon. In the same year it was almost completely destroyed by fire and, when the popes returned to Rome in 1378, they transferred to the Vatican. In 1586 Sixtus V commissioned Domenico Fontana to rebuild the Lateran as a summer palace, and this is the building you can see today. It is a rather unsuccessful emulation of the PALAZZO FARNESE, lacking the inventiveness of its model and giving the impression of sheer size without grandeur. In fact, later popes preferred to make the PALAZZO DEL QUIRINALE their summer residence, and the Lateran is now the seat of the Rome Vicariate.

LUDOVISI QUARTER (Quartiere Ludovisi)
*Map **6**G7. Metropolitana: Barberini.*
This area is named after the now-vanished Villa Ludovisi, which succumbed to urban development at the end of the last century. It is a smart residential enclave, lying to the W of Via Veneto, and boasts a number of expensive hotels.

MAMERTINE PRISON   The prison where St Peter is said to have been held was later consecrated as the chapel of SAN PIETRO IN CARCERE.

MAUSOLEUM OF AUGUSTUS (Mausoleo di Augusto) ★
*Via di Ripetta. Map **5**G5.*
This great Imperial family tomb still retains much of its ancient dignity, its mellowed brickwork warmed by the sun and ringed with cypresses. The mausoleum was known in Classical times as the Augusteum, and the ground around it was laid out in groves and public walks. The entrance to the enormous circular drum was flanked by two pink obelisks, since removed to PIAZZA DEL QUIRINALE and Piazza dell' Esquilino (outside SANTA MARIA MAGGIORE). The drum itself was surmounted by an earthen tumulus, at the center of which stood a colossal bronze statue of Augustus. We have no more precise details than these of the mausoleum's appearance, but it is possible that cypresses were planted in rings leading up to the top of the mound.

In the 12thC it was turned into a fortress by the Colonna family, a fate that also befell the Mausoleum of Hadrian when it was converted into the CASTEL SANT' ANGELO. Later on, the Augusteum was transformed into an amphitheater for bullfighting, a sport that was not banned until 1829. At the end of the 19thC the building was in use as a circus and concert-hall, and it was not until 1926-36 that significant archeological exploration was accomplished. Three niches were found, one of which must have contained the urn holding the ashes of the Emperor — who died in August, AD14 (the month named after him) — and of his wife Livia. The other niches contained the ashes of his sister Octavia and of his nephews Caius and Lucius Caesar. Members of the public are not admitted, but you can walk round the deep perimeter path surrounding the building and get a glimpse of the interior through the entrance on the s side.

MAUSOLEUM OF HADRIAN   This huge circular structure, converted to a fortress from the 3rdC, is better known as the CASTEL SANT' ANGELO.

MONUMENT TO VICTOR EMMANUEL II (Monumento Vittorio Emanuele II)
Piazza Venezia. Map 9I6.

An enormous amount of time, expense and marble went into the construction of this gigantic memorial to the first king of a united Italy. The

gleaming white mountain is strikingly out of character and scale with the neighboring city-scape, and was aptly nicknamed the wedding cake by Allied troops in World War II. It has inevitably become something of a landmark. Designed by Giuseppe Sacconi, it took from 1885 to 1911 to construct. The **Tomb of the Unknown Soldier** is on the first level, at

the foot of the **Altare della Patria** (Altar of the Fatherland) by Zanelli. From the top level, there are spectacular views across the entire city.

MOOR FOUNTAIN (Fontana del Moro)
Piazza Navona. Map 5H5.

This attractive fountain at the s end of PIAZZA NAVONA is the work of Giacomo della Porta (1575). The central figure of the Moor grasping a dolphin was an addition by Giovanni Antonio Mari, from a design by Bernini (1654). The surrounding tritons are 19thC copies of the late 16thC originals.

MOSES FOUNTAIN (Fontana del Mose)
Piazza San Bernardo. Map 6G7. Metropolitana: Repubblica.

Also known as the Fontana dell' Acqua Felice, this is the first of the monumental Post-Renaissance fountains. Commissioned by Sixtus V in 1587 and designed by Domenico Fontana, it is in the form of a triumphal arch. In the side niches, scenes in high relief represent Joshua leading the Hebrews across the Jordan, and Aaron leading the Hebrews to drink. In the central niche stands the colossal figure of Moses, which Venturi called "the most shameful parody of Michelangelo's work in Rome." It was traditionally held to be by Prospero da Brescia, who was said to have died of grief following the derisive reception given to his work. In fact, he was only a collaborator of the true sculptor, Leonardo Sormani.

MUSEO NAZIONALE ROMANO This museum occupies part of the old Carthusian monastery erected among the ruins of the BATHS OF DIOCLETIAN. It contains a superb collection of early Greek and Roman sculpture.

MUSEO NAZIONALE DI VILLA GIULIA An important collection of Etruscan art, housed in Julius III's tranquil hilltop retreat, the VILLA GIULIA.

MUSEO DI PALAZZO VENEZIA This museum in the PALAZZO VENEZIA contains some very fine tapestries, as well as a good collection of paintings, sculpture, ceramics, porcelain, silver and Majolica.

NAIADS' FOUNTAIN (Fontana delle Naiadi)
Piazza della Repubblica. Map 6G8. Metropolitana: Repubblica.
Realistically modeled on the curvaceous Vittoria Placidi, Mario Rutelli's fountain shocked prudish opinion at its inauguration in 1901, but is now regarded as the best of the modern fountains in Rome. It consists of four bronze groups, each representing a naiad grappling with a sea monster. The central male figure was added in 1912. The powerful spray and spectacular play of water can best be appreciated when the fountain is floodlit at night.

NERO'S GOLDEN HOUSE (Domus Aurea) ★
Via Labicana 136. Map 10I8 ▦ ✗ compulsory. Open Tues-Sun 9am-1pm. Closed Mon. Metropolitana: Colosseo.
Few ruins in Rome do less to inspire visions of the glories of ancient times than what remains of Nero's fabulous house. The rooms are dank and dark, the walls in places wet with condensation, but this gives a gloomy and false impression and hopefully one that has been eradicated by recent restoration work. The tyrant's house was once situated high up on a terrace, and its splendid chambers were light and airy. It is not possible to see anything like the whole extent of the original buildings, because succeeding emperors demolished large portions. Trajan, especially, swept away much of the original fabric in order to build his great Baths (104-109). He completely covered over the residential wing of the house — the part that has been excavated and can be seen today — to provide the foundations for libraries and other recreational areas.

Nero's house was called golden because the main facade was entirely gilded. The building was of complex design, and the furnishings of the utmost luxury: coffered ivory ceilings concealed apertures that sprayed mists of scent on the rooms below, and the internal baths were supplied with both sea water and water from the sulfur springs. The architects were Severus and Celeres, and they lived up to their patron's most exotic expectations. Nero commissioned leading painters to execute murals, the most famous of which are from the hand of Fabullus. The discovery of these paintings in the 16thC caused tremendous excitement, and inspired the "grotesque" style of painted decoration, so called because they were found in underground rooms that were like grottoes or caves. The house was once filled with superb pieces of sculpture, and it is even possible that some of these still lie buried beneath later construction and have yet to come to light.

One of the few rooms that convey something of the original atmosphere is the famous domed **octagonal hall**, or dining room, where sumptuous banquets were held. It is a beautifully proportioned room. According to Suetonius, it "revolved slowly, day and night, in time with the heavens." Others describe a revolving table at which the reclining guests would not need to bestir themselves to reach for the dish of their choice. At one end of the room, cooling water cascaded over stepped tiles to a channel below, continuously refreshing the atmosphere.

The guided tour usually includes the **cryptoporticus**, frequented by Raphael and other 16thC artists who came to study the paintings. These are not easy to see (they are distinguished by their white backgrounds), but are fascinating examples of the Fourth Pompeian style.

ORATORY COMPLEX ㎜

Corso Vittorio Emanuele. Map 4H4.

The Congregation of the Oratory of St Philip Neri needed various buildings besides the CHIESA NUOVA. These included a sacristy, living quarters, and a large library. Borromini began as co-architect with Paolo Maruscelli in 1637, but the latter soon resigned and left Borromini in sole charge of the project. In spite of the large scale of the task, progress was rapid, and by 1650 the program was completed with the building of the **clock tower** overlooking Piazza dell' Orologio, the square to which it gave its name.

Standing in Piazza della Chiesa Nuova, you can admire Borromini's genius in the curving facade of the **Oratory of the Filippini** (★). The design is a masterly play of convex and concave, topped by a strange, almost Gothic, broken pediment (see illustration on page 28). The wealth and complexity of the detail make for an effect of great richness, all the more remarkable in that the material used is brick.

PALATINE HILL (Palatino) ★

Via di San Gregorio ☎6790333. *Entrance from E end of Roman Forum, S of Arch of Titus along Clivus Palatinus. Map 9J7* ▦ *(combined with Roman Forum)*
✗ *with advance notice* ◀ *Open Mon, Wed-Sat 9am-5pm; Tues, Sun 9am-2pm. Metropolitana: Colosseo.*

At a height of approximately 50m (164 feet), the Palatine provides an unusual combination of beauty and wilderness, the former provided by trees, shrubs and gardens, and the latter by complex archeological

KEY **1** House of Augustus **2** Temple of Apollo **3** House of Livia **4** Domus Tiberiana **5** Farnese Gardens **6** Palace of Caligula **7** Cryptoporticus **8** Antiquarium **9** Domus Flavia **10** Domus Augustana **11** Domitian's Stadium **12** Domus Severiana **13** Paedagogium **14** Temple of Cybele **15** Hut of Romulus **16** Lupercal **17** S. Maria Antiqua **18** S. Anastasia **19** To Roman Forum

remains, which are more than usually difficult to unravel. This is due to soil subsidence and structural weakness, which together prevent inspection of important buildings, and to current archeological research, which cannot be disturbed. Yet the Palatine is well worth visiting, not only for its historical interest, but for the park-like atmosphere of its grassy enclaves. It is an ideal spot in which to have a picnic lunch.

The history of the Palatine precedes that of the ROMAN FORUM, and it has been called the cradle of Roman civilization. It was here, according to legend, that Romulus in 753BC yoked oxen to a plow and traced the lines of the city boundaries. Whether or not that story is true, indisputable remains of Early Iron Age huts (9thC BC) have been found here.

During the years of the Republic, many prominent citizens such as Catullus and the orator Hortensius made their homes here. The air was fresher at this height, and the fine views made it popular. Their houses were concentrated in the area to the w known as the **Germalus**, one of the Palatine's three crests. Augustus was born here, and having taken over Hortensius' house (later renamed the **House of Augustus (1)**), he built the **Temple of Apollo (2)**, one of the sumptuous edifices with which he surrounded his comparatively simple house. The front of the temple, with its beautiful statue of Apollo by Scopas, was surmounted by a gilded chariot that reflected the rays of the sun. To the e are the remains of the **House of Livia (3)** (✰), now considered to be outbuildings of the first house and not the home of his wife.

Augustus was succeeded by Tiberius, and from this time onward the Palatine became the most important center of political and social life in Rome. Tiberius leveled all the private houses to the NW of the Germalus, to build the **Domus Tiberiana (4)**. Large remains of the substructure are visible, and some vaulted rooms are still preserved along the Clivus Victoriae. But most of the palace remains unexcavated beneath the beautiful **Farnese Gardens (5)** (✰), laid out for Cardinal Alessandro Farnese in the 16thC and still very well kept. The terrace of the gardens provides a splendid view across the Forum and toward the CAPITOLINE HILL. Caligula extended the Domus toward the Roman Forum and built a bridge to connect it with the Capitol. The ruins of this later addition are known as the **Palace of Caligula (6)**. On the e boundary of the Domus is the *cryptoporticus* **(7)**, a vaulted passage decorated with splendid stuccoes; the originals are in the **Antiquarium (8)** or Palatine museum.

To the SE of the *cryptoporticus* are the extensive ruins of the splendid palace complex built by Domitian at the end of the 1stC using the foremost architect of the time, Rabirius. The construction entailed leveling and merging large areas of the Palatine so that the original crests of the Germalus and **Palatium** (in the s) could no longer be distinguished. The complex consisted of the **Domus Flavia (9)** (the official palace of the Imperial government, in the portico of which Domitian was later assassinated), the **Domus Augustana (10)** (the emperor's residence) and **Domitian's Stadium (11)**.

However, the best-preserved and most evocative ruins on the Palatine are those of the **Domus Severiana (12)** (✰) or Palace of Septimius Severus. Its massively arcaded front was designed to form a monumental approach to the area, and hid the confusion of structures behind. The remains include part of the baths. Somewhere to the SE of the Domus stood Septimius Severus' **Septizodium**, a fabulous three-tiered structure that was notable for its profusion of fine marble columns.

On the extreme w of the Palatine are the **Paedagogium (13)** *(closed to the public)* and ruined **Temple of Cybele (14)**. Close by is the Iron Age **hut of Romulus (15)** and the **Lupercal (16)**, a sanctuary of the greatest antiquity, being the grotto where Romulus and Remus were supposedly suckled by the wolf. The spot where the twins are reputed to have drifted ashore is near the entrance of the Lupercal.

PALAZZO BARBERINI �XX A grand Baroque palace, built for Urban VIII, the Barberini Pope, from 1625-33. Since 1949 it has housed the GALLERIA NAZIONALE D'ARTE ANTICA, the earlier part of the National Art Collection.

PALAZZO BORGHESE ⌂
Piazza Borghese. Map 5G5.

Due to its curious shape, this large and sumptuous palace is known to Romans as **Il Cembalo** (The Harpsichord). It was begun around 1560, possibly to a design by Vignola, and was later purchased by Cardinal Borghese (Pope Paul V from 1605). He arranged for its completion by Flaminio Ponzio. It remains in the family's possession to this day. It was here that the Borghese's patronage of the arts resulted in a collection of enormous size and sybaritic indulgence. Founded by Paul's nephew, Cardinal Scipione Borghese, the collection was housed in the palace until 1891, when it was transferred to the Casino in the Villa Borghese, now known as the BORGHESE GALLERY.

PALAZZO BRASCHI   A fine late 18thC palace, which since 1952 has been the home of the ROME MUSEUM.

PALAZZO DELLA CANCELLERIA ⌂
Corso Vittorio Emanuele. Map 4H4.

One of the finest Renaissance palaces in Rome, this great building has a beautiful easterly facade overlooking the piazza named after it. The palace was built for Raffaele Riario, a nephew of Sixtus IV, between 1485 and 1513. Its authorship remains a mystery, although the design of the courtyard has often been attributed to Bramante. Incredibly, Riario won a third of the small fortune that the palace cost him to build in a single night's gambling with Francesco Cybo, nephew of Innocent VIII. The palace later became the Chancellery; hence its present name.

PALAZZO CHIGI ⌂
Piazza Colonna. Map 5H6.

Facing PIAZZA COLONNA and flanking Via del Corso, this palace was begun in 1580 for the Aldobrandini family, and only passed to the Chigi in 1659. The architects included Carlo Maderno and Felice della Greca. At one time it contained a famous library, started by Alexander VII (Fabio Chigi). This was presented to the Vatican by the State in 1923. The palace is closed to the public, but from the entrance you can glimpse the beautiful inner courtyard with its 17thC stuccoes and fountain bearing the Chigi coat-of-arms.

PALAZZO COLONNA ⌂ ★
Piazza Santi Apostoli ☎6794362. Entrance in Via della Pilotta 17. Map 5H6
▨ *(gallery). Open Sat only, 9am-1pm. Closed Aug.*

One of the largest and most sumptuous palaces in Rome, the Palazzo Colonna was begun by Pope Martin V (1417-31), but the bulk of the present building dates from a refurbishment in 1730. The church of SANTI APOSTOLI forms part of the complex but, apart from this, the **Galleria Colonna** is the only part of the palace that may be visited.

Antonio del Grande started work on the gallery in 1654, but when he died in 1671 the project was taken over by Girolamo Fontana. The gallery was finally opened in 1703 by Filippo Colonna. The frescoed ceiling depicts the *Battle of Lepanto,* at which a Colonna ancestor had distinguished himself, and is the work of Giovanni Coli and Filippo Gherardi. The large collection of pictures includes works by Rubens, Van Dyck, Tintoretto, Veronese, Paul Brill and Salvator Rosa. The undoubted masterpiece is Annibale Carracci's *Bean-eater*(★), an early work of earthy realism by an artist whose later style was supremely Classical.

PALAZZO CORSINI ▥

Via della Lungara, 10. Map 4I4. Gallery ▨ Open Tues-Fri 9am-7pm (closes 1hr earlier on holidays); Sat 9am-2pm; Sun 9am-1pm. Closed Mon.

Originally built in the 15thC for Cardinal Domenico Riario, this palace later became the residence of Queen Christina of Sweden, who died here in 1689. From 1732-36, Ferdinando Fuga extensively remodeled the building, adding the long and elegant facade you can see today. The palace houses the art collection started by Cardinal Neri Corsini in the 18thC. Among the Italian works, two Caravaggios, *Narcissus* (★) and *St John the Baptist,* are powerful dramatizations of youthful beauty, while Salvator Rosa's sensitive portrait study of his wife is an unusual work by an artist better known for his landscapes. Paintings by foreign artists who lived in Rome include three fine works by Le Valentin, Caravaggio's most faithful follower, Rubens' early *St Sebastian* and Van Dyck's *Rest on the Flight into Egypt* (★), a tender meditation.

PALAZZO DORIA ▥ ★

Via del Corso ☎6794365. Entrance in Piazza del Collegio Romano Ia. Map 5H6. Palace and gallery ▨ ✗ compulsory. Private apartments. Open Tues, Fri, Sat, Sun 10am-1pm. Closed Mon; Wed; Thurs.

This building dates from 1435, but is a composite of many styles and periods. The facade overlooking the Corso is by Gabriele Valvassori (1734), that on the Via del Plebiscito by Paolo Ameli (1743), and that on the Piazza del Collegio Romano by Antonio del Grande (c.1660). They all mask older fabric, and the foundations of the whole rest on ruins of Classical times. The palace was founded by the cardinals of the nearby diocese of Santa Maria in Via Lata, passed through the hands of the della Rovere, the Aldobrandini and the Pamphili, and eventually became the property of the Doria family.

The **Galleria Doria Pamphili** contains the Doria family's important collection of paintings and *objets d'art* and is the finest such patrician collection in Rome. It consists of four long galleries surrounding a courtyard, with various rooms issuing from them. The first gallery contains a number of outstanding pictures: Titian's *Religion Succoured by Spain;* Correggio's *Allegory of Virtue;* Raphael's *Double Portrait;* Titian's *Salome;* and three paintings by Caravaggio, *St Mary Magdalen, The Rest on the Flight into Egypt* and *St John the Baptist.* Also in this room is Alessandro Algardi's bust of *Olimpia Maidalchini,* Innocent X's formidable sister-in-law, and the butt of many pasquinades.

The sequence of small rooms at the end of the second gallery contains several fine small-scale works, including Parmigianino's *Adoration of the Shepherds* and *Virgin and Child* and Pieter Brueghel the Elder's *Bay of*

Naples. At the end of the third gallery there is a small room containing Velázquez's superb portrait of *Innocent X Pamphili* (★), as well as a bust of the pope by Bernini. The fourth gallery displays a magnificent collection of 17thC landscapes, including works by Claude Lorrain and Gaspard Dughet, as well as Annibale Carracci's *Flight into Egypt* and *Entombment*.

The **private apartments**, which are still lived in, contain some very fine family portraits, of which the best is Sebastiano del Piombo's portrait of *Andrea Doria* (★), the famous admiral. The yellow salon, lined with superb Gobelins tapestries made for Louis XV, is the most impressive.

PALAZZO FARNESE 🏛 ★
Piazza Farnese. Map 4I5.

The finest Renaissance palace in Rome is unfortunately no longer open to the public. It was begun in 1514 for Cardinal Alessandro Farnese (later Paul III) by the Florentine architect Antonio da Sangallo the Younger, who completed the main and side facades but, just before his

death in 1546, found himself forced to relinquish the project to Michelangelo. The hand of the later architect can be seen in the raised, strongly projecting cornice and in the inverted emphasis of the recessed central window, both typical Mannerist touches. The building was finally com-

pleted by Giacomo della Porta in 1589. Since 1871 it has been the French Embassy. Inside, the gallery has superb frescoes by Annibale Carracci, notably the *Triumph of Love* (1597-1604).

PALAZZO MADAMA 🏛
Corso del Rinascimento. Map 5H5.

A 16thC palace of fine proportions built for the Medici, this sumptuous building takes its name from Madama Margherita d'Austria, the illegitimate daughter of the Emperor Charles V. She was first married to Alessandro de' Medici, and subsequently to Ottavio Farnese. The grand facade dates from 1649, when the building was extended by Paolo Maruscelli. The palace is now the seat of the upper house of the Italian parliament.

PALAZZO MASSIMO ALLE COLONNE 🏛
Corso Vittorio Emanuele. Map 4I5.

The present palace was designed by Baldassare Peruzzi to replace one destroyed in the Sack of Rome of 1527. It was completed after the architect's death in 1536. The curved facade was unique at this date, and Peruzzi's audacity is also evident in the squat columns of the entrance, which almost look as if they are being crushed by the weight of masonry above them. It is not possible to go inside, but you may catch a glimpse of the stuccoed ceiling of the vestibule and even of the courtyard beyond. The princely family of the Massimo, one of the oldest in Rome, is recorded even earlier than the Colonna or the Orsini.

PALAZZO DI MONTECITORIO ▥
Piazza di Montecitorio. Map 5H5.
Designed by Bernini for Pope Innocent X, who intended it for his Ludovisi relations, this palace was begun in 1650. After long interruptions it was completed by Carlo Fontana in 1694, as Innocent XII's Palace of Justice. Bernini's sober facade dominates the Piazza di Montecitorio but is no longer the main entrance. Since 1871, the building has been the seat of the lower house of the Italian parliament.

PALAZZO ORSINI
This extraordinary 16thC palace, named after the family that owned it in the 18th and 19thC, occupies a unique position on top of the THEATER OF MARCELLUS, built by Julius Caesar and Augustus.

PALAZZO PAMPHILI ▥
Piazza Navona. Map 5H5.
The Pamphili Pope, Innocent X, reputed to be the ugliest man in Rome and the subject of a famous portrait by Velázquez in the PALAZZO DORIA, commissioned this palace from Girolamo Rainaldi in 1644. It formed part of his grand design to make PIAZZA NAVONA a social focus, a plan that largely succeeded.

The palace then became the residence of the notorious Donna Olimpia, the Pope's sister-in-law. The interior, with splendid rooms designed by Borromini, and a long gallery frescoed by Pietro da Cortona with the *Story of Aeneas* (1651-54), is closed to the public. The building is now the Brazilian Embassy.

PALAZZO PICCOLA FARNESINA ▥ ★
Corso Vittorio Emanuele 168 ☎6540848. Map 4I5 ▩ (museum). Open Tues, Thurs 9am-2pm, 5-8pm; Wed, Fri, Sat 9am-2pm; Sun 9am-1pm. Closed Mon.
This enchanting palace reveals the more intimate and personal side of Renaissance culture that is often overlooked amid so much grandeur. It was built for a French prelate called Thomas le Roy, who had acted as an intermediary between Francis I of France and Pope Leo X; the grateful King allowed le Roy to incorporate the fleur-de-lis into his coat of arms.

These heraldic lilies appear on the outside of the palace, and their confusion with the Farnese lilies gave the palace its name. Begun in 1523, probably to a plan by Antonio da Sangallo the Younger, it was completed in 1546 by le Roy's nephew. The facade toward Corso Vittorio dates from around 1900, when the destruction of some old houses left this side of the palace exposed.

The building is now the property of the City of Rome and houses the **Barracco Museum**, a small but fine collection of Classical sculpture assembled by Baron Giovanni Barracco. The quality of the Greek pieces is outstanding: note especially the *Head of a Woman* — a work of great sensitivity — and four low-relief panels showing warriors fighting.

PALAZZO DEL QUIRINALE 血 ★

*Piazza del Quirinale ☎4699. Map **5**H6 🖭 𝑘 compulsory. Admission by appointment only, after written application to Ufficio Intendenza, Palazzo del Quirinale, 00137.*

Since 1947 the Quirinal has been the official residence of the Italian President. The splendid site was chosen originally by Cardinal Ippolito d'Este (the illegitimate son of Alfonso d'Este and Lucrezia Borgia) for his town palace, and the present building was begun in 1573 by Martino Longhi. A distinguished list of architects followed him, including Carlo Maderno, Bernini, Domenico Fontana and Ferdinando Fuga. In 1592 Clement VIII decided to move here from the supposedly unhealthy environs of the Vatican, and his example was followed by later popes. Before 1870, conclaves were held in the Cappella Paolina (built to the same dimensions as the Sistine Chapel), and the cardinals were housed in comfort in the long monotonous wing known as the *manica lunga*, or long sleeve, that overlooks Via del Quirinale.

The principal entrance is by Maderno; the tower to the left of it, on which the national flag flies, was added at the time of Urban VIII. The spacious inner court is by Fontana. Visitors are taken round the palace in small groups on a tour lasting about an hour. One of the finest sights is Melozzo da Forlì's superb fresco on the grand staircase of *Christ in Glory* (★) — a fragment from his masterpiece, formerly in the church of SANTI APOSTOLI. At the top of the stairs, the **Sala Regia** and **Cappella Paolina** were both designed by Maderno. The fine stucco decoration in the latter is the work of Martino Ferabosco. The tour takes you through a series of sumptuously decorated apartments that include a chinoiserie salon and a room with magnificent Murano glass chandeliers. The **Cappella dell' Annunciata** has frescoes by Guido Reni, and the **Gallery of Alexander VII** has frescoes executed under the direction of Pietro da Cortona by a number of celebrated artists including Gaspard Dughet.

PALAZZO SENATORIO

This is the central building of the palace complex designed by Michelangelo for PIAZZA DEL CAMPIDOGLIO. The original plans were somewhat modified after his death, and the facade was finally built by Giacomo della Porta and Girolamo Rainaldi (1582-1605).

PALAZZO SPADA 血 ★

*Piazza Capo di Ferro ☎6561158. Map **4**I5. Gallery 🖭 Open Mon-Sat 9am-1.30pm; Sun 9am-1pm. State Rooms 🖭 𝑘 compulsory. Admission by appointment only, after written application to Ufficio Intendenza, Palazzo Spada, Piazza Capo di Ferro 13, 00186.*

Built for Cardinal Capo di Ferro in 1540, and once the property of Cardinal Bernardino Spada, this palace is remarkable for the exquisite stucco decoration that adorns the **facade** and **courtyard**, the work of Giulio Mazzoni (1556-60). In the course of renovating the palace, Borromini added a cunning illusionist design on the s side of the garden. The *trompe l'oeil* of the perspective gives the appearance of a long colonnade ending in a court, over which a Classical statue presides. In fact the colonnade is only about 9m (30ft) long, and the statue is tiny. It is a rare example of Borromini's less serious work. The palace is now the seat of the Council of State, but permission can be obtained to visit the very fine State Rooms when they are not in use.

The **Galleria Spada** is a small but select collection of works acquired by Cardinal Spada and later generations of his family. Of the four rooms, the first three are the most interesting. In Room I, you can compare the portraits of Cardinal Bernardino Spada by Guido Reni and Guercino. Room II has Titian's unfinished *Portrait of a Musician,* and Room III, Guercino's grandiose *Death of Dido* and Rubens' *Portrait of a Cardinal.* Also in Room III are Giovanni Battista Gaulli's *Triumph of the Name of Jesus,* a sketch for the ceiling of the GESÙ, and *Christ and the Samaritan Women,* both showing his debt to Bernini.

PALAZZO VENEZIA 🏛 ★
Via del Plebiscito ☎6798865. Map 5I6. Museum 🚾 Open Tues-Sat 9am-2pm (Thurs 9am-7pm); Sun 9am-1pm. Closed Mon. Garden Court 🚾 ✗ compulsory. Admission by appointment only, after written application to Ufficio Intendenza, Palazzo Venezia, Via del Plebiscito 1, 00186.

Originally called the Palazzo di San Marco, the Palazzo Venezia was the first substantial Renaissance palace to be built in Rome. It was begun in about 1455 for Cardinal Barbo (later Pope Paul II), but the identity of the architect remains in doubt. With the Palazzetto Venezia and the church of SAN MARCO, it forms a large, unified complex.

One floor of the palace now houses the **Museo di Palazzo Venezia (Sezione Medioevale)**, a heterogeneous collection of medieval art, sculpture, ceramics, weaving, jewelry and other artifacts. Opened in May 1985, it is, for a Roman museum, strikingly modern, well lit and generously laid out. The finest exhibit is Nino Pisano's *Head of a Woman.*

The other treasures of Palazzo Venezia — its splendid Italian, German and Flemish tapestries and its Renaissance paintings — are still being rearranged and are not on show. Special permission must be obtained to visit the beautiful **garden court**, with its unfinished 15thC loggia by Giuliano da Maiano and 18thC fountain, representing *The Marriage of Venice and the Sea,* by Carlo Monaldi.

PANTHEON (Temple of All the Gods) ★
Piazza della Rotonda. Map 5H5. Open Mon-Sat 9am-2pm; Sun 9am-1pm.

The Pantheon is the best preserved of all the ancient monuments of Rome. It has stood solidly and majestically for close on 2,000 years, defying architectural change all around, and there is something comforting and reassuring about its very presence. The building is particularly impressive after dark, when floodlighting emphasizes the grandeur of the 16 soaring monolithic granite columns, 12.5m (41 feet) high (see illustration on page 26). In front of the portico, and echoing its solemn statement, is Giacomo della Porta's **fountain** (1578), incorporating into its restrained design an **obelisk** of the time of Rameses II.

The Pantheon was built by the Emperor Hadrian between 119 and 128, despite the bold inscription on the pronaos stating *M. AGRIPPA L.F.*

COS TERTIUM FECIT (Marcus Agrippa, son of Lucius, Consul for the third time, built this). Such modesty was typical of Hadrian. He refused to have his name inscribed on any of his buildings, even though they included the TEMPLE OF VENUS AND ROME, the greatest temple in the city, and an enormous and complex villa at TIVOLI (see EXCURSIONS). Agrippa in fact built the original Pantheon, which was destroyed by fire, and Hadrian must have wanted to perpetuate his name on the new building.

How was it that the Pantheon was saved from the fate of so many other ancient monuments of Antiquity, which were used as quarries for grandiose building projects? The reason is that in 609 it was given by the Byzantine Emperor Phocas (in whose patrimony it was) to Boniface IV, who consecrated it as the church of Santa Maria and Martyres (the name being an allusion to the martyrs' bones that were transferred here from the catacombs).

However, desecration did take place. Sheets of gilded bronze were stripped from the dome (by Constans II in 655) and the bronze from the beams of the portico was removed for the making of the baldacchino of SAINT PETER'S (by Urban VIII) — two unforgivable acts of vandalism.

Moving through the portico, you reach the great **bronze doors** — the finest extant from Antiquity — and pass into the interior. This is dominated by the huge **dome**, its surface coffered and carefully proportioned to give a subtle interplay of light and shade. The great central oculus is open to the skies, and on a typical Roman day the sun pours in, throwing a brilliant roundel of light against the marble interior. The dome has a superb span, 43m (142 feet), wider than that of St Peter's (42m/138 feet) and dwarfing St Paul's, London (31m/101 feet). It is equal in height to the width of the building, just one example of the harmonious proportions that are in a large part responsible for the great beauty of the Pantheon.

The interior has changed little since ancient times. Although restored, the fine pavement retains its original design, and the great apse, the eight aedicules or shrines and the six recesses remain as before. The statues of the gods that once filled them have long since gone, and the building is now the burial place of two Italian kings — Victor Emmanuel II and Umberto I — and some of Italy's greatest artists, notably Raphael and Annibale Carracci.

PAOLA FOUNTAIN (Fontana Paola)
Via Garibaldi. Map 7J4.
This handsome Baroque fountain, with its monumental facade of five arches and six granite columns, was inspired by the earlier MOSES FOUNTAIN in Piazza San Bernardo. It was built for Paul V between 1610-12, by Flaminio Ponzio assisted by Giovanni Fontana. It is supplied with water from the Acqua Paola aqueduct, which was constructed at the same time. The basin was added later, by Carlo Fontana (1690).

PIAZZA BOCCA DELLA VERITÀ ⸿
Map 8J6.
This attractive garden square is overlooked by the Romanesque bell tower of SANTA MARIA IN COSMEDIN, guardian of the legendary **Bocca**

della Verità, or Mouth of Truth, from which the name derives. On the N side is the **Casa dei Crescenzi**, which once belonged to one of the most powerful families in the city. Like many other medieval buildings, it included Classical fragments in its construction. The piazza also boasts the well-preserved TEMPLE OF VESTA and TEMPLE OF FORTUNA VIRILIS.

PIAZZA DEL CAMPIDOGLIO 🏛 ★
Map 9/6 ◄€

This imposing palace complex centers on the ancient ridge or *asylum* between the twin summits of the CAPITOLINE HILL, where the Capitol of ancient Rome once stood. It is the architectural masterpiece of Michelangelo, who organized the space and was responsible for the basic design of the palaces. The buildings gradually come into view as you ascend the gentle flight of steps known as **La Cordonata**. In front of you is the **Palazzo Senatorio** (built over the remains of the ancient **Tabularium**, where the state archives are kept), with the **Palazzo Nuovo** and **Palazzo dei Conservatori** to left and right (the last two comprise the CAPITOLINE MUSEUMS). On either side of the steps at the entrance to the square stand the colossal Roman statues of the *Dioscuri*, the horse-tamers Castor and Pollux. There is a similar pair in PIAZZA DEL QUIRINALE.

The magnificent bronze equestrian statue that stood in the center of the piazza has been removed for security reasons, but will eventually be replaced by a facsimile. It represents the *Emperor Marcus Aurelius* (★) but was believed in the Middle Ages to show the first Christian Emperor, Constantine, a fact which may explain its survival. It once stood in front of the LATERAN PALACE, but was moved here by order of Paul III, and against the wishes of Michelangelo, who then designed its base.

PIAZZA CAMPO DEI FIORI
Map 4/5.

Rich in historical associations and local color, this is one of the most interesting and delightful of Rome's many piazzas. It is first and foremost a market place, with makeshift stalls selling flowers, fruit and vegetables (see SHOPPING). In the SE corner is the **Palazzo Pio**, partly incorporating the ancient Theater of Pompey (although none of it is now visible). It is hard to believe that these peaceful surroundings were once the scene of public executions (the diarist John Evelyn witnessed one in 1644) and that the figure of Giordano Bruno in the center of the piazza is a memorial to his death by burning in 1600, for heresy. Yet before this date Campo dei Fiori was a place of fashion, with some of the best-known inns in Rome. Now boasting two hotels, and with several trattorie in close proximity, it has perhaps regained its former character.

PIAZZA COLONNA
Map 5H6.

This fine central square is dominated by the COLUMN OF MARCUS AURELIUS and is overlooked by the PALAZZO CHIGI to the N and the **Palazzo**

Wedekind to the w. The 19thC facade of the Palazzo Wedekind incorporates 16 splendid Ionic columns from a Classical building at Veio.

PIAZZA DELLA MINERVA
Map 5H5.
Tucked away in the heart of the old city, this little square is dominated by the plain brick facade of SANTA MARIA SOPRA MINERVA. It was in the immediate vicinity that the Temple of Minerva originally stood. In front of the church is Bernini's charming *Elephant Supporting an Obelisk,* which carries an inscription by Alexander VII, and was unveiled in 1667. The text states that a robust intelligence is needed to support the burdens of wisdom, and this group was the unusual and endearing consequence.

PIAZZA NAVONA ★
Map 5H5.
Considered by many to be the finest of Rome's piazzas, this elongated "square" occupies the site of the Circus Agonalis, the stadium of Domitian from which, via the corruption *n'Agona,* it derives its name. Used in ancient times for athletic contests and displays, the arena survived into the 17thC as a place for jousting and other tournaments. Innocent X transformed it into a Baroque masterpiece by commissioning Bernini's FOUNTAIN OF THE FOUR RIVERS and the church of SANT' AGNESE IN AGONE.

Rome in the 17thC loved pageantry, and the custom of partially flooding the piazza dates from this period. The nobility would have their carriages decked out in festive style, and then drive them through the water to the delight of the attendant crowds — a vestige of the *naumachia* or mock sea fights performed in Domitian's stadium. These water-pageants persisted into the mid-19thC, every weekend in August.

The surface of the square is now flat and can no longer accommodate artificial lakes, but the carnival spirit lingers on and crowds still congregate in this now pedestrian area. They gather around the three splendid fountains (to the s, the Baroque MOOR FOUNTAIN, to the N, the **Neptune Fountain**, only completed in 1878), or stroll past the artists who exhibit their work along the edges of the piazza. Occasionally, a mild flutter among the crowd announces that an instant cartoonist has once again made his mark with a willing member of the public.

A children's market is held here from mid-December (see ROME FOR CHILDREN).

PIAZZA DEL POPOLO ☆
Map 5F5. Metropolitana: Flaminio.
The revolutionary design of this great oval piazza was largely the inspiration of Giuseppe Valadier (1816-24). He abandoned the traditional concept of the enclosed space, and opened up the E side to include the pine-covered slopes of the PINCIO as a spectacular backcloth. At the SE corner are two small Baroque churches — **Santa Maria di Montesanto** and **Santa Maria dei Miracoli** — both begun by Rainaldi and

111

completed by Bernini and Carlo Fontana. They divide the three streets that lead into the piazza from the s: Via del Babuino, Via del Corso and Via di Ripetta.

In the center stands one of the obelisks salvaged and re-erected by Sixtus V, to serve as a landmark for pilgrims to the Holy City. Beyond the obelisk is the impressive **Porta del Popolo**, marking the entrance to the city from Via Flaminia. It was commissioned by Pius IV in 1561, but the facade overlooking the piazza was added by Bernini in 1655, to mark the entry of Queen Christina of Sweden. Next to this, standing sideways onto the center of the piazza and therefore easily missed, is the important church of SANTA MARIA DEL POPOLO. Toward Via del Babuino and Via di Ripetta are two fashionable cafés, **Canova** and **Rosati** (see BARS, CAFÉS AND ICE CREAM SHOPS).

PIAZZA DEL QUIRINALE
Map 5H6 ◀≣

This hilltop piazza, with its splendid view over the city, is dominated by the great mass of the PALAZZO DEL QUIRINALE, the official residence of the President, and in the center by the great stone figures of the *Dioscuri,* the horse-tamers Castor and Pollux. The statues are Roman copies of Greek originals and once adorned the Baths of Constantine. An obelisk from the MAUSOLEUM OF AUGUSTUS and a 19thC fountain complete the group.

PIAZZA SAN PIETRO (St Peter's Square)
Map 3H3.

Signaling the approach to the greatest church in Christendom, Bernini's piazza is a masterpiece of architectural planning. The free-standing, oval colonnade is four columns deep, and above it, 140 statues of saints are silhouetted against the sky (see illustration on page 29). In the center of the piazza stands the first obelisk to be re-erected in modern times. Sixtus V ordered it to be brought here from the s side of the basilica, and the task was achieved by Domenico Fontana in 1586, with the assistance of some 900 men, 140 horses and 44 windlasses.

On either side of the obelisk, which was originally brought to Rome by Caligula, are two spectacular fountains, one by Carlo Maderno (1613), the other by Carlo Fontana (1677). In this magnificent setting, huge, enthusiastic crowds of Romans and pilgrims from all over the world gather on Christmas Day and Easter Sunday to receive the Pope's blessing (see PAPAL AUDIENCES, page 45).

PIAZZA DI SPAGNA ☆
Map 5G6. Metropolitana: Spagna.

This colorful square with its palm trees and flower barrows is named after the **Palazzo di Spagna** in the sw corner, which was built in the early 17thC as the residence of the Spanish ambassador to the Vatican. At about the same time, the piazza became a center for tourists and expatriates and has remained so ever since. The list of illustrious Europeans who have stayed or lived in the immediate vicinity is prodigious:

Wagner, Liszt, Balzac, Stendhal, Rubens, Tennyson, Byron and Keats, to name but a few.

For many, the Piazza di Spagna is still the heart of Rome, if not its center. Radiating from it are the smartest shopping streets in the city. Via Condotti and Via Frattina are thankfully both now banned to traffic, but beware at the intersections with other streets, where cars are still allowed to cross. Via delle Carrozze takes its name from the long-distance touring carriages that were maintained and parked here.

At the s end of the piazza, the great stairway known as the SPANISH STEPS sweeps up majestically to the Baroque church of TRINITÀ DEI MONTI.

Flanking the Spanish Steps is the KEATS-SHELLEY MEMORIAL, the house where Keats died. **Babington's Tea Rooms** is a favorite haunt on hot summer days, and, just down Via Condotti, the **Caffè Greco** is another notable establishment (see REFRESHMENTS for both).

PINACOTECA   This simply means "picture gallery" but usually refers to the **Pinacoteca (Vaticana)** in the VATICAN MUSEUMS. There is another in the CAPITOLINE MUSEUMS, known as the **Pinacoteca Capitolina**.

PINCIO ☆
Piazza del Popolo. Map 5F5 ◀ *Metropolitana: Flaminio.*
These popular music gardens were laid out by Giuseppe Valadier in 1809-14, on the site originally occupied by the formal terraced Gardens of Lucullus (1stC). The land was later owned by the Pinci family (4thC), whence the name derives. The gardens adjoin the public park of the VILLA BORGHESE to the N and E and the private gardens of the VILLA MEDICI to the SE. The winding paths of the Pincio are a favorite strolling place, particularly on weekends, and the view from the terrace at the top is justly celebrated. This is at its most spectacular in the early evening, when you can see the dome of SAINT PETER'S and the western skyline silhouetted against the sunset.

PONTE SANT' ANGELO ★
Map 4H4.
Unquestionably the most beautiful of Rome's ancient bridges, the Ponte Sant' Angelo has spanned the muddy waters of the Tiber for nearly 2,000 years. It connects the old city with the CASTEL SANT' ANGELO, formerly the **Mausoleum of Hadrian**. The parapets are adorned by statues of St Peter and St Paul (1530) and ten angels in a splendid variety of poses, from the school of Bernini (1668). The three central arches belong to the original bridge, the Pons Aelius, built by Hadrian in 133-134. The original outer arches had to be replaced in 1892-94 after the widening of the river caused by the building of the Lungotevere embankment. The bridge is now barred to traffic.

PORTA MAGGIORE ▥
Piazza di Porta Maggiore. Map 10 I10. Metropolitana: Manzoni.
Originally the Porta Prenestina, this solemn Imperial structure was erected in 52 by Claudius as a gateway at the intersection of the Via

Prenestina and the Via Labicana. Its two lofty arches carried the conduits of the Aqua Claudia and Anio Novus, two of the finest Roman aqueducts. The gateway was not incorporated into the AURELIAN WALL until 272-279, which explains the contrast between its light travertine and the brick of the Wall.

PORTA PIA

Via XX Settembre. Map 6F8. Museum 🖭 *Open Tues and Thurs only, 9am-1pm.*
Commissioned by Pius IV in 1561, this historic gateway was one of Michelangelo's last works but was reconstructed in 1853-61 by Virginio Vespignani, who was also responsible for the outer face. It was through breaches made in the adjacent walls that the armies of a united Italy entered Rome in 1870. Inside the gateway building, the **Museo Storico dei Bersaglieri** contains military memorabilia.

PORTA PORTESE 🏛

Via Portuense. Map 8K5.
The present gateway is an early 17thC replacement of the ancient Porta Portuensis. A large and lively market is held here on Sunday mornings (see SHOPPING).

PORTA SAN PANCRAZIO

Janiculum Hill. Map 7J4.
High up on the Janiculum Hill, the Porta San Pancrazio featured dramatically in the defense of the Roman Republic in 1849, when soldiers of Garibaldi's legion withstood charge after charge by numerically superior French forces until, weeks later, they were compelled to yield. The gateway was rebuilt in 1854. It was once known as the Porta Aurelia, since it marked the beginning of the Via Aurelia of antiquity. Today the Via Aurelia Antica starts about 200m (220 yards) to the w of the gateway.

PORTA SAN PAOLO 🏛

Piazza di Porta San Paolo. Map 9L6. Museum 🖭 *Open Tues and Sat only, 9am-1pm. Metropolitana: Piramide.*
In Antiquity this great fortified gateway was called the Porta Ostiense. It now takes its name from the basilica of SAN PAOLO FUORI LE MURA, to which it leads. Sturdy defensive towers built in the 6thC flank the gate. The structure was restored on the outer side by Honorius in 402, but the inner face is basically still the same as when Aurelian built it in the 3rdC. Inside the massive gateway building, the **Museo della Via Ostiense** provides a foretaste of a visit to the ruins of the port of OSTIA ANTICA (see EXCURSIONS).

PORTA SAN SEBASTIANO 🏛

Via di Porta San Sebastiano. Map 10L8.
This magnificent gateway, flanked by two imposing towers, is the best preserved and most impressive of any in the AURELIAN WALL. Known as the Porta Appia in Antiquity (replacing the earlier Porta Capena in the

Servian Wall), it was reconstructed in the early 5thC by the Emperor Honorius, and restored by Belisarius and Narses in the 6thC.

PORTICO OF OCTAVIA (Portico d'Ottavia)
Via del Portico d'Ottavia. Map 4/5.
This once-impressive portico was originally built by Quintus Caecilius Metellus in 146BC. It was reconstructed by Augustus between 27 and 23BC and dedicated to his sister Octavia, and restored again in AD203 by Septimius Severus. It originally consisted of about 300 columns set in a large, double-colonnaded rectangle, and enclosed temples dedicated to Jupiter and Juno, as well as numerous pieces of Greek sculpture. Inside now is the church of **Sant' Angelo in Pescheria**, where Cola di Rienzo and his followers assembled prior to their ill-fated seizure of the Capitol (1347). Looking at the surviving monumental entrance, note how the balance has been upset by the brick relieving arch that was added in the Middle Ages to replace two of the elegant Corinthian columns. Nearby, and in the **Via del Portico d' Ottavia**, are several medieval and early Renaissance houses.

PRE-CONSTANTINIAN NECROPOLIS   The site, discovered in 1940 underneath the **Vatican Grottoes**, beneath ST PETER'S, contains a simple monument believed to mark St Peter's grave.

PROTESTANT CEMETERY (Cimitero Protestante)
Via Caio Cestio 6. Map 8L6. Open 8-11.30am, 3.20-5.30pm. Metropolitana: Piramide. To gain entry, ring bell at the gate.
Close to the PYRAMID OF CAIUS CESTIUS and the PORTA SAN PAOLO, this cemetery is divided into two parts, the **Old Cemetery** and the **New Cemetery**. Many famous people were laid to rest here: in the Old Cemetery, the English poet John Keats, who died in 1821, and his friend Joseph Severn; and in the New, Percy Bysshe Shelley, who died by drowning in 1822, Edward Trelawney (died 1881) and John Addington Symonds (died 1893). Keats' tombstone bears the inscription *Here lies one whose name was writ in water,* words that the poet himself had asked to be included. The house he and Severn once stayed in, overlooking the SPANISH STEPS, is now the KEATS-SHELLEY MEMORIAL.

PYRAMID OF CAIUS CESTIUS (Piramide di Caio Cestio)
Piazzale Ostiense. Map 8L6. Metropolitana: Piramide.
This solemn structure, faced in white marble and standing just outside the PORTA SAN PAOLO, is the tomb of Caius Cestius, praetor and tribune of the people. He died in 12BC, and his grandiose tomb monument stands 27m (88 feet) high, which is small by Egyptian standards, but impressive enough in Rome.

QUATTRO FONTANE (Four Fountains)
Via delle Quattro Fontane. Map 6H7 ◁€ Metropolitana: Barberini.
At the intersection on the highest point of the QUIRINAL HILL, four lazily-splashing Baroque fountains fit neatly into four corner niches (1588-

93). The figures represent the Tiber, the Arno, Diana and Juno. On a clear day, the famous quadrilateral view takes in three distant obelisks — in PIAZZA DEL QUIRINALE and in front of TRINITÀ DEI MONTI and SANTA MARIA MAGGIORE — as well as the PORTA PIA.

QUIRINAL HILL (Quirinale)
Map 5H6.

The highest of the seven ancient hills of Rome, the Quirinal was originally a Sabine settlement. Its name derives either from a temple of Quirinus (the name given to Romulus after his deification) or from Cures, the town from which the Sabines are supposed to have come. The summit is now crowned by the obelisk of PIAZZA DEL QUIRINALE.

RAPHAEL STANZE   Almost as famous as the **Sistine Chapel**, these frescoed apartments are the second greatest draw of the VATICAN MUSEUMS. The decorative scheme of the second room, the **Stanza della Segnatura**, includes Raphael's masterpiece, the *School of Athens*.

ROMAN FORUM (Foro Romano)
Via dei Fori Imperiali. Map 9I6 (combined with Palatine Hill) ✗ with advance notice. Open Wed-Sat, Mon 9am-5pm; Tues, Sun 9am-2pm. Begin by viewing Forum from Via del Campidoglio, off Piazza del Campidoglio. Then enter Forum from Via dei Fori Imperiali (opposite Via Cavour).

To visit the Forum for the first time, even with some knowledge of its history, can be something of a disappointment. You will find areas cordoned off for archeological research, and arches and columns undergoing restoration, veiled in scaffolding and green netting. Shattered temples and basilicas lie scattered over the ground in apparently random heaps; columns stand here and there in isolation, only occasionally linked by fragmentary architraves. But in fact, the remains of the Forum are not nearly as haphazard as they at first appear.

It is helpful to start with an overview of the general layout, from the terrace in Via del Campidoglio. However, before attempting to single out any individual features, it is worth remembering that the gradual development of the Forum spanned a period of more than 1,000 years. In the earliest times, before the peace between Romulus and the Sabine leader Titus Tatius, said to have come to pass in 753BC, the area now comprising the Forum was little more than a marshy plain between the CAPITOLINE HILL and PALATINE HILL, choked by debris from the primitive settlements on the hills. These consisted mainly of shepherds' huts, and it was only when the population began to become more sophisticated — shepherds turning into farmers and finally soldier-farmers — that the comparatively large area of flat, albeit marshy, land became desirable for the erection of uncomplicated, easily defensible buildings. Tradition has it that the earliest monuments, such as the Curia and the Temple of Vesta, can be credited to the time of the kings. And it is to the last of the kings that Livy gives credit for canalizing the stagnant waters underground.

The development of the site fulfilled a variety of purposes, political, legal and mercantile. But above all, it was the obvious place to build temples. Long after less crucial activities had dispersed to other locations, the Forum remained the special home of religious worship, with the Temple of Vesta as the symbolic center of such activity. A large central area, roughly rectangular in shape, was consecrated but kept unenclosed, and buildings and temples were erected around it. This is where the farmer-soldiers gathered to sell their produce, when the Forum was in the true sense of the word a market place, with rows of shops on either side. In the course of time, however, this mercantile character was lost, the traders were banished from the exclusive area, and the first steps were taken to make the Forum respectable and solemn, with the construction of civil buildings known as basilicas.

Now looking down from your vantage point on the Capitoline Hill, you can see immediately beneath you the 12 surviving columns of the **Portico of the Dii Consentes (1)**, built by the Flavian emperors to honor the 12 principal Roman gods. To your left are three fine Corinthian columns supporting a fragmentary architrave, all that remains of the **Temple of Vespasian (2)**, built by Domitian to honor his father. Beyond this stood the **Temple of Concord (3)**, founded in the 4thC BC to celebrate the conclusion of peace between patricians and plebs, and reconstructed by Tiberius in the early 1stC AD. It was later used as a museum of art, housing Greek sculptures and paintings, but now only part of the pavement remains.

Still in the foreground to your left, you can see the **Arch of Septimius Severus (★) (4)**. This well-proportioned, highly decorated triumphal arch was raised by the Senate to celebrate the tenth anniversary of Septimius Severus' accession to the throne (203), and to honor his victories over the Parthians, Arabians and Assyrians. Included in the original inscription were the names of his sons Caracalla and Geta, but when Caracalla subsequently murdered his brother, Geta's name was replaced by a further inscription in praise of Caracalla. The holes made for the original lettering are still visible. The arch had an enormous influence on monumental architecture, acting as a prototype for the ARCH OF CONSTANTINE, and thence for many others both ancient and modern. The sculpted figures of reclining gods in the spandrels are almost certainly derived from a Greek idea.

Looking to the right and almost ahead of you, you will see the eight surviving granite columns of the **Temple of Saturn (5)**, a romantic ruin seen to best advantage against the evening sky. Most of what can be seen today is a reconstruction (42BC), the last of many, but the original (c. 497BC) was one of the oldest temples in Rome. The Romans believed that Saturn had taught them the skills of agriculture, and was therefore responsible for their wealth, which explains why this temple was also used as the State Treasury. Vast hoards of gold and silver bars were stored inside. Here also, the December festival of the Saturnalia took place.

Over to the far left, beyond the Arch of Septimius Severus, you can see the last substantial monument at this, the W end of the Forum: the well-preserved if somewhat austere brick structure of the **Curia (6)** or Senate House. The Curia was burned down and replaced several times. The present building was begun in 80BC, continued by Julius Caesar and

KEY: 1 Portico of the Dii Consentes 2 Temple of Vespasian 3 Temple of Concord 4 Arch of Septimius Severus 5 Temple of Saturn 6 Curia 7 Column of Phocas 8 Imperial Rostra 9 Sacra Via 10 Arch of Tiberius 11 Basilica Giulia 12 Honorary Columns 13 Basilica Aemilia 14 Temple of Antoninus and Faustina 15 Temple of Castor and Pollux 16 Temple of Julius Caesar 17 Regia 18 Temple of Vesta 19 House of the Vestal Virgins 20 Arch of Augustus 21 Basin of Juturna 22 Shrine of Juturna 23 Oratory of the Forty Martyrs 24 S. Maria Antiqua 25 Via Nova 26 Temple of Romulus 27 Forum of Vespasian 28 Basilica of Maxentius 29 S. Maria Nova 30 Antiquarium Forense 31 Arch of Titus 32 Temple of Venus and Rome

partly or wholly visible
barely visible or disappeared

0   50   100m
0   50   100yds

finally completed in 29BC by Augustus. It was restored by Diocletian after a fire in AD283. The existing bronze doors are copies of the originals, which went to adorn Borromini's SAN GIOVANNI IN LATERANO. Originally the building was clad in marble and stucco, which would have given it a much less grim and uniform appearance than now.

In the center of your view, and just in front of a tall column, the **Column of Phocas (7)** (taken from an Imperial building and erected on this spot in 608), you should be able to make out the long "wall" of brick, which is all that remains of the **Imperial Rostra (8)**, or orators' platform. It was moved here from its earlier position in front of the Curia by Julius Caesar. The original platform was clad in marble, traces of which remain, and decorated by the bronze beaks or *rostra* of ships captured at the Battle of Antium in 338BC.

If you now look on either side of the Rostra and Column of Phocas you will see the two branches of the **Sacra Via (9)**. The N road once led under the Arch of Septimius Severus, the S one under the **Arch of Tiberius (10)**, of which there are only scanty remains. To the right and flanking the S road is the vast area of the **Basilica Giulia (11)**, of which very little is left, although the outline of the plan is quite clear. It was begun by Julius Caesar in 54BC, completed by Augustus in AD12, and restored by Diocletian in AD305 following a fire. An enormous building, the basilica measured 101 by 49m (330 by 160 feet). It was the central courthouse, the meeting place of the four civil tribunals. In front stood seven **honorary columns (12)**, of which fragments survive.

Looking to your left again, beyond the Curia are the remains of the **Basilica Aemilia (13)**, another vast rectangular hall. It was originally built by the Censors M. Aemilius Lepidus and M. Fulvius Nobilior in 179BC, but was reconstructed several times following fires. The ruins you see today are the consequence of Alaric's sack of Rome in AD410.

Beyond this basilica the large mass of the **Temple of Antoninus and Faustina (★) (14)** stands out clearly, its Corinthian portico especially distinctive. The remarkable preservation of this temple, which was erected in 141 to commemorate the death of Faustina, wife of the Emperor Antoninus, is entirely the result of its having been converted into a church (San Lorenzo in Miranda) in the 11thC. The facade was added in 1602.

Returning your gaze to the right side of the Forum, you will see three exquisite columns, all that remains of the **Temple of Castor and Pollux (15)**. Built originally in 484BC by Aulus Postumius, it commemorates the divine intervention of the heavenly twins at the Battle of Lake Regillus (499BC), which put an end to the hopes of the Tarquin dynasty of regaining sovereignty over Rome. The temple was rebuilt on several occasions, notably by Quintus Caecilius Metellus in 117BC and by Augustus in AD6.

The remaining large buildings cannot be made out clearly from this viewpoint, so the rest of the Forum is best seen at ground level. Entering from Via dei Fori Imperiali, you pass the Temple of Antoninus and Faustina on your left and the remains of the Basilica Aemilia on your right. Having reached the Sacra Via, you can see ahead of you the remains of the **Temple of Julius Caesar (16)**, erected by Augustus in 29BC in honor of the deified Julius, over the spot where his body was cremated. To the left of this are the foundations of the **Regia (17)**, the official residence of the Pontifex Maximus.

Turning left from here, past the Temple of Antoninus, and then right, you arrive at one of the most interesting places in the Forum, the circular **Temple of Vesta (18)** and the adjoining **House of the Vestal Virgins (19)**. The "house" was in fact more like a palace, with 50 rooms on the ground floor alone. Here the Vestal Virgins led a life of extreme simplicity, completely cut off from the world outside. The building was originally called the Atrium Vestali, because the rooms were designed to look inward to the garden court. The court has regained some of its former beauty and serenity now that the pools have been repaired and filled, and the garden planted with roses and other flowers. The Vestal Virgins were obliged to dress simply and to honor a strict code of conduct, the breaking of which led to savage punishments. If they lost their virginity, they were buried alive. All the same, they possessed remarkable privileges, and could retire after 30 years with a generous dowry from the state.

The most important of the Vestal Virgins' duties was to tend the sacred fire in the Temple of Vesta. The extinction of the fire was considered a national catastrophe, and the person held responsible could expect to be scourged by the Pontifex Maximus. The original temple was almost certainly made of wood, in the shape of the circular huts of the earliest settlements, and this distinctive shape was retained in all subsequent rebuildings. The present remains, which were assembled in 1930, are all that can be seen of the last reconstruction by Septimius Severus and his wife Julia Domna at the beginning of the 3rdC. Inside were housed the *pignora imperii,* the secret pledges of the duration of Rome, which included the *Palladium,* the statue of Pallas Athene that was reputedly saved from Troy by Aeneas. The exact nature of the *pignora imperii* was known only to the Vestal Virgins and the Pontifex Maximus.

Just to the w of the Temple of Vesta are the scanty remains of the **Arch of Augustus (20)**, and to the s the path leads to the **Basin of Juturna (21)**, the site of the spring where, according to legend, Castor and Pollux watered their horses after announcing the news of the victory at Lake Regillus. The square basin of the fountain that was subsequently built here is clearly visible. Just s of the basin is the restored **Shrine of Juturna (22)**, goddess of the healing waters. Beyond is the **Oratory of the Forty Martyrs (23)**, a converted 1stC building that contains remnants of 8thC frescoes recording the martyrdom of 40 Armenian soldiers under Diocletian. s of this is the oldest church in the Forum, **Santa Maria Antiqua (24)**. It contains many remarkable early frescoes, but has been closed to the public for a long time and is likely to remain so. The straight road leading past Santa Maria Antiqua is the **Via Nova (25)**, much of the surface of which still survives.

Now retrace your steps past the Temple of Vesta, bearing right into the main part of the Sacra Via. To your left, you will see the circular **Temple of Romulus (26)**, a splendidly preserved 4thC brick construction dedicated to Romulus, the son of Maxentius, who died in his youth in 309 and was deified. The bronze doors are exceptionally well preserved. Behind is the FORUM OF VESPASIAN (**27**), in part of which stands a structure remodeled by Maxentius and later converted into the church of SANTI COSMA E DAMIANO. It was originally perhaps the audience hall of the city prefect.

The Sacra Via continues (for long stretches virtually intact) past the great mass of the **Basilica of Maxentius** (★) (**28**), also known as the Basilica of Constantine, substantial parts of which have survived. This extraordinary building is of great intrinsic interest, but its sheer size has the effect of dwarfing its surroundings to an uncomfortable degree, and this must have been even more true when it was intact. The basilica was begun by Maxentius (306-312), and completed by Constantine along modified lines. In the vast vaulted structure of brick and concrete, covering an area of 100 by 65m (328 by 213 feet), six enormous piers carried the three bays of the groined vault over the central area. The three extant rounded arches on the N side have been the inspiration of many architects from the Renaissance onward. Here was a successful attempt to apply the construction methods of the great Roman baths to the building of a basilica.

The Sacra Via from this point veers slightly s, but passes quite close to the church of **Santa Maria Nova** (**29**), more commonly known as Santa Francesca Romana. The handsome Romanesque bell tower is visible from most parts of the Forum, and inside there is a fine 12thC mosaic of the *Madonna Enthroned with Saints*. In the adjacent 14thC cloisters is the **Antiquarium Forense** (**30**) or Forum museum *(open 9am-noon)*, containing sculptural fragments and reconstructions. The Sacra Via now leads directly to the **Arch of Titus** (★) (**31**), a beautifully proportioned triumphal arch erected in 81 to honor the victories of Titus and Vespasian in the Judaean War.

The arch is especially interesting for the sculptural reliefs on the inside surfaces. Each represents part of the triumphal procession. On one side, the symbolic figure of Rome guides the Imperial quadriga; on the other, victorious soldiers bear the seven-branched candelabra and other spoils from the Temple of Jerusalem. High relief and superb animation make these friezes noted masterpieces of Roman honorific sculpture.

From this point there is a way out of the Forum past the TEMPLE OF VENUS AND ROME (**32**) in the direction of the COLOSSEUM.

ROME MUSEUM (Museo di Roma)
Piazza San Pantaleo ☎6875880. Map 5H5 ▨ Now used only for temporary exhibitions, so check opening times. Details of exhibitions may be found in Il Messagero, La Repubblica, Un Ospite di Roma *and* This Week in Rome.

Now housed in the late 18thC **Palazzo Braschi**, this museum was founded in 1930 to illustrate various aspects of Roman life from the Middle Ages onward. Most of the paintings, sculptures and artifacts are therefore of socio-historic interest.

The entrance to the palace is impressive. At the foot of a magnificent open staircase, probably designed by Valadier (1802-4), stands Francesco Mochi's colossal group of *Christ Baptized by St John* (1629-34). The exhibits are mainly on the first and second floors. Of particular interest are a number of paintings showing the great pageants of 16th and 17thC Rome. *Joust of the Saracen at Piazza Navona* is one of several canvases recording famous tournaments, and *Festival at Palazzo Barberini for Christina of Sweden* depicts the colorful spectacle that the Barberini family laid on for the Queen in 1656.

The collection also includes frescoes, removed from other palaces during the course of demolition, and, in the **Salone d'Onore**, some fine Gobelins tapestries. At street level, off the courtyard, stands **Pius IX's railway carriage**, constructed in Paris in 1857 for his journeys between Rome and Frascati.

SANT' AGNESE IN AGONE 𝖒 † ☆
Piazza Navona. Map 5H5.

This church is often thought to be entirely the work of Borromini, but it in fact represents the saddest story of his career. It was begun by Girolamo and Carlo Rainaldi, father and son, in 1652, of whom Carlo contributed the most. Borromini was obliged to adapt the Rainaldi plan, but then Carlo was recalled in 1657, and the work was not completed as Borromini intended. His great rival Bernini also had a hand in the changes, and the result was a richer, more ornate interior and some modification to the exterior design.

Borromini's genius is most evident in the concave and elegant facade, with towers on either side that unify the front of the church and the dome. The towers, however, are the work of other hands, and were completed in 1666, when Bernini's pediment was added as a central feature.

The decoration inside is lavish, and contains some fine examples of High Baroque art, notably Ercole Ferrata's relief of the *Stoning of St Emerenziana,* Antonio Raggi's *Martyrdom of St Cecilia,* and the frescoes by Ciro Ferri in the dome and by Giovanni Battista Gaulli in the pendentives.

Beneath the church is the heavily restored pre-Carolingian oratory containing Alessandro Algardi's last work, a marble relief of *The Miracle of the Hair of St Agnes*. This relates the traditional story of the miraculous growth of the saint's hair to cover her nakedness when she was thrown into a brothel after refusing to renounce her faith. Although there is little doubt that St Agnes was martyred close to this spot, her remains now lie buried under the basilica of SANTA' AGNESE FUORI LE MURA.

SANT' AGNESE FUORI LE MURA 𝖒 † ☆
Via Nomentana ☎ 8320743. Map 12C4. Catacombs ▨ 𝒦 compulsory. Open Mon-Sat 9am-noon, 3-6pm; Sun 3-6pm. Bus 36 from Stazione Termini or 60 from Piazza Venezia or Piazza Barberini.

St Agnes was reputedly martyred in 304, during Diocletian's persecutions, and while it is thought that she was put to death on the spot where SANT' AGNESE IN AGONE now stands in Piazza Navona, her remains almost certainly lie buried under this basilica, some 2.5km ($1\frac{1}{2}$ miles) from the city center. The church is well worth visiting when combined with the catacombs and the nearby church of SANTA COSTANZA.

SANT' ANDREA AL QUIRINALE

The original church of Sant' Agnese fuori le Mura was built by Constantia, daughter or grand-daughter of the Emperor Constantine, in 342. It was constructed right into the side of the hill in order to be immediately above the saint's tomb, as is the present church, erected in the 7thC and most recently restored by Pius IX (1855-56). To enter the church, you descend a long shallow staircase, lined with fragments of inscriptions.

Inside, the 19thC restoration has not robbed the church of its Early Christian character. The 7thC mosaics are among the finest Byzantine works in Rome, and feature St Agnes in Byzantine court dress, with the sword of her martyrdom at her feet. Behind the tabernacle, the alabaster statue of the saint is an early 17thC restoration of a Classical figure. Over the altar there is a fine canopy dating from the same period. It is an octagonal dome, inlaid with colored marble, supported by four slender antique porphyry columns.

The **catacombs of St Agnes** probably date from the late 3rdC. They are well preserved, and you can see numerous inscriptions as well as the burial niches or *loculi,* some of which remain intact. Visitors are taken round in small groups — a pleasant change from the massed guided tours of the more famous catacombs.

SANT' AGOSTINO ☫ †
Piazza di Sant' Agostino. Map 5H5.
This church is one of the earliest examples of Renaissance architecture in Rome. After its plain facade, dating from 1479, the sumptuous 18thC interior comes as something of a surprise. Immediately to the right of the main door is the *Madonna del Parto.* This greatly venerated group was executed in 1521 by Jacopo Sansovino, and the left foot of the Madonna is now worn smooth by the attentions of countless devotees. Other outstanding artistic treasures are Caravaggio's *Madonna of Loreto* (★) (1605), in the first chapel of the left aisle; Andrea Sansovino's *Madonna and Child with St Anne* (1512), which stands below Raph-ael's celebrated *Prophet Isaiah* (★) (1512), by the third pillar on the N side of the nave; and the Byzantine *Madonna,* brought from Constantinople, over Bernini's high altar.

SANT' ANDREA AL QUIRINALE ☫ † ★
Via del Quirinale. Map 6H7.
This exquisite little church with its elegantly curved facade was designed by Bernini and built between 1658-71 for Cardinal Camillo Pamphili, nephew of Innocent X. Entering, you find yourself in an oval church, faced by two pairs of magnificent pink and white marble columns that stand in front and on either side of the main altar. In an opening in the concave pediment above, St Andrew is seen soaring in space in a highly dramatic pose that is characteristic of Bernini, although the statue is in fact the work of his pupil Raggi. A clever touch is provided by the relatively great height of the dome, which creates the effect of a much larger church. A predominance of gilding gives a warmth to the whole interior.

SANT' ANDREA DELLA VALLE ㎡ †
Corso Vittorio Emanuele. Map 4l5.

Perhaps best known as the fictional setting of the first act of Puccini's *Tosca*, this large Baroque church was begun in 1591 by Giacomo della Porta and Francesco Grimaldi, and continued by Carlo Maderno from 1608. Maderno was responsible for the magnificent dome, largest in Rome after that of SAINT PETER'S, but the sumptuous facade, which has recently been renovated, was mainly the work of Carlo Rainaldi (1655-65). Inside, the church is vast, ornate and impersonal. Few people visit it, and the huge areas of marble seem almost wasted. However, the **frescoes** in the pendentives of the dome, by Domenichino (1624-28), are worth making a detour for. The painting of the dome itself was left to Domenichino's rival, Lanfranco.

SANTI APOSTOLI ㎡ †
Piazza dei Santi Apostoli. Map 5H6.

The original church was probably erected by Pelagius I in the 6thC, but the present structure is now a mixture of Renaissance, Baroque and Neoclassical styles. It was almost entirely rebuilt by Francesco Fontana (1702-08) and Carlo Fontana (1708-14), the latter continuing the work after his son's death. The majestic portico of nine arches, enclosing a Classical Roman relief, is the work of Baccio Pontelli and dates from the end of the 15thC, but the rest of the facade is by Valadier (1827). Inside, eight spirally fluted columns in the **Chapel of the Crucifix** (at the end of the s aisle) are the only remains of the original church. The present church contains a number of fine tombs of the della Rovere family, dating from the Renaissance, as well as the **Tomb of Clement XIV**, Canova's first work in Rome.

SAN BARTOLOMEO ㎡ †
Isola Tiberina. Map 4l5.

Neither the 12thC tower rising above the ISOLA TIBERINA nor the Classical 17thC facade give a true indication of the age of this church, which was founded at the end of the 10thC by Otto III. It was originally dedicated to St Adalbert and only became the church of St Bartholomew when the relics of the latter were transferred here. The columns in the nave are original, but because of its location the church has been damaged by flooding on several occasions, and substantial restorations have taken place. A unique feature is the small **marble well-head** of the 12thC, especially interesting because it is likely that the church was built over the site of the Temple of Aesculapius, the God of Healing. It is thought that near the temple there was a spring with healing properties.

SAN CARLO AI CATINARI ㎡ †
Piazza Cairoli. Map 4l5.

Rosato Rosati was the architect of this large and harmoniously proportioned Baroque church (1612-20), but he was not responsible for the handsome facade, added later by Giovanni Battista Soria (1635-38).

Domenichino painted the *Cardinal Virtues* (★) in the pendentives of the dome (1630), but his is just one of the many famous names associated with the interior decoration. Paintings over the various altars of the church and in the sacristy include works by Mattia Preti, Andrea Sacchi, Giovanni Lanfranco, Pietro da Cortona and Guido Reni. The high altar was designed by Martino Longhi, and in the sacristy there is a **bronze crucifix** by Alessandro Algardi.

SAN CARLO ALLE QUATTRO FONTANE �III ✝ ★
Via del Quirinale. Map 6H7.
Borromini's tiny church, familiarly known as **San Carlino**, is very near to Bernini's SANT' ANDREA AL QUIRINALE, and it is interesting to compare the two churches. The spontaneous warmth and exuberance of Bernini's style may be more immediately appealing, but given time the subtlety and complexity of Borromini is no less rewarding. Borromini had to deal with a restricted site at the corner of an intersection, but he used the limited space to masterly effect. He built cloisters and lodgings for the adjacent monastery as well as the church, and his personal involvement with the project lasted from 1634 until his death in 1667.

Work on the church itself began in 1638, and the structure was complete by the following year. The basically oval design is achieved by means of highly sophisticated geometrical calculations. But this in no way produces a sense of heaviness. As you look up into the dome, which is divided into hexagonal, octagonal and cross-shaped coffers that diminish in size as they near the top, it seems suspended in space. Returning to earth, you can hardly fail to admire the fine detail of the Corinthian columns and the coolness of the gently curving ground-plan.

The slightly earlier cloisters are unusually confined, but show Borromini's customary originality and ingenuity. Even more remarkable is the facade of the church, which was begun only two years before the architect's death, but follows his design. Shaking off all two-dimensional restraints, it is a triumph of concavities and convexities.

SANTA CECILIA IN TRASTEVERE �III ✝ ★
Piazza di Santa Cecilia. Map 8J5 📷 *(convent). Open Tues, Thurs 10am-noon; Sun 11am-noon.*
The church is approached through a beautiful enclosed garden with an ancient white marble vase in the center. The facade of the church is the work of Ferdinando Fuga (1741), but the portico, incorporating Classical columns, is medieval. To the right is the fine 12thC campanile. As so often in Rome, the general outward character of the church gives no clue of its real age. Santa Cecilia was built by Paschal I between 817-824 on the site of a much earlier church, probably of the 5thC. Major restorations took place in 1725 and 1823. The latter drastically altered the character of the church, robbing it of any appearance of antiquity: Classical columns are now embedded in solid piers (for structural reasons), and the decoration is predominantly late Baroque.

The most famous work of art in the church is Stefano Maderno's touching and beautiful statue of the martyred *Santa Cecilia* (★). The saint is shown lying on her side wrapped in a golden robe, just as she was found when her tomb was opened in 1599, at which time Maderno saw the body and made a drawing of it. St Cecilia was martyred in either the 3rd or 4thC. She came from a patrician family, as did her husband, St Valerian, who was also martyred. In Maderno's work you can see the cuts in her neck caused by the three blows of the executioner's sword that failed to kill her outright. St Cecilia is traditionally said to have invented the organ, and she is the patron saint of music.

The statue of the saint lies beneath the high altar, which is graced by an outstanding canopy by Arnolfo di Cambio (c. 1293). In the apse behind is a 9thC mosaic, similar in subject to a mosaic in one of Paschal's other churches, SANTA PRASSEDE, though not of such fine quality. Yet there is much to admire in this scene of St Peter and St Paul presenting St Cecilia and St Valerian to Christ, in the company of St Agatha and Pope Paschal (singled out by the square halo of the living).

The convent attached to the church contains a superb fresco of the *Last Judgment* (★) by Pietro Cavallini, a contemporary of Giotto. This fragment, dating from around 1293, is Cavallini's masterpiece.

SAN CLEMENTE 🏛 † ★
Via di San Giovanni in Laterano. Map 10J8 🚇 *(lower church). Open Mon-Sat 9-11.30am, 3.30-6.30pm; Sun 10-11.30am, 3.30-6.30pm. Metropolitana: Colosseo.*

San Clemente is one of the best preserved of all the ancient sites in Rome, and is of exceptional interest. There are substantial remains here of a 1stC *domus* or palace and a 3rdC Mithraic temple, and above these two, of a 4thC church dedicated to St Clement. Above this, and making three levels in all, is the main church built in 1110-30. The whole complex site has been in the care of Irish Dominicans since 1677.

The **upper church** has a typical basilican plan with a nave and two aisles separated by antique columns, plain and fluted. The 12thC inlaid **pavement** is the lovely creation of the Cosmati, the name given to the celebrated mosaic workers of this period. Much of the marble-paneled **schola cantorum** dates from the 9thC and was brought from the lower church; so were the **pulpits**, one with an exquisitely-decorated Cosmatesque **candlestick**. The elegant **canopy** over the high altar may also have been taken from the lower church, at least in part.

One of the most beautiful features of the upper church is the superb mosaic in the apse, depicting the *Triumph of the Cross* (★). Against a gold background, the Tree of Life — of which the Cross forms a part — thrusts out branches of curling leaves that fill the whole of the conch of the apse. It is a work of intense symbolism, with the Cross shown as a support for all life, both human and animal. The many figures among the foliage include the four Doctors of the Latin Church, Augustine, Ambrose, Gregory and Jerome, as well as exotic birds and animals. This fantastic work dates from the 12thC, but it is thought to have been inspired by the design of an earlier mosaic that once adorned the 4thC church below. The fresco beneath, representing *Christ and the Virgin Mary between the Twelve Apostles,* is of the 14thC.

Returning to the very beginning of the left aisle, you come upon the **Chapel of St Catherine**, with the earliest Renaissance paintings in Rome. It is famous for its **frescoes** (★) by Masaccio's collaborator, Masolino da Panicale (c. 1428). The scenes feature events in the lives of St Catherine of Alexandria and St Ambrose, a ravishing *Annunciation* over the entrance arch, and a *Crucifixion* on the rear wall. The new interest in perspective and depth is apparent in these frescoes, but it is allied to a grace and lightness of touch that are not always found later on.

Off the right aisle is the entrance to the **lower church**. This has a wide nave interrupted by the foundations of the piers for the church above. Every effort has been made to preserve the frescoes, but they have faded badly as a result of exposure. Fortunately, copies were made at the time of their discovery, when they were still well preserved following their concealment under layers of damp earth and rubble. The original frescoes, dating from the 9th-11thC, include the *Marriage at Cana,* the *Crucifixion* and the *Ascension,* as well as the later *Story of St Alexis* and *Story of Sisinnius.* The last is particularly interesting because it not only recounts an extremely picturesque legend from the life of St Clemente, but also contains some of the earliest examples of written Italian. Among the frescoes of interest in the right aisle are an 8th or 9thC *Madonna* and a 9th or 10thC *Christ.*

At the end of the left aisle, a staircase leads down to the level of the 1stC **domus** and 3rdC **Mithraic temple**. The *domus* was originally of palatial dimensions and has been only partly excavated. The *triclinium* or banqueting hall of the temple was used for the religious feasts of the Mithraic ritual. In the center of this room is a low-relief representing Mithras, the sun-god, slaying a bull. The atmosphere is noticeably damp when you are this deep underground, and you can hear the constant sound of rushing water as an underground channel conveys water to the nearby CLOACA MAXIMA.

SANTI COSMA E DAMIANO ▥ † ★

Via dei Fori Imperiali. Map 9I6. Metropolitana: Colosseo.
This church was founded by Felix IV in 527, when one of the halls of the FORUM OF VESPASIAN was converted for the purpose. It was restored in 1632 under Urban VIII, at which time the mosaics were also repaired. The church is reached from Via dei Fori Imperiali through the cloisters of the adjoining convent, and cannot be entered from the ROMAN FORUM, even though the **Temple of Romulus** serves as a vestibule.

The chief glories of the church are the 6thC **mosaics** (★) of the apse and triumphal arch. These were admired to such an extent in the early centuries of the Roman Church that they became a prototype for several other churches. The design and craftsmanship are both of the highest order. In the apse, the Savior is seen standing in golden robes in the full glory of the Risen Christ, against a dramatic dawn sky. On either side stand St Peter and St Paul, with the two Arabian doctors (both martyred under Diocletian) to whom the church is dedicated; beyond them are St Theodore, and Felix (remade 1632) carrying his church. Below, facing the central Lamb of God, are two lines of sheep, six on either side, emerging from the towns of Bethlehem and Jerusalem. On the triumphal arch, the Mystic Lamb is shown surrounded by seven golden candlesticks, four angels, and the symbols of the Evangelists. Below, the 24 Elders offer up crowns.

SANTA COSTANZA 🏛 ✝ ☆

Via Nomentana. Map 12C4. Bus 36 from Stazione Termini or 60 from Piazza Venezia or Piazza Barberini.

Barely 2.5km (1½ miles) from the city center, this magnificent Early Christian church is best combined with a visit to SANT' AGNESE FUORI LE MURA. It was originally built in the early 4thC as a mausoleum for Constantia and Helena, daughters of the Emperor Constantine. It was subsequently used as a baptistry, and only consecrated as a church in 1254, when it was dedicated to Santa Costanza, who in spite of her name had no connection with Constantia.

The original building is preserved almost intact, with a dome carried over the central space by 12 pairs of composite columns. This colonnade is surrounded by a high barrel-vaulted ambulatory, its vaults decorated with **mosaics** (☆) dating from the 4thC that are unrivaled anywhere in Rome. The invention, design and execution are of the highest order, the colors exquisitely fresh. The background is white, unlike the gold of Byzantine mosaics, and the content is often said to be purely secular. Certainly there are no pictures of saints, but the images were soon endowed with Christian significance, even if they were originally pagan in mood.

The exceptional grace of line and richness of detail are what make these mosaics so memorable, and their beauty can be enjoyed whatever their meaning. It is a great shame that the mosaics in the dome have not survived; 16thC drawings record their content and give some idea of their quality.

The church contains a replica of Constantia's **sarcophagus** (the original is now in the VATICAN MUSEUMS), an interesting example of Early Christian art that features reliefs of lambs, peacocks, and cherubs harvesting grapes.

SANTA CROCE IN GERUSALEMME 🏛 ✝

Piazza Santa Croce in Gerusalemme. Map 10J10. Metropolitana: San Giovanni.

This is one of the seven pilgrim churches of Rome, said to have been built to house the precious relics of the True Cross brought to Rome from Jerusalem by St Helena, the mother of Constantine. The original church may have been a converted hall in the Palazzo Sessoriano (c.320), but the present building is much later. The Romanesque tower is one of the few visible signs of Lucius II's 12thC restoration, and the interior has been remodeled in a predominantly Baroque style. The main reminders of the church's great age are the eight large antique marble columns of the nave and the Cosmatesque pavement, a typical example of this late medieval inlay work. The church contains two notable works of art dating from the late 15thC. The unusual **fresco** in the apse of the *Invention of the True Cross* is probably by Antoniazzo Romano, while the fine **mosaic** (★) in the **Chapel of St Helena** (behind the high altar, to the right) was almost certainly designed by Melozzo da Forlì, with later intervention from Baldassare Peruzzi.

SANTA FRANCESCA ROMANA   The more familiar name of **Santa Maria Nova**, at the E end of the ROMAN FORUM.

SAN GIOVANNI IN LATERANO (St John Lateran) † ★
Piazza di San Giovanni in Laterano. Map 10J9. Metropolitana: San Giovanni.
This basilica is the cathedral church of Rome, the titular see of the Pope in his role as Bishop of Rome. It is the mother and head of all the churches of the city and of the world. Its name derives from the fact that it was built on the land of a Roman family called the Laterani. It was originally dedicated to Christ as Redeemer, and only later to St John the Baptist and St John the Evangelist. The 4thC basilica was five-aisled, but the church you see now dates from much later. The Lateran has suffered even more than the other ancient churches of Rome, having been sacked by the Vandals and destroyed by fire and earthquake a number of times. That it retains a distinctive character in spite of all it has gone through is one of its greatest charms.

The facade, by the 18thC architect Alessandro Galilei, was one of the few high points in a century of architectural mediocrity in Rome, but the full majesty of the basilica only becomes apparent as the visitor enters the building. (Inside the portico, notice the antique bronze central doors, removed from the **Curia** in the ROMAN FORUM.) The **interior** (★) has its detractors and is certainly a shock to those who hanker for the splendors of Early Christian gold mosaics, but it is a masterpiece. Innocent X gave Borromini the task of restoring the church in 1646, and the work was completed by 1650. The old structure had become both unattractive and unsound, and Borromini's solution, which harmonized with the fine 16thC wooden ceiling, was to create a subtle and cool white and gray interior. It is the least exuberant but perhaps the most illustrious of all his inventions, a notable instance of artistic restraint and care.

Borromini preserved as much of the old church as he could, including the earlier tombs and the 13thC apse **mosaic** by Jacopo Torriti and Jacopo da Camerino. The mosaic was reset in the 19thC, but the design retains much of its force. The basic scheme with the head of Christ and the Cross may recall an earlier design, but the figures of St Francis and St Anthony of Padua date from the time of Nicholas IV (13thC) and refer to the fact that the church was administered by Franciscans.

In the center of the crossing stands the **papal altar**, at which only the Pope can celebrate Mass, and above it soars the fine Gothic **canopy** made for Urban V in 1367 by Giovanni di Stefano. In front of the altar, at the foot of the steps to the *confessio,* a bronze **tomb slab** records Martin V, who died in 1431. It is an early Renaissance work by Simone Ghini. A custom has arisen of throwing coins onto the tomb.

Opinions may differ over the merits of Borromini's nave, but few visitors to the Lateran fail to be enchanted by the adjoining **cloisters** (★), reached through the last chapel of the left aisle. Tranquil and serene in atmosphere, they are the finest achievement of Jacopo and Pietro Vassalletto, among the most brilliant of the Cosmati, the school of Roman marble-workers and inlayers, whose work, renowned throughout Europe, reached its high point in the mid-13thC. The mosaics on the small paired columns, some straight, some twisted, are not all perfectly preserved, but the atmosphere of the place is unaffected. Fragmentary remains of the old basilica, including reliefs from the marvelous **Tomb of Cardinal Annibaldi** by 13thC sculptor Arnolfo di Cambio, add to the slightly decaying charm.

Baptistry Ⅲ ✝ ☆

Entrance from Piazza di San Giovanni in Laterano. Open 8am-noon, 4-6pm.

This octagonal building is the sole remaining edifice of great antiquity in the Lateran complex, and therefore of unusual interest. It was built in the reign of Sixtus III (432-440), to replace an earlier (4thC) baptistry that had been sacked by the Goths. Inside, eight porphyry columns enclose the font and support eight marble columns that in turn bear the dome. The font itself is an ancient basin of green Egyptian basalt, with a 17thC bronze cover. In it, probably, the Anglo-Saxon King Caedwalla was baptized in 689. The eight *Scenes from the Life of St John the Baptist* around the drum of the cupola are by Andrea Sacchi.

The sacristan will show you the chapels. The **Chapel of St John the Baptist** was built by Hilarius (461-468). Its heavy bronze doors, said to come from the BATHS OF CARACALLA, make a strangely musical sound when opened. The **Chapel of St Rufina** contains 5thC **mosaics (☆)** of exceptional beauty, with branches and acanthus leaves entwined against a brilliant blue background. Next there is the **Chapel of St Venantius**, built in 640 by John IV to house the relics of the martyrs of Salona in the Adriatic. John, a Dalmatian, adorned the chapel with **Byzantine mosaics**. They show a group of Dalmatian saints round the Madonna, and include representations of Bethlehem and Jerusalem. Finally, the **Chapel of St John the Evangelist**, also built by Hilarius in the 5thC, has a vaulted roof decorated with mosaics of the Holy Lamb surrounded by birds and flowers. The bronze doors were made in 1196.

Scala Santa Ⅲ

Open 6am-12.30pm, 3-7pm (May-Sept 3.30-7pm).

The 28 marble steps of this staircase are traditionally said to have come from Pilate's palace in Jerusalem and to have been ascended by Christ during his trial. They were supposedly brought here by St Helena, the mother of Constantine. The steps now lead to the Chapel of the Sancta Sanctorum, and many devout Catholics will only ascend them on their knees, following the example of several popes from Gregory the Great (590-604) to Pius IX (1846-78). The Sancta Sanctorum was the private oratory of the popes until 1308 and was the only part of the original LATERAN PALACE to survive the devastating fire of that year. The chapel is not open to the public but can be seen through the grating. Here, on a panel of cedar wood, is the celebrated picture of Christ known as the *Acheiropoeton* ("not painted by human hands"). This icon probably dates from the 6thC and was believed to have been painted by angels.

SANTI GIOVANNI E PAOLO 🏛 ✝ ★
Clivo di Scauro, off Via di San Gregorio. Map 9J7. Metropolitana: Circo Massimo.
The present church is the last of several that have been built on this spot, following man-made or natural disasters. The original 4thC basilica was believed to have been built on the site of the house of John and Paul, two officers in Constantine's army, who were executed in 362 on the orders of Julian the Apostate. Their bodies are said to have been secretly buried in the house.

Following wanton destruction by Alaric in 410, an earthquake in 442 and demolition by Robert Guiscard in 1084, rebuilding began under Paschal II (1099-1118) and Adrian IV (1154-59). Adrian, who is perhaps better known as Nicholas Breakspear, was responsible for the fine **Romanesque campanile** (★). He also built the handsome **portico** of six granite Ionic columns, and two marble Corinthian columns, as well as the beautiful **apse** with its arcaded loggia. The striking upper facade with its five arches on 3rdC columns belongs to the original 4thC basilica.

Inside, the church was remodeled in 1718, losing all trace of its ancient past. Of immeasurably greater interest is a visit below ground level to the *confessio* (★), often held to be part of the house of John and Paul. (Ask the sacristan to take you down there.) Some pagan frescoes now visible were once covered up, presumably by the Christians who lived here. Among the religious frescoes, one is especially interesting. It shows two men and a woman being beheaded, and must relate to the legend that Crispin, Crispinian and Benedicta were martyred after being found at the tomb of John and Paul.

SAN GREGORIO MAGNO 🏛 ✝
Via di San Gregorio. Map 9J7. Metropolitana: Circo Massimo.
A fine Baroque facade by Giovanni Battista Soria (1629-33) disguises the antiquity of this church's origins. Gregory II built a church here in the 8thC and dedicated it to his illustrious predecessor St Gregory the Great (590-604). According to tradition, the first Gregory turned his estate on this site into a Benedictine monastery in about 575, and it was from here that he is reputed to have sent St Augustine to convert England. Rebuildings in the 17th and 18thC have completely altered the original aspect of the church, but some interesting tombs and fragments remain. Especially notable is the beautiful altar of 1469 by Andrea Bregno in St Gregory's Chapel.

The sacristan will show you the **three chapels** set back from the gardens to the left of the church, dedicated to St Sylvia (Gregory's mother), St Andrew and St Barbara. An important group of early 17thC **frescoes** (★) includes Guido Reni's *Choir of Angels* and Domenichino's *Flagellation of St Andrew*.

SANT' IGNAZIO 🏛 ✝
Via Sant' Ignazio. Map 5H6.
This church was built to honor the canonization of Ignatius Loyola, founder of the Jesuit order. It was begun in 1626 to the designs of Padre Orazio Grassi. The imposing facade derives from the earlier

GESÙ, but the church is above all famed for the magnificence of its interior. Particularly remarkable are the **frescoes** (★) by Padre Andrea Pozzo, especially the ceiling painting representing the *Entry of St Ignatius into Paradise*. Even in a city where Baroque illusionism is relatively common in ceiling decoration, the *trompe l'oeil* effect here is outstanding. The best place from which to see the illusion is on a small disc in the pavement in the middle of the nave.

SANT' IVO 🏛 † ★

Corso del Rinascimento. Entrance from courtyard of Palazzo della Sapienza. Map 5H5. Open Sun morning only.

Like Borromini's other masterpiece, SAN CARLO ALLE QUATTRO FONTANE, this church is more remarkable for the ingenuity of its design than for any grandeur of scale. Sant' Ivo was commissioned in 1642 and completed in 1660; it stands at the E end of the late 16thC **Palazzo della Sapienza**, beyond Giacomo della Porta's fine arcaded courtyard. Borromini's complex ground plan is based on the hexagon, with alternately pointed and rounded ends to the arms. This strange system produces a uniquely stylish and fanciful dome, but the external appearance of the church, with its bizarre spiraling lantern, is yet stranger.

SAN LORENZO FUORI LE MURA 🏛 † ★

Piazzale di San Lorenzo. Map 12C4. Bus 71 from Piazza San Silvestro, or 11 from Colosseo or Stazione Termini.

Lawrence was martyred in 258 and buried in this area. Constantine built the first church over the burial place (c.330), and Sixtus III added a second church (432-440), dedicated to the Virgin, backing onto the first. Constantine's church was enlarged and rebuilt by Pelagius II (579-590). The process of joining up the two churches by destroying the apses was begun by Adrian I in the 8thC, but the rebuilding of Sixtus' nave was not effected until the early 13thC by Honorius III — the date also of the campanile and splendid six-columned **portico** (★).

Today you see a remarkable hybrid of styles. The majestically proportioned nave, with its cool Ionic columns, is rich in Cosmatesque decoration. The **pavement**, **pulpits** (★) and **paschal candlestick** date from the early 13thC. The altar stands directly over the crypt containing the remains of St Lawrence, St Stephen and St Justin, and marking the level of the earlier church of Pelagius. Steps lead up to the 13thC choir inserted between Pelagius' arcades. The difference between the two churches is striking. Here, perfectly matched Corinthian columns of precious marble support a flat architrave with carved frieze. Above this are the slender columns and high arches of the gallery. High up on the triumphal arch an original (6thC) **mosaic** shows Pelagius, with Lawrence and other saints, offering his church to Christ.

At the beginning of the choir, the **canopy** over the *confessio* is a work of great beauty, signed by the master masons Johannes, Petrus, Angelus and Saxo (1148). Behind the high altar is an **episcopal throne** with fine Cosmatesque decoration, dating from the 13thC. A sacristan will accompany you to the 12thC **cloisters** and the **catacombs of St Cyriaca**.

SANTI LUCA E MARTINA ⅏ †

Via dei Fori Imperiali. Entrance from Clivus Argentarius. Map 9I6. Open Sun only 10-11am.

Built among the ruins of the ROMAN FORUM, this consists of two churches, one of them now below ground level. The first was constructed in the 6thC over the remains of the Secretarium Senatus, the place where tribunals sat in judgment over senators, and was dedicated to St Martina. During the Renaissance it became the church of the Academy of St Luke, with a special significance for artists. But following the rediscovery of the body of St Martina, a new, upper church was built by Pietro da Cortona between 1634-50, on a Greek-cross plan. The imposing, complex facade is constructed of travertine and blends perfectly with the elegant dome. It is Cortona's architectural masterpiece.

SAN LUIGI DEI FRANCESI ⅏ † ☆

Piazza di San Luigi dei Francesi. Map 4H5.

This is the French national church in Rome. It was founded in 1518 by Cardinal Giulio de' Medici, later Clement VII, but was not completed until 1589. The fine Renaissance facade, attributed to Giacomo della Porta, has recently been restored. The richly marbled interior contains some outstanding works of art. In the second chapel on the right, **frescoes by Domenichino** (☆) (1613-14) tell the *Story of St Cecilia* with great sensitivity and beauty. In the fifth chapel on the left are three **early Caravaggios** (☆) (1597-1602). To the left is the *Calling of St Matthew,* a solemn scene in a realistic setting. The altarpiece shows *St Matthew and the Angel,* a subdued effort that replaced the more shocking first version that the clergy had rejected, and on the right is the melodramatic *Martyrdom of St Matthew.*

SAN MARCO ⅏ †

Piazza Venezia. Map 8I6.

An elegant Renaissance facade, Romanesque bell tower and lush Baroque interior belie the origins of one of the oldest churches in Rome. The first church here was founded by St Marcus in 336 but was destroyed by fire, and a long history of reconstructions and destructions followed. The fine apse **mosaic** (☆) dates from the time of Gregory IV's rebuilding in the first half of the 9thC. It shows Gregory offering his church to Christ in the company of St Mark the Evangelist and other saints. A further reconstruction was undertaken by Pietro Barbo, later Paul II, from 1455-71, and the beautiful gilded ceiling dates from then.

SANTA MARIA DEGLI ANGELI

This church, converted out of the central hall of the BATHS OF DIOCLETIAN by Michelangelo, was later reoriented and refurbished in Baroque style by Vanvitelli.

SANTA MARIA DELL' ANIMA ⅏ †

Via dell' Anima. If closed, ring the bell at Piazza della Pace 20. Map 5H5.

This fine Renaissance church dates from 1500-23 and is the German national church in Rome. The impressive three-tiered facade is no

133

longer attributed to Giuliano da Sangallo, nor the bell tower to Bramante, but the three pseudo-Classical **portals** are the undisputed work of Andrea Sansovino. The *Madonna between Two Souls,* in the tympanum of the middle portal, gave the church its name (literally, Madonna of the Soul).

Inside, the curious hall-like design is the work of an unknown northern architect. The church contains many notable works of art, including Giulio Romano's *Holy Family and Saints* (★) over the high altar. To the right of this is the imposing *Monument to Adrian VI* (Adrian Florenz of Utrecht, who reigned from 1522-23 and was the last non-Italian pope before John Paul II).

SANTA MARIA ANTIQUA   This is the oldest church in the ROMAN FORUM. It contains important early Christian frescoes, but is unfortunately closed to the public.

SANTA MARIA D'ARACOELI ⏹ ✝ ★
Piazza d'Aracoeli. Entrance from Piazza d'Aracoeli or from behind Palazzo Nuovo (Capitoline Museums). Map 8l6.
Ever since the beginnings of recorded history, the N summit of the CAPITOLINE HILL has been one of the most revered places in Rome. It was originally the site of the *Arx* or citadel and of the early Roman Temple of Juno Moneta. And it was here, some three centuries later, that Augustus is said to have seen the Virgin and Child in a vision. The altar he raised to commemorate the event was called the *Ara Filii Dei* or *Ara Coeli* (Altar of Heaven), hence the name of the Franciscan church that was built here c.1260. It replaced a much smaller church called Santa Maria in Capitolio, dating from the 8thC.

Entrance is made up 122 steep marble steps from Piazza d'Aracoeli or through the s doorway, which is surmounted by a fine Cavallinesque mosaic of the *Virgin and Child with Two Angels.* The interior has an impressive assortment of Classical columns and a fine Cosmatesque **pavement**. These merit more attention than the highly ornate gilded ceiling that celebrates Marcantonio Colonna's *Victory at Lepanto* (1571).

The church is full of treasures. In the **Bufalini Chapel** at the beginning of the right aisle are superb **frescoes** (★) by Pinturicchio, depicting the *Life of St Bernardino.* Facing the high altar are two **pulpits** reconstituted from a single pulpit by Lorenzo and Giacomo Cosma (c.1200). The **Savelli Chapel** in the s transept contains the splendid **tombs of Luca and Jacopo Savelli**. Jacopo became Honorius IV (1285-87), and the tomb of his father, Luca, consists of an ornate Roman sarcophagus surmounted by a statue. The high altar, which was once adorned with Raphael's *Madonna of Foligno,* now has a small 10thC Byzantine *Madonna;* in the N transept is the **Chapel of St Helena** or Cappella Santa. Its elegant eight-columned shrine (1605) is said to stand on the site of the altar erected by Augustus; at the end of this transept is the beautiful Cosmatesque **Monument to Cardinal Matteo d'Acquasparta** (died 1302), a general of the Franciscan order, mentioned by Dante; the fresco of the *Madonna and Two Saints* is attributed to Pietro Cavallini.

To the right is the entrance to the **Chapel of the Holy Child**, sanctuary of the figure of the *Santo Bambino,* the most venerated object in the church. The Bambino is said to have been carved from the wood of one of the olive trees in the Garden of Gethsemane. He used to be taken to visit the sick and dying in an old brown coach, which would receive instant recognition and right of way. Today he is driven in a taxi, but still brings comfort to many people.

SANTA MARIA IN COSMEDIN ⅏ † ☆
Piazza Bocca della Verità. Map 9J6 ✿

One of the most beautiful medieval churches in Rome, Santa Maria in Cosmedin graces PIAZZA BOCCA DELLA VERITÀ with a handsome seven-story bell tower and disarmingly simple facade. The original church was constructed in the 6thC, making use of materials from more ancient buildings. It was later enlarged by Adrian I (772-795) and given to the Greek colony that had grown up in the surrounding district. The church became known as the *Schola Graeca* or Santa Maria in Cosmedin — the latter name deriving from the Greek word meaning ornament, and probably referring to Adrian's additions. It was extensively remodeled in the 12thC.

Skillful restoration of the interior has revealed much of the original fabric, and the antique marble columns, with their fine Corinthian capitals, are especially worthy of attention. The church is also rich in Cosmati marble work. The magnificent **pavement** (☆) and **paschal candlestick** date from the 12thC, while the bishop's throne is slightly later. The **canopy** is signed and dated by Deodato di Cosma: *Deodatus Me Fecit 1294.* There are fragments of 8thC mosaics in the **sacristy**, and the tiny **crypt** can be visited if the sacristan is in attendance.

Outside, in the portico, is the notorious **Bocca della Verità** or Mouth of Truth. This great, round, weatherbeaten face of stone was used by the ancient Romans as a drain-cover. In the Middle Ages a legend grew up that anyone who held his right hand in the gaping mouth and told a lie would lose his fingers. Even to this day, few young visitors can resist taking up the challenge.

SANTA MARIA IN DOMNICA ⅏ † ☆
Via della Navicella. If closed, ring the bell at Piazza della Navicella 5. Map 9J7.

The present church dates from the reign of Pope Paschal I (817-824), and from restorations by Giovanni de' Medici (later Leo X) in the early 16thC, but the foundation is far more ancient. The name is possibly a corruption of *dominicum,* the word used in early Christian times to describe a holy place. The church is also known as **Santa Maria della Navicella**, after the fountain in the form of a boat or *navicella* that stands outside. The fountain was one of Leo X's embellishments.

The fine Renaissance facade, with its elegant Doric portico, is by Andrea Sansovino (1513-14). Inside, the church is dominated by Paschal I's glorious 9thC **mosaic** (★) in the apse. The Virgin and Child are shown enthroned in the midst of a flowering paradise garden, with Paschal (wearing the square halo of the living) kneeling at their feet. The wide nave has 18 gray granite columns, with marble Corinthian capitals. The beautiful 16thC frieze above the windows is by Perin del Vaga, from designs by Giulio Romano. It includes the heraldic devices of yoke, lion and triple ostrich plumes, all referring to the Medici family.

SANTA MARIA MAGGIORE ⅲ † ★

Piazza di Santa Maria Maggiore. Map 6H8. Metropolitana: Cavour.

One of the great patriarchal churches of Rome, Santa Maria Maggiore crowns the N summit of the ESQUILINE HILL with its monumental presence. But nothing on the outside prepares you for the revelation of the near-perfect basilica within. The church was built by Sixtus III in the years following the Council of Ephesus in 431, and its dedication reflects the Council's reverence for the cult of the Virgin. It is also known as the **Basilica Liberiana** or **Santa Maria della Neve** (Snow), following association with an earlier basilica built on the Esquiline by Liberius. The site of Liberius' church was indicated by a miraculous midsummer snowfall.

The beautifully proportioned nave, equal in width and height, is divided from the side aisles by 40 antique columns, 36 of marble and four of granite. The bases and capitals were added (and the columns streamlined) by Ferdinando Fuga (1741-43), who was also responsible for remodeling the external aspect of the church. The **ceiling** is coffered and reputedly gilded with the first gold to have reached Europe from America around the turn of the 16thC. The fine **Cosmatesque pavement** is a later reconstruction of the 12thC original.

The **nave mosaics** (★) are hard to see without binoculars, but they are a fascinating series of narrative scenes from the Old Testament, marking the very end of the antique, Classical tradition. In total contrast are the **mosaics of the triumphal arch** (★), also done for Sixtus III, but glistering with gold and Byzantine ceremony. The stories are of the *Infancy of Christ,* with the Virgin of the Annunciation shown as an empress, regally clothed and bejeweled, and the Christ Child receiving the gifts of the Magi in splendid isolation on a magnificent throne.

The conclusion of all these mosaics is the 13thC **apse mosaic** by Jacopo Torriti. It is no doubt based on a 5thC original, although the way of depicting the *Coronation of the Virgin,* with Mary and Christ seated side by side, is more modern. The best time to see the mosaics is at Mass on Sunday and feast days, when they are illuminated. But this is only possible if you are attending a service.

Later periods added to the richness of the interior decoration, but not always entirely successfully. The two great Baroque showpieces are the

Sistine Chapel and **Pauline Chapel**, off the right and left aisles respectively. Their sumptuous ornamentation is nothing less than excessive, even by Baroque standards. Beneath the Sistine Chapel is the ancient **Oratory of the Crib**, redesigned by Arnolfo di Cambio in the late 13thC. At the end of the right aisle is the **Tomb of Cardinal Consalvo Rodriguez** (died 1299) by Giovanni Cosma, a fine example of the superb marble inlay work for which all the Cosmati were famed.

The **campanile** of the basilica (1377) is the highest in Rome. In Piazza dell' Esquilino, to the N of the basilica, you can see an **obelisk** that originally stood in front of the MAUSOLEUM OF AUGUSTUS. It was brought here in 1587 by Sixtus V.

SANTA MARIA SOPRA MINERVA 🏛 † ★
Piazza della Minerva. Map 4H5.
Concealed behind a plain Renaissance facade is the only Gothic church in the whole of Rome. Founded in the 8thC on the site of a temple of Minerva, it was rebuilt in its present form c.1280, but has suffered a number of heavy restorations over the centuries, notably in the 15th and 19thC.

Some of the 20 chapels within are richly endowed with works of art. Most important is the **Carafa Chapel** in the right transept, containing superb **frescoes** (★) by Botticelli's associate, Filippino Lippi (1488-92). Next to this, in the seventh chapel of the right aisle, is the fine Renaissance **Tomb of Diego de Coca** (1477) by Andrea Bregno, with a fresco by Melozzo da Forlì. In the next chapel along is Federico Barocci's typically dramatic *Last Supper* (1594). Turning back toward the choir, at the foot of the steps you will see Michelangelo's celebrated *Redeemer* (★) (1519-21), the suffering figure of Christ taking up the Cross. The second chapel to the left of the choir contains the **Tomb of Giovanni Arberini** (1473), incorporating a Roman sarcophagus with a low-relief of *Hercules and the Lion*. Finally, returning down the left aisle, you will see at the end the **Tomb of Francesco Tornabuoni** (1480), a masterpiece by Mino da Fiesole.

SANTA MARIA DELLA NAVICELLA
The name sometimes given to SANTA MARIA IN DOMNICA, after the boat or *navicella* that forms the basis of the fountain outside the church.

SANTA MARIA NOVA
This is more commonly known as Santa Francesca Romana. It stands at the E end of the ROMAN FORUM, marked by a fine Romanesque bell tower.

SANTA MARIA DELLA PACE 🏛 † ★
Vicolo della Pace. Approach from Piazza Navona along Via Lorenesi. Church open only during Sun morning service. For entrance to cloisters, ring bell at Via Arco della Pace 5. Map 5H5.
This tiny church, lying tucked away among the narrow streets of the medieval city, is rich in artistic treasures. It was built by Sixtus IV (1471-84), possibly to a design of Baccio Pontelli, and restored under

Alexander VII by Pietro da Cortona (1656-57). The beautiful Baroque facade, with its charming little semicircular porch, dates from the time of the restoration.

Inside, the first chapel on the right contains the celebrated *Sibyls* (★) of Raphael, painted for the founder of the chapel, Agostino Chigi, in 1514.

The four prophets above the sibyls form part of the same decorative scheme, but may have been executed by Raphael's former teacher, Timoteo Viti. Over the altar of the first chapel on the left there is a fresco by Baldassare Peruzzi of the *Madonna with Sts Bridget and Catherine and Cardinal Ponzetti,* and above the richly decorated **high altar** by Carlo Maderno (1611) is the much-venerated image of the *Madonna della Pace,* dating from the 15thC. The image is said to have bled on being struck by a stone and was the inspiration for Sixtus' church. The **cloisters** (★) by Bramante (1500-4), commissioned by Cardinal Oliviero Carafa, are among the finest and most harmonious of Bramante's works in Rome, consisting of a simple arcade surmounted by an elegant colonnade.

SANTA MARIA DEL POPOLO �XIII † ★
Piazza del Popolo. Map 5F5. Metropolitana: Flaminio.

Santa Maria del Popolo is one of the treasure houses of Rome, mainly thanks to the lavish patronage of the della Rovere popes Sixtus IV and Julius II. The handsome early Renaissance facade is probably by Andrea Bregno, but the light and spacious interior was remodeled by Bernini in the Baroque style.

Starting with the **first chapel** on the right, there are important frescoes by Pinturicchio (1485-89), especially the *Adoration of the Child* over the altar. Also worthy of note is the joint tomb of Cardinal Cristoforo and Domenico della Rovere (1477) by Bregno. The **second chapel**, rich in marble inlay, is the work of Carlo Fontana (1682-87). The altarpiece, by Carlo Maratta, shows the artist's debt to Raphael. The **third chapel**, frescoed by pupils of Pinturicchio, contains another fine tomb, that of Bishop Girolamo Foscari (died 1463). A corridor leads from the s transept to the **sacristy**, where there is a marble altar by Bregno, commissioned in 1473 for the high altar by Rodrigo Borgia (later Pope Alexander VI).

Returning to the main body of the church, you come to the apse behind the high altar. The architectural design is by Bramante, while the **frescoes** (★) in the vault are probably Pinturicchio's finest works in Rome. They depict the *Coronation of the Virgin,* the *Evangelists,* the *Fathers of the Church* and the *Sibyls.* In one of the roundels, St Luke can be seen putting the finishing touches to a framed icon of the Virgin. The apse contains two splendid tombs, of **Cardinal Girolamo Basso della Rovere** (1507) and **Cardinal Ascanio Sforza** (1505). Together they constitute Andrea Sansovino's greatest work.

The **high altar** itself is adorned with the *Madonna del Popolo,* a picture of great sanctity that is reputed to have been painted by St Luke, but probably dates from the 13thC.

The **first chapel of the left transept** (★) houses two masterpieces by Caravaggio (1601-2), the *Conversion of St Paul* and the *Crucifixion of St Peter,* as well as the *Assumption of the Virgin* by Annibale Carracci. All three are wonderful paintings, but the drama and intensity of Caravaggio's lighting were utterly novel and remain unequaled. Continuing back down the nave, the penultimate chapel is the octagonal **Chigi Chapel** (★). Agostino Chigi was an immensely wealthy Sienese banker who wanted only the best, and he employed Raphael to build his chapel. Raphael was also to be responsible for all the decoration, including the mosaics and statues, but the project was not in fact completed until the 17thC.

The altarpiece of the *Birth of the Virgin* is by Sebastiano del Piombo, and the statues of *Habakkuk* (on the right of the altar) and *Daniel* (to the left of the entrance) are the work of Bernini. On either side are the remarkable pyramidal **tombs** of Agostino (1512) and his brother Sigismondo (1526).

SANTA MARIA IN TRASTEVERE 血 † ★
Piazza di Santa Maria in Trastevere. Map 7J4.

The exact origins of this undoubtedly ancient church have become confused over the centuries and it is therefore not clear whether it was founded by St Calixtus in 221 or by St Julius in 341. All that is certain is that this was the first church in Rome to be dedicated to the Virgin.

The church was rebuilt by Innocent II (1130-43), at which time the Romanesque campanile was added, along with the mosaics in the upper apse. The portico was an even later addition (1702), by Carlo Fontana. The facade, with its heavily restored 12th-13thC **mosaics**, has been the subject of much controversy. The Madonna is flanked by ten female figures, sometimes said to be the Wise and Foolish Virgins. The fact that only two of the figures carry unlighted lamps casts doubts on this interpretation, although it is just possible that three of the lamps could have been altered in restoration.

The **mosaics** inside the church are of exceptional quality. In the **upper apse** (★) the Virgin is shown seated on the same throne as her Son; with one hand on her shoulder, he holds open a book to reveal the words *Veni, electa mea, et ponam in te thronum meum* ("Come, my chosen one, and I will place my throne in you"). These powerful figures are the work of Greek or Greek-trained Roman mosaic workers of the 12thC. The Virgin is crowned with a diadem of gold and jewels like a Byzantine empress, and the faces are solemn yet marvelously expressive — the hallmark of the Byzantine masters. Christ and the Virgin are flanked by St Calixtus, St Lawrence and Innocent II (presenting his church) on one side, and by St Peter, St Cornelius, St Julius and St Calepodius on the other.

In the **lower apse** (★) are six 13thC mosaics by Pietro Cavallini, representing *Scenes from the Life of the Virgin.* They are full of animation and vigor, and contrast splendidly with the timeless majesty of the Byzantine work above. Below them, another mosaic by Cavallini shows the donor, Bertoldo Stefaneschi, being presented to the Virgin.

SANTA MARIA IN VALLICELLA   Long known as the CHIESA NUOVA or "New Church," following a rebuilding in the late 16thC by St Philip Neri.

SANTA MARIA DELLA VITTORIA ⚏ ✝ ✫
Via XX Settembre. Map 6G7. Metropolitana: Repubblica.
This fine Baroque church was built by Carlo Maderno (1608-20) and the facade added by Giovanni Battista Soria (1624-26). The church was originally dedicated to St Paul, but was renamed after the donation of a small picture known as the *Madonna della Vittoria*. The picture had been discovered, unharmed, among the ruins of the Castle of Prague after the defeat of Frederick of Bohemia by the Catholic armies (1620).

The interior has some of the richest Baroque decoration in the whole of Rome, and Bernini's extraordinary **Cornaro Chapel** (✫) is the main showpiece (last chapel on the left). The commission gave him a wonderful opportunity to indulge his love of the dramatic and to combine his gifts in architecture, sculpture and painting. The work was begun after the Venetian Cardinal Federigo Cornaro settled in Rome in 1644. Bernini had the novel idea of grouping eight members of the Cornaro family in recesses on either side of the chapel, so that they look as if they are in boxes at the theater (although in fact theater boxes only came into existence later). The scene they are witnessing is the *Ecstasy of St Teresa,* as her heart is pierced by the fiery arrow of Divine Love. In her own words, "It was the sweetest caressing of the soul by God." Bernini shows her swooning, her arms limp, her mouth half open, the weightlessness of her body conveyed by the multitudinous folds of her billowing drapery. The work has received almost equal amounts of praise and criticism, but is now accepted as one of Bernini's most characteristic and notable achievements.

SANTA MARTINA E LUCA   This church was originally dedicated to St Martina and later became associated with St Luke. It is better known as the church of SANTI LUCA E MARTINA.

SAN PAOLO FUORI LE MURA ⚏ ✝ ✫
Via Ostiense. Map 11D3. Cloisters open 9am-1pm, 3-6pm. Metropolitana: San Paolo Basilica.
St Paul was beheaded at Aquae Salviae (now Tre Fontane), some 3km (2 miles) s of where this great basilica now stands. His remains were wrapped in linen and handed over to a pious Roman matron, Lucina, who had the body buried in her family tomb just off the Via Ostiense. Here a *martyrium* or memorial chapel was built, which drew large numbers of pilgrims. Two and a half centuries later, Constantine had the body encased in a double sarcophagus of marble and bronze and built the first church here. In time even this became inadequate to contain the huge crowds that flocked to the martyr's shrine, and in 385

plans were drawn up by Valentinian II for a new basilica, as an offering from himself and his two co-emperors, Theodosius and Arcadius. The building was completed by the year 400.

The magnificent new basilica was modeled on Constantine's St Peter's, but it was larger, measuring 120 by 60m (390 by 195 feet). Like old St Peter's, it had an immense nave with two aisles on either side, but it was superior in having superb matched fluted columns with Corinthian capitals, whereas old St Peter's had a random selection. The Middle Ages saw many splendid additions in the form of mosaics and frescoes, and San Paolo became the most finely decorated church in Rome.

Disaster struck on the night of July 15, 1823, when the basilica was gutted by fire. The left side collapsed and the right-hand columns were calcinated. By modern methods, much of the original fabric — including many mosaics and frescoes — could have been salvaged, but at the time little effort was made to save the old church. As a result, the building you see today is almost entirely a work of the 19thC. Fortunately, the dignity and grandeur of the original have been retained, and it is the detail rather than the overall effect that has been altered.

The **mosaics** of the apse are heavily restored but are still of interest. They show Christ blessing in the Byzantine manner, flanked by Sts Peter, Paul, Andrew and Luke, with Honorius III at his feet. On either side there are mosaics by Pietro Cavallini, which once adorned the facade. Other treasures that survived the fire include the superb 12thC **paschal candlestick** (★) by Nicolò di Angelo and Pietro Vassalletti, a masterpiece of the art of bronze casting, and the **canopy** (★) over the shrine of St Paul by Arnolfo di Cambio (1285), showing the artist's combined talents as sculptor and architect at their most enchanting. The badly damaged **bronze doors**, which were made in Constantinople in 1070 by Staurachios of Chios, have recently been restored and are on view.

The early 13thC **cloisters** (★) are undoubtedly the most lovely in all Rome. They were almost certainly created by Pietro Vassalletto, who was also partly responsible for the cloisters of SAN GIOVANNI IN LATERANO. The Vassalletti family were arguably the supreme exponents of the Cosmatesque style of decoration. Here, every detail is different and fascinating, from the variations of the paired colonnettes to the sculpture of the frieze and the rich mosaics. The delightful rose garden in the middle is a perfect complement to the setting.

SAINT PETER'S (Basilica di San Pietro in Vaticano) 🏛 ✝ ★
Piazza San Pietro ☎6984466. Map 3H2. Open Oct-Apr 7am-6pm; May-Sept 7am-7pm.

For the many thousands for whom a journey to the eternal city is above all a pilgrimage, St Peter's is the climax of the entire itinerary. But it is almost unthinkable that anyone should visit Rome and not go to see this great basilica. Even so, the first sight of it may come as something of a disappointment, for Carlo Maderno's overweight and formless facade is hardly its most impressive feature.

The history of the rebuilding of St Peter's — earlier attempts to save Constantine's 4thC basilica having failed — begins with the destruction of the old church at the command of Julius II, who appointed Bramante as his architect. The foundation stone of the new basilica was laid in 1506, and Bramante's design consisted of a Greek cross, with a great central dome and four satellite cupolas. When he died in 1514, the four central piers and the great arches to carry the dome had been completed.

Following Bramante's death, competition to complete the church was fierce, with many disparate designs, in particular an ungainly scheme by Antonio da Sangallo the Younger (1539) that was only partially realized. It is remarkable that order eventually prevailed, due largely to the intervention in 1546 of an unwilling Michelangelo at the insistence of Paul III. The great master expressed enormous admiration for Bramante's original project, but was of the opinion that Antonio's labored work needed a surgeon's rather than a draftsman's hand. He substituted a beautifully simple design in place of Sangallo's over-complicated system of major and minor crosses. Paul III, watching the wholesale destruction of Sangallo's outer shell with some apprehension, nevertheless gave his architect a free hand. Michelangelo's plan of square cross and covering dome was put into effect and by the time of his death in 1564 the basilica was completed as far as the base of the dome. The dome itself should have been lower and flatter than the one you can see today (height, including lantern and cross, 136.5m (448 feet) above ground), but Michelangelo's design was considerably altered by Giacomo della Porta. However, the basic conception, and beautiful garlands and paired columns at the base, are Michelangelo's.

The decision to transform the shape of the church came from Paul V in 1605, when a Latin cross design was deemed desirable to cover Constantine's old basilica and atrium. Paul directed his architect Carlo Maderno to demolish what was left of the old basilica, and to extend the nave as far as the old Piazza San Pietro, adding a facade (1607-14). At last, on November 18, 1626, Urban VIII consecrated the new basilica, 1,300 years after the original consecration. Bernini was appointed chief architect in 1637 and was responsible for the overwhelmingly Baroque style of the interior.

The basilica is fronted by the great central **portico**, above which is the benediction loggia from which the Pope traditionally gives his blessing. The portico, with pavement designed by Bernini and a fine stuccoed ceiling, has five entrances to the basilica leading off it. The **Porta Santa**, the portal farthest to the right, is opened only every 25 years (in Holy Years). The great central **bronze doors** (★) were taken from old St Peter's and were made by Antonio Filarete for Eugenius IV between 1433 and 1445. Eugenius presided over the Council of Florence in 1439, and the reliefs depict exotic visitors to the Council — Africans, Ethiopians and Greeks — as well as the Pope himself, and the figures of St Peter and St Paul. In the tympanum above the central entrance (looking back toward the light) are the rather sorry remains of Giotto's *Navicella,* a famous but much-restored work that was rescued from the old basilica. At the right end of the portico, behind the door leading to the vestibule of the **Scala Regia**, stands the equestrian statue of *Constantine* (★) by Bernini.

N

Tomb of Paul III
St Leo Turning Attila away from Rome
Tomb of Urban VIII
Throne of St Peter
Colonna Chapel
Baldacchino
Tomb of Alexander VII
Confessio
St Longinus
Monument to Pius VIII (to Treasury)
to Vatican Grottoes
St Peter Enthroned
Tomb of Leo XI de' Medici
Tomb of Innocent VIII
Monument to Clementina Sobieski (to dome)
Canova's Monument to the Last Stuarts
Baptistry
Pietà
Scala Regia
Constantine
Bronze Doors
Porta Santa
Portico
Navicella

Entering St Peter's for the first time is an unforgettable experience. You expect everything to be on a vast scale, as befits the largest church in the world — inside length 186m (610 feet), maximum width 135m (443 feet), height of nave 44m (144 feet) — and yet the impression of great size is not at first apparent, so harmonious are the proportions. However, the sight of tiny figures far up the nave soon reveals just how vast it is.

The first chapel on the right contains Michelangelo's *Pietà* (★) of 1499. This superb depiction of maternal affection and grief was executed when the artist was 25 and is his only signed work. It has been expertly restored after the 1972 attack and is protected from further damage by a toughened glass screen. At the end of the nave, on the right, is Arnolfo di Cambio's bronze statue of *St Peter Enthroned* (★), the right foot worn down by the veneration of ages.

The high altar is dominated by Bernini's spectacular bronze **baldacchino** (★). Half architecture, half sculpture, this enormous structure is the height of the Palazzo Farnese and manages to fit in perfectly with its surroundings. It represents an incredible achievement in casting, with its four great fluted columns soaring upward in barley-sugar fashion to support the canopy, anchored by four gilded angels. The columns swarm with Barberini bees, referring to Urban VIII, who commissioned the monument. The great space of the dome is defined by four piers, each containing a colossal statue. Of these, Bernini's *St Longinus* (★) in the NE pier is the most arresting.

A deep sunken area lies in front of the high altar, and steps lead down to the richly marbled *confessio* by Maderno, where the figure of *Pius VI* by Canova (1820) kneels in prayer.

The apse is thrillingly concluded by the *Throne of St Peter* (★), again by Bernini (1656-65), a dynamic rush of movement and vitality, which represents the glory of the Church Triumphant guided by the Holy Spirit. On either side of the throne, which seems to float on clouds amid a host of joyous angels and cherubs, are the Doctors of the Church. St Ambrose and St Augustine stand for the Latin Church, and St Athanasius and St John Chrysostom for the Greek. The ancient wooden chair of St Peter is encased within the bronze of the existing throne, invisible among all this splendid exuberance. In either side of the altar below are two very fine **tombs** (★), the one on the right designed by Bernini for his great patron *Urban VIII* (1642-47), and the one on the left by Guglielmo della Porta for *Paul III* (1551-75).

The left aisle contains a richer succession of treasures than the right. Walking back down it, notice especially the **Colonna Chapel**, which contains a fine relief by Alessandro Algardi (1646-50) depicting *St Leo Turning Attila away from Rome* (★). In the passage leading to the left transept is Bernini's **Tomb of Alexander VII** (★), a late work (1672-78). Crossing the transept and turning to your left, you will see Algardi's fine **Tomb of Leo XI de' Medici** (★) (1642-44) and, in the next passageway, Antonio Pollaiolo's splendid **Tomb of Innocent VIII** (★) (1498), one of the rare monuments transferred from the old basilica to the new.

In the last passageway before the portico there is a monument of special interest to British visitors, **Canova's Monument to the Last Stuarts** (★) (1817-19) with busts of James and Charles Edward, the Old and Young Pretenders, and also of Henry, Cardinal of York. Finally, the **Baptistry** at the end of the aisle (to your right) contains an upended cover of a porphyry sarcophagus, now used as the font. It formerly covered the tomb of the Emperor Otto II, which is now buried in the **Vatican Grottoes** (see opposite).

Treasury

🚻 *Access from left aisle, just E of transept, under Monument to Pius VIII. Open Oct-Apr 9am-4.30pm; May-Sept 9am-6pm.*

The Treasury houses the **Museo Storico-Artistico di San Pietro**, an absorbing collection of sacred relics, chalices, reliquaries, vestments, illuminated manuscripts and ornaments, many of great value. In Room III is the magnificent **Tomb of Sixtus IV** (1493) by Antonio Pollaiolo.

Ascent to dome

⊠ ✻ ⊰ *Access from beginning of left aisle, under monument to Clementina Sobieski. Open Oct-Apr 8am-4.45pm; May-Sept 8am-6.15pm.*

An elevator takes you up to the roof, where there are marvelous views across Bernini's Piazza San Pietro and the Castel Sant' Angelo. From this level you can eventually reach, via 537 steps, the loggia of the **lantern**, from which there is a stupendous view of the entire city and the surrounding countryside.

Vatican Grottoes

⊡ *Entrance from NE pier of crossing, under St Longinus' statue. Open Oct-Apr 7am-3.30pm; May-Sept 7am-6pm.*

The grottoes follow the outline of the basilica above, and are divided into Old and New. On descending you arrive at the **New Grottoes**, with chapels arranged off a passage shaped like a horseshoe. Among them are the **Tomb of Pius XII** (died 1958) and the unfinished **Tomb of Paul II** (✰) (died 1471) by Mino da Fiesole.

In the **Old Grottoes** you can see many altars and tombs of great interest, some old, for example the 15thC **Altar of the Virgin**, and some new, such as the **Tomb of John XXIII**, always covered in flowers, and the **Tomb of Paul VI**.

Pre-Constantinian Necropolis ✰

⊠ ✖ ✗ *compulsory. Admission by appointment only. Apply in writing (giving address and telephone number) to Prefettura Casa Pontificia, Città del Vaticano, 00120, or in person to Ufficio Scavi (Vatican tourist office) on S side of Piazza San Pietro.*

In 1940, engineers were working in the **Vatican Grottoes** (see above), engaged in excavations for the Tomb of Pius XI. They hit upon some masonry that later proved to be part of a Roman mausoleum. This discovery led Pius XII to order a full-scale examination of the entire area beneath the papal altar. Could it be proved by archeology that this was indeed the site of St Peter's burial? Nine years of excavations followed. The engineers had to cope with subterranean waters and with underpinning and buttressing the basilica above, but their labors paid off. They brought to light not only a pagan Roman cemetery, untouched since it was buried by Constantine's workmen, but also a rudimentary monument believed to mark the burial place of St Peter.

The **monument**, a simple marble slab set between two niches, is set into a red cement wall facing an open courtyard now underlying Maderno's *confessio*. The plausible theory is that while making the red wall, 2ndC builders hit upon a deeply buried grave, which was promptly identified as that of St Peter and duly marked. Greek inscriptions on a wall nearby add weight to the argument. Behind the monument, the Vatican excavators found a huge store of coins of many ages and countries, and, in a fissure reaching under the foundations of the wall, the bones of an elderly and powerfully built man. Paul VI declared these to be the bones of St Peter, and the spot has since been honored by throngs of pilgrims.

The guided tour also includes the **pagan tombs**, which are built exactly like houses. Formerly they would have been roofed, but now they are immediately under the nave of the present basilica. There are 22 tombs, mostly built between 125 and 200. Those buried here came from well-to-do families; many have Greek names, and were probably merchants. The insides of many of the tombs are luxuriously decorated with frescoes and terra-cotta and stucco reliefs, and once contained many articles of everyday use. They were evidently regarded as residences of the dead.

SAN PIETRO IN CARCERE †

Clivus Argentarius (near Via San Pietro in Carcere) ☒ *Open Wed-Mon, Oct-Apr 9am-4pm; May-Sept 9am-12.30pm, 2-6.30pm. Closed Tues. Entrance under church of San Giuseppe dei Falegnami. Map 9I6.*

This gloomy chapel is better known as the notorious **Mamertine Prison**, where St Peter is said to have been imprisoned by Nero. Before that, it was probably a cistern. The lower level was once called the *Tullianum* and served as a dungeon. Among those who were thrown down here to die from starvation or strangulation were Jugurtha and Vercingetorix. The prison was turned into a chapel in the 16thC but even now still recalls its grisly past.

SAN PIETRO IN MONTORIO ▥ † ☆

Via Garibaldi. If closed, ring the bell at the door to the right of the church. Map 7J4.

This church was built on the supposed site of St Peter's crucifixion, which in actual fact probably took place in the Circus of Nero, beneath the Vatican Hill. Mentioned as early as the 9thC, the church was rebuilt from 1481 for Ferdinand IV and Isabella of Spain.

Inside, on the right side of the nave, the first chapel is entirely decorated with **frescoes** (☆) by Sebastiano del Piombo, including the

Flagellation, for which Michelangelo provided drawings. The second chapel has a fresco of the *Coronation of the Virgin* by Baldassare Peruzzi. The fourth chapel contains the fine **tombs of Antonio and Fabiano del Monte** (1550-53) by Bartolomeo Ammannati. Crossing to the other side of the church, the overall design of the second chapel is the work of Bernini (c. 1640).

In the nave are the **tombs of Hugh O'Neill of Tyrone** and **Roderick O'Donnell of Tyrconnel**, leaders of the revolt against James I of England. Beatrice Cenci is buried under the steps of

Tempietto

the high altar, although no inscription marks the spot. Raphael's *Transfiguration* graced the apse until 1809, when it was removed to the Vatican Museums.

In the courtyard outside the church is Bramante's celebrated **Tempietto** (★). Close adherence to Classical forms and perfectly balanced proportions make this little temple one of the masterpieces of the Italian High Renaissance. Built in 1502, it was at one time thought to mark the exact spot where St Peter was martyred.

SAN PIETRO IN VINCOLI ▥ † ☆

Piazza di San Pietro in Vincoli. Map 9I7. Metropolitana: Cavour.

This church was founded by the Empress Eudoxia in 432, to house the chains that had bound St Peter during his captivity in Jerusalem. It was then restored by Adrian I (774-795), by Giuliano della Rovere, later Julius II (1471-1503) — at which time the elegant colonnaded portico was added — and by Francesco Fontana at the beginning of the 18thC. Fontana was responsible for adding the Ionic bases to the 20 ancient Doric columns of the nave.

The church is not only famous for its precious relics — kept in a tabernacle in the *confessio* beneath the high altar. It is the celebrated resting place of substantial parts of Michelangelo's **Tomb of Julius II** (far end of right aisle). The figure of *Moses* (★) is one of the artist's greatest masterpieces. This majestic bearded figure is shown holding the tablets of the Ten Commandments, and looks as if he may shatter them at any moment. The sense of power, both physical and spiritual, is overwhelming. The much calmer but very beautiful figures of *Leah* and *Rachel* on either side, which may symbolize the active and contemplative life, are also by Michelangelo. The figures in the upper register of the tomb, in contrast, are by pupils. The tomb was Michelangelo's most ambitious venture and was intended to include 42 figures, but it was never completed. Constant problems with Julius and his successors caused the project to founder, and what had been planned as the centerpiece of Saint Peter's ended up as the glory of San Pietro in Vincoli.

Other notable works of art in the church are the gilded bronze **doors** of the tabernacle of the *confessio,* with reliefs attributed to Caradosso (1477), and a fine Early Christian **sarcophagus** (4thC) in the crypt.

SANTA PRASSEDE ▥ † ☆

Via Santa Prassede (off Piazza di Santa Maria Maggiore). Map 10I8.
Metropolitana: Cavour.

Paschal I built this often-restored church in 822 and dedicated it to Santa Prassede, sister of the saint who gave her name to the nearby church of SANTA PUDENZIANA. Prassede and Pudenziana were the daughters of a Roman senator named Pudens, an early convert and friend of St Peter. Although not herself a martyr, Prassede is said to have witnessed the execution of 23 Christians whom she had been sheltering, and to have collected their blood with a sponge and squeezed it down a well. The site of the well is marked by a porphyry disc let into the Cosmatesque pavement, toward the rear of the nave.

The church is full of **mosaics** (★) dating from the time of Paschal I. Those on the **triumphal arch** show Christ flanked by two angels in the Heavenly Jerusalem of the Apocalypse, with, below, the Virgin Mary, St John the Baptist, St Paul and the Apostles. Moses and Elijah are on either side, and at the gates of the city are two more angels. The **apse mosaics** show the two daughters of Senator Pudens being presented to the Redeemer by Sts Peter and Paul, the apostles each with a hand on one of the sisters' shoulders. Also present are St Zeno and Paschal, carrying his church.

These mosaics all betray some Byzantine influence, which is even more marked in the small **Chapel of St Zeno** (★), the chief glory of the church. The chapel was built by Paschal as a mausoleum for his mother, Theodora. On either side of the entrance are two very rare black granite columns, supporting an elaborate cornice. The entire surface of the walls and vaulted ceiling is encrusted with mosaic, predominantly of glittering gold, and of such quality that the Romans in medieval times called it the Garden of Paradise. In the vault, the head of Christ in a medallion is supported by four angels. In a niche behind the altar the Madonna and Child are shown between the sisters Prassede and Pudenziana. To the left you can see Theodora, with the square halo of the living (indicating that the chapel was built during her lifetime). To the right is the **Column of Flagellation**, which was brought from Jerusalem in 1223. It is believed to be part of the column to which Christ was tied while being scourged, and is an object of great veneration.

Another place of special interest in this church is the *confessio*, in which Paschal stored the many relics of popes, bishops and martyrs that he removed from suburban cemeteries to save them from the clutches of relic hunters. It was a time when the continuing spoliation of the cemeteries was at its peak. These relics are now largely dispersed, but the Early Christian sarcophagi containing the relics of Prassede and Pudenziana still remain.

SANTA PUDENZIANA ⋔ ✝ ★
Via Urbana. Map 6H7. Metropolitana: Cavour.

According to legend, this church was built on the site of the house of a Roman Senator called Pudens, the father of Pudenziana and of the saint to whom the nearby church of SANTA PRASSEDE is dedicated. Baths were constructed over the house in the 2ndC and in part incorporated into the 4thC church, which is one of the most ancient and attractive in all Rome. It was rebuilt in the 8thC and several times restored, notably in the early 13thC when the handsome bell tower was added, and in 1589 by Francesco da Volterra for Cardinal Enrico Caetani. The present facade dates from 1870 but incorporates 8thC fragments in the form of two white spiraling columns and a frieze featuring Pudens, his two daughters, St Pastor and the Holy Lamb.

The chief glory of the church is the **apse mosaic** (★), one of the finest Early Christian mosaics in Rome. The mosaic was executed between 384 and 399 and shows Christ seated on a golden throne, surrounded by his Apostles and two women often identified as Pudenziana and Prassede. High above the figure of Christ is a triumphal cross of gold, studded with jewels and flanked by symbols of the Evangelists. The background represents an ideal vision of the city of Jerusalem.

The execution of these mosaics is of the highest order. The coloring is soft and sensitive, the attention to detail superb. During restoration of the church in the late 16thC the lower part of the mosaic was cut off and the sides trimmed, with consequent losses to the outermost figures. Subsequent restorations of the mosaic itself have significantly altered the character of some of the heads.

Ask the sacristan to show you the remains of the 2ndC baths behind the apse and the **Marian Oratory**, containing 11thC frescoes. Entrance is through a door in the left aisle, usually kept closed.

SANTI QUATTRO CORONATI ṁ †
Via dei Santi Quattro Coronati. Map 10J8. Metropolitana: Colosseo.
Part church, part fortress, Santi Quattro Coronati has an interesting history dating back to its foundation in the 4thC. In the Middle Ages it was part of a fortified abbey, used to defend the nearby basilica of SAN GIOVANNI IN LATERANO. In 1084 it was destroyed by the Normans. The present church was built by Paschal II from 1111, using antique columns, and has a fine **Cosmatesque pavement**.

The Quattro Coronati were four Roman soldiers who were martyred for refusing to worship a statue of Aesculapius. Five sculptors suffered the same fate for having refused to carve the statue, and the small but exquisitely fashioned **cloisters** (★) are the dedicated work of 13thC sculptors in memory of their predecessors. The adjoining **Oratory of San Silvestro**, containing a fine series of 13thC **frescoes**, may be visited on request.

SAN SABA ṁ †
Via di San Saba. Map 9K6. Metropolitana: Piramide.
An ancient church now set in a quiet residential district, San Saba sports an unusually hybrid exterior, even by Roman standards. A 13thC portico stands in front of the Romanesque facade, and on it is superimposed an elegant late 15thC **loggia**. The church, founded in the 7thC by Eastern monks fleeing the Arab invasion of the Holy Land, has three apses in the Greek manner. It was sacked by the Normans in 1084, rebuilt in 1205 and eventually restored in 1465.

The superb marble inlay work in the **main door, pavement** and in fragments of the **schola cantorum** (now in the nave) is by Jacopo Cosma (13thC). Fragments of sculpture relating to San Saba's history are exhibited in the sacristy corridor.

SANTA SABINA ṁ † ★
Via di Santa Sabina. Map 9J6. Cloisters open 3.30-5.30pm.
Located high up on the AVENTINE HILL, with magnificent views over the city, this church is a fine and distinctive example of a 5thC basilica. It was built by a priest called Peter of Illyria, probably on the site of a Roman house belonging to a woman called Sabina, who had become confused with the saint of that name.

Construction began in 422, not long after the Sack of Rome by the Goths. The church was restored and embellished in 824, and again in 1216, shortly before being given to St Dominic in 1222 for his new order. Domenico Fontana remodeled the interior in 1587, and it was only after the restorations of Muñoz and Berthier in 1914-19 and 1936-38 respectively that it regained its original simplicity and majesty.

The atrium is reached through a 15thC portico and contains perhaps the greatest of Santa Sabina's treasures: the 5thC carved cypress-wood panels of the **west doors** (✿). Eighteen of the original 28 panels survive: they demonstrate parallels between the Old and New Testaments, as shown by the lives of Moses and Christ. The *Crucifixion* is one of the very earliest representations of this subject.

The interior of the church is impressive: on either side of the wide nave there is a superb **arcade** of fluted Corinthian columns, plundered from a nearby temple. This is notable as the first instance in Rome of an arcade replacing the more traditional colonnade, and the arches are decorated with fine 5thC marble inlay. The beautiful **windows** above were reconstructed from original fragments and date from the 9thC. So too do the similarly restored *schola cantorum*, **pulpits** and **bishop's throne**.

The mosaic decoration of the apse did not survive, but Taddeo Zuccaro's fresco (1560) probably reproduces its subject. The only **mosaic** decoration that remains is above the w door. Here, an inscription that includes the names of the founder and of Celestinus I, in gold letters against a blue background, is flanked by two austere female figures representing the Church of the Jews and the Church of the Gentiles. In the center of the nave is the **mosaic tombstone** of Muñoz de Zamora (1300), the only example of this type of tomb in Rome. The beautiful 13thC **cloisters** in the adjacent convent are only open at certain times, but are well worth visiting.

SANTO STEFANO ROTONDO ▥ ✝ ✿
Via di Santo Stefano Rotondo. Entrance through convent door to right of portico. Map 10J8.

It is tragic that one of the most interesting of all the ancient churches in Rome should be in such a dismal state of repair, so reduced in grandeur and majesty. The church is closed to the public for the moment, except during occasional services held there. This magnificent round structure was probably built in the 5thC at the height of the cult of St Stephen, and consecrated by Simplicius (468-483). At one time it consisted of a central space and two ambulatories, which were separated by circles of majestic antique columns.

The church gained special significance for being an exact replica of Constantine's great Church of the Holy Sepulchre in Jerusalem, at the time one of the most famous churches in all Christendom. Even today, vast amounts of geometrical data and legend are sometimes cited to support the theory that this is "the New Jerusalem of the Book of Revelation," or, failing that, at least the most important church ever built in the West. Certainly the sheer magnificence of the marbles, mosaics and frescoes once lavished on it by Pope John I (523-526) and Pope Felix IV (526-530) leaves little doubt that it was considered, even in Rome, a church of outstanding importance. These superb decorations are unfortunately lost, and today we know of them only from accounts given by pilgrims.

Recent excavations have revealed that the church was built over a military barracks and a Mithraic temple, which must both have been leveled by 350. Major restorations took place under Adrian I in 795 and

Innocent II in 1143, but the real damage was done by Nicholas V in 1453. He had the outer circle of the building demolished and the outer ring of arches walled in, thus diminishing the size of the church and spoiling its appearance.

At the time of the Counter-Reformation, Gregory III did the church a further disservice by causing the inside face of the new walls to be frescoed with depictions of the most horrific martyrdoms. The frescoes are now, like the rest of the church, in an appalling state of repair. Perhaps one day they will be removed and the church restored, if not to its former dimensions, at least to something of its former glory.

SANTA SUSANNA 𝍤 †
Via XX Settembre. Map **6***G7. Metropolitana: Repubblica.*

This church is said to have been founded on the site of the home of Susanna, a niece of Pope Caius, who was martyred under one of Diocletian's persecutions. It was rebuilt in 1475 under Sixtus IV, but the present appearance is largely due to Carlo Maderno. His **facade** (★) of 1603 is one of the masterpieces of the early Baroque style, elaborate but always beautifully controlled. The complexity of the rhythm is balanced by the vertical continuity, with Corinthian columns below and pilasters above. Santa Susanna is now the American national church in Rome.

SAN TEODORO 𝍤 †
Via di San Teodoro. Map **9***I6. Open Wed-Mon 4-6pm. Closed Tues.*

This small, round church, tucked away at the foot of the PALATINE HILL, is approached down a flight of steps and through a pretty **courtyard** designed by Carlo Fontana (1705). The church was founded toward the end of the 6thC, although several times restored, and may originally have served as a baptistry. An ancient custom certainly existed of bringing children here to be blessed on recovery from illness. The **mosaics** in the apse date from the time of the building's construction but, like the rest of the fabric, have been heavily restored.

SCALA SANTA   These highly-venerated steps are said to have come from Jerusalem and to have been ascended by Christ. They are best visited at the same time as the basilica of SAN GIOVANNI IN LATERANO.

SERVIAN WALL   This fortified wall was built in the 4thC BC and encircled a much smaller area than the later AURELIAN WALL. Substantial remains can be seen in front of STAZIONE TERMINI.

SISTINE CHAPEL   The overwhelming power and nobility of Michelangelo's *Creation* and *Last Judgment* are legendary, but this chapel in the VATICAN MUSEUMS also contains outstanding frescoes by Botticelli, Ghirlandaio and Perugino. Years of patient restoration have returned Michelangelo's work to as near to their original appearance as modern methods permit, financed by Japanese television in exchange for exclusive TV rights to the operation.

SPANISH STEPS (Scalinata della Trinità dei Monti)
Piazza di Spagna. Map 5G6. Metropolitana: Spagna.
This elaborate and graceful flight of steps leads up from PIAZZA DI SPAGNA to the church of TRINITÀ DEI MONTI, after which the steps are more correctly named. They were built between 1723 and 1726 by Francesco de Sanctis, and remain one of the most popular of all Rome's tourist sights. In the days of Goethe and Dickens, artists' models used to pose on the low walls and balustrades in colorful costumes, but today their place has been taken by street sellers offering cheap jewelry, leather goods, and pictures. In spring, the steps are decked out with a mass of azaleas, and the terraces become a riot of color.

STAZIONE TERMINI ▥
Piazza dei Cinquecento. Map 6H8. Metropolitana: Termini.
Perhaps the most impressive modern building in Rome (see illustration on page 29), Stazione Termini is as functional within as it is visually striking without. Begun under Mussolini by Angiolo Mazzoni del Grande, it was not completed until 1950, largely to the designs of Eugenio Montouri. The vast interior provides every service you could hope to find at a major rail terminal — shops, restaurant, sauna, massage, hairdressing — as well as the usual bookstalls and kiosks. Car-rental facilities are available, and there is a branch of **EPT**, the tourist information service.

In the forecourt, to the N of the station, are substantial remains of the **Servian Wall**, which dates from about 378BC and was once 11km (7 miles) long.

TEMPIETTO ▥   In this tiny but perfectly proportioned circular temple, closely modeled on antique sources, Bramante expressed the High Renaissance ideals that were to inspire his plans for the rebuilding of ST PETER'S. The temple stands in the courtyard outside the church of SAN PIETRO IN MONTORIO, said to mark the exact spot of St Peter's martyrdom.

TEMPLE OF FORTUNA VIRILIS (Tempio della Fortuna Virile)
Piazza Bocca della Verità. Map 8J6.
This elegant little temple stands close to the circular structure of the TEMPLE OF VESTA on the E bank of the Tiber. It is a delightful example of a Republican temple and is in excellent condition for its age (late 2ndC BC). Six free-standing fluted Ionic columns grace the front and sides of the pronaos, and half-columns (also of travertine) are incorporated into the tufa walls of the *cella* or sanctuary. The original dedication of the temple is unknown, but may have been to Portunus, the river god.

TEMPLE OF VENUS AND ROME (Tempio di Venere e Roma)
Piazza del Colosseo. Map 9I7. Metropolitana: Colosseo.
Little remains of the largest temple ever built in Rome, but surviving columns have been re-erected and part of the area ingeniously laid out as a shrub-garden. The missing columns are indicated by privet, the steps by box and the walls by laurel.

The temple was founded by Hadrian in 121 and dedicated in 135, but rebuilt by Maxentius in 307, after a fire. It was a unique double-apsed structure, with the two apses placed back to back in the center. The apse facing the ROMAN FORUM was dedicated to Rome and is now incorporated into the cloisters of **Santa Maria Nova**. The apse facing the COLOSSEUM was dedicated to Venus and has also survived: you can still see the diamond coffering on the vault.

With 56 magnificent Corinthian columns (ten at either end), gilded bronze roof tiles, and 150 granite and porphyry columns in the enclosing colonnade, this temple was one of the great sights of Rome. It stayed in use until 391 — longer than most Roman temples — and remained almost intact until 625, when Honorius I removed the gilded bronze tiles for old St Peter's.

TEMPLE OF VESTA (Tempio di Vesta)
Piazza Bocca della Verità. Map 8J6.

Like the nearby TEMPLE OF FORTUNA VIRILIS, this fine circular temple does not bear its original name. It was once dedicated to Hercules Victor but became known as the Temple of Vesta because of its resemblance to the temple of that name in the ROMAN FORUM. Dating from the late 2ndC BC, it is the oldest surviving marble temple in Rome. Marble was rarely quarried in Italy at that time, and the marble of the circular *cella* or sanctuary probably came from Greece. The temple was restored by the Emperor Tiberius, and the 20 surrounding Corinthian columns (one missing except for its base) date from this later period. The ancient entablature and roof have long since disappeared.

THEATER OF MARCELLUS (Teatro di Marcello) ★
Via del Teatro di Marcello. Map 9I6.

This enormous building, 120m (393 feet) in diameter, was capable of holding 20,000 spectators, and even in its present gaunt and fragmented state is one of the most impressive ancient monuments in Rome. It was begun by Julius Caesar and finished under Augustus in 11BC. Only 12 out of the original 41 arches in each of the two tiers are extant, and they would not be there at all if the building had not been used as a fortress in the Middle Ages and partly converted into a palace in the 16thC. The palace is now known as the **Palazzo Orsini**, after the family who owned it for two centuries. The three Corinthian columns standing to the N of the building are all that remain of the **Temple of Apollo**, first built in 433-431BC, and reconstructed in 34BC.

TORRE DELLE MILIZIE   A fortified medieval tower overlooking TRAJAN'S MARKETS.

TORTOISE FOUNTAIN (Fontana delle Tartarughe)
Piazza Mattei. Map 4I5.

Small, graceful and imaginative, this late Renaissance fountain has a gaiety and lightness of touch that betray the Florentine origins of its sculptor, Taddeo Landini. The overall design is by Giacomo della Porta

(1581-84). Each of the four youths, cast in bronze, restrains a dolphin, one foot planted firmly on the head and one hand grasping the tail. With their free hands they reach up to support four bronze tortoises that are struggling to drink from the bowl above. The tortoises were a 17thC addition.

TRAJAN'S COLUMN ★   Superb low-reliefs, and the fascinating narrative they relate in their upward spiral, make this one of the greatest surviving monuments of ancient Rome. The column stands in the FORUM OF TRAJAN.

TRAJAN'S MARKETS (Mercati Traianei) ✫
Via 4 Novembre ☎67103613. Entrance near steps of Via Magnanapoli. Map 9I6 🚾 but 🚹 on last Sun of month. Open Oct-Apr, Tues-Sat 9am-1.30pm, Sun 9am-1pm; May-Sept, Tues-Sat 9am-1pm, Sun 9am-1pm. Closed Mon.

In Trajan's time, these brick-faced concrete buildings formed a carefully planned shopping center, accessible at two different levels. They are probably the work of Apollodorus of Damascus (early 2ndC), the architect of the FORUM OF TRAJAN, and are remarkably well preserved. The lower level, built in a hemicycle to match the semicircular portico on the NE side of the Forum, consists of three tiers of shops. Little remains of the third tier, which faces away from the Forum onto a street known as the Via Biberatica and a second level of shops. To the left is the **great hall**, a three-story covered market.

High above the markets is the 13thC **Torre delle Milizie**, the largest remaining fortified tower in Rome. It was originally even taller, but lost its top story in the 14thC. It is also mistakenly known as **Nero's Tower**, because of the popular legend that Nero watched Rome burning from its battlements.

TREVI FOUNTAIN (Fontana di Trevi) ★
Piazza di Trevi (Via delle Muratte/Via della Stamperia). Map 5H6 ♣ Metropolitana: Barberini.

Years of pollution and grime were removed from this, the most spectacular and famous of all Rome's many fountains, during extensive renovations to smarten the city for the 1990 World Cup. The work was

completed and the fountain's gala reopening finally took place in summer 1991. Only weeks later, unsightly green algae began to appear. There is a tradition that anyone who throws a coin into the water will return to Rome, and few tourists seem willing to risk doubting the legend. They continued to hurl their small change when the fountain was dry during renovation, despite the admonishments of the municipal signs. At the confluence of several narrow streets, near the junction of the Corso and Via del Tritone, the fountain is not the easiest place to find. But as you approach, the roar of the waters and raised voices of the crowds will act as your guides.

Fountain detail

The fountain is the work of Nicolò Salvi and is supplied with water from the Acqua Vergine aqueduct. It was completed in 1762, but only after more than a century of planning following Bernini's abandonment of the project on the death of Urban VIII in 1644. The Trevi probably takes its name from the *tre vie*, three of the streets that meet at this point. The backdrop to the cascading exuberance of marble and water is formed by the side of **Palazzo Poli**. Neptune dominates the design from his central niche, flanked by allegorical figures and overlooked by statues of the four seasons. Below, two tritons control their seahorses: the one on the left seems to be having some trouble with his steed — Salvi's representation of the ocean in ugly mood — while his conch-blowing companion represents a calm sea.

TRINITÀ DEI MONTI ⅢⅢ ✝
Piazza Trinità dei Monti. Map 5G6 ◀≦ Metropolitana: Spagna.
Dominating the SPANISH STEPS and PIAZZA DI SPAGNA, Carlo Maderno's handsome Baroque facade is one of the best-known sights in Rome and is perhaps a more satisfactory architectural synthesis than his grandiose design for the facade of ST PETER'S. The church was begun in 1502 by Louis XII of France and completed in 1585. It was richly endowed by successive French kings and cardinals, and the interior was sumptuously decorated. Many of the furnishings were plundered during the Napoleonic occupation, but restored under Louis XVIII in 1816.

The most notable works of art are Daniele da Volterra's *Assumption* in the third chapel on the right, and his *Deposition* in the second chapel on the left, generally regarded as his masterpiece. From the piazza outside there are spectacular views across the city. Pius VI erected the 2ndC **obelisk** here in 1788.

TRITON FOUNTAIN (Fontana del Tritone)
Piazza Barberini. Map 6G7. Metropolitana: Barberini.
This marvelously imaginative work, one of Bernini's unquestioned masterpieces, was commissioned by Urban VIII in 1643. Constructed out of travertine rather than the more usual marble, the realism of the design was also remarkable. Four dolphins, mouths wide open, suck up the waters of the Acqua Felice. Perched on their tails is a wide scallop shell. Seated on it is the Triton, blowing water through a conch held to his mouth. The water cascades down over his magnificent torso, drenching the papal tiara and Barberini bees beneath his seathrone.

VATICAN CITY (Città del Vaticano)
Map 4G2.
The Vatican City, home of the great basilica of SAINT PETER'S, is an independent sovereign state, established by the Lateran Treaty of 1929. It covers an area of 43 hectares (108 acres) and, with the exception of PIAZZA SAN PIETRO, is surrounded by walls. Within this small area, the Vatican is entirely self-sufficient in its administration and public services. It has its own civil and judicial systems, post office, bank, news-

paper, radio station and rail station, a supermarket and several garages. An added benefit for the thousand residents is that many commodities are untaxed.

VATICAN GROTTOES   These lie under the basilica of SAINT PETER'S and are the traditional burial place of the popes. They contain many fine tombs and altars.

VATICAN MUSEUMS (Musei Vaticani)
Viale Vaticano ☎ 6983333. Map 3G3 ▆▆ but ▨ on last Sun of month
✗ ▆ Open Oct-June, Mon-Sat 9am-2pm; July-Sept, Mon-Fri 9am-5pm, Sat 9am-2pm. Closed Jan 1 and 6; Mar 19; Easter and Easter Mon; May 1, 8 and 9; June 29; Aug 14 and 15; Nov 1; Dec 8, 25 and 26; and Sun (except last Sun of month) 9am-2pm. Metropolitana: Ottaviano. Alternatively, take a bus through the Vatican gardens, from outside the Ufficio Scavi (Vatican tourist office) on the s side of Piazza San Pietro.

No museum in the world has a finer collection of antiquities than the Vatican. But the fame of this magnificent complex has brought disadvantages, in the sheer number of people who flood through its gates every year, intent on homing in on the star attractions. To ease congestion at particularly popular spots and to help visitors make best use of the time at their disposal, the museum authorities now offer a choice of four tours, each linked to a color code posted clearly along the route. Not everyone will wish to follow the official routes, but at the very least they are convenient rough guides. It is not impossible to change direction mid-route, but it can be difficult. Codes are as follows:

(A) (violet)	**(B)** (beige)	**(C)** (green)	**(D)** (yellow)
$1\frac{1}{2}$ hours	3 hours	$3\frac{1}{2}$ hours	5 hours

Inevitably the recommendations that follow are highly selective. In describing such a vast complex, it is only possible to mention outstanding examples.

EGYPTIAN MUSEUM (C) (D): Founded by Gregory XVI in 1839, this has eight rooms. In Room V is the colossal statue of *Queen Tuia,* mother of Rameses II, and the sandstone *Head of the Pharaoh Mentuhotep* of the 11th dynasty (20thC BC). In Room VIII is the basalt statuette of a priest carrying a small temple — the *Naophorus* (525BC).

CHIARAMONTI MUSEUM (C) (D): Named after its founder, Pope Pius VII (1800-23), it changed little in appearance since it was first laid out by Canova. Displayed here are a huge number of antique portrait busts, statues, urns and sarcophagi. Especially fine are the *Portrait of a Roman* (Section XIX) and the fragmentary relief of *Penelope* (★) (Section XXIII), a Greek original of about 450BC. Beyond is the **Lapidary Gallery**, displaying Roman and early Christian inscriptions (closed to general public).

PIO-CLEMENTINE MUSEUM (C) (D) (★): The museum is named after Pius VI and Clement XIV, who were largely responsible for assembling the magnificent collection of sculpture. Due to the flow arrangements, visitors now enter by Room XII and leave from Room I (**Greek**

Cross Room). Room XII (**Square Vestibule**) contains a sarcophagus of *Lucius Cornelius Scipio the Bearded,* in gray tufa. Room X has a fine Roman copy (1stC) of the *Apoxyomenos* (★) by Lysippus (c. 320BC), the athlete looking decidedly weary after his exertions.

Room VIII (**Octagonal Court**) has some of the greatest treasures in the museums. These are contained in the *gabinetti* or recesses of the four corners. Moving clockwise, first on the left is the *Apollo Belvedere* (★) (see illustration on page 33), a marvelous Roman copy (c.AD130) of Leochares' original (c.330BC), which once stood in the Agora in Athens. The legendary *Laocoön* (★) was rediscovered in 1506 near NERO'S GOLDEN HOUSE and bought by Julius II.

The Ancients considered this marble group to be one of the greatest pieces of sculpture in the world. According to Pliny the Elder, it was the work of the Rhodian sculptor Hagesandros and his sons Polydoros and Athenodoros. It represents Laocoön, a priest of Apollo, and his two sons, vainly struggling against serpents entwined among their limbs. *Hermes,* with his cloak thrown over his left shoulder, is a Roman copy of a Greek original (4thC BC). Lastly, Antonio Canova's elegant *Perseus Triumphant with the Head of Medusa* (★) (1800) shows the strong influence of the Apollo Belvedere.

Room V (**Gallery of Statues**) features the *Apollo Sauroktonos* (★), in which the god watches a lizard he is about to kill, a Roman copy of a 4thC BC bronze original by Praxiteles. Room VII (**Cabinet of Masks**) contains the *Cnidian Venus* (★), an important and much admired copy of another work by Praxiteles. Room III (**Room of the Muses**) is famed for the *Belvedere Torso* (★), a badly damaged piece that nevertheless shows the superb skill of the sculptor Apollonios, son of Nestor, who signed it (1stC BC). The torso, of a powerful man bending forward, was greatly admired by Michelangelo.

Room II has a floor decorated with ancient mosaics from Otricoli and contains the *Jupiter of Otricoli,* a Roman version of a well-known 4thC BC Greek representation of Zeus. Room I contains two monumental sarcophagi. **The Sarcophagus of St Helena** (★) came from the tomb of Constantine's mother in the Tor Pignattara (4thC). The dark red Egyptian porphyry sarcophagus is decorated with reliefs of victorious soldiers, and was perhaps initially meant for her husband. On the other side of the room, the **Sarcophagus of Constantia** (★) came from the church of SANTA COSTANZA. Dating from 350-360, it is similar in style, made of porphyry, and decorated with reliefs of lambs, peacocks, and cherubs harvesting grapes.

GREGORIAN-ETRUSCAN MUSEUM (B) (D) (★): This museum was founded in 1837 by Gregory XVI. Besides having one of the finest collections of Etruscan artifacts in the world (Rooms I-IX), a stairway that displays Assyrian reliefs, and a distinguished collection of Greek and Italiot vases (Rooms X-XIV), it also houses four rooms of fragmentary Greek statues and reliefs.

Outstanding among the exhibits in Room II are the furnishings of the **Regolini-Galassi Tomb** (★), excavated near Cervéteri in 1836. The 7thC BC tomb contained the remains of a richly adorned man and woman and,

KEY

1 Egyptian Museum
2 Chiaramonti Museum
3 Lapidary Gallery
4 Pio-Clementine Museum
5 Gregorian-Etruscan Museum
6 Gallery of the Candelabra
7 Gallery of the Tapestries
8 Gallery of the Maps
9 Apartment of Pius V
10 Raphael Stanze
11 Borgia Apartments
12 Collection of Modern Religious Art
13 Vatican Library
14 Pinacoteca
15 Gregorian-Profane Museum
16 Pio-Christian Museum
17 Missionary-Ethnological Museum
18 Historical Museum

LOWER FLOOR

UPPER FLOOR

Cortile del Belvedere

Cortile della Biblioteca

Cortile della Pigna

Cortile della Pinacoteca

Cortile delle Corazze

Giardino Quadrato

Sistine Chapel

BRACCIO NUOVO

Entrance

Loggia of Raphael

Chapel of Nicholas V

Sobieski Room

Sala dei Palafrenieri

Room of the Immaculate Conception

Room of the Biga

N

in an urn, the ashes of a third person. All the various ornaments and objects that were found with them are on display. Room III contains several bronzes, culminating with the superb *Mars of Todi* (★), impressive both for its sheer size and for the quality of its invention. In the **Room of the Greek Originals** the outstanding pieces are a splendid *Head of Athene* (★) and a funerary **stele** (★) showing a young athlete and servant.

The vase collection includes many amphorae, hydriae, wine jugs and craters of superb quality. The majority were discovered in Etruscan tombs, proof of the thriving export trade from Greece. Room XII, the Hemicycle, contains the collection's masterpiece, Exekias' black-figured amphora of *Achilles and Ajax playing Morra* (★) of about 530BC, a work of exquisite delicacy.

Other notable pieces are the cup by the "Brygos Painter" of *Hermes Having Stolen the Cattle of Apollo,* in the same room, and the hydria by the "Berlin Painter" of *Apollo Sitting on the Delphic Tripod,* in the upper Hemicycle, Room XIV.

ROOM OF THE BIGA (D) (★): The superb two-horsed chariot or *biga* is an 18thC work by Franzoni, incorporating Classical fragments of a 1stC original — probably a votive chariot dedicated to Ceres.

GALLERY OF THE CANDELABRA (A) (B) (C) (D): The gallery takes its name from the pairs of ancient marble candelabra that decorate its six sections. It contains a number of important statues, including a 2ndC copy of *Diana of the Ephesians.*

GALLERY OF THE TAPESTRIES (A) (B) (C) (D): The tapestries displayed here are known as the New School, to distinguish them from the Raphael originals or Old School in the **Pinacoteca** (see page 163). Both series were made in Brussels, but the New School was worked from designs by Raphael's pupils and dates from the time of Clement VII (1523-34).

GALLERY OF THE MAPS (A) (B) (C) (D): A long, barrel-vaulted gallery splendidly frescoed with 16thC maps of Italy.

APARTMENT OF PIUS V (A) (B) (C) (D): Contains a good collection of tapestries, including important 15thC works from Tournai in Belgium.

SOBIESKI ROOM (A) (B) (C) (D): Named after the huge painting by Jan Matejko, depicting John III Sobieski, King of Poland, liberating Vienna from the Turks in 1683.

ROOM OF THE IMMACULATE CONCEPTION (A) (B) (C) (D): A display of books and manuscripts presented to Pius IX after his proclamation of the dogma of the Immaculate Conception in 1854.

RAPHAEL STANZE (C) (D) (★): These four rooms comprise the official apartments of Julius II (1503-13) and his successors up until the time of Gregory XIII (1572-85). In 1508, Julius II decided to entrust the redecoration of the entire apartments to a young painter from Urbino. Raphael was only 26, and this commission marked the start of his short but brilliant Roman career. It was to occupy him until his untimely death in 1520.

Room I: Stanza dell' Incendio (1514-17). The earlier vault decorations are by Perugino. There are four main works by Raphael and his assistants: the *Coronation of Charlemagne in St Peter's;* the *Battle of Ostia;* the *Self-defense of Leo III;* and the *Fire in the Borgo* (★). The last shows how Leo IV extinguished the fire raging in Borgo Santo Spirito by making the sign of the Cross, and is a fine example of Raphael's complex last manner.

Room II: Stanza della Segnatura (1508-11). The scheme of decoration works from the four sections of the ceiling down through the walls, with the personifications of Theology, Philosophy, Poetry and Justice becoming the *Disputà,* the *School of Athens,* the *Parnassus* and the *Institution of Civil and Canon Law* respectively. The earliest fresco, the *Disputà* (★), might more correctly be described as the Triumph of the Christian Religion. In the upper part Christ is shown between God the Father above and the Dove of the Holy Spirit below, with the Virgin on his right and St John the Baptist on his left. To either side are rows of saints and prophets, while below, the body of the faithful gather round an altar bearing the Eucharist. The balanced but animated throng of the faithful comprises popes, cardinals, bishops and laymen, some anonymous, others deliberately identifiable. Most notable are Dante, Fra Angelico and the patron's uncle, Sixtus IV.

On the opposite wall is Raphael's masterpiece, the *School of Athens* (★). The composition is centered around the two majestic figures of Plato and Aristotle, representing Natural and Moral Philosophy; the former may be a portrait of Leonardo da Vinci. They stand beneath the magnificent span of a coffered vault, an architectural dream inspired by the plans of Raphael's cousin Bramante for the new SAINT PETER'S. We do not know now exactly how many of the figures are supposed to be portraits, whether of Classical or contemporary persons, but the man leaning on a block and writing has always been taken to be Michelangelo as Heraclitus. However, the overall sense of intellectual ferment is plain enough. In artistic terms, it is Raphael's supreme achievement to have created a noble and perfectly harmonious world of study that is never boring or monotonous. Within a composition of great symmetry, he ensures that every detail is worthy of contemplation.

In the center of the *Parnassus* (★) above the window sits Apollo surrounded by the Muses, with groups of poets and writers on either side. The blind Homer is flanked by Dante (in profile) and Virgil. Farther down, Sappho is identified by a scroll, but most of the figures remain unnamed, although Boccaccio and Tebaldeo are said to be among their number. This exquisite, flowing composition makes light of the inconvenience of the shape Raphael was obliged to fill, and is in many ways the most natural of all the frescoes in the room.

It is faced by allegorical figures of *Prudence, Fortitude* and *Temperance,* and, below them, scenes of *Justinian Receiving the Pandects* and *Gregory IX Approving the Decretals.* The lower section of this wall is the only part of the *Stanza* where the intrusion of Raphael's workshop is apparent.

Room III: Stanza di Eliodoro (1512-14). The theme of the frescoes here is the miracle of Divine intervention. Raphael gave *Leo I Repulsing Attila* a Roman setting, although the actual event probably took place near Ravenna. It shows Leo I, with the features of Leo X, advancing on a white mule. Work began while the latter was a cardinal and finished during his papacy. The *Mass of Bolsena* (★) celebrates the miracle that befell a doubting priest, who, while celebrating Mass in Bolsena, saw blood pour forth from the Sacred Host. The event gave rise to the Feast of Corpus Christi and the construction of Orvieto Cathedral. Julius II is pictured on the right, surrounded by kneeling Swiss Guards. The *Expulsion of Heliodorus from the Temple* (★) derives from a story in the Apocrypha, telling how Heliodorus was sent to seize the treasure of the Temple of Jerusalem and was driven out by an angelic horseman. The dramatic mood of the fresco shows a very real development from the calmer world of the previous Stanza. The *Liberation of St Peter from Prison* (★) is visualized in three parts that work perfectly as a whole, while the effects of nighttime and supernatural radiance are brilliantly rendered. The angel is shown waking Peter and leading him past the sleeping guards.

Room IV: Sala di Costantino (1517-24). This room contains four frescoes, some perhaps based on Raphael's designs, although most of the work was completed after his death in 1520. They are the *Baptism of Constantine,* which is set in the Baptistry of SAN GIOVANNI IN LATERANO and attributed to Francesco Penni; the *Battle of the Milvian Bridge,* showing Constantine's victory over Maxentius, mostly by Giulio Romano; the *Apparition of the Cross,* by Giulio Romano; and the *Donation of Constantine,* attributed to Giulio Romano and Francesco Penni.

LOGGIA OF RAPHAEL (C) (D): This so-called loggia is the middle of three arcades, built one upon the other, begun by Bramante and finished after his death by Raphael (1519). The second loggia was also decorated by Raphael, in collaboration with his pupils. (The ground-floor and top loggias were decorated by Giovanni da Udine, but both are closed to the public.) The decorative surrounds, involving stuccoes and grotesques, derive from Antiquity, while the scenes in the vaults depict Old Testament stories, with four from the New Testament in the last bay. The series is known as Raphael's Bible.

SALA DEI PALAFRENIERI (C) (D): Also known as **The Room of the Chiaroscuri** for its late 16thC monochrome frescoes, this room contains a **model of the dome of St Peter's**, a copy of one of Michelangelo's own models. A door bearing the name and coat-of-arms of Julius II leads to the Chapel of Nicholas V.

CHAPEL OF NICHOLAS V (C) (D): The walls of the chapel were decorated with **frescoes** (★) by Fra Angelico between 1447 and 1451. They show scenes from the lives of St Stephen (upper level) and St Lawrence (lower level). The exquisite coloring and charm of these compositions are typical of the style of this most holy of painters.

BORGIA APARTMENTS (C) (D): These take their name from Alexander VI (1492-1503), who used the whole of the first floor of the palace of Nicholas V as his personal apartments. The chief interest of these rooms centers on the **frescoes** (★) by Pinturicchio, executed between 1492-94. The richly decorated **Room of the Saints** (Room V) is considered by many to be his masterpiece.

COLLECTION OF MODERN RELIGIOUS ART (C) (D): This huge collection of modern paintings, sculpture and graphic art was set up by Paul VI and is well displayed in 50 rooms, including the first rooms of the **Borgia Apartments** (see previous page).

SISTINE CHAPEL (A) (B) (C) (★): The chapel was built by Baccio Pontelli between 1475 and 1480, by order of Sixtus IV. The interior decoration was at first a team effort involving the leading painters of the time: Perugino, Botticelli, Ghirlandaio and Rosselli, assisted by Pinturicchio, Piero di Cosimo and Bartolomeo della Gatta; later they were joined by Signorelli. This work was begun in 1481 and completed two years later, at which time the chapel was consecrated by Sixtus and dedicated to the Virgin Mary, who was honored in a central fresco on the w wall.

Side walls (★). Proceeding from the altar wall, the scenes depict the lives of Moses on the right and Christ on the left, in both cases illustrating the divine prerogative of the papacy. The finest of the Moses frescoes are Botticelli's *Moses Kills the Egyptian* (★) (2) with the Burning Bush and other scenes, and the *Punishment of Corah, Dathan, and Abiron* (★) (5). Of the New Testament scenes, Ghirlandaio's *Calling of Peter and Andrew* (★) (3), with its gallery of contemporary portraits, and Perugino's *Christ Giving the Keys to St Peter* (★) (5), using a Renaissance piazza as a backdrop to the action, are outstanding. The end walls originally had frescoes by Perugino (altar end), Ghirlandaio and Signorelli. These were destroyed and replaced by Michelangelo's *Last Judgment* and inferior late 16thC versions.

Ceiling (★). In 1508 Michelangelo began to paint the ceiling of the chapel for Julius II. There is no doubt that the sculptor was reluctant to accept this exacting commission, but when the work was finally unveiled four years later, after intense labor under most unfavorable conditions, it was clear that he had created a supreme masterpiece. The narrative element of the ceiling consists of nine rectangular panels telling the stories of the Creation, the Fall and Noah, starting from the altar wall, although painted in reverse order.

The scenes are as follows:

(**1**) the *Separation of Light from Darkness;* (**2**) the *Creation of the Sun, Moon, and Stars;* (**3**) the *Separation of Land and Water;* (**4**) the *Creation of Adam;* (**5**) the *Creation of Eve;* (**6**) the *Fall, and Expulsion from Paradise;* (**7**) the *Sacrifice of Noah;* (**8**) the *Flood;* and (**9**) the *Drunkenness of Noah*.

Although many of these pictures are very familiar, the ceiling never fails to impress. The sheer size of the task is staggering, but it is the mastery of the nude, the nobility of the expressions, and above all the assurance of the compositions, that make the ceiling unique. The Genesis scenes form only the central part of a complex arrangement, however, with the *Ignudi* (nudes) supporting them, and the *Prophets* and *Sibyls* below. These men and women, brothers and sisters of Michelangelo's *Moses* in SAN PIETRO IN VINCOLI, show him at his most monumental and heroic. In the spandrels between them are the shadowy figures of the *Ancestors of Christ,* revealing the darker and more pessimistic side of the artist's character. Finally, in the corners are four scenes showing *Moses,*

David, Esther and *Judith,* which convey a violence and distortion that look forward to the world of the *Last Judgment.*

Last Judgment (★). Michelangelo began preparations for this work, the masterpiece of his later years, in 1533, only six years after the terrible Sack of Rome. Although Paul III — a leader of the movement for spiritual regeneration that swept through the church at this time — approved the work, the message represented Michelangelo's personal view and is utterly uncompromising. The figure of Christ, a beardless and Herculean figure, turns in a dynamic twisting movement, his right hand raised in the direction of the desperate figures of the Damned, who tumble and free-fall to the depths below. Charon, a ghastly black figure, smites with an oar his boat-load of captives.

The mood of the entire work is somber. Even the Blessed who rise up on the left side of the picture show more wonder than joy at the sight that greets them. There are 250 figures in the painting, all originally nude: this shocked some, including Paul's Master of Ceremonies, whom Michelangelo had already included among the figures of the Damned, as Minos entwined with a serpent (extreme bottom right corner). Outraged, the official appealed to his master to have it removed, and the Pope is supposed to have replied: "From purgatory I might have been able to obtain your release — but over hell I have no power." Later on, drapery was added, but this certainly formed no part of Michelangelo's scheme for his compellingly powerful painting.

VATICAN LIBRARY (A) (B) (C) (D): Because of the one-way system, the visit now begins with Room XIII and ends with Room I. Room X contains the *Aldobrandini Wedding* (★), a justly admired Roman fresco dating from Augustan times. Room V is the Library Reading Room, used for temporary exhibitions.

BRACCIO NUOVO (C) (D): This "new wing" of the **Chiaramonti Museum** (see page 156) was inaugurated in 1822. It contains an impressive collection of Classical statuary, including a famous reclining statue of the *Nile,* probably a 1stC copy of a Greek original, and the *Augustus of Porta Prima* (★), the finest statue of the Emperor still in existence.

PINACOTECA (B) (D): It is not easy to select individual paintings from such an extraordinarily rich collection, but some pictures are particularly outstanding.

Room II has Giotto's *Stefaneschi Altarpiece* (★), originally in old St Peter's, and one of his very rare surviving panel pictures.

Room IV is dominated by the work of Melozzo da Forlì, and contains his fresco of *Sixtus IV Appointing Platina as Vatican Librarian* (★) as well as several fragments from the fresco that was originally in the church of SANTI APOSTOLI. The lovely *Musician Angels* (★) are particularly delightful.

Room VIII contains three masterly altarpieces by Raphael. The *Coronation of the Virgin* of 1502-3 came from the church of San Francesco at Perugia, while the *Madonna of Foligno* (★) of 1512 was the high altarpiece of SANTA MARIA D' ARACOELI, and shows Raphael at his most tender and Classical. The *Transfiguration* (★), completed in the last year of his life, is a dramatic departure that suggests Raphael would have conquered new worlds but for his tragic death at the age of 37. The walls are lined with ten **tapestries** (★) designed by Raphael for the Sistine Chapel and woven in Brussels.

Room IX offers Leonardo da Vinci's ill-treated *St Jerome* (★) and Giovanni Bellini's *Pietà* (★), two very different expressions of the spirit of the Renaissance.

Room XII is dominated by four superlative early Baroque altarpieces: Caravaggio's powerful *Deposition* (★), Guido Reni's somber *Crucifixion of St Peter* (★), Domenichino's moving *Last Communion of St Jerome* (★) and Poussin's unexpectedly brutal *Martyrdom of St Erasmus* (★).

GREGORIAN-PROFANE MUSEUM (B) (D): This collection of pagan antiquities was founded by Gregory XVI in 1844 and transferred from the LATERAN PALACE in 1970. It consists mainly of statues and sarcophagi excavated within papal territory.

PIO-CHRISTIAN MUSEUM (B) (D): This collection was founded by Pius IX in 1854 and moved from the Lateran Palace in 1963. It is particularly interesting for its large collection of Christian sarcophagi and for the statue of the *Good Shepherd* (★), a memorable and rare example of a free-standing Early Christian sculpture.

MISSIONARY-ETHNOLOGICAL MUSEUM (B) (D): Yet another Lateran foundation, begun in 1926 and transferred to the Vatican in 1970: an extensive collection of artifacts from the missionary countries.

HISTORICAL MUSEUM (B) (D): Established in 1973 by Paul VI, this museum exhibits carriages used by popes and cardinals, and militaria of the papal armed forces, disbanded in 1970.

VIA DELLA CONCILIAZIONE
Map 3H3.

As far back as the 15thC, the idea had been mooted of opening up the view in front of SAINT PETER'S with a grand processional route, but construction did not begin until 1936, under Mussolini. Many ancient buildings were demolished to make way for this straight, broad thoroughfare, but the impact of the basilica and its lovely colonnade is in fact only diminished by the scale of the new approach. The district on either side is known as the BORGO.

VILLA BORGHESE
Map 5F6 ❀ *Metropolitana: Flaminio.*

This magnificent park was created in the 17thC by Cardinal Scipione Borghese, and now covers an area more than 6km ($3\frac{1}{2}$ miles) in circumference. In 1902, it was bought by Umberto I, King of Italy, and given to the city with the new name of Villa Umberto I. The name never caught on, but, for all that, the gift has been appreciated by generations of Romans for its landscaped beauty and wide-open spaces. The whole area is crisscrossed by roads, but you can easily escape the traffic and enjoy the shaded plantations of oak and pine, the fountains and the lakes. The gardens of the PINCIO are to the SW and the **zoo** to the NE (see PARKS AND ZOOS in ROME FOR CHILDREN).

VILLA FARNESINA ▥ ★
Via della Lungara. Map 4/4 ▣ *Open Mon-Sat 9am-1pm. Closed Sun.*

This elegant Renaissance villa was built between 1508-11 by Baldassare Peruzzi, for the Sienese banker, Agostino Chigi, and was once richly frescoed, both inside and out. The exterior frescoes on the facade have long since vanished and the plain walls left behind look strangely bare without their decoration.

The **loggia** was originally open, but has been glazed in order to protect one of Raphael's most beguiling works, the fresco cycle of *Cupid and Psyche* (★) (1517). Although the concept and design are Raphael's, the execution was largely entrusted to his assistants, notably Giulio Romano, Francesco Penni and Giovanni da Udine. Evidence of his hand alone is found in the *Galatea* fresco (★) in the adjoining room, where simple geometry is allied to a seductive lightness of touch. Other important frescoes in this room include the *Constellations* of Peruzzi, and the *Metamorphoses* and *Polyphemus* by Sebastiano del Piombo. Upstairs is Peruzzi's intriguing **Sala delle Prospettive**, with illusionistic views of Rome seen through a screen of painted columns and, in the next room, Sodoma's *Marriage of Alexander and Roxanne* (★), this Sienese artist's undoubted masterpiece. Also here is the **Gabinetto Nazionale delle Stampe**, a very fine collection of prints.

VILLA GIULIA ▥ ★
Viale delle Belle Arti ☎ *3601951. Map 5E5. Gardens and museum* ▨ ▉ *Open Tues-Sat 9am-2pm; also Wed 3-7pm (Oct-Apr 2-6pm); Sun 9am-1pm. Closed Mon.*

The Villa Giulia was built for Julius III between 1551 and 1553 and is one of the most attractive examples of late Renaissance architecture in Rome. Vignola's impressive and almost stern **facade** (see illustration on page 27) contrasts splendidly with the animation and grace of his inner **courtyard** and **hemicycle** (★). The **loggia** at the end of this court is by Bartolomeo Ammannati, as, to a certain extent, is the **nymphaeum** (★) beyond, where Ammannati was assisted by Vasari. The collaboration of three of the most fertile imaginations at work in mid-16thC Rome ensured that the villa would be as charming as it is tranquil. It remains, as ever, a pleasant refuge from the rush of the city.

The villa now houses the **Museo Nazionale di Villa Giulia**, an important collection of Etruscan art which is splendidly displayed in a combination of frescoed rooms and more recent additions. The collection is vast, and sometimes the interest is more archeological than artistic. But there are some very fine Greek vases, which were excavated from Etruscan tombs and provide evidence of an extensive export trade from Greece.

Etruscan civilization, the precursor of Roman culture, is often mysterious, but its finest achievements are both haunting and impressive. The fragmentary 6thC BC group *Apollo and Hercules* (★), from Veii, is one of the masterpieces of Etruscan sculpture. Another is the **sarcophagus** (★) from Cervéteri, which shows a husband and wife reclining as if at a banquet (see illustration on page 244). They must have been buried together, but their wonderfully enigmatic smiles do not reveal why.

VILLA MEDICI 🏛

Viale Trinità dei Monti. Gardens open Wed 9-11am, but check with Ufficio Intendenza, Villa Medici, Viale Trinità dei Monti, 00187. Map 5F6. Metropolitana: Spagna.

Built by Annibale Lippi in 1564, this handsome if somewhat austere building was purchased by Cardinal Ferdinando de' Medici in 1580. Napoleon acquired it in 1803 and transferred the National Academy of France here. The **gardens** are little changed in ground plan since they were laid out in the 16thC, and are graced by a number of fine antique sculptures.

KEY TO MAP PAGES

MAPS 1-10 : ROME CITY

KEY TO CITY MAP SYMBOLS

▨	Place of Interest or Important Building
▢	Built-up Area
⬛	Park
⬛	Cemetery
†	Church
✡	Synagogue
⊞	Hospital
i	Information Office
⊠	Post Office
☝	Police Station
☎	Parking Lot / Garage
Ⓜ	Metropolitana Station
⊥⊥⊥	Stepped Street
—	Ancient Wall
5	Adjoining Page No.

```
0          250        500m
├────┬────┼────┬────┤
0          250        500yds
```

Key to city map symbols is located on first page of this city map section

Key to city map symbols is located on first page of this city map section

3

1 2

E
F

RAI-TV

2 3

PIAZZALE CLODIO

1

VIALE

VIA M. C. MIGLIOLI

VIA SARD

GIUSEPPE

PIAZZA D. PRATI D. STROZZI

CIRCONVAL

VIALE

VIALE

TRIONFALE

PRA

VIA TELESIO

CAMPANELLA

VIA S. PIETRO

VIA CAMOZZI

V. D. MEDAGLIE D'ORO

CIRC. TRIONFALE

VIA B.

T

VIA

TRIONFALE

LARGO TRIONFALE

RUZZO

F

G

PIAZZALE DEGLI EROI

VIA A.

VIA LEONE IV

VESPASIANO

VIA BARLETTA

OTTAVIAN

VIA

VIA

VIA LUIGI

CIPRO

MELORIA

VIA

CANDIA

VIA OTTAVIANO

VIA

DEL

S. M. dei Miracoli

VIALE

VATICANO

PIAZZA DEL RISORGIMENTO

BRAMANTE

VIA

VIA

V. D.

ANGELO

VATICANO

CITTÀ DEL VATICANO

Musei Vaticani

VIA D. PORTA ANGELICA

BORGO

BORGO

G

H

Governatorato

Radio

STAZ.

S. Pietro in Vaticano

PIAZZA S. PIETRO

VIA D. C

VIALE

VATICANO

VIA NICOLÒ V

AURELIA

VIA

V. DI PORTA CAVALLEGGERI

VIA STAZ. DI S. PIETRO

V. D. PAOLO

VIA NICOLÒ III

V. D. INVERSIONE

S. M. alle Fornaci

VIALE

G

VIA AURELIA

H
I

STAZ. S. PIETRO

Maria Addolorata

DELLA

DELLE

VIA AURELIA NUOVA D. FORNO

AURELIO

AURELIA

VIA NERINA

VILLA

ABAMELEK

Pl. D. G.

Casa del Sole

I
J

1 2

VIA

AURELIA

2 3

7

ALINA

TRIONFALE

Key to city map symbols is located on first page of this city map section

Key to city map symbols is located on first page of this city map section

7

2 3 S. M. alle Fornaci
STAZ. S. PIETRO

Maria Addolorata

3

VILLA

ABAMELEK

I
J

VILLA DORIA PAMPHILI

S. Pancrazio

J
K

K
L

PIAZZALE QUATTRO VENTI

M

GIANICOLENSE
2 3

Osp. S. Camillo

3

S. Onofrio

3 4

LUNG. GIANICOLENSE

G. SANGALLO

Villa Farnes

Pal. Corsini

PIAZZALE G. GARIBALDI

VIA PORTA S. PANCRAZIO

S. Pietro in Mont.

T R A S T E

VILLA SCIARRA

PIAZZA I. NIEVO

CIRCONVALLAZIONE GIANICOLENSE

Sacro Cuore

PIAZZA FLAVIO BIONDO

STAZ. TRASTEVERE

PIAZZA DELLA RADIO

3 4

Key to city map symbols is located on first page of this city map section

Where to stay

Making your choice

As a capital city and cultural center of international standing, Rome offers an excellent choice of accommodations, ranging from simple boarding houses, with rudimentary facilities, to unashamedly luxurious palaces that rank among the world's great hotels. In between are a vast number of comfortable, well-run establishments, and you can take your pick from antique charm and old-world courtesy, slick modernity and streamlined service — or, ideally, a subtle blend of old and new.

In any case, the exterior of a hotel can be no guide to the standard of accommodations within. Crumbling and dilapidated walls can mask the most elegant and shining of interiors, where polished marble floors and mellow antique furniture create an unmistakable atmosphere of fine and gracious living.

The *pensione,* a uniquely Italian institution, usually offering bed-and-breakfast or half-board, officially no longer exists. The Roman authorities have reclassified all such accommodations as "hotels." That hasn't stopped establishments persisting with the name, however, and to all intents and purposes *pensioni* remain a feature of the city. Prices differ widely according to location and the standard of furnishings and food provided, but are generally reasonable.

Many religious houses in the Vatican City and on the nearby Janiculum Hill offer a similar type of accommodation. Prices are again very reasonable, and people of all faiths, or none, are welcomed. For travelers alighting from overnight trains or for anyone arriving in Rome with no base to go to and a few hours to spare, the *albergo diurno* or day hotel at **Stazione Termini** is a useful place to freshen up with a shower and perhaps a shave, although no sleeping facilities are provided. Another *albergo diurno* offering similar facilities on the other side of the river is **Cobianchi** *(Via Cola di Rienzo 136a).*

Standards of all types of accommodations are strictly monitored by the Regional Board of Tourism.

NOISE
Narrow streets, tall buildings and a long and honorable tradition of horn-blasting among drivers and scooter-riders make Rome one of the noisiest cities in Europe. On hot, dusty summer days and nights, concerted use of hooters and klaxons can reach fever pitch. Bear this in mind when choosing accommodations and, if you're intent on staying

in the city center, at least ask for a room facing away from the main street, perhaps onto a courtyard or quiet alley at the back. The room may be darker and have a less attractive view, but these are minor considerations when set against the relative peace and tranquility.

Of course, you may well decide to stay in a quieter (and probably cheaper) off-center area, in which case you will have to weigh up the inconvenience and time wasted in traveling to and fro.

"Quiet hotel" (▭) symbols applied in the following listings do not guarantee absolute quiet, but indicate relatively peaceful locations.

RESERVING

The peak tourist season lasts from April to October, but good, low-cost accommodations are always heavily reserved and, whatever price category you aim for, always try to make advance reservations. (See *Sample reservation letter* in WORDS AND PHRASES.) British travelers can obtain a brochure listing recommended hotels from **ENIT — Italian State Tourist Office** *(1 Princes St., London, W1R 8AY ☎ (071) 408-1254)*. The same brochure, together with a list of religious houses offering accommodations, is available in Rome from offices of **EPT — Ente Provinciale per il Turismo** *(Via Parigi 11 ☎ 4881851)*. There are branches at **Fiumicino Airport**, **Stazione Termini** and highway service areas at **Salaria Ovest** (when arriving from Florence) and **Frascati Est** (when arriving from Naples).

PRICE

Price categories given in the following listings are intended only as rough guides to average prices. There are five bands: cheap, inexpensive, moderate, expensive and very expensive. See HOW TO USE THIS BOOK on page 7 for the approximate prices they correspond to.

Prices can vary considerably within one hotel, according to the size and position of the rooms. If you are making a reservation in person, it is therefore advisable — and quite acceptable — to ask to see the types of room available. Rates are displayed by law in every room but may be quoted exclusive of tax, service and breakfast. You should therefore always ask for an inclusive rate. Other extras could be air conditioning and, for rooms without a bathroom *en suite*, use of bath. On the plus side, many hotels have off-season rates between November and March, which are worth inquiring about.

TIPPING

Tips are expected by commissionaires and by the porter who carries your cases to your room. You should also give something to the room maid when you leave.

MEALS

Inflation and high staff costs have in recent years played havoc with the restaurant facilities of smaller hotels. Family-run establishments have generally managed to maintain their restaurants, but many others have been forced to abandon the attempt. A few do not even serve breakfast, but there will be numerous excellent bars around the corner and you will suffer no great hardship. (See REFRESHMENTS.) Many of the larger hotels such as the **Cavalieri Hilton**, **Ambasciatori Palace**, **Lord Byron** and **Atlante Star** have excellent restaurants that attract nonresidents as well.

LOCATION

The area around **Via Veneto**, just s of the Villa Borghese, boasts the greatest number of large, first-class hotels. Those around **Piazza di Spagna** and the **Pantheon** tend to be smaller but equally exclusive. More modest establishments and what were formerly called *pensioni* can also be found in all these areas, but predominate on the other side of the river, in the **Borgo** and **Prati**, where relative peace and quiet can be traded for a short bus ride into the city center.

Like most city rail terminals, **Stazione Termini** is surrounded by a vast array of accommodations. The district has lost its former cachet and has become distinctly seedy. The area directly in front of the station has become a market place for hard drugs and is best avoided. However, a few fine hotels linger on, maintaining consistently high standards in an atmosphere of change and decay. They are convenient for most of the sights of ancient Rome and well placed for public transportation. You can also stay right outside the city center, above the **Villa Borghese** or on **Monte Mario**, where the air is cleaner and fresher but the city's sights and other attractions are less accessible.

The selection in this book has been made not only to give a wide choice of price and area, but also with other factors in mind: atmosphere, relative quiet and space. Addresses, telephone and fax numbers (and telex where appropriate) and nearest Metropolitana stations are given, as well as symbols showing which hotels are particularly luxurious (▥) or simple (▤), and which represent good value (♣). Other symbols show price categories, charge/credit cards, and a resumé of the facilities that are available. See KEY TO SYMBOLS on page 7 for the full list of symbols.

☎ The **telephone prefix (area code)** for Rome is **6**.

Rome's hotels A to Z

ALEXANDRA
Via Vittorio Veneto 18, 00187 ☎*4991943* ▣*622655* ▣*490011*. Map **6G7** ▥
45 rms, all with bathrm ▦ ▣ ▣ ▣ ▨
▢ ▣ ▨ ▨ ▣ Metropolitana: Barberini.
Location: At the s end of Via Veneto, within walking distance of the Spanish Steps. Modest hotels cost over the odds in this still-popular location, and the Alexandra is no exception. Rooms for the most part are large and lofty, if rather shabby, and the atmosphere is

one of faded gentility. The Via Veneto is busy 24 hours a day, and a room at the back is advisable.

AMBASCIATORI PALACE ▥
Via Vittorio Veneto 70, 00187 ☎*47493* ▣*610241* ▣*4743601*. Map **6G7** ▥
147 rms, all with bathrm ▣ ▣ *by arrangement* ▧ ▦ ▣ ▣ ▨ ▨ ▵ ▢
▣ ▨ ◁ ▨ ▨ ▣ Metropolitana: Barberini.
Location: On the main sweep of Via

HOTELS CLASSIFIED BY AREA

PANTHEON AND PIAZZA NAVONA
Cesari ▥
Colonna Palace ▥
Genio ▥
Portoghesi ▥
Raphael ▥
Sole al Pantheon ▥
Tiziano ▥

PARIOLI AND MONTE MARIO
Cavalieri Hilton ▥ ▥
Lord Byron ▥

PIAZZA DI SPAGNA
Fontana ▥
Hassler-Villa Medici ▥ ▥
D'Inghilterra ▥
Delle Nazioni ▥
De la Ville ▥
Valadier ▥

TERMINI AND COLOSSEUM
Anglo Americano ▥
Britannia ▥
Diana ▥ ♣
Edera ▥
Esperia ▥
Forum ▥
Grand ▥ ▥
Londra e Cargill ▥

Massimo d'Azeglio ▥
Milani ▥
Napoleon ▥ ♣
Quattro Fontane ▥ ♣
Quirinale ▥
Villa delle Rose ▥ ♣

VATICAN AND PRATI
Arcangelo ▥
Atlante Garden ▥
Atlante Star ▥ ▥
Columbus ▥ ♣
Diplomatic ▥
Giulio Cesare ▥
Jolly Leonardo da Vinci ▥

VIA VENETO
Alexandra ▥
Ambasciatori Palace ▥ ▥
Bernini Bristol ▥ ▥
Eden ▥ ▥
Excelsior ▥ ▥
Flora ▥
Imperiale ▥
Jolly ▥
Marcella ▥ ♣
Savoia ▥
Victoria ▥ ♣

Veneto, backing onto the elegant Ludovisi Quarter. Impeccable service, palatial rooms and fine furnishings keep this long-established hotel in the luxury class. Despite having been completely renovated, it continues to be run on very traditional lines. The popular but somewhat pricey **ABC** terrace restaurant can be reached directly from the Via Veneto.

ANGLO AMERICANO ♣
Via Quattro Fontane 12, 00184 ☎*472941* ▣*4746428. Map* **6**H7 ▥ *120 rms, all with bathrm* ▤ ⬛ ▦ ⬛ ⬛ ▦ ✷ ▢ ▧ ▤ *Metropolitana: Barberini.*
Location: *In the middle of the Quirinale district, near Piazza Barberini.* An inexpensive hotel with 4-star facilities, very conveniently located. Decor is modern but stylish and the staff pleasantly courteous.

ARCANGELO
Via Boezio 15, 00192 ☎*6896459* ▣*613010* ▣*6893050. Map* **4**G4 ▥ *33 rms, all with bathrm* ▤ ⬛ ⬛ ▦ ✷ ▢ ▧ ▼ ▤
Location: *Close to Castel Sant' Angelo; Via Boezio runs parallel to Via Cola di Rienzo.* A now pleasant although not palatial hotel following extensive renovation in recent years. Situated in a quiet area, it is nevertheless handy both for the stores of Cola di Rienzo and the Vatican. A roof garden commands a somewhat restricted view of St Peter's.

ATLANTE GARDEN
Via Crescenzio 78, 00193 ☎*6872361* ▣*623172* ▣*6872315. Map* **3**G3 ▥ *43 rms, all with bathrm* ▤ ▦ ⬛ ⬛ ▦ ✷ ▢ ▧ ▟ ▼ ▤ *Metropolitana: Ottaviano.*
Location: *Close to the Vatican and Via*

Cola di Rienzo; Via Crescenzio runs from Piazza del Risorgimento to Piazza Cavour. Less luxurious sister of the **Atlante Star** and without the views, this is nevertheless a comfortable and well-run establishment in a quiet quarter near to St Peter's. Rooms can be had at lower prices, but the standards of service remain high, and guests are welcome at the Star's rooftop restaurant a block and a half away.

ATLANTE STAR 🏨
Via Vitelleschi 34, 00193 ☎6873233
622355 ✆6872300. Map **3**G3
61 rms, all with bathrm 🖩 📷 ➡ 🅰️ 🔘
🔘 📼 ❄ ⟨⟨ ✳ ☐ 🚹 🐎 Ƴ ⌂ 🖂
Metropolitana: Ottaviano.
Location: Between Castel Sant' Angelo and the Vatican; the hotel is a short walk from both. The reputation of this, one of the most agreeable hotels in Rome, continues to grow. Its loyal clientele significantly includes Italian businessfolk on expense accounts as well as visiting celebrities and leading foreign politicians. The rooms are comfortable, if compact, and were stylishly decorated and ingeniously designed by architect Giuseppe Luzzi. A youthful staff manages to generate an atmosphere of friendly efficiency under the watchful eye of proprietor Benito Mencucci. The hotel's *terrazza* commands superb views of the entire city, particularly the dome of St Peter's. Much money has been spent recently to extend the *terrazza* around the whole of the top floor, and the result is certain to be the envy of Rome's hoteliers. Swallows wheel around the rooftop garden, which is so far above the bustle of the city that the birdsong is never drowned out by traffic noise. Courtesy cars pick guests up from the airport, and a private plane and business office can be arranged. It boasts one of the most romantic and enjoyable restaurants in the city. (See **Les Etoiles**, page 199.)

BERNINI BRISTOL 🏨
Piazza Barberini 23, 00187 ☎4883051
610554 ✆4824266. Map **6**G7
125 rms, all with bathrm 🖩 📷 by

arrangement ➡ 🅰️ 🔘 📼 📺 ✳ 🚹 ☐
📼 🐎 ❄ Ƴ Metropolitana: Barberini.
Location: At the foot of Via Veneto and well placed for main sights, shops and cafés. Facing Bernini's magnificent TRITON FOUNTAIN, the solid, marble-clad entrance advertises the traditional virtues of this comfortably conservative hotel. The presidential suite has an attractive roof garden with fine views over the city and a price to match, and every room has independent air conditioning and a refrigerator bar.

BRITANNIA
Via Napoli 64, 00184 ☎4885785
611292 ✆4882343. Map **6**H7
32 rms, all with bathrm 🖩 ➡ 🅰️ 🔘 🔘
📺 ✳ ☐ 📼 Ƴ 🖂 Metropolitana: Termini or Repubblica.
Location: Close to Stazione Termini and other public transportation. A small, efficiently-run hotel, not far from the great patriarchal basilica of SANTA MARIA MAGGIORE. The interior has been recently modernized and redecorated and every room now has a sun lamp, refrigerator bar and, for the security-conscious, a personal safe.

CAVALIERI HILTON 🏨
Via Cadlolo 101, 00136 ☎31511
625337 ✆31512241. Map **1**D2
387 rms, all with bathrm 🖩 ➡ 📷 ➡ 🅰️
🔘 🔘 📼 🏠 ✳ ⟨⟨ ☐ 📼 ❄ ⟨⟨ 🐎 Ƴ
🖂 🌡 🡆
Location: On Monte Mario, N of the Vatican City. Admittedly the view from the Hilton is breathtaking, but you have to decide whether it makes up for the inconvenient situation well outside the center of Rome. In summer, when the city becomes intolerably hot, the choice is not too difficult. Service and facilities are all you could wish for, including sauna, massage, a swimming pool and tennis facilities, and a courtesy bus winds its way up and down the slopes of Monte Mario at frequent intervals, providing an efficient link-up with the city.

Perhaps the most attractive feature of the hotel is **La Pergola**, the delightful roof-top restaurant where you can enjoy spectacular views over the entire city while you dine.

CESARI

Via di Pietra 89a, 00186 ☎*6792386* ⟠*6790882. Map* **5**H6 ⬚ *51 rms, 40 with bathrm* ▭ 𝔸 ⊡ ⊠ ▦ ✱ ⌂ ⚲ ⬜
Location: Just off the busy Corso, and reasonably close to the Pantheon and Piazza Navona. Authentic without, completely renovated and modernized within, this 18thC hotel in bygone days accommodated Mazzini and Garibaldi. Nowadays it has no pretensions to grandeur, but the central location and friendly bar have earned it many faithful patrons.

COLONNA PALACE

Piazza di Montecitorio 12, 00186 ☎*6781341* ⟠*621467* ⟠*6794496. Map* **5**H5 ⬚ *100 rms, all with bathrm* ▭ ▭ ⊡ *by arrangement* 𝔸 ⊡ ⊠ ▦ ⌂ ✱ ⚴ ⬜ ⌂ ⚲
Location: In the old city, close to the Pantheon and Piazza Navona. A first-class hotel situated in a quiet square, opposite Bernini's grandiose PALAZZO DI MONTECITORIO, now the lower house of the Italian parliament. Renovated in 1991, it is comfortably but unexcitingly furnished in a nondescript modern style. Excellent service is guaranteed.

COLUMBUS ♣ ▥

Via della Conciliazione 33, 00193 ☎*6867796* ⟠*620096* ⟠*6864874. Map* **3**H3 ⬚ *107 rms, 80 with bathrm* ⊠ ▭ 𝔸 ⊡ ⊠ ▦ ✱ ⬜ ⌂ ⚲
Location: Between St Peter's and the Castel Sant' Angelo. The hotel takes up the greater part of the Palazzo dei Penitenzieri, built in the 15thC for Cardinal Domenico della Rovere, and retains much of the original decoration. The magnificent lounge, formerly the main hall, has a superb *cassettone* beamed ceiling, and elsewhere there are frescoed vaulted galleries. Fine period furniture and paintings blend discreetly into their palatial surroundings, creating an atmosphere of gracious living that is a real bargain at rates such as these.

DIANA ♣

Via Principe Amedeo 4, 00185 ☎*4827541* ⟠*611198* ⟠*486998. Map* **6**H8 ⬚ *187 rms, all with bathrm* ▭ ▭ 𝔸 ⊡ ▦ ✱ ⌂ ⚲ *Metropolitana: Termini.*
Location: Between Stazione Termini and Santa Maria Maggiore. An efficiently-run second-class hotel, conveniently located for public transportation and the airport buses from Via Giolitti. Furnishings are plain and unpretentious, but the place is well geared to the needs of tourists.

DIPLOMATIC

Via Vittoria Colonna 28, 00193 ☎*6833775* ⟠*610506* ⟠*6832685. Map* **5**G5 ⬚ *35 rms, 7 with bathrm* ▭ ⚓ *by arrangement* ▭ 𝔸 ⊡ ⊠ ▦ ✱ ⬜ ⚓ ⊟
Location: Between Ponte Cavour and Piazza Cavour, near Castel Sant' Angelo. Four-star accommodations on the right side of the river for the Vatican but only a bridge away from the livelier quarters of the city.

EDEN ▥

Via Ludovisi 49, 00187 ☎*4743551* ⟠*610567* ⟠*4821584. Map* **6**G7 ⬚ *110 rms, all with bathrm* ▭ ⊠ *by arrangement* 𝔸 ⊡ ⊠ ▦ ▭ ⌂ ✱ ⬜ ⌂ ⟪ ⚴ ⚲ ⚴ *Metropolitana: Barberini.*
Location: In the exclusive Ludovisi Quarter, w of Via Veneto. A long-established top-class hotel, with a high standard of service and the lowest rates of all the hotels in this class. The restaurant, **La Terrazza dell' Eden**, offers a spectacular panorama of the city, taking in the Villa Medici to the N and the Quirinal to the S.

EDERA

Via Poliziano 75, 00184 ☎*7316341* ⟠*738275. Map* **10**I8 ⬚ *46 rms, 42 with bathrm* ⚓ ⊠ *by arrangement* 𝔸 ⊡ ⊠ ▦ ⌂ ✱ ⚴ ⬜ ⌂ ⚵ ⚲ *Metropolitana: Colosseo or Vittorio Emanuele.*
Location: Off Via Merulana in the Colle Oppio district, above the Colosseum. A more peaceful and convenient location for a hotel in Rome would be hard to find. The Edera was completely redecorated in a bland, modern color-

scheme. The only really attractive feature of this face-lift is the small patio with white garden furniture in the well of the building. But quiet it certainly is: wishing to preserve the tranquility of his hotel, the owner does not accept groups.

ESPERIA

Via Nazionale 22, 00184 ☎*4744245*
🖅*614635* 🖻*4744245*. Map *6*H7 ⅢⅢ
98 rms, all with bathrm ▦ ▣ *by*
arrangement 🆑 ⊙ ⊙ 🖸 ✱ ▢ 🖾 🦐
❖ *Metropolitana: Repubblica.*
Location: Near Stazione Termini and other public transportation. A 19thC hotel that offers traditional service with a convenient if noisy location. The public rooms remain much as they were at the turn of the century, but most of the bedrooms have been completely renovated. If traffic noise bothers you, a back room is essential.

EXCELSIOR 🏨

Via Vittorio Veneto 125, 00187 ☎*4708*
🖅*610232* 🖻*4826205*. Map *6*G7 ⅢⅢ
394 rms, all with bathrm ▦ ▣ ⇉ 🆑 ⊙
⊙ 🖸 ✱ ⟁ ▢ 🖾 🦐 ♨ ❖ ♪
Metropolitana: Barberini.
Location: On the E side of Via Veneto, not far from the Villa Borghese. Everything about this splendid hotel is palatial: the number of bedrooms, the sumptuous bathrooms, the grand scale of the public rooms, the Oriental silk rugs that cover the marble floors, the beautiful antique furnishings. In keeping with the leisurely, relaxed air of the whole establishment, breakfast is served until 10.30am, and a piano bar provides nostalgic evening entertainment far into the night. One of the prestigious CIGA chain, the Excelsior rates high among the top hotels of Rome.

FLORA

Via Vittorio Veneto 191, 00187 ☎*497821*
🖅*622256* 🖻*4820359*. Map *6*G7 ⅢⅢ
177 rms, all with bathrm ▦ ▣ *by*
arrangement 🆑 ⊙ 🖸 ✱ ▢ 🖾 🦐 ♨
♨ ❖ ▣
Location: At the top of Via Veneto, near the Porta Pinciana and Villa Borghese.

An old-fashioned, comfortably-furnished hotel with first-class traditional service to match. The public rooms have an aura of faded elegance, with muted color schemes, Oriental carpets and antique furniture. Upstairs, the bedrooms are on a grand scale, and many of them have superb views across the pine-studded park beyond the AURELIAN WALL.

FONTANA

Piazza di Trevi 96, 00187 ☎*6786113.*
Map *5*H6 ⅢⅢ *28 rms, all with bathrm* ▦ 🆑
⊙ 🖸 ✱ ▢ 🖾 ❖ *Metropolitana:*
Barberini.
Location: In a wonderfully central position, within walking distance of Piazza Navona, Piazza di Spagna, Via Veneto and the Roman Forum. Facing the TREVI FOUNTAIN, one of the city's most spectacular Baroque creations, this hotel scores high on convenience of location, but low on seclusion and tranquility. Outside, from dawn until far into the night, the thundering waters and chattering crowds of sightseers fight hard to be heard. But if you can stand the noise, there is always plenty going on outside your window. The hotel is in fact older than the fountain, for the building was once part of a medieval monastery, although it is now much restored. You may even be lucky enough to be allocated a room converted from two monks' cells. Among its clientele the hotel boasted the late president, Sandro Pertini, who lodged here while his own apartment nearby was converted to splendor befitting the Republic's number one citizen.

FORUM

Via Tor de' Conti 25, 00184 ☎*6792446*
🖅*622549* 🖻*6786479*. Map *8*I6 ⅢⅢ
76 rms, all with bathrm ⬤ ▦ ▣ ⇉
(closed Sun) 🆑 ⊙ ⊙ 🖸 ⌂ ✱ ⟁
▢ 🖾 🦐 ◁◁ ☎ ❖ *Metropolitana:*
Colosseo.
Location: Between the Colosseum and Piazza Venezia, overlooking the Imperial and Roman Forums. A converted Renaissance palace, originally built out of material plundered from the

ancient ruins nearby. Intriguing Classical fragments include the Corinthian columns visible in the interior. The star feature is the marvelous view from the roof-top restaurant over the Forums and toward the Palatine Hill. In summer, sun-lovers may lunch or dine on the open terrace alongside the restaurant. Bedrooms are smallish but comfortable.

GENIO

Via G. Zanardelli 28, 00186 ☎*6833781* ⊠*6547246. Map* **4H5** ▥ *61 rms, all with bathrm* ▦ �〓 🅰 🅿 🆑 ▩ ⊛ ✆ 🔲 🖾 ☕ 🖃

Location: Just a few paces from Piazza Navona and close to the beautiful antique stores of the Via dei Coronari. The hotel has been completely renovated, and apart from its location it has the advantage of panoramic views from a *terrazza*. An elegant hotel that nevertheless tries to maintain a family atmosphere.

GIULIO CESARE

Via degli Scipioni 287, 00192 ☎*3210751* ⊠*613010* ⊠*3211736. Map* **4F4** ▥ *90 rms, all with bathrm* ▦ ➤ 🅰 🅿 🆑 🖾 ⊛ 🔲 🖾 ☕ ☕ 🖃

Location: Close to Metropolitana Lepanto and handy for the Piazza del Popolo, just across the river. Rather pricey for a hotel in this off-center quarter, perhaps due to its noble past as the villa of a countess. After the war it was converted into a school, and became a hotel about 35 years ago. It now provides a comfortable retreat for those who like a quieter life.

GRAND 🏨

Via Vittorio Emanuele Orlando 3, 00185 ☎*4709* ⊠*610210. Map* **6G7** ▥ *168 rms, all with bathrm* ▦ 🖾 ➒ 🅰 🅿 🆑 🖾 ⊛ ♿ 🔲 🖾 ⊛ ⚓ ☕ 🖃

Metropolitana: Repubblica.

Location: Between Piazza della Repubblica and Piazza San Bernardo, near Stazione Termini. When this imposing Neoclassical palace opened in 1894, it stood in one of the most fashionable quarters of the city. Piazza della Repubblica and the surrounding streets have long since lost their chic, but the Grand soldiers on, an oasis of luxury and good taste. It is still the top hotel in Rome of the illustrious CIGA chain, and the natural choice for visiting royalty and VIPs. The majestically proportioned rooms, sumptuous decorations and discreet service are all that you might expect of a top-class hotel, and the facilities include hairdresser, beauty parlor and sauna. A café (**Le Pavillon**) and restaurant cater to all occasions.

HASSLER-VILLA MEDICI 🏨

Piazza Trinità dei Monti 6, 00187 ☎*6782651* ⊠*610208* ⊠*6789991. Map* **5G6** ▥ *100 rms, all with bathrm* ▦ 🖾 ➓ 🅰 🅿 🖾 ⊛ ♿ 🔲 🖾 ⚓ ⊛ ☕

Metropolitana: Spagna.

Location: Above the Spanish Steps. This hotel's glorious position is the envy of Rome's hoteliers. Basking in the Baroque grandeur of TRINITÀ DEI MONTI, it overlooks the graceful SPANISH STEPS and the city beyond. Inside, squared marble columns and exquisite furnishings create an atmosphere of quiet affluence that has proved irresistible to international jet-setters. The roof-top restaurant, famed for its stupendous views over the city, is open to nonresidents.

IMPERIALE

Via Vittorio Veneto 24, 00187 ☎*4826351* ⊠*621071* ⊠*4826351. Map* **6G7** ▥ *85 rms, all with bathrm* ▦ ➓ ⊛ 🔲 🖾 🖃

Location: Rubbing shoulders with some of the most expensive hotels in Rome. If you want to stay in what was once Rome's most fashionable street but don't feel like paying the exorbitant rates of the luxury hotels, this is for you. But a *cappuccino* at any of the cafés nearby will cost up to ten times the price paid in an ordinary bar.

D'INGHILTERRA

Via Bocca di Leone 14, 00187 ☎*672161* ⊠*614552* ⊠*6840828. Map* **5G6** ▥ *105 rms, all with bathrm* ▦ 🅰 ➤ 🅿 🆑 🖾 🖾 ⊛ 🔲 🖾 ⚓ ☕

Location: Close to Piazza di Spagna, in the center of the city's fashionable shop-

ping district. Not so long ago this was a rather dowdy establishment with a dated charm and exotic history. Writers such as Anatole France, Henry James and Ernest Hemingway used to stay here when they came to Rome. The historical associations linger on, but recent modernization has removed all trace of mustiness and decay. Smartness and elegance prevail, and prices have skyrocketed in tandem.

JOLLY

Corso d'Italia 1, 00198 ☎ *8495* 📠 *612293* 📠 *8841104. Map* **6**F7 ▥ *200 rms, all with bathrm* ▦ ⬛ ▤ ⬛ 🅰🅵 ⬛ ⬛ 🆅 ❖ ▢ ▱ ◀ ▲ ♈

Location: Overlooking the Villa Borghese, just E of Via Veneto. This is an ultramodern glass and steel affair, located in a prime position on the edge of the park. Vast public rooms and functional furnishings create a cold and rather impersonal atmosphere, but standards of comfort and efficiency are high. Bedrooms are small, although some have beautiful views over the park.

JOLLY LEONARDO DA VINCI

Via dei Gracchi 324, 00192 ☎ *32499* 📠 *611182* 📠 *3610138. Map* **4**F4 ▥ *256 rms, all with bathrm* ▦ ⬛ ▤ 🅰🅵 ⬛ ⬛ 🆅 ❖ ▢ ▱ ▲ ♈ ♉ ▤

Metropolitana: Lepanto.

Location: Just off Cola di Rienzo, close to the river. This used to be the Grand Hotel L. da Vinci until the Jolly chain got hold of it and turned it into one of its homogeneous but efficient modern facilities. It was completely redecorated and remodeled between 1986 and 1988, a process that has ensured every mod con and removed most of its character. Facilities exist here for massive conferences. There's a third sister, the **Jolly Midas**, located out of town — details may be obtained from central reservation.

LONDRA E CARGILL

Piazza Sallustio 18, 00187 ☎ *4880298 (for reservations* ☎ *460298)* 📠 *622227* 📠 *4746674. Map* **6**G8 ▥ *105 rms, all*

with bathrm ▦ ▤ ⬛ 🅰🅵 ⬛ ▨ ▱ ❖ ▰ ▢ ▱ ◢ ▲ ♈ ▤

Location: Off Via XX Settembre, not far from Stazione Termini and Via Veneto. The exterior might be that of any anonymous late 19thC *palazzo* but, inside, all is gleaming, clean-lined modernity. Bedrooms are simply but attractively furnished. A large conference room, recently renovated, is available.

LORD BYRON

Via G. de Notaris 5, 00197 ☎ *3224541* 📠 *611217* 📠 *3224541. Map* **5**E6 ▥ *50 rms, all with bathrm* ▦ ⬛ ▤ 🅰🅵 ⬛ ⬛ 🆅 ▱ ❖ ▢ ▱ ♉ ⧉ ▲ ♈

Location: Parioli district on the edge of the Villa Borghese. A delightfully secluded hotel not far from the Villa Giulia, Julius III's tranquil summer retreat. No hotel in Rome can be more beautifully furnished, and staying here is like living in an elegant private house.

For most people, the disadvantage of being based outside the city center is more than offset by the quiet parkland location. Riding facilities are available. The hotel also has a restaurant of some distinction in **Le Jardin** (see EATING AND DRINKING).

MARCELLA ❖

Via Flavia 106, 00187 ☎ *4746451* 📠 *621351* 📠 *4815832. Map* **6**G8 ▥ *70 rms, all with bathrm* ▦ ⬛ *by arrangement* 🅰🅵 ⬛ ⬛ 🆅 ⧉ ❖ ▢ ▱ ♈ ▤ Metropolitana: Repubblica.

Location: Just off Via XX Settembre, equidistant from Stazione Termini and Villa Borghese. Comfortable rooms, some with excellent views, and elegant furnishings. The atmosphere is of a cool retreat from the city in which the Marcella is centrally located. It's a small step to Via Veneto, but a giant leap in prices.

MASSIMO D'AZEGLIO

Via Cavour 18, 00184 ☎ *4880646* 📠 *610556* 📠 *4827386. Map* **6**H8 ▥ *200 rms, all with bathrm* ▦ ⬛ ▤ 🅰🅵 ⬛ ⬛ 🆅 ❖ ▢ ▱ ▲ ♈ ▤ Metropolitana: Termini.

Location: Close to Stazione Termini and other public transportation. First opened in 1875 when the district was more salubrious than it is now, the Massimo d'Azeglio has refused to be dragged into the 20thC and, for many people, this is the essence of its appeal. The interior decorations convey more than a hint of nostalgia, and somewhat old-fashioned standards of service prevail. It is a well-run, comfortable hotel, and these solid virtues extend to the excellent restaurant.

MILANI
Via Magenta 12, 00185 ☎4457051
▥614356 ▣4462317. Map 6G8 ▥
78 rms, all with bathrm ▣ *by arrangement*
⬥ ☐ ▱ ☗ *Metropolitana: Termini.*
Location: Near Stazione Termini. An unpretentious, pleasantly furnished hotel in an unexciting but very convenient situation, almost next door to the main rail station, Metropolitana, and city and airport bus terminals. A good choice for those who want modern facilities and services without the expensive wrappings and trappings.

NAPOLEON ✿
Piazza Vittorio Emanuele 105, 00185
☎4467264 ▥611069 ▣4467282. Map
10l8 ▥ *82 rms, all with bathrm* ▥ ▣ *by*
arrangement ▭ ▨ ▣ ▥ ▥ ⬥ ▱ ⛏
☗ ♪ ▭ ☐ *Metropolitana: Vittorio Emanuele.*
Location: Between Stazione Termini and the Colosseum. This first-class hotel faces onto a grandiose 19thC piazza. Despite improvements to the square, however, the surrounding area remains rather seedy. The hotel is reasonably well situated for the Colosseum, the Forums and public transportation; one of the city's most colorful street markets is situated in the piazza. Air-conditioned bedrooms shut out unwelcome noise from traffic and the market beyond, and service is quietly efficient. A pianist plays in the lounge after dinner on Thursday and Saturday, a sign of the hotel's reassuringly traditional style.

DELLE NAZIONI
Via Poli 7, 00187 ☎6792441 ▥614193
▣6782400. Map 5H6 ▥ *83 rms, all with*

bathrm ▥ ▬ ▨ ▨ ▣ ▥ ▥ ⬥ ☐ ▱
⛏ ▭ *Metropolitana: Barberini.*
Location: Near the Trevi Fountain, within walking distance of Piazza di Spagna and most major sights. The central situation is the chief virtue of this once-stuffy hotel. Behind the still-sober facade, a recent modernization has introduced ultra-modern styling, which is perhaps of rather limited appeal.

PORTOGHESI
Via dei Portoghesi 1, 00186 ☎6545133
▥6876976. Map 5H5 ▥ *27 rms, 20 with*
bathrm ▥ ▣ ▥ ▱ ⬥ ▱
Location: Between Piazza Navona and the Mausoleum of Augustus. Nestling beside the church of Sant' Antonio, which is adorned with works by such artists as Canova, in an attractive Renaissance street, this small hotel scores mainly through its wonderfully central position. Not long ago it was one of the cheapest hotels in the old city, but prices went up with the installation of an elevator and general modernization. Atop the Torre dei Frangipane opposite the hotel is a lamp, put there in thanks to the Virgin Mary for saving the life of a baby carried up the tower by a monkey in the 17thC, a story that these days guarantees good behavior among the hotel's younger guests.

QUATTRO FONTANE ✿
Via delle Quattro Fontane 149, 00184
☎4819559. Map 6H7 ▥ *38 rms, 34 with*
bathrm ⬥ ▱ *Metropolitana: Barberini.*
Location: In one of the less frenetic streets in the heart of the city separating the Palazzi Barberini and Quirinale. This offers comfortable lodgings in a conveniently central location at bargain prices.

QUIRINALE
Via Nazionale 7, 00184 ☎4707
▥610332 ▣4820039. Map 6H7 ▥ *210 rms, 200 with bathrm* ▥ ▣ *by*
arrangement ▭ ▨ ▣ ▥ ▥ ⬥ ♿ ☐
▱ ⛏ ⛏ ☗ *Metropolitana: Repubblica.*
Location: Near Piazza della Repubblica and Stazione Termini. A grand hotel with even grander operatic con-

187

nections, the Quirinale was designed by the architect of the adjacent Teatro dell' Opera, to which it has its own private entrance. Verdi stayed here in 1893 for the première of *Falstaff*, and close associations between hotel and opera house continue, the bar of the Quirinale being a favorite rendezvous for pre-curtain drinks.

In Verdi's day, Via Nazionale was not the thundering thoroughfare it is today, and a room at the back was not so essential.

RAPHAEL

Largo Febo 2, 00186 ☎6838881
🖷622396 🖹6878993. Map **5H5** ⅢⅢ
51 rms, all with bathrm ▦ ➡ ᴁ ▣ ▥
▥ ⌂ ⇕ ☐ ⌂ ⟪ ♉ ▤
Location: In the old quarter of the city, close to Piazza Navona. Loaded with style and atmosphere, this ultra-chic hotel conceals a fine blend of antique furniture, *objets d'art* and Oriental rugs behind its vine-covered walls. Bedrooms are on the small side, but some have marvelous views over Renaissance Rome and beyond. Politicians come here en route for the nearby parliament buildings, which gives the added bonus for nervous guests of a 24-hour police guard. The central location is also perfect for sightseers and pilgrims. The hotel is being completely renovated in an attempt to win a fifth star, so the number of rooms available has been temporarily reduced — and the price is soon likely to rise.

SAVOY

Via Ludovisi 15, 00187 ☎4744141
🖷611339 🖹4746812. Map **6G7** ⅢⅢ
120 rms, all with bathrm ▦ ➡ ᴁ ▣ ▥
▥ ⌂ ⇕ ☐ ⅋ ⌂ ♨ ♨ ♉ ♩
Metropolitana: Barberini.
Location: In the smart Ludovisi Quarter, w of Via Veneto. A solid, Neoclassical exterior advertises the sterling virtues of this comfortable, well-run hotel. Inside, all is on an expansive scale, although efforts have been made to make the piano bar and snack bar more intimate, and good service can be guaranteed.

SCALINATA DI SPAGNA ♣

Piazza Trinità dei Monti 17, 00187
☎6793006 🖹6840598. Map **5G6** ⅢⅢ
15 rms, all with bathrm ᴁ ▥ ▱ ⟪ ♠ i
☐ ▤ Metropolitana: Spagna.
Location: Above the Spanish Steps. Smallish, with a marvelous view from its commanding position at the top of the Spanish Steps. It is comfortably furnished and well run. The view is even better from the roof terrace, where breakfast is served in summer.

SOLE AL PANTHEON

Via del Pantheon 63, 00186 ☎6780441
🖹6840689. Map **5H5** ⅢⅢ *28 rms, 25 with bathrm* ⇕ ▱ ♉
Location: Overlooking the Pantheon, in the heart of the old city. This small hotel began life as an inn in the late 15thC and is rich in historical associations. Ariosto, author of the spirited epic *Orlando Furioso*, lodged here in 1513, and Mascagni, composer of the late 19thC operatic perennial, *Cavalleria Rusticana*, wrote several of his works here. Recent renovations have effected a modest face-lift, but the facade retains its Renaissance charm.

TIZIANO

Corso Vittorio Emanuele 110, 00186
☎6865019 🖷6865019 🖹6833827.
Map **5H5** ⅢⅢ *50 rms, 45 with bathrm* ➡
▦ ᴁ ▣ ▥ ▥ ⇕ ▱ ♉ ☐ ▤
Location: Near Piazza Navona, Pantheon and Piazza Venezia. A second-class hotel on one of the busiest streets in Rome, a short bus-ride away from St Peter's. The building began life as a stately patrician palace, but the vast public rooms are now decked out with a curious mix of antique and modern furnishings. Extremely effective double glazing now manages to cut out all noise from the bustling traffic below.

VALADIER

Via della Fontanella 15, 00186 ☎3610592
🖷620873 🖹3201558. Map **5G6** ⅢⅢ
40 rms, 38 with bathrm ▦ ᴁ ➡ ▥ ☐
♉ ♨ ▤
Location: Off the Via del Babuino, close to some of the city's most exclusive

shops. No expense was spared during recent renovations, and guests are left with the impression of being adrift aboard an extremely luxurious ocean liner. An excellent base for the well-heeled who intend spending a lot of time — and money — in the quarter's elegant shops.

VICTORIA ✿

Via Campania 41, 00187 ☎*473931* ᐧ610212 ᐧ4941330. Map **6F7** ▥
110 rms, all with bathrm ▦ ◨ ᐧ ◉ ◧
◱ ✦ ♿ ▢ ◪ ◉ ♨ ♀ ▣

Location: Close to the Villa Borghese and Via Veneto. Tucked away in a quiet street facing the AURELIAN WALL, this is one of the most delightful hotels in the whole of Rome, renowned for its stylish interior and high standard of service. Upstairs, from the upper rooms and roof terrace, there are splendid views over the park. Be warned: visitors tend to become hooked on the Victoria's charms and feel the need to return here again and again.

VILLA DELLE ROSE ✿

Via Vicenza 5, 00185 ☎*4451795. Map* **6G8** ▥ *37 rms, all with bathrm* ◒ ◪ ◉

◨ ▩ ✦ ▢ ◪ ♨ ♀ ▣ *Metropolitana: Termini.*

Location: Close to Stazione Termini and other public transportation. A small, clean, efficiently-run hotel, on the more salubrious side of the central rail station. At one time a fine private residence in this erstwhile elegant district, it still recalls that vanished era with its beautifully proportioned drawing-room (now the lounge) and delightful shady garden, complete with burbling rock pool.

DE LA VILLE

Via Sistina 69, 00187 ☎*67331* ᐧ620836 ᐧ6784213. Map **5G6** ▥ *194 rms, all with bathrm* ◒ *by arrangement* ▦ ◨ ◨ ◪ ◉ ◧ ▩ ♿ ♨ ✦ ▢ ◪ ♨ ♨ ♠ ♀ *Metropolitana: Spagna.*

Location: Near the Spanish Steps. A first-class hotel, well situated for the fashionable shops and cafés around Piazza di Spagna and in Via Veneto. Its elegant image is now somewhat overshadowed by the swanky **Hassler** up the road, but an attractive *al fresco* garden restaurant and spectacular views from the upper bedrooms and roof terrace keep it popular.

Inexpensive hotels (formerly "pensioni")

Although cheaper accommodations can still be found in Rome, don't expect the charming *pensioni* of 19thC grand tours. These days, this type of hostelry is strictly for the young and sturdy who don't mind sharing. They all seem to be located up at least one flight of stairs, and are almost invariably full. Rucksack toters would do well to check the electronic board at Stazione Termini to see what is available — and then double-check by phone. The following list begins with a reasonably detailed description of the best (costing between Ł30,000 and Ł60,000) and is followed by a selection of the rest (mostly under Ł30,000, some well under).

ADRIATIC

Via Vitelleschi 25, 00193 ☎*6869668. Map* **3G3** ▥ *32 rms, 30 with bathrm* ◒ ✦ *Metropolitana: Ottaviano.*
Location: A few yards from Castel Sant'

Angelo. Convenient for the Vatican and Prati shops, this 2-star hotel has comfortable rooms (many with bath/shower) and a TV lounge. Eat out in the many good *trattorie* in the district.

FORTI'S GUEST HOUSE 🏠
Via Fornovo 7, 00192 ☎3212256. Map
4F4 ▢ 22 rms, 10 with bathrm ▱
Metropolitana: Lepanto.
Location: In Prati, across the Tiber from
the city center, but within walking dis-
tance of Piazza del Popolo. This is a
clean and friendly establishment, run
by the American owner and his Italian
wife.

GOLDEN
Via Marche 84, 00187 ☎493746
▣4821660. Map 6G7 ▥ 13 rms, 11 with
bathrm ▦ ▧ ▱ ☀ ▤ *Metropolitana:*
Barberini.
Location: Near the Aurelian Wall, Villa
Borghese and Via Veneto. A modern,
impeccably clean *pensione* on the first
floor of an old house. Cool, off-white
decor and one small, carpeted lounge-
cum-breakfast room. The fashionable
central location and extra facilities
(such as refrigerator bar in every room)
make it slightly expensive for this type
of accommodation.

KATTY 🏠 ♧
Via Palestro 35, 00185 ☎4041216. Map
6G9 ▢ 9 rms, none with bathrm.
Metropolitana: Termini.
Location: Close to Stazione Termini,
city and airport bus termini and Metro-
politana. Modest but well-kept accommodations in an unexciting but
convenient area. Cheap rates make this
pensione a real bargain for students

who don't mind sharing three or four to
a room.

DELLA LUNETTA
Piazza del Paradiso 68, 00186
☎6861080. Map 4I5 ▢ 30 rms, 13 with
bathrm.
Location: A few steps from Piazza
Campo dei Fiori and Piazza Navona.
A pleasant and inexpensive hotel in the
heart of Renaissance Rome, run by a
very friendly family. It is located in an
excellent part of the city for good restaurants with modest prices.

PENSION SUISSE ♧
Via Gregoriana 56, 00187 ☎6783649.
Map 5G6 ▢ 28 rms, 9 with bathrm ☀
Metropolitana: Barberini.
Location: Near the Spanish Steps. A
long-established and efficiently run
pensione, on two floors of an old building in a smart and very central area. The
rooms are large, well-furnished and
kept spotlessly clean, and there's a
lounge as well as a breakfast room.

SOLE AL BISCIONE
Via del Biscione 76, 00186 ☎6540873.
Map 4I5 ▢ 64 rms, 25 with bathrm.
Location: Campo dei Fiori is around
the corner. A simple, quiet and comfortable hotel in one of the most picturesque parts of the city. The garage is
a salvation for anyone contending with
the difficulties of finding a parking
place in this part of town.

BASIC BUT INEXPENSIVE
Accommodations in the following are likely to be on the spartan side,
and bathrooms and bedrooms will probably be communal. However,
the rates are low.

Alimandi Via Veniero 60 ☎318404, map **3**G2
Amati Via V. Veneto 155 ☎493651, map **6**G7
Athena Via Pasquali ☎426379
Azzurra Via del Boccaccio 25 ☎4746531, map **5**G6
Ca' d'Oro Via XX Settembre 91 ☎4755338, map **6**G8
Enotria Via Nazionale 13 ☎4743717, map **6**H8
Isa Via Cicerone 35 ☎380253, map **5**G4
Italia Via Venezia 18 ☎4745550, map **6**H7
Lella Via Palestro 9 ☎484940, map **6**G8
Locanda Marini Via Palestro ☎4047380, map **6**G8

Piemonte   Via Vicenza 34 ☎4452240, map **6**G8
Primavera   Piazza San Pantaleo 3 ☎6543109, map **7**K3

Office-from-office

For the traveling executive who needs more than a hotel room, special
facilities are gradually becoming available. Here are three.

Atlante Star
Via Vitelleschi 34 ☎*6879558* 🖳*622355* 🖳*6799907* ≟ *Map 3G3.*
Complete office for rent within the hotel, including phone, fax, telex, typewriter
and personal bilingual secretary. Extensive conference facilities available. (See
page 182 for hotel details.)

Pinciana Office
Via di Porta Pinciana 4 ☎*4754143* 🖳*621489. Map 5G6.*
Specialists in the provision of offices for rent in a prestige location close to the Via
Veneto, with phone, telex and multilingual secretaries.

Pisana Palace
Via della Pisana 374 ☎*66690* 🖳*620062* 🖳*66161190. Map 5G6.*
This hotel, located in a residential area of Rome, provides a daytime office service,
including access to a fax and a personal computer as well as the assistance of a
multilingual secretary.

Eating and drinking

Dining out in Rome

"Italian cooking" is a misnomer, a catch-all for a hypothetical assemblage of regional, provincial, local and family styles of preparing food with the grace that emanates so spontaneously from Italian hands. But even if *la cucina italiana* did exist, Rome would not be its capital.

Instead, Rome remains — gastronomically — a regional center with some renowned "Roman" specialties, although several were borrowed from outlying places and popularized in the city's *trattorie* and *osterie*. Still, Rome has, undeniably, a way of cooking or, more to the point, a way of eating all of its own. And even if the city's restaurants rarely garner top ratings in the guidebooks, dining out in them can be a delight, a carnival of colors, flavors, odors, moods and sounds, uniquely and unabashedly Roman.

One of Rome's pleasures is *al fresco* dining, whether the setting is a manicured garden, a terrace under a shady pergola, or rickety tables and chairs set nonchalantly in a narrow street. From April to October they become not only places to eat but also centers for the favored Roman pastime of people-watching, a diversion highlighted by the parade of street musicians and impromptu entertainers who may pass round the hat in scores of places in an evening, but who are especially evident in Trastevere and around Piazza Navona.

Cooking in Italy has become more uniform in recent times, as country traditions have given way to urban expediencies. Beside the omnipresent *pizzerie,* there are ever more *tavole calde* and *tavole fredde* (hot and cold buffets), snack bars and fast-food shops catering to people with no time for a five-course meal. For anyone in a hurry or on a tight budget, they provide an often tasty alternative for at least one meal of the day.

Despite these trends, however, regional cooking continues to thrive. Rome so dominates Latium that *la cucina romana* has come to represent the region, even if the city's cooks tend to interpret the fare more flamboyantly than do their rural counterparts.

Roman cooking is not, as a rule, refined. Although hints of ancient Roman recipes remain (notably in combinations of sweet and sour), the lavish concoctions of the papal and royal courts and the bourgeoisie of olden days are mostly forgotten. What survive are the clever improvisations of the poor. Authentic Roman dishes are often based on rudimentary, even coarse, ingredients — pasta, chickpeas, tripe, salt cod, broad beans, sweetbreads, artichokes, brains, oxtails, pig's trotters, mussels, anchovies and salt pork, flavored with garlic, herbs, vinegar, mint, wine and sharp *pecorino* cheese. But the results are hardly humble: Roman cooking is as flavorful and sensuous as any in Italy.

Nor is there a complete lack of luxury. Baby lamb *(abbacchio),* kid *(capretto)* and sucking pig *(porchetta)* are preferred meats. Fresh Mediterranean seafood is devoured in the capital, despite its high cost. And the Roman countryside provides exquisite fresh greens and vegetables, which arrive daily at the open-air markets.

THE MENU

A complete Roman repast starts with *antipasti,* sometimes selected from a table laden with a dazzling assortment of cold cuts, cooked and raw vegetables, omelets, olives and shellfish.

Then comes pasta, here, as elsewhere, more often than not the high point of a meal. Pasta is part of what is generally known as the *primo piatto* (which also takes in soups, risottos, polenta, crepes and dumplings). But more than a course or a category, pasta is a national institution. Rome's specialties include *spaghetti alla carbonara* (tossed with bacon, garlic, pepper, grated cheese and raw beaten eggs); *bucatini all' amatriciana* (thin tubes with chili peppers, bacon, often tomatoes and grated *pecorino); penne all' arrabbiata* (short, ribbed tubes with a sauce hot enough to make your eyes water); and *fettuccine al burro* (light egg noodles with butter, cream and Parmesan).

For a fuller understanding of the menu, refer to the MENU DECODER on page 268.

Many restaurants provide a choice between meat or fish for a main course. You will notice that restaurants always specify on the menu whether their fish is fresh or frozen, as required by law. Whichever, fish is invariably expensive — payment is often by the *etto* (100g) — and when you select it you will in effect lift the restaurant into a higher price band than we have indicated in HOW TO USE THIS BOOK on page 7.

If you are serious about fish it is wise to select a place noted for fresh products (**La Rosetta**, for instance, where grilled *scampi* are the specialty). Be sure also to try lamb or chicken *alla cacciatora* (with rosemary, garlic and vinegar), *saltimbocca* (veal fillet with *prosciutto* and sage cooked in butter and white wine) and *coda alla vaccinara* (stewed oxtail). Vegetables or salad are usually served separately. Peas are excellent in season, and also not to be missed are artichokes, whether *carciofi alla romana* (sautéed in oil, garlic and mint) or *carciofi alla giudia* (flattened like flowers and deep-fried).

Fresh dessert cheeses may follow: perhaps *ricotta* sprinkled with sugar and ground coffee, or *ovoline,* small "eggs" of *mozzarella.* Romans often conclude with fresh fruit or the fruit cup known as *macedonia. Gelato* is always good in Rome and, in some places, cakes and tarts are irresistible. The final touch to any meal is a thick *espresso.*

Although some Italian restaurants have adopted the French-inspired set menu, Romans prefer to order *à la carte.* The bill will include bread and cover charge, food and drinks, service (usually 15 percent) and VAT. On top of this, the waiter will expect a personal tip of around 10 percent.

The *menu turistico* at a fixed price includes bread and cover charge, first and second course with vegetables and fruit or dessert, sometimes wine, and service and tax. The price may be attractive, but in Rome the food will be more likely to include leftovers than the house's best. You would probably be better off at a *tavola calda* or *pizzeria*.

SELECTING A RESTAURANT

Rome's thousands of eating places vary widely in type, price and quality. In theory, the *ristorante* is the largest and most elegant establishment. The word *trattoria* suggests simplicity, often with home cooking and family-style service. The *osteria* or *hostaria* should be simpler still: in Roman terms a place where open wine is served by the liter (or half or quarter) and customers can dine on simple dishes or sandwiches or even on food of their own. But in practice the breakdown is not always so clear. Some *ristoranti* are rather cramped and modest; some *trattorie* are large, luxurious and expensive; and some *osterie* are fully-fledged restaurants (the **Hostaria dell' Orso**, for instance, is one of the most famous and fancy places in Rome).

As an international center, Rome has several foreign restaurants — French, Chinese, Spanish, German, Arab, American, Japanese — although few that are inspiring. A better bet, if you feel like something other than Roman, would be one of the many regional restaurants, such as **El Toulà** (Venetian), **Taverna Giulia** (Genoese) and **Il Buco** (Tuscan).

Although fast-food outlets are beginning to change Roman eating habits, most Italians are brought up to relish their food and the ceremony surrounding its preparation and consumption. As a consequence, they tend to linger over their meals, so reservations are always advisable, even on "quiet" weekday evenings. Traditionally, weekend evenings are reserved for the family excursion to the pizzeria, so choose another night if a peaceful atmosphere is desired.

Our A to Z selection of restaurants has been made not only to give a good choice of price and area, but also with consideration to atmosphere and the style of cuisine. Addresses, telephone numbers and nearest Metropolitana stations are given, as well as symbols showing particularly luxurious (△) or simple (📟) restaurants, and those that represent good value (♦). Other symbols show price categories, charge/credit cards and other noteworthy points. See KEY TO SYMBOLS on page 7 for the full list of symbols. Times are specified when restaurants are **closed**.

A selection of fast-food shops follows the main list of restaurants.

Drinking in Rome

Rome, despite appearances to the contrary, is a wine town of sorts. Romans still seem to prefer "local" wines, mostly white, from the Castelli Romani: Frascati, Marino, Colli Albani, Velletri and less specific *appellations*. These can be eminently drinkable when young. Because they are soft, rather full-bodied for whites and well-rounded, they serve

RESTAURANTS CLASSIFIED BY AREA

PANTHEON/PIAZZA DEL POPOLO
Alfredo alla Scrofa
Alfredo L'Originale
L'Angoletto
Dal Bolognese
La Buca di Ripetta
Il Buco
La Campana
La Capricciosa
L'Eau Vive to
La Fontanella
Hostaria dell' Orso
La Majella
L'Orso Ottanta
Pino e Dino
La Rosetta
El Toulà

PARIOLI
Ambasciata d'Abruzzo
Le Jardin

PIAZZA NAVONA
Trattoria l'Antiquario
Il Convivio
Passetto

PIAZZA DI SPAGNA AND TREVI
Da Mario
Al Moro
Otello alla Concordia to
Ranieri
Re degli Amici

PRATI
Les Etoiles
Taberna dei Gracchi

PONTE VITTORIO AND LARGO ARGENTINA
Amapola
Angelino a Tor Margana
Arnaldo
Da Pancrazio
Polese
Taverna Giulia

TERMINI AND COLOSSEUM
Da Nazzareno
Da Nerone
Taverna Flavia

TRASTEVERE
Comparone
Romolo
Sabatini I and II

TRIONFALE AND MONTE MARIO
La Caravella
Nuraghe Sardo

VIA VENETO AND CORSO D'ITALIA
ABC
Al Fogher
George's
Il Giardino
Giovanni
Girarrosto Toscano
Piccolo Mondo
Sans Souci

---

as a soothing counterpoint to the somewhat aggressive flavors of much Roman food. Sometimes, though, they can be so unpalatable — especially the open wines served in many *trattorie* and *osterie* — that the only solution is to dilute them with bubbly mineral water, as the Romans often do.

Most good Roman restaurants provide bottled wines from the Castelli and elsewhere in Latium, along with nationally known types such as Chianti, Orvieto, Verdicchio, Pinot Grigio and Barolo. Italy has more than 200 zones of *denominazione di origine controllata,* and wines so labeled are authentic but not necessarily of high quality. Some of Italy's — and Latium's — best wines are categorized simply as *vino da tavola* (table wine). Latium's rarities include the red Torre Ercolana, Colle Picchioni, Castel San Giorgio and the red and white Fiorano, grown just outside Rome. Also worth trying are Maccarese, the red Cesanese, Cervéteri red and white and the bizarrely titled Est!Est!Est!

Serious students of Italian wine can browse through well-stocked shops such as the **Enoteca Trimani** *(Via Goito 20, map 6 G8)*, which carries bottles from every region and most nations, the **Enoteca Costantini** *(Piazza Cavour 16b, map 4 G4)*, the **Enoteca Palombi** *(Piazza Testaccio 40, map 7 L4)*, the **Enoteca Roffi-Isabelli** *(Via della Croce 76a, map 5 G6)* and **Il Goccetto** *(Via dei Banchi Vecchi 14, map 4 H4)*. In some *enoteche*, such as **Cavour 313** *(Via Cavour 313, map 9 I7)* and **Cul de Sac 1** *(Piazza Pasquino 73, map 4 H5)*, you can buy a good bottle chosen from a vast selection of wine or dine on the best regional products, such as cheese and charcuterie.

The traditional *aperitivo* is vermouth, light or dark, dry or semisweet, with a shaving of lemon peel and, in summer, ice. Other favorites are Campari Soda, Punt e Mes and Aperol, all with a bitter taste that stimulates the appetite. Increasingly popular as an aperitif is a flute of sparkling wine, preferably a *brut spumante* from Pinot or Prosecco grapes.

The classic finale to a Roman meal is the anis-flavored *sambuca* with *le mosche* (flies) — three coffee beans to munch on while you sip. Similarly sweet are *amaretto* and Strega, although these days Scotch whisky seems to be the leading *digestivo,* and there are many good Italian grappas and brandies to choose from. A lighter alternative would be a glass of sparkling Asti Spumante.

Rome's restaurants A to Z

ABC
Via Veneto 66 ☎ *4740950. Map* **6**G7 ▥
▤ ▢ ♠ ▦ ⊕ ▣ ▦
In the restaurant of the **Ambasciatori Palace** (see WHERE TO STAY), you are guaranteed top service and elegant surroundings. From May to October, meals can be enjoyed on the hotel's *terrazza,* which is probably the best way to enjoy the Via Veneto. Across the street is the building in which Brig. Gen. Robert T. Frederick set up his HQ on the eve of the liberation of Rome in June 1944 — now the American embassy.

ALFREDO ALLA SCROFA ♣
Via della Scrofa 104 ☎ *6540163. Map* **4**H5
▥ ▢ ▭ ♠ ▦ ⊕ ▦ ↻ *Closed Tues.*
Way back in the 1930s, Douglas Fairbanks and Mary Pickford presented Alfredo, "King of Fettuccine," with a golden fork and spoon. Thereafter, to have your pasta served with these celebrated implements was an honor reserved only for the very rich and famous, whose photographs literally paper the walls. Nowadays, even common mortals can enjoy this favor, but doubts have been expressed as to the authenticity of the fork and spoon. When Alfredo died, many years ago, his son left the restaurant to his father's partners and founded one of his own, and indeed there are now several restaurants in Rome of this name, all under different management. The son now claims exclusive possession of the true fork and spoon, and the whereabouts of the Fairbanks-Pickford originals remain one of Rome's many mysteries, although the owners here will swiftly produce a set from a drawer under the till. Alfredo alla Scrofa is still a good restaurant, but it is hard to maintain a famous reputation over more than half a century. All the pasta dishes are still superb, and the rest is more than acceptable so long as you avoid the elaborate dishes. Added attractions are a good wine list and soulful guitar player.

ALFREDO L'ORIGINALE
Piazza Augusto Imperatore 30 ☎*6878734.*
Map 4G5 ▥ ▭ ▰ ▮ ▱ ▤ ▨ ▩
Closed Sun.
Another set of golden cutlery, and more
walls lined with photographs of the famous, can be found in this restaurant
just off the Via del Corso, where the
third-generation Alfredo keeps the
tradition of the royal family of *fettuccine*
alive and spreads the fame by cheerfully posing for photographs tossing
pasta for all and sundry. His claim to be
the original Alfredo to whom Fairbanks
and Pickford presented the fork and
spoon may rather stretch the truth — he
can only have been a noodle in his
father's eye at the time — but, publicity
aside, a mean bowl of *fettuccine* is produced here. Unashamedly aimed at the
tourist with musicians who are old
enough to have serenaded Fairbanks
and Pickford, it is nonetheless most enjoyable.

AMAPOLA
Via Panico 83 ☎*6873666. Map 4H4* ▥
▤ ▭ ▮ ▰ ▤ ▨ ▩ *Closed Sun.*
Columns and potted palms set off the
austere elegance of Mario Forte's excellent restaurant, near Ponte Sant' Angelo,
where the digestion of a fine meal is
assisted by able musicians.

AMBASCIATA D'ABRUZZO ♣
Via Tacchini 26 ☎*8078256* ▣*874964.*
Map 5D6 ▥ ▭ ▰ ▤ ▨ ▩ *Closed Sun;*
three weeks in Aug.
This Parioli restaurant is nothing special
to look at either inside or out, but it has
loads of atmosphere and the food is
excellent. As soon as you've sat down,
you'll be given a basket of assorted
salami to nibble at while you concentrate on choosing the serious food. This
could be *raviolini* made with fresh *ricotta* from the mountains, or a delicately flavored mutton stew made with
castrato. Both cheese and meat are de-
livered daily from Abruzzo, from where
the Montepulciano wine also comes.
There is a vast choice of regional
cheeses to round off the meal, and
owner Italo Poggi takes a personal in-

terest in the Abruzzi wines he brings in
to lubricate the whole affair.

ANGELINO A TOR MARGANA
Piazza Margana 37 ☎*6783328. Map 8I6*
▥ ▭ ▰ ▮ *Closed Sun; Aug.*
Angelino used to be a kind of artistic
center as well as a good restaurant.
There was even a Tor Margana Prize,
much sought after by painters and
writers. Now Angelino rests on its lau-
rels and the names of the famous are
kept only to ennoble the less traditional
items on the menu, such as *Pigeon à la
Sartre.* The simple Roman dishes are
best. This is a delightful place to eat in
summer, when candlelit tables are set
in the piazza outside. It's a quiet corner
of old Rome, relatively free of traffic,
with only a few stray cats to bother you.

L'ANGOLETTO
Piazza Rondanini 51 ☎*6861203. Map 4H5*
▥ ▭ ▤ ▨ ▩ ▤ *Closed Mon; one
week in Aug.*
A lively, noisy, extrovert *trattoria* specializing in fish, and just the place to go
for rowdy badinage with droll waiters
— assuming your Italian is good
enough to keep up with them. The hectic style of L'Angoletto was originally
the creation of one Alfredo Pantalone;
since his departure, older habitués
claim that the place has become too
sedate and respectable. You may not
agree. Try to resist the lure of the in-
numerable mouthwatering *antipasti,* or
you won't have room for the superbly
fresh fish or enormous Mediterranean
prawns — some say the very best seafood in Rome. Mushrooms are another
Angoletto specialty: from late summer
to late fall, they have the finest *porcini*
and freshest *ovoli.*

ARNALDO ♣
Via Grotta Pinta 8 ☎*6861915. Map 4I5* ▥
▭ ▰ *Closed Tues; Aug.*
Arnaldo's can be hard to find. It's near
Piazza Campo dei Fiori, tucked away in
a narrow street that still follows the
curve of the ancient Theater of Pompey,
and only advertises its presence by a
small nameplate beside the door. Ar-

naldo is painter turned chef, and his restaurant and food both reflect his fascination with the unusual. Surrounded by Art Nouveau lanterns and photographs of the dance, you can spend a delightful evening experiencing the ultimate variations on the theme of pasta (with corn, grapes or even cabbage sauce). And if you gain Arnaldo's confidence, he will charm you with his personal reminiscences of the world of ballet, of which he is a devoted fan. Nureyev and Fracci have been seen dining here, but don't ask for autographs: Arnaldo is very jealous of his clients' privacy. There is a good choice of wines, despite Arnaldo's total abstinence.

DAL BOLOGNESE ♣
Piazza del Popolo 1-2 ☎ *3611426. Map* 5F5 ▥ ▭ ▰ 🚗 *Closed Sun evening; Mon; two weeks in Aug. Metropolitana: Flaminio.*

Dal Bolognese is an eminently fashionable place to be seen at, and critics might argue that the glamorous outfits of the female clientele are even more remarkable than the cooking — which is, of course, Bolognese in inspiration. But all must agree that the *gran carrello misto dei bolliti* — trolley of boiled meats (tongue, chicken, beef and stuffed pigs' trotters) served with *salsa verde* (parsley and garlic sauce) or *mostarda di Cremona* (fruit in aspic) — is really outstanding. Service is fast and reliable and you can dine on the terrace all year round (behind glass screens in winter). The restaurant is decorated with a fine collection of modern paintings, but these can't compete with the Baroque splendor of PIAZZA DEL POPOLO outside even though the view from Dal Bolognese is slightly restricted. To appreciate the whole piazza, go next door to **Rosati** (see REFRESHMENTS) for your *aperitivo* or your coffee.

LA BUCA DI RIPETTA ☕ ♣
Via di Ripetta 36 ☎ *3219391. Map 4G5* ▥ ▤ ▭ *Closed Sun evening; Mon; Aug.*

A small, friendly *trattoria,* where you must arrive very early indeed if you

have not reserved. Its popularity is well-deserved, for the prices are very reasonable and the good-natured *padrone* is in constant attendance. The food, which has just a slight bias toward Roman specialties, is wholesome and straightforward. The restaurant consists of one room only, its high walls cheerfully festooned with ornamental bric-à-brac — enormous bellows, great copper pans, even rustic ox-harnesses.

IL BUCO ♣
Via Sant' Ignazio 8 ☎ *6793298. Map* 5H6 ▥ ▤ ▭ ▰ 🆔 🌐 *Closed Mon; Aug 15-31.*

This Tuscan *osteria* was opened in 1891 by Raffaele Masini and used to be so small that it earned itself the nickname of *il buco* (the hole). Now, three generations later, Il Buco is a large and celebrated restaurant. Nicola, the present owner, is proud of the fact that he gets all his basic ingredients from the Tuscan *campagna,* and his fall *porcini* (mushrooms) and winter game from the Tuscan woods. Start your meal with *crostini* (usually liver canapés), and follow these with the *ribollita,* the traditional thick cabbage soup. Remember that the enormous *fiorentina* steak serves two. And you'll want to leave room for the *cantuccini di Prato,* delicious little almond biscuits that you dip into sweet, rich *vin santo.* You can't escape the Chianti wine, and the service is a bit rough, but that's all part and parcel of the great Tuscan tradition.

LA CAMPANA ☕ ♣
Vicolo della Campana 18 ☎ *6867820. Map* 4G5 ▥ ▤ ▭ 🆔 *Closed Mon; Aug.*

The first mention of La Campana as an inn appears in the Roman census of 1518, so don't be surprised if the menu concentrates on plain, traditional Roman fare. You should also be prepared for a limited choice of wines (this too is Roman tradition), but Ida Jacobini's superb cooking will more than compensate for the deficiencies of the cellar. Try the *vignarola,* a traditional vegetable soup (served only in the evening), or the less well-known

Roman specialties, *stufatino al sedano* (stew with celery) and *alicette gratinate* (anchovies au gratin).

LA CAPRICCIOSA ✿

Largo dei Lombardi 8 ☎ *6878636. Map 5G5* ▯▯ ▭ 🚗 🅰🅴 ⊙ *Closed Tues; two weeks in Aug.*

Better known as a *pizzeria*, this is in fact a general *trattoria,* with loads of room (except Sunday lunchtime) downstairs and on the first floor. There is an unusually wide selection of Roman and regional dishes — a score of variations on the theme of *pasta* and twice that number of main courses — plus some excellent *antipasti* and mouthwatering desserts. Pizzas are served after 7.30pm. The restaurant naturally claims that the now ubiquitous *pizza capricciosa* (the one with a bit of everything on it) was their own invention and that theirs are still the best in Rome.

LA CARAVELLA ⛴

Via degli Scipioni 32b ☎ *3729159. Map 4F4* ▯ ▭ 🍴 *Closed Thurs; Jan. Metropolitana: Ottaviano.*

A reliable, family-run *trattoria,* serving plain, wholesome Roman fare and *vino da tavola* in simple, unpretentious surroundings. Prices are very reasonable, and the close proximity to the VATICAN MUSEUMS makes this an ideal place to enjoy a relaxing lunch during a daylong tour of the galleries.

COMPARONE

Piazza in Piscinula 47 ☎ *5816249. Map 8J5* ▯▯ ▭ 🚗 🅰🅴 ⊙ 🈺 *Closed Mon.*

This is the place for an authentic evening out in Trastevere, so don't allow yourself to be herded into the garish tourist traps nearby, which seem to have an arrangement with the driver of every coach and horse-drawn cab in Rome. If you sit out on the terrace of the restaurant, you are surrounded by medieval buildings, and the cooking is equally authentic — mainly Roman, with traditional dishes of brains, sweetbreads, liver and tripe. For the less adventurous there is a good variety of grills, cooked either *ai ferri* (over char-

coal) or *alla piastra* (on a hotplate). As in all good Roman restaurants, the *padrone* will tell you that Marcello Mastroianni is frequently to be seen dining there, but in this case one can believe him, for the actor has a house just around the corner.

IL CONVIVIO

Via dell'Orso 44 ☎ *6869432. Map 4H5* ▯▯ ▰ 🅰🅴 ⊙ 🆑 🈺 *Closed Sun.*

The brothers Troiani opened this restaurant in 1989, and it immediately won a reputation as one of the finest in Rome. Angelo Troiani's creative cuisine, chosen from a menu that changes every few weeks, is an unfailing surprise and delight to the palate. Other commendable features are a vast and intelligent wine list, extremely polite service (on the slow side), and a general atmosphere of calm sophistication. Given all this, the bill is reasonable.

L'EAU VIVE

Via Monterone 85 ☎ *6541095. Map 4H5* ▯▯ *(tourist menu) to* ▯▯▯ 🍽 ▭ 🍴 *lunchtime only* 🅰🅴 🈺 *Closed Sun; Aug.*

In a grand 16thC palace built for Pope Leo X, this unusual restaurant is run by the *Vergini laiche cristiane di azione cattolica missionaria per mezzo del lavoro* (Christian Virgins of Catholic Missionary Action through Work). Their mission is to run restaurants in all parts of the world, spreading the twin gospels of Christianity and (mainly) French cuisine. Evangelization has been successful, judging from the crowds of prelates and politicians from the nearby Senate. Even the present Pope, when still a cardinal, was a habitué. For tourists, the main attraction is the lay virgins themselves, who come from the French ex-colonies and dress in colorful national costumes. The food — classic French and French colonial dishes — is less compelling, even when enriched with exotic fruits. The lunchtime tourist menu is, however, a real bargain. The special dish — changed daily — may originate anywhere from the Philippines to North Africa. The wine list is comprehensive but unexceptional.

Don't be surprised if, at 10pm, the piped music is switched off so that the assembled company, led by the waitresses, can sing hymns in honor of the Virgin Mary.

LES ETOILES △

Via Vitelleschi 34 ☎*6873233. Map* **4G4** ▥ ▭ ▬ ⊑ ⛨ ≪ *AE* ⊙ ⊙ *VISA*

The restaurant of the **Atlante Star** (see WHERE TO STAY), commanding one of the finest views in Rome. You're so close to St Peter's that it's sinful not to say grace, but Sardinian chef Lino Pisu quickly brings the mind back to matters worldly with beautifully presented *antipasti* that are as artfully arranged as they are tasty. The rest of the meal lives up to the promise, and the wine list is excellent. Classical music adds to the magic of watching the sun disappear behind the dome of St Peter's. A memorable evening is assured.

AL FOGHER

Via Tevere 13b ☎*8417032. Map* **6F8** ▥ ▭ ⊑ ⛨ ⛝ *AE* ⊙ *Closed Sun.*

Two decades ago, Signora Pina Gaspardis d'Eva realized a lifetime's ambition by opening her own restaurant. She called it Al Fogher, which means "at the hearth" in the dialect of her native Friuli. It soon established a reputation as one of the best restaurants in Rome. Signora Gaspardis' *forte* are her *risotti*, prepared with such loving care and devotion that they are veritable works of art. She is especially proud of her midwinter specialty made with apples, *risotto alla mele della Val-di-non*. The menu also boasts an exotic list of hams. Forget the humble pig, forget wild boar — Al Fogher offers you chamois ham and the ham of the saiga from the steppes of Kazakhstan. The wines naturally come from the Friuli. Merlot, Refosco and Cabernet di Friuli are the principal reds, while outstanding among the whites are Sauvignon, Pinot Bianco and Ribolla. The restaurant is just outside the old city walls, near both the VILLA BORGHESE and the PORTA PIA.

LA FONTANELLA ✿

Largo della Fontanella di Borghese 86 ☎*6871582. Map* **5G5** ▥ ▭ ⛨ *AE* ⊙ *VISA Closed Mon; Sat lunch.*

A deservedly popular restaurant, brimming over with old-world charm and efficiency. In summer you can eat outside in the shadow of the PALAZZO BORGHESE. The Tuscan cuisine, which includes a magnificent *pappardelle al sugo di lepre*, always attracts a quorum of deputies from the nearby Parliament.

GEORGE'S △

Via Marche 7 ☎*484575. Map* **6G7** ▥ ▭ ⊑ ⛨ ⛛ ⋔ *AE* ⊙ *VISA Closed Sun; Aug.*

George, ex-barman and skilled dice-player, created this restaurant just after the war to cater to the rich *Dolce Vita* of nearby Via Veneto. Those balmy days are long since gone, but George's successfully maintains the discreet luxury and hushed elegance of that vanished era. It remains one of the city's most prestigious restaurants. Signor Pavia, manager and *maître,* runs an impeccable service in the softly-lit rooms and on the really enchanting garden terrace. The food is unexceptional, however, and you'd be well advised to steer clear of some of the more bizarre-sounding items on the menu. You'd do just as well — if not better — sticking with simple *pastas,* the *piatto del giorno* and perhaps a *crème brûlée,* although you can't go wrong with the special salad *(insalata alla Morra)* or *carpaccio.* George's has one of the best cellars in Rome, and a piano bar provides evening entertainment. Reservation is recommended, and jacket and tie are obligatory for men.

IL GIARDINO ⛝ ✿

Via Zucchelli 29 ☎*4885202. Map* **5G6** ▥ ⛝ ▭ ⛨ *AE* ⊙ *VISA Closed Mon; one week in Aug. Metropolitana: Barberini.*

Il Giardino is typical of the best type of simple, inexpensive Roman trattoria. All that matters is the food: the look of the place is simply irrelevant. In summer, you have the choice of eating inside (on two floors) or under a canopy of vines in the little garden past the kitchen. The business is run by a consortium of the waiters, which seems to guarantee excellent quality and service.

GIOVANNI

Via Marche 64 ☎*4821834. Map* **6***G7* ▦
▤ ⊏⊐ ⚍ ▣ ▨ *Closed Fri evening; Sat;*
Aug.

Close to the bright lights of the Via Veneto is one of the city's many regional restaurants. Founded by Giovanni Sbrega, it is now largely run by son Franco and daughter Lilli. The family come from the Adriatic sea town of Ancona, as does the marvelously fresh fish they serve. But seafood is not the only attraction here: a fine range of good honest dishes is conjured up in the family kitchen, with soups prepared from the purest beef and chicken broths. The wonderfully warming lentil soup, *zuppa di lenticchie di Castelluccio,* is only available in winter. The *calamaretti dell' Adriatico ai ferri* are also seasonal; these are small grilled squid, even smaller and more delicately flavored than those from the Tyrrhenian sea, but only available for a couple of months in the spring. The pasta, freshly made every day by mother, includes *tagliolini al fegato d'oca* in a delicious goose-liver sauce.

GIRARROSTO TOSCANO

Via Campania 29 ☎*4821899. Map* **6***G7*
▦ ⊏⊐ ⚍ ▣ ▣ ▨ ▨ *Closed Wed.*

Concealed in the cellar of a huge building facing onto the ancient AURELIAN WALL, Girarrosto Toscano is a prize-winning restaurant of special appeal to the night-owls of the Via Veneto. Last orders are not until 12.30am. The food is mainly top-quality beef and veal, grilled on an open wood-fired oven. But first you can indulge in melon, Parma ham and *ovoline* (small *mozzarella* cheeses), which, like all the best *antipasti,* arrive at your table almost the moment you sit down. Fast in the daylight hours if you are planning to dine here: portions are generous and the desserts are superb. Girarrosto is expensive but not over-priced, and the service is meticulous.

HOSTARIA DELL' ORSO ⌂

Via dei Soldati 25 ☎*6864250. Map* **4***H5*
▦ ⊏⊐ ⚍ ▾ ◐ ⋔ ▣ ▣ ▨ *Open*
evenings only. Closed Sun.

With or without its fabulous setting, L'Hostaria dell' Orso would be a first-class restaurant, but the beautiful 13thC palace is nevertheless the main attraction. A lofty, richly decorated chamber serves as dining room, and the atmosphere is about as far removed from the 20thC as the old wooden beams that may have looked down on such illustrious diners as Dante and Rabelais in the days when this was just a simple inn. Nowadays L'Hostaria is one of the most expensive restaurants in the capital, boasting a piano bar and a nightclub upstairs.

LE JARDIN ⌂

Via G. de Notaris 5 ☎*3224541. Map* **5***E6*
▦ ⊏⊐ ▣ ▣ ▣ ▣ ▨ *Closed Sun.*

In a beautiful setting above the Villa Borghese, Le Jardin is the restaurant of the **Lord Byron** hotel (see WHERE TO STAY) and a rare Italian link in the prestigious Relais et Châteaux chain. It's easy to understand how the owner, Amedeo Ottaviani (to whom the luxurious Regency Umbria hotel in Florence also belongs), has managed to overcome the usual native mistrust of all things French and foreign. Peaceful surroundings, impeccable service and a very reliable international cuisine have made Le Jardin one of the top restaurants in Rome, with a reputation quite independent of its excellent but perhaps less celebrated mother hotel. It's ideal for important business lunches, and special dinners can be arranged with reasonable notice. Obviously, expect to pay top prices.

LA MAJELLA ♣

Piazza Sant' Apollinare 45 ☎*6864174.*
Map **4***H5* ▦ ▤ ⊏⊐ ⊞ ▣ ▣ ▣ ▨
Closed Sun; Aug 10-25.

In a central location close to PIAZZA NAVONA, this is a colorful *trattoria* with reliably good food and loads of atmosphere. The building is mid-16thC, with great brick arches separating the high, beamed ceilings of the rooms. There is a wide variety of dishes, with the emphasis on specialties from Abruzzo.

DA MARIO ♣
Via della Vite 55 ☎*6783818. Map* **5**G6 ▨▢
▤ ▭ ▰ ▣ ◈ ▨ *Closed Sun; Aug 5-30.*
Stuffed birds in the window give the game away about Mario Mariani's seasonal specialty. And inside, near the door, is another clue to this restaurant's identity: a large glass bottle full of *cannellini* (white beans) simmering in oil. These are *fagioli al fiasco,* as much a constant of Tuscan wining and dining as the Chianti flasks set on the tables. One of Mario's great virtues is that he creates fine Tuscan food without the pompous rhetoric and parochial pride common among Tuscan restaurateurs. There are *frittate* (vegetable omelets) and the usual *crostini* (in this case, liver canapés) to start the meal. Or you can have *ribollita* (heavy but delicious cabbage soup) or *pappa col pomodoro* (a dish made with tomatoes and bread, very simple and very good). If you are lucky you can eat (three times a week) *stracotto* (beef stewed in wine and tomato sauce). Failing that, settle for the customary but excellent *bistecca alla fiorentina* (serves two). The only fish worth considering is the superb *baccalà* (dried cod), but this is served only on canonical Friday. If you stick to the good house wine you can eat here for a very reasonable sum, and that's why it's hard to find an empty table.

AL MORO
Vicolo delle Bollette 13 (off Via del Lavatore) ☎*6783495. Map* **5**H6 ▨▢ ▤ ✿ ▭ ▰
Closed Sun; Aug.
Il Moro (the Moor), the owner of this restaurant, starred in one of Fellini's movies as an arrogant and pompous upstart in the decadent reign of Nero. Something of the master's screen example must have brushed off on the waiters, for they can boast of being the bluffest in Rome since Antiquity. The food is really excellent, however: good Roman fare, with many original dishes, all prepared from the freshest and best

quality ingredients. If you can endure noise, crowds and scornful waiters, you will have one of the best meals in Rome. Reserve a table before you go — and good luck!

DA NAZZARENO ☕ ♣
Via Magenta 35-37 ☎*4957782. Map* **6**G8
▢ ▭ ▰ ▣ ◈ ▨ *Closed Wed; last two weeks in Aug. Metropolitana: Termini.*
A bustling, fast-moving *trattoria,* only one block away from Stazione Termini, the main rail station. Entirely without sophistication, it owes its popularity to a happy combination of good, mainly Roman food and low prices.

DA NERONE
Via delle Terme di Tito 96 ☎*4745207. Map* **9**I7 ▨ ▭ ▰ *Closed Sun; Aug.*
Despite the daily cavalcade of buses driving up to park on the Colle Oppio, the phlegmatic Eugenio de Santis seems almost unaware of the thousands of tourists flocking to the nearby COLOSSEUM. Thus his small family restaurant facing the overgrown ruins of NERO'S GOLDEN HOUSE has far more Roman atmosphere than the flashier eating places down below in Piazza del Colosseo. The fairly limited menu will not tax the tourist's vocabulary: the *antipasti* are good and, if you like a rare steak, the *filetto* is recommended. One concession Eugenio makes to foreign visitors is a never-ending supply of French fries. It is surprisingly easier to get a table here at night than at lunchtime.

NURAGHE SARDO
Viale Medaglie d'Oro 50a ☎*382485. Map* **3**F2 ▨ ▤ ✿ ▭ ▰ *Closed Wed; Aug.*
If you've just spent the day in the VATICAN MUSEUMS and feel like eating somewhere reasonably cheap and irresistibly cheerful, try this off-center restaurant in the Trionfale Quarter. Rome is full of restaurants that specialize in regional cooking, but Nuraghe Sardo does more than re-create characteristic Sardinian dishes. Through its colorful rustic atmosphere it succeeds in conveying something of the island's spirit as well. Surrounded by festoons of garlic,

chilies and Sardinian *salami,* and banks of wine bottles, you can tuck into a hearty *spaghetti alla bottarga* — pasta flavored with gray mullet roe — and *maialetto sardo* — mouthwatering roast sucking pig. Wash them down with the white Vernaccia di Oristano or the fruity rich red Canonau — both from the island — and mop them up with *pane sardo* — home-baked rye bread. To round off your meal, don't miss the fresh Sardinian *pecorino.*

L'ORSO OTTANTA (L'Orso 80)
Via dell' Orso 33 ☎ *6864904. Map 4H5* ▨ 📧 🐾 ⟱ 🅰🅱 🅾 🆑 🎴 *Closed Mon; Aug 8-20.*

Like many Roman restaurant owners, Antonio Valerii comes from the Abruzzi. He married the sister of another Abruzzese restaurateur, and the resulting husband-and-wife partnership has been immensely successful. Their reputation is well-deserved, for the restaurant itself is pleasant — in spite of the alpine-look pine-wood paneling — and the cooking even more so. This is the place to come for classic *pasta* dishes, good fresh fish and simple, homemade desserts. You'll be plied with delicious *antipasti,* and there are freshly baked pizzas and bread from a capacious red-brick oven. The house wine from Frascati is very tolerable.

OTELLO ALLA CONCORDIA 🍽 ♣
Via della Croce 81 ☎ *6791178. Map 5G6* ⟱ *(set menus) to* ▨ 🌿 ⟱ 🍴 🐾 *Closed Sun; two weeks at Christmas.*

This ia a small, colorful, family-run *trattoria,* just off Via della Croce. It's approached down a narrow alley and through a small shady garden. Inside, the walls run riot with a dazzling array of oil paintings, doubtless not unconnected with the proximity of the artists' quarter around Via Margutta — although whether these works were received as barter or gifts, it might be indiscreet to ask. The food is simple and traditional, attractively served and reasonably priced. The set menus are remarkably good value for such a picturesque restaurant in the heart of

one of the world's most fashionable shopping areas.

DA PANCRAZIO
Piazza del Biscione 92 ☎ *6861246. Map 4I5* ▨ ⟱ 🚗 🅰🅱 🅾 🆑 🎴 *Closed Wed; Aug 10-18.*

Hidden away in an attractive but somewhat dilapidated corner of the old town, between Sant' Andrea della Valle and Campo dei Fiori, this old-established restaurant is in part of the ancient THEATER OF POMPEY, long since so over-built by additions as to be unrecognizable, except by its oval ground-plan. You can either dine on the ground floor or descend to the converted cellar below, where the coldness of the massive stone-blocked walls is offset by subtle lighting. Da Pancrazio is strong on atmosphere, but the food is nothing special.

PASSETTO
Via Zanardelli 14 ☎ *6540569. Map 5H5* ▨ ⟱ 🍽 🅰🅱 🅾 🆑 🎴 *Closed Sun; Mon lunchtime.*

Native Romans are quick to recommend this restaurant, and a walk along the antique stores of Via Coronari can be agreeably capped by a lunch or dinner here, with its Italian and international cuisine. Be careful not to spend too much on the way if you plan a banquet.

PICCOLO MONDO
Via Aurora 39 ☎ *485680. Map 6G7* ▨ ⟱ 🍽 🎶 🅰🅱 🅾 🆑 🎴 *Close Sun, Aug. Metropolitana: Barberini.*

Hospitable Benito Camponeschi runs this recently restored restaurant assisted by three sons and a daughter. The menu includes some Roman specialties, and the cellars boast a sparkling white wine from a brother's vineyard. Musicians add to the atmosphere.

PINO E DINO 🍽
Piazza di Montevecchio 22 ☎ *6861319. Map 4H5* ▨ ⟱ *Closed Mon; Aug; ten days at Christmas.*

Just off Via dei Coronari — a street of small, picturesque antique stores —

Pino and Dino, a southerner from Taranto and a northerner from Venice, together run this small restaurant with enormous devotion and almost embarrassing kindness. Dishes from Taranto such as *pasta e broccoli* and from Venice such as *polenta brustoada* form only part of a menu offering specialties from every Italian region. There is excellent and inexpensive game in season, and an uneven choice of wines with some pleasant surprises. The atmosphere is elegant and intimate, the clientele young and chic.

POLESE ☕ ♣

Piazza Sforza Cesarini 40 ☎*6861709. Map 4H4* ▢ ▭ ☰ 🐟 *Closed Tues; Aug 15-31.*

A typical Roman *trattoria,* Polese offers good, inexpensive food in simple, unpretentious surroundings. It occupies the back of a rather murky square, but at night does its best to look cheerful dressed up in a garland of red and white lampshades. The restaurant itself is fairly large, including the vaulted cellars downstairs, and can seat about 130 people; in summer you can also eat outside under the trees. The food has a slight Genoese bias, and the *antipasti* are especially good.

RANIERI

Via Mario de' Fiori 26 ☎*6791592. Map 5G6* ▦ ▤ ▭ ☰ 🄰🄴 🄲 🄳 ▦ *Closed Sun; two weeks in Aug.*

Since its foundation in 1865, Ranieri has made little attempt to keep up with the times. This is of course its special charm, for the quietly deferential service and dated furnishings make it the ideal place to lunch or dine in gracious style. The name derives from the founder, Giuseppe Ranieri, a Neapolitan who at one time was chef to Queen Victoria — hence the decidedly royalist bent of the menu. Her Majesty herself is remembered in the *mignonettes Regina Vittoria*. A convenient restaurant for lunch if you are shopping in the Via Condotti area, Ranieri is stronger on old-world atmosphere than gastronomic prowess.

RE DEGLI AMICI

Via della Croce 33b ☎*6795380 or 6782555. Map 5G6* ▦ ▭ 🄰🄴 🄲 ▦ *Closed Mon; last three weeks in June.*

This seemingly immortal *trattoria* has been serving traditional Roman food since 1927. Competitive prices and a prime location close to PIAZZA DI SPAGNA ensure its continuing popularity. Excellent pizzas are served after 7.30pm, and there is room to seat more than 200 people.

ROMOLO

Via Porta Settimiana 8 ☎*5818284. Map 4I4* ▦ ▭ ☰ 🐟 🄰🄴 🄲 ▦ *Closed Mon; last three weeks in Aug.*

Rich in historical associations and romantic atmosphere, Romolo is one of the most popular restaurants in Trastevere. The ancient building is full of surprises, but the main attraction is the enchanting courtyard, bounded by the AURELIAN WALL. You can dine out here on summer evenings, savoring the building's colorful past. Local dialect poet Trilussa dined here daily, and there is a legend that this is where La Fornarina, Raphael's mistress, once lived.

LA ROSETTA

Via della Rosetta 9 ☎*6861002. Map 4H5* ▦ ▤ 🍴 ▭ ☰ 🄲 ▦ *Closed Sun; Mon lunchtime; Aug.*

According to a 25-year-old legend, Carmelo Riccioli, a native of Sicily, gave up a double career as sports editor and boxer when he won this restaurant in payment of a bet. Fish, fresh every day from Sicily, is the big lure of the place. At La Rosetta, you can freely indulge in everything that swims or crawls in the sea — and this is one of the few restaurants in Rome where you can eat shellfish with absolute safety. To enjoy these privileges, Romans crowd every night into small, cramped rooms and pay enormous bills without blinking an eyelid. The waiters, dressed in black, are as breezy as the Straits of Messina in a *scirocco,* and there is nowhere to hang your coat — but who cares? A delectable mussel soup is only minutes away — or a plate of plump, juicy scampi or other *frutti di mare*. Good white Sicilian wines.

SABATINI-I
Piazza Santa Maria in Trastevere 13
☎5812026. Map 7J4 ▥ ▢ ⬛ ⬛
Closed Wed; two weeks in Aug (when branch below open).

SABATINI-II
Vicolo Santa Maria in Trastevere
☎5818307. Map 8J5 ▥ ▢ ⬛ ⬛
Closed Tues; two weeks in Aug (when branch above open).

Sabatini has a fine reputation as a fish restaurant, but above all it's a place to soak up authentic Trastevere atmosphere. The building itself is full of character, with its old beams and frescoes, but in summer you can also dine outside in the *piazza* and enjoy the golden, floodlit mosaics of the church. This is a popular spot, and reservation is advisable. If you can, try to get a table in the Vicolo Santa Maria branch, especially if you are eating outside. Sitting in the piazza in front of a thousand passers-by, you begin to feel like a lobster in Sabatini's aquaria.

SANS SOUCI ⬟
Via Sicilia 20 ☎4821814. Map 6G7 ▥ ▦
▢ ⬛ ⬛ ⬛ ⬛ ⬛ ⬛ ⬛ *Closed lunchtime; Mon; Aug 6-Sept 1.*

Just off the Via Veneto, this is the place for an intimate dinner in luxurious surroundings, but not on a budget. You pay dearly for impeccable service and decor that would make Louis XIV feel at home. The wine list may be among the best in Rome. A classical guitar covers a stream of hushed commands to an army of anxious waiters, and later in the evening Italian love songs bring a tear to the eye — as does the bill. Try *filleto in crosta alla salsa di Madera e tartufo nero*. Along with **El Toulà**, a serious contender for the title of Rome's most luxurious gastronomic experience.

TABERNA DEI GRACCHI
Via dei Gracchi 266-268 ☎3216958. Map 4F4 ▥ ▦ ⬛ ⬛ ⬛ ⬛ *Closed Sun; Mon lunch.*

Owner Dante Mililli has in recent years turned this into a star among Roman restaurants, serving excellent fare in an atmosphere of genial efficiency. Opened in 1962 but recently completely renovated, it is well worth a visit. Visitors would be well advised to reserve, even out of season. The clientele included soccer-player Maradonna during his controversial Italian sojourn. Businessfolk and lovers will appreciate the private tables — everyone else the food.

TAVERNA FLAVIA
Via Flavia 9 ☎4745214. Map 6G8 ▥ ▢
⬛ ⬛ ⬛ ⬛ ▥ ⬛ ⬛ *Closed Sun; Aug 15-20.*

In the heady days of *La Dolce Vita*, Mimmo gave up a career in law to open this restaurant, and it has been a favorite of movie stars and directors ever since. With the Italian movie industry now in decline, fewer celebrities visit regularly, but the pictures and autographs lining the bright, red-brick walls are a constant reminder of the good times, and the atmosphere is still chic. Mimmo's menu is appropriately adventurous, with such exotic concoctions as *insalata Veruschka*, a mouthwatering salad made with truffles. The wine list is excellent.

TAVERNA GIULIA
Vicolo dell' Oro 23 ☎6893720. Map 4H4
▥ ⬛ ▢ ⬛ ⬛ ⬛ ⬛ ⬛ *Closed Sun; Aug.*

Conveniently situated for the Vatican, just s of Ponte Vittorio Emanuele, this is a restaurant of some distinction, despite the scruffy exterior of the building. Down below in the semi-basement the decor has been smartened up considerably, although the whitewashed pebbled walls will not be to everyone's taste. The food is really excellent: an unusually good selection of Genoese dishes with plenty of *pesto* for basil-lovers.

EL TOULÀ ⬟
Via della Lupa 29b ☎6873750. Map 5G5
▥ ▢ ⬛ ⬛ ⬛ ⬛ ⬛ ⬛ *Closed Sun; Sat lunchtime; Aug.*

Still considered by many to be among the best restaurants in Rome, El Toulà scores high on most counts. The food is superb, the service impeccable, the surroundings unashamedly luxurious. The menu is predominantly Venetian in inspiration, but draws on many international sources for the creation of its culinary extravaganzas. El Toulà attracts more than its fair share of famous faces — millionaire tycoons and stars of screen and stage. Evening reservations and a substantial income are essential, and don't be put out if asked to dine in the bar area — some of El Toulà's best customers think it a privilege.

TRATTORIA L'ANTIQUARIO
Piazzetta di San Simeone 27 ☎ *6879694. Map 5H5* ▥ ⊏⊐ ⋝ ᴀᴇ ᴄᴅ ᴠɪsᴀ *Closed Sun; Aug.*

Giorgio Nisti has run a trattoria here for a quarter of a century, extensively renovating it in recent years. Although the chef, Galliano Fracassi, is Tuscan, the cuisine is international, and this is an excellent place in which to pause for lunch during a shopping expedition along the Via dei Coronari. Alternatively, have an *aperitivo* in one of the bars of Piazza Navona, and make this the location for an enjoyable evening meal.

Other options

In the unlikely event that Italian cuisine begins to pall, diners are assured of a refreshing change at a number of Chinese restaurants, where oriental culinary skills are applied to the humble noodle with appetizing results. **Golden Crown** (*Via in Arcione 85* ☎ *6789831, map 5H6* ⊏⊐ ▤ ᴀᴇ ⊡ ᴄᴅ ᴠɪsᴀ *closed Mon*), **La Taverna di Bambu** (*Via di S. Dorotea 2* ☎ *5806065, map 4I4* ⊏⊐ ▤ ᴠɪsᴀ *closed Mon; Aug*) and **Yu Yuan** (*Via delle Quattro Fontane 27* ☎ *483484, map 6H7* ▥ ⊏⊐ ◼ ▤ ᴄᴅ) are three of the best.

In Italy, the birthplace of the pizza, fast food runs counter to the national culture. These days, however, more and more places are springing up for tourists who have OD'd on pasta, pizza and pastry. "Takeouts," or, as they are known in Italian, *mangia dove vuoi*, can be purchased from:

Italy & Italy   In Piazza Barberini, map 6G7, where it has replaced the Piccadilly restaurant, and Via Cola di Rienzo, map 4G4: pasta dishes, hamburgers, grills, salads, French fries and ices

New Point   Corso Vittorio Emanuele 137, map 5H5, open 11.30am-midnight, closed Mon

Willy's   Corso Vittorio Emanuele 213, map 5H5, closed Wed

Burghy   Piazza Rotonda, map 4H5, closed Wed

C & C Burger   Corso Vittorio Emanuele 310, map 5H5

MABurger   Via del Mascherino 56-58, map 3G3

Speedyburger   Via P. Emilio 17, map 4F4

Big Burg   Via di Propaganda 17-19, map 5G6; Piazza Istria 28-29; Viale Giulio Cesare 120, map 4F4; Piazzale Flaminio 22, map 5F5; and Via del Tritone 212, map 5H6

For homesick Americans, even **McDonald's** can now be found, at Piazza della Repubblica 40, map 6G-H8, and in Piazza di Spagna, map 5G6.

Refreshments

BARS

The Italian bar is the hub of local life, acting as pub, café, corner store and telephone booth all in one. Even the smallest, most rudimentary of bars performs a wide range of services, selling both alcoholic drinks and coffee, and a variety of *tost* (snacks). It is also a *latteria* (the only place you can buy milk) and usually provides the only public telephone in the vicinity. The bigger the bar, the greater the number of facilities on offer. Slightly larger bars take on additional roles of *pasticceria* and *gelateria,* selling pastries and ice creams; very often these are prepared on the premises. The grandest bars also provide *tavola calda* and *tavola fredda* (hot and cold pre-prepared food) and sometimes have a small restaurant area as well. They may also include shops selling chocolates, candies and cookies, and a *tabaccheria* for postcards, stamps and cigarettes.

Briskly efficient service (orders at the bar arrive almost instantly), mingled smells of fresh coffee and pastries, and shining-clean stainless steel tops and mirrored walls give the larger Roman bars a specially attractive atmosphere. Although chairs and tables are usually provided, it is most unusual to sit down in such establishments. Unless your legs are giving out and you don't mind doubling your bill (and waiting twice as long), it's best to do as the Romans and consume your coffee and *cornetto* (sweet croissant) standing up at the bar. In all but the smallest bars, you pay before being served. Go first to the *cassa* (cash desk) and state your order. Having paid, take the receipt to the bar, hand it over and repeat your order.

CAFÉS

Whereas bars are found all over Italy, cafés are a phenomenon peculiar to Rome — a capital city's desire to emulate the boulevard lifestyle enjoyed by Parisians. In the 19thC the **Caffè Greco** was the haunt of expatriate writers and composers such as Byron and Liszt. Later, the **Café de Paris** became the chic meeting place for the international jet set. Reputations change — but prices remain high.

For the best coffee in Rome, go to the **Sant' Eustachio** or **La Tazza d'Oro**. The nicer cafés are good places to rendezvous, and they offer some of the few acceptable public rest rooms in Rome.

ICE CREAM

Roman ice cream is justly celebrated, and every resident and visitor has a favorite *gelateria*. The best ice cream is made only with eggs, milk, cream, sugar and fresh fruit (or other natural flavorings). Certain bars produce one excellent ice cream and several indifferent varieties; even their specialties can vary from day to day.

Most discerning Romans agree that the best ice cream in the city comes from **Bar San Filippo**, which is tucked away in fashionable Parioli, although **Giolitti** and the **Gelateria della Palma** also have their devotees.

ACCADEMIA

Via del Tritone 54/56 ☎*6793585. Map 6G7* ▦ ▨ ⫽▢

Pastries, ice cream and terrific coffee in relaxing surroundings, near the busy Piazza Barberini.

ALEMAGNA

Via del Corso 181 ☎*6792887. Map 5H6* ▨ ⊑ ▨ ⫽▢ *Open 7.30am-10pm. Closed Sun.*

Gilded candelabra on lofty mirrored walls make this one of the grandest bars in Rome. It is also one of the largest, busiest and most central. *Tavola calda, frullati* (milk shakes) and a shopping area are included.

BABINGTON'S TEA ROOMS

Piazza di Spagna 23 ☎*6786027. Map 5G6* ▨ ▨ ⫽▢ *Open 9am-10.30pm. Closed Thurs.*

Opened in 1896 by Miss Anna Maria Babington and still serving homemade scones and muffins prepared to her original recipes, this pseudo-English establishment continues to attract wealthy shoppers from nearby Via Condotti. Prices go over the top, and have even inspired some barbed remarks in the celebrity visitors' book, but Babington's remains one of the few places in Rome where you can drink reasonable tea.

BAR DELLA PACE

Via della Pace 5 ☎*6861216. Map 4H5. Open 10-3am. Closed Mon.*

This is one of the most popular bars in town. The cozy interior, with its Roman column, marble tables and wooden decor, hasn't changed since it opened in the late 19thC. Romans go there in the afternoon for a selection of delicious cakes and hot drinks. After dark, it becomes one of the city's main meeting places.

BAR SAN FILIPPO

Via di Villa San Filippo 8 ☎*879314. Map 11C3. Open 6am-midnight. Closed Mon.*

Specializes in ice cream cakes for birthday parties and other celebrations, although it also sells smaller portions to casual callers, from a choice of 60 ice creams and water ices. The zabaglione is recommended.

BELLA ROMA

Via Panico 28 ☎*6861414. Map 4H4. Closed Mon.*

At the foot of the Via dei Coronari, spend whatever small change is left from an expedition to the antique stores on an enjoyable sandwich, a coffee and an ice cream.

BERNASCONI

Largo di Torre Argentina 1 ☎*6548141. Map 4I5. Open 8am-9pm. Closed Mon.*

Selling ice creams and pastries as briskly as a takeout burger joint, this bar has the added attraction of a telephone room downstairs, equipped with 18 telephones. Buy a coffee ice on your way down there.

BIANCANEVE

Piazza Pasquale Paoli 1 ☎*6540227. Map 4H4. Open 7am-1am. Closed Tues.*

This café has made a specialty of the *mela stregata* it serves — a "bewitched apple" of chocolate and zabaglione ice creams, coated in chocolate and topped with cream. This over-priced concoction has perhaps lost its magic, and the service also seems to have fallen under a bad spell.

CAFFÈ GRECO

Via Condotti 86 ☎*6782554. Map 5G6. Open 8am-9pm. Closed Sun.*

The most famous café in Rome, the Caffè Greco dates from the early 18thC, and throughout the 19thC was a celebrated meeting place for writers, musicians and artists from all over Europe. The original 1860 interior has been preserved and past patrons are recorded in an impressive collection of paintings and medallions: in particular, note the portraits of Ludwig I of Bavaria, Nikolai Gogol and Hans Christian Andersen. Illustrious visitors still drop by. Prices are high, but it is a comfortable retreat from the hurly-burly of Via Condotti.

CAFÉ DE PARIS

Via Vittorio Veneto 90 ☎*4885284. Map 6G7* ▦ 🄰🄴 🄲🄳 ▥ 🅅🅂🄰 ▯▢ *Open 8am-2am. Closed Thurs.*

The *Dolce Vita* days of this café are long since gone, and it is now less fashionable than **Doney**, the rival establishment across the road. The tables outside may have lost their chic, but the air-conditioned bar offers generally courteous service and an excellent choice of *tavola fredda*. Prices go over the odds, and faint muzac imparts an international flavor.

CANOVA

Piazza del Popolo 16 ☎*3612231. Map 5F5* 🄰🄴 🄲🄳 ▥ 🅅🅂🄰 ▯▢ *Open 7.30am-11.30pm. Closed Mon.*

Well-heeled Roman women meet for lunchtime parties in this glittering modern café — and pay through the nose. Service is slow and ice creams indifferent. **Rosati** (see below) on the other side of the piazza offers fewer facilities but loads more atmosphere.

COLOMBIA

Piazza Navona 88 ☎*659647. Map 5H5* 🄰🄴 🄲🄳 ▥ 🄲🄳 ▥ 🅅🅂🄰 ▯▢ *Open 7am-1.30am. Closed Mon.*

The best Colombian coffee and generally excellent ice creams make this café worth visiting. A useful pizzeria is included at the back, and tables outside allow the comfortable contemplation of the delights of Piazza Navona.

DONEY

Via Vittorio Veneto 145 ☎*4821788. Map 6G7* 🄰🄴 🄲🄳 ▥ 🄲🄳 ▥ 🅅🅂🄰 ▯▢ *Open 8am-1am. Closed Mon.*

Business is booming on the sunny side of the street, and Doney has become more fashionable than the once-celebrated **Café de Paris**. A restaurant behind the sun terrace is a recent addition.

EUROPEO

Piazza San Lorenzo in Lucina 33 ☎*6876300. Map 5G5. Open 8am-11pm. Closed Mon.*

Visit this tiny bar for Sicilian specialties

— pastries filled with *ricotta,* and *cassata* ice cream.

GELATERIA DELLA PALMA

Via della Maddalena 20 ☎*6540752. Map 5H5. Open noon-midnight. Closed Wed.*

Opened in 1981, this *gelateria* offers more than 100 different flavors of ice cream, specializing in exotic fruits such as mango, paw-paw, kiwi and wild strawberry. *Semi-freddi* (semifrozen creams) and *cremolati* (water-ices) are specialties.

This is the biggest ice cream shop in Rome, and there is plenty of room to sit down and indulge.

GIOLITTI

Via Uffici del Vicario 40 ☎*6794206. Map 4H5. Open 7am-2am. Closed Mon.*

King of the *gelaterie* for more than 30 years, Giolitti still serves up reliable ice creams and moderately-priced *tavola calda.*

HARRY'S BAR

Via Vittorio Veneto 150 ☎*484643. Map 6G7* 🄰🄴 🄲🄳 *Open 11am-1am. Closed Sun.*

Don't be misled by the gloomy and rather tatty interior. Since 1961 Harry's Bar has been a fashionable meeting place for anyone who is anyone (especially politicians and actors), and the hushed voices around you may be discussing important affairs of state. Head barman Guido Lanfranconi will produce a Harry's Special on request.

MICHELE DI RIENZO

Piazza della Rotonda 9 ☎*6869097. Map 5H5. Open 7.30am-2.30am. Closed Tues.*

Just next door to the Pantheon, this bar serves eggs and bacon and the most delicious chocolate ice cream you will find anywhere in Rome.

ROSATI

Piazza del Popolo 4 ☎*3611418. Map 5F5. Open 7.30am-midnight. Closed Tues.*

The nicest café in Rome has been in the Rosati family for three generations and offers old-fashioned elegance with first-class service, as well as a view of one of the finest Baroque squares in Europe.

The 1922 Liberty-style decorations have been preserved throughout. Period glass jars filled with candies line the walls on carved wooden shelves, against a pink and cream background. A huge chrome and glass cake-stand displays Rosati's homemade specialties: liqueur chocolates, jellies, candies and cakes. Cocktails are another forte — all original, of course — and high prices are justified. Upstairs there is a spacious tearoom, which caters to special or festive occasions.

SANT' EUSTACHIO
Piazza Sant' Eustachio 82 ☎6861309. Map 5H5. Open 8am-1am. Closed Mon.
Famed for its *espresso* and *cappuccino*, this café is also worth visiting for its superb coffee *granita*.

LA TAZZA D'ORO
Via degli Orfani 84 ☎6789792. Map 5H5. Open 7am-10pm. Closed Sun.
Huge sacks of coffee beans piled against the walls and an enticing aroma prepare you for one of the best *espressos* in town. This bar sells nothing but coffee and coffee *granita*, and single-minded dedication has paid off.

TRE SCALINI
Piazza Navona 30 ☎6541996. Map 4H5. Open 7am-2.30am. Closed Wed.
Tartufo is the wicked specialty here. This is a rich chocolate ice cream, to which pieces of broken chocolate and whole cherries have been added. Served with a topping of whipped cream, it certainly lives up to all expectations.

Nightlife and entertainment

Rome by night

The eternal city may not keep as wide awake at night as New York, but it is a lot livelier than many other capital cities. Theaters and restaurants keep later hours than in London, for example. Curtains rise between 8.30-9.30pm, and it is usual to dine from 9.30pm-12.30am. A number of cafés and bars stay open until 1 or 2am, and many clubs and discotheques don't close their doors until 5am at weekends.

Despite all this, the reveling Roman rises early next morning to begin work at 9am — fortified, no doubt, by the prospect of an agreeable long lunch and siesta ahead (1 to 3.30 or 4pm). If you propose to explore Roman nightlife, you would do best to follow suit and catch up on some sleep in the afternoons.

Performing arts

BALLET AND OPERA
The official opera seasons runs from November to June at the **Teatro dell' Opera** *(Piazza Beniamino Gigli 1* ☎ *4881755, map 6H7)*, but the same company also gives summer performances in July and August in the Baths of Caracalla. The Teatro dell' Opera is not in the same international class as La Scala (Milan), and the open-air summer productions (where quality matters less than atmosphere) tend to attract more visitors.

Ballet is included in the winter season, and in October there is an experimental program that sometimes features jazz. Postal reservation is available, and remaining tickets go on sale two days before the performance. Charge/credit cards are not accepted, and the box office is closed on Monday.

Tickets for the summer season can be bought at the Teatro dell' Opera box office, or at the Baths of Caracalla on the day of the performance only, from 8-9pm. Check *This Week in Rome, Il Messaggero* or *La Repubblica* for times of performances.

CHAMBER MUSIC, RECITALS AND CONCERTS
Rome is rich in musical activity, often enhanced by the beautiful settings in which concerts and recitals take place. Although a number of

established orchestras, choirs and chamber groups give regular concerts, the keyword to the Roman musical scene is spontaneity. A profusion of one-off concerts and choral recitals are held throughout the year in basilicas such as **San Giovanni in Laterano**. In summer a number of villas, including **Villa Ada**, present festivals featuring themes such as African or Indian music. Regular summer concerts are held at the **Basilica of Maxentius** in July and August *(Via dei Fori Imperiali* ☎ *6793617, map 9 I6)*.

The official concert season runs from October to June. In a class of its own, and playing host to numerous international stars, is the **Accademia di Santa Cecilia**. The Accademia holds orchestral concerts at the **Auditorio di Via della Conciliazione** *(Via della Conciliazione 4* ☎ *6541044, map 3 H3)*, near Piazza San Pietro, and other recitals at the **Sala Accademica di Via dei Greci** *(Via dei Greci 18, map 5 G5-6; box office Via Vittoria 6* ☎ *6790389, map 5 G6)*.

The **Accademia Filarmonica** *(Via Flaminia 118* ☎ *3601752)* generally performs in the **Teatro Olimpico** *(Piazza Gentile da Fabriano 17* ☎ *3234936, map 1 D3)*, and the **RAI** (Italian radio orchestra) invariably in the **Foro Italico** *(Piazza Lauro De Bosis* ☎ *36865625, map 1 C3)*. Concerts and recitals are also given by the orchestra of the **Teatro dell' Opera** (see BALLET AND OPERA); by the **Gonfalone** *(Via del Gonfalone 32a* ☎ *6875952, map 4 H4)*; and at the **Auditorio San Leone Magno** *(Via Bolzano 38* ☎ *853216)*.

CINEMA

The Italian movie industry has been in decline since around 1965, and three out of every four movies shown in Rome are American. This might be good news for English-speaking tourists were it not that every foreign movie is dubbed in Italian. Many Italian movie-goers also resent this practice and would prefer to see the original versions with subtitles. They and discerning expatriates frequent **Pasquino** *(Piazza Santa Maria in Trastevere* ☎ *5803622, map 7 J4)*, the only public movie theater that shows undubbed English and American movies.

The *cinema d'essai* (art cinema) club scene is lively and well worth investigating. The clubs can be joined on the spot for a nominal fee, and present a variety of experimental programs, exploring unusual themes and concepts. European and American art movies are sometimes shown in their original versions, and young independent Italian movie-makers are well represented. Rock movies are often screened to boost the takings. The following small theaters are especially recommended.

Caravaggio Via Paisiello 24 ☎ 8554210, map **6**E7
Grauco Cinema Via Perugia 34 ☎ 7551785
Labirinto Via Pompeo Magno 27 ☎ 312283, map **4**F4
Politecnico Via Tiepolo 13a ☎ 3227559, map **2**D5

Less recherché but equally exciting are the open-air summer movie festivals held in one of several ancient settings. August is not the best month to be in Rome: temperatures soar; all theaters, most movie theaters and many shops are closed; and the city itself has the appearance of a deserted movie set. To keep the city-bound populace happy (and with the same good and wise intentions that must have inspired the building of the Colosseum) the authorities rig up a huge screen on the Arch of Constantine or some other ancient monument, and set out thousands of chairs in the surrounding streets. Bumper packages of up to five movies per sitting are shown every evening throughout August. Programs last from about 8pm to 4am and a small fee is payable. Theatrical lighting effects and hot-dog stands add to the festivities. For the current venue, check *Il Messaggero*.

JAZZ, FOLK AND ROCK MUSIC

The same rules of spontaneity and surprise apply to jazz and rock as to the classical music scene. Jazz features in many of the festivals that crop up during the summer months, and rock events are frequently laid on at breathtakingly short notice.

Jazz has a permanent home at the **Mississippi Jazz Club** *(Borgo Angelico 16* ☎ *6540348, map 3 G3)*, and folk music at the **Folkstudio** *(Via Frangipane 42* ☎ *4871063, map 9 I7)*.

Venues for major rock concerts include **Tenda Strisce** (the Striped Tent) *(Via Cristoforo Colombo)* and the **Sports Palace** (or *Palaeur*) in EUR. Tickets for these events are obtainable from nominated box offices throughout the city, listed in *This Week In Rome,* along with details of visiting big names.

THEATER

The Roman theater season is short, beginning in October and ending in May, but attendances are on the increase, and more than 100 companies now compete for audiences. Standards of acting are variable, however, and fringe theater groups *(teatri off)* have ill-disguised political motivations.

The staple diet at the established theaters is Pirandello, well seasoned with Goldoni, de Filippo and French and English classics (in translation) as well as the somewhat less-than-classic, such as *Niente Sesso, Siamo Inglesi* (better known as *No Sex Please, We're British*).

In the list of major theaters below, **Piccolo Eliseo** has a lighter program and **Sistina** stages musicals.

Argentina   Largo Argentina 53 ☎ 6544601, map 4I5
Delle Arti   Via Sicilia 59 ☎ 4880141, map 6G7
Delle Muse   Via Forlì 43 ☎ 8831300
Eliseo   Via Nazionale 183 ☎ 4882114, map 6H7
Flaiano   Via S.S. del Cacco 15 ☎ 6796496, map 3I3
Ghione   Via delle Fornaci 37 ☎ 6372294, map 3I3
Parioli   Via Borsi 20 ☎ 8083523, map 2D7
Piccolo Eliseo   Via Nazionale 183 ☎ 4885095, map 6H7
Quirino   Piazza dell'Oratorio 73 ☎ 6794585, map 5H5
Sistina   Via Sistina 129 ☎ 4826841, map 5G6
Valle   Via Teatro Valle 23a ☎ 6543794, map 4H5

For all but the most popular productions, tickets can usually be bought right up to the day of the performance, but no theater will accept payment by charge/credit card.

During the summer months, regrouped companies stage open-air performances outside Rome, at Classical sites such as **Ostia Antica**. Excellent listings of both winter and summer performances are given every Thursday in *La Repubblica* and every Friday in *Il Messagero*.

Nightlife

NIGHTCLUBS AND DISCOS

Rome is almost too well provided with places in which to dance the night away. For every fun spot there are three or four sad and empty clubs where the champagne buckets sit on the tables just for show and are never filled with ice. Bypassing the area around Via Veneto could spare you some of the least inspiring tourist traps, but would also mean missing out on some of the liveliest discos. Instead, follow the recommendations given here, from which all known "cowboy clubs" have been excluded, and you should escape being stung.

The city has more than 70 night spots, catering to all tastes and ages. At the bottom end of the scale are noisy discos with neon lights and plenty of space for energetic dancing. At the top end are a couple of exclusive clubs where the clientele is glamorous, lights subdued and dance floors small.

Somewhere in the middle are less pretentious establishments where dress is unimportant and an evening's enjoyment does not depend upon being seen by the right people.

Glamor is a transient quality, and fashions change at a whim. The most important ingredient of a nightclub is its clientele, and this fickle crowd takes off like a flock of migrant birds once its nest has been discovered. Thus smart clubs hit the doldrums through no fault of their own.

In Rome, the terms nightclub and discotheque are used loosely. Exclusive clubs call themselves discotheques, and the sleaziest discotheques masquerade as clubs. None of the clubs listed has a members-only policy, but you are likely to be excluded from the very few "in" places on those alleged grounds if your face doesn't fit.

In more expensive clubs, payment is built into the cost of the drinks. Elsewhere, the entrance fee allows one "free" drink, and the previous rule applies thereafter.

LA CABALA

Hostaria dell' Orso, Via dei Soldati 25 ☎6864250. Map 4H4 ▥ ● ▮ ⇉ ▦ ▣ ▦ *Open 10.30pm-3am. Closed Sun.*
Over the restaurant **Hostaria dell' Orso**, housed in a fine palace dating from the 13thC. Unexciting, but you can dress smartly or otherwise, dance to American funk and be served expensive drinks by posh-looking waiters.

CLUB 84

Via Emilia 84 ☎4827538. Map **6**G7 ▥ ● ▮ ↑ ▦ ▣ ▦ *Open 10pm-3.30am.*
This long-established club features live music from 11.30pm-1am and 1.30-3am. The singers are generally Italian and the songs romantic. Between times you can dance the night away to American funk.

DIVINA

Via Romagnosi 11a ☎ *3611348. Map* **4F5** ▦ ◉ ◪ *Open 11.30pm-3.30am.*

Once upon a time known as the Atmosphere, this club was opened in 1980 by Gil, in his other incarnation the make-up artist of **Gilcagné** (see BEAUTY CENTERS on page 220). After some time, however, Gil sold his interest in it and, as a result, the place went decidedly downscale after its glamorous beginnings. These days, however, Divina is winning back a decent reputation under a new name and new management.

GILDA

Via Mario de' Fiori 97 ☎ *6784838* ▦ ◉ ◪ ⇉ ▨ ◙ ▩ *Open 10pm-5am. Closed Mon.*

Probably the most glamorous nightclub in Rome, Gilda attracts a luminous clientele of film and music stars, politicians and high society. Jet-setters hold their exclusive private parties here. It has an expensive but indifferent restaurant and a piano bar, which opened recently.

KRIPTON

Via Schiaparelli 29 ☎ *3221360. Map* **2E6** ▦ *to* ▦ ◉ ♫ *Open 11pm-3am, Sat and Sun also 4-8pm. Closed Mon.*

Since opening in a converted movie theater in 1978, this club, which was at various points in its history called Acropolis and Much More, has offered a lively disco with special lighting effects and frequent live rock. Now mainly a place for the young, during its more exclusive reincarnations it attracted such celebratedly seasoned night owls as Marcello Mastroianni, Alberto Moravia, Helmut Berger and Christopher Lee.

MAKUMBA IN

Via Lidia 44 ☎ *7858291. Map* **10L9** ▦ ❧ ◉ ♫ *Open 10pm-5am.*

To the N of fashionable Parioli, Rome's growing population of African emigrés has made this lively club its night-time home. You can dance under the stars till dawn to the best sounds from all over the African continent, both live and recorded.

OPEN GATE

Via San Nicola da Tolentino 4 ☎ *4824464. Map* **6G7** ▦ ◉ ♫ ⇉ ▨ ◙ ▩ ▦

Don't be fooled by the name — exclusivity is the hallmark of this combination of restaurant, piano bar and disco. Manager Pietro Loreti maintains absolute discretion about his famous clientele, a sure sign that this is the haunt of the rich, celebrated and amorous. To join them may cost. The best way is probably to reserve for dinner, and afterwards drift discreetly onto the dance floor. You may be lucky enough to fall in with a partner who can afford to pay your restaurant bill.

PIPER 90

Via Tagliamento 9 ☎ *8555398. Map* **6E8** ▦ ▨ ◉ ▨ ◙ ▩ ▦ *Open 10pm-3am, Sat and Sun, also 4-7.30pm. Closed Mon.*

This disco is still buzzing with excitement. It's young, loud, and energetic, with an atmosphere all of its own. The latest craze, whatever it may be, is always catered to. Video, movie and lighting effects, plus a whole room of computer games, add to the sense of fun.

ROSE CAFÉ

Via della Purificazione 9 ☎ *4745578. Map* **5G6** ▦ ◉ ◪ *Open 11pm-3.30am.*

Once called "Easy Going," that former appellation still applies to the spirit of this gay club, tucked away along the street that takes you from Piazza Barberini to the back of the Via Veneto. With piano music replacing the pulsating glam rock of earlier days, this has become more of an intimate meeting place for the likeminded than the open house it once was.

XANADU

Piazza dei Ponziani 3 ☎ *5814555. Map* **8J5** ▦ ♟ ▨ ◙ ▨ *Open 10pm-3.30am.*

Xanadu shares quarters with Prugna 2, a popular and lively piano bar (see PIANO BARS), which has recently been relaunched.

PIANO BARS

Nightclubs are where you go with someone special or a group of friends. Piano bars are more for single people, and are an easy way to make friends in a strange city.

Rome is well provided with such bars, and they turn up in the most unlikely places, frequently tucked away at the back of discotheques, the singers hoarse from competition with the loudspeakers next door. The poshest restaurants and clubs have piano bars, and so do the scruffiest. They are cherished almost like club mascots or household gods — and the show *always* goes on. However, in recent years, the term "piano bar" has taken on a dubious ambiguity, and some establishments now have more in common with London's Soho than Saint Peter's. So beware street touts drumming up trade for "piano bars" in the back streets. Those listed here are respectable venues, but off the beaten track you may fall among thieves.

Among the mass of indifferent and merely average musicians who perform in these bars, a few genuine artists attract appreciative audiences from all over Rome. Sometimes playing solo, sometimes accompanied by a guitar or another singer, they generally have a wide range of styles, and they welcome requests.

When you go into a piano bar, you should take one of the high seats round the piano (as they're always grand pianos, there's usually room). You are expected to join in the entertainment: a skilled performer will weave his audience into his show, making each and every one feel like a celebrity.

Highly recommended for a quiet and sociable evening, good piano bars should leave you brimming with *Casablanca*-style nostalgia and just about as mellow.

L'ARCILIUTO
Piazza Montevecchio 5, off Via dei Coronari ☎6879419. *Map* **4H5** ▥ ☙ ♪ *Open 10pm-2am. Closed Sun.*
Neapolitan proprietor Enzo Samaritani sings and plays guitar, accompanied on the piano. Enzo writes his own songs and will sing in most European languages, depending on the audience present. His excellent pianist plays light jazz and popular classics between times.

L'INCONTRO
Via della Penna ☎3610934. *Map* **5F5** ▥ ☙ ♪ ▣ ▣ ▣ *Open 10pm-3.30am.*
The name means "meeting," which gives a rough idea of the ambience. There's Brazilian music and two floors of discotheques if the Rick's Café syndrome becomes overwhelming.

LITTLE PIANO
Via Gregoriana 54 ☎6796386. *Map* **5G6**.
Near to the Spanish Steps, which at night must be one of the most romantic spots in the world. Eugenio Capponi and Maurizio Marcilli provide the music.

PRUGNA 2
Piazza dei Ponziani 3 ☎5890555. *Map* **8J5** ▥ ☙ ▣ ▣ ▣ *Open 10pm-3.30am.*
Successful successor to La Prugna, this piano bar has recently been redecorated and relaunched.

TARTARUGHINO
Via della Scrofa 2 ☎6786037. *Map* **5H5** ▥ ☙ ♪ ≡ *Open 9pm-3am. Closed Sun.*
Rome's most exclusive piano bar accepts only the highest standards of dress and can be difficult to get into

because it is so small. Upstairs, the tiny, exquisitely decorated restaurant is a favorite haunt of top politicians. Downstairs, you may drink without dining and listen to the excellent pianist. In July and August the whole ensemble, chef and pianist included, moves to Sardinia for the summer season.

TONY'S BAR
Via Ludovisi 11 ☎*4744141. Map 6G7* ▥
▯ ♫ ☷ ▨ ▣ ▥ ▦ *Open 8pm-2am.*
Closed Sun.
Part of the Savoy hotel in an elegant quarter of Rome, and quite intimate, considering the rather imposing furnishings of the hotel proper.

CABARET AND COCKTAILS
Certain musical experiences do not fit neatly into any of the previous categories, but any brief survey of Roman nightlife would be incomplete without them. Here is an assorted selection.

BLATUMBA
Piazza in Piscinula 20 ☎*5896421. Map 8J5. Opens 10.30pm-late. Closed Mon.*
Across the river at Isola Tiberina, this club specializes in Latin American music, led by Giancarlo Biagini and Jose Maria Salvador. Recommended for setting the pulse racing.

CLUB MILLEUNO
Via Lazio 31 ☎*4744242. Map 6F7* ▥ ♫
Open 8pm-2am.
Floor shows nightly, including some internationally known acts.

ST MORITZ
Via Sicilia 57 ☎*4759160. Map 6G7* ▥
Opens 10pm.

Just off the Via Veneto, this venue stages acts throughout the night, gathering pace after midnight.

FANTASIE DI TRASTEVERE
Via di Santa Dorotea 6 ☎*5817343* ▩*625865. Map 714* ▥ ➠ ➤ ♫ ▨ ▣ ▥ *Open 8pm-midnight. Closed Sun.*
This well-known tourist attraction will either thrill or revolt you — there is no half measure. The food is indifferent but you have to eat if you want to see the show. Singers dressed in Tyrolean costumes, purporting to be Roman peasants, deliver hearty folk songs to loud, brassy accompaniments. Later, strolling musicians tour the tables with a selection of tear-jerking opera classics.

Shopping

Where to go

Concentrating the very best of Italian design and craftsmanship into one conveniently small area, Rome is one of the finest shopping centers in the world. It is where you go to find quality, and quality that you are prepared to pay for. Beautifully-made articles created out of the very best materials can never be cheap, and this is not the place to look around for cut-price bargains. Leather and silk goods predominate, but Rome is also an important center for jewelry, antiques and general prêt-à-porter fashion. And, to ensure that face and body do justice to fabulous jewels and elegant clothes, beauty centers abound.

The main shopping area centers on **Via Condotti** and extends across just four main blocks, to **Via della Croce** in the N and **Via Frattina** in the S. This network of narrow streets, bordered by **Via del Corso** in the W and **Piazza di Spagna** in the E, is entirely free of traffic, and shoppers can stroll at leisure, unjostled by fellow pedestrians and unmolested by traffic fumes. The atmosphere is hushed and elegant, almost heavy with the savor of affluence.

In Italy, department stores are the exception rather than the rule. Romans, like other Italians, prefer to shop in boutiques, and the Via Condotti area has little shops selling everything from shirts to gloves. This specialization originates in the craft stores from which the smart shopping village has grown, and generally ensures top quality and personal service. Many of the boutiques have been in one family of craftsmen for generations, and the shopkeeper is often the craftsman or factory owner as well.

The grandeur of Roman shops is legendary. More money is lavished on opulent decorations than in any other shopping center in the world. There is, however, a very thin line between stylish opulence and brash vulgarity. Bulgari's small-scale palace is delightfully elegant, while the flashy interiors of some of the newer shops are pure nouveau-riche.

Shopkeepers have the bearing and manners to match these fine surroundings, and the customer is also expected to play the part. The richer you look, the less likely you are to receive courteous but dismissive treatment.

Such high standards of dress and deportment apply particularly to Via Condotti and Via Borgognona, but are also worth bearing in mind if you intend shopping in the parallel street of Via Frattina or in some of the little cross-streets, or in Piazza di Spagna or Via del Babuino. Other shopping districts are less formal, and many of these are worth investigating: **Via del Tritone** and the streets around the Trevi Fountain, **Via Cola di Rienzo** across the Tiber and N of the Vatican, **Piazza San Lorenzo in Lucina** and the streets around **Piazza Campo dei Fiori** are all areas where you will find cheaper leather bags and shoes. Streets to avoid are Via del Corso and Via Nazionale. These are much like main streets anywhere else in the world and often have the poor or uneven quality you might expect to find there. **Via Veneto** also has more of an international flavor, but contains some of the city's most expensive shops.

Vying with Via Condotti as a peculiarly Roman shopping attraction are the city's colorful **street markets**. Offering a vast selection of top-quality fruit, flowers, vegetables, *prosciutto,* salami, cheeses, meat and fish, as well as cheap clothes, these regular events explain why food stores, like department stores, are not found in the city center.

STRATEGIES

Straight bargaining is an accepted practice in clothes markets, but elsewhere transactions are conducted in a more roundabout way. At food stalls where cheeses and other weighed items have *prezzi fissi* (fixed prices), and in nearly all clothes stores, you can try asking for a *sconto* (discount). Reasons for meriting a *sconto* may be numerous — buying two articles at once is a good example — but if you are bold you will ask for a *sconto* for no good reason at all, and will usually get one. This practice applies to all but the very grandest shops.

Shoppers from outside the EC do not have to pay Value-Added Tax on certain purchases. This rule does not apply to small articles such as shoes, bags, clothing and porcelain. Larger items such as Oriental carpets or antique furniture do not qualify for VAT provided that they are exported independently of the purchaser. This means that if you want to walk out of the shop carrying your purchase you must pay VAT.

Surprisingly few shopkeepers speak English, but in the larger shops there is usually one person on hand who understands enough to be able to help you. Regular late-evening shopping may be a novelty for many visitors (see SHOPPING HOURS on pages 42-43), but it is nevertheless best to shop in the mornings if you can. Sales people can get understandably tired and testy by 7.30 or 8pm, particularly as this is the time of day when most Italians like to make their purchases and the shops are at their most crowded.

ANTIQUES

The grandest antique stores can be found in **Via del Babuino** *(map* **5***F5-5 G6),* where **W. Apolloni** at #133 has drawings as well as paintings and furniture, and **Adolfo di Castro** at #80, **Nicola e Angelo di Castro** at #92 and **Amadeo di Castro** at #77 all have furniture and *objets d'art.* The last di Castro claims no connection with the first two, and to confuse the issue still further another professedly independent general dealer of that name, **Alberto di Castro**, operates from nearby *(Piazza di Spagna 5, map* **5** *G6),* while **Aldo di Castro** sells prints at #71 Via del Babuino. On the same street, **Carlo** and **Cesare Lam-**

pronti, at #69 and 67 respectively, have paintings as well as furniture, and **Antonacci**, at #146, just furniture. **Emporio Floreale**, close by *(Via delle Carrozze 46, map 5 G6)*, specializes in Art Nouveau and Art Deco glass, furniture and paintings. None of these takes charge/credit cards.

Via dei Coronari *(map 4 H5)*, a charming street in the old part of the city, is worth wandering down even if you are not interested in buying anything. The *coronari* used to make rosaries to sell to pilgrims on their way to St Peter's, and most of their workshops are now tiny antique boutiques. The open shop-fronts have been covered with glass, allowing the contents to be viewed easily from the street — an unusual bonus as far as shopping for antiques is concerned. **Via Giulia** *(map 4 H-I4)*, s of Corso Vittorio Emanuele, has similar, but fewer, antique boutiques, as well as some modern art galleries.

BEAUTY CENTERS

Hairdressing salons in Rome are grand affairs, offering a full range of beauty treatments besides the traditional manicure. Cheaper, younger-style hairdressers are strangely lacking, mainly because nearly all Italian girls wear their hair long and thick. Some of the fashionable salons are worth trying out if you have money to spend and feel like being pampered. A herbalist and perfumery are also included in this section.

DE PAOLA
Via della Croce 23 ☎*6789607. Map* **5G6**
A□ □
This extremely popular shop has been doing brisk business in Via della Croce since 1946. It is Rome's biggest perfumery and has by far and away the widest selection. Go early to avoid the crush.

FILIPPO PARRUCCHIERE
Via Condotti 91 ☎*6794907. Map* **5G6**.
Filippo is more famous as a fashion designer than as a hairdresser, but this salon still offers one of the least expensive cuts in town.

GILCAGNÉ
Via del Babuino 173 ☎*3613291. Map* **5G6**
A□ □ □ □
Two white Corinthian columns set at an angle lead to the shop that displays Gilcagné's impressive range of make-up. Deep-cleansing, massage and hairdressing are available in the salon behind the shop, while in the makeup studio Gil shows you how to make the best of your individual features or how to change your image. If your name is Amanda Lear or Liza Minelli, or you are

some other well-known habituée of Gil's club, these sessions may be conducted for free. Otherwise, the cost could be substantial.

L'ISOLA DI MOD
Via dei Cappuccini 11 ☎*4746072. Map* **5G6**. *Closed Mon.*
Stylist Gianni Modafferi writes a beauty column and appears on Italian TV as a beauty consultant. Here, there's sauna, massage, solarium and hairdressing — for men too.

ERBORISTERIA DI M. MESSÉGUÉ
Piazza San Silvestro 8 (Galleria RAS) ☎*6797294. Map* **5H6**.
Maurice Mességué, herbalist and author, personally grows and harvests in Fleurance, France, all the herbs that go into the preparation of his cosmetics, medications and teas. This is a friendly and attractive little shop, run by disciples Antonio Barbieri and Maria Luisa Lisandrelli — both qualified herbalists who are happy to give expert advice.

MICHEL
Via Sistina 143 ☎*4740761. Map* **5G6**.
A beauty center within reasonable

economic reach, Michel's is nevertheless quite an experience. The unprepossessing entrance on the first floor leads to a labyrinth of mirrored pillars and potted plants. Look behind each pillar and you will find Michel and his staff hard at work beautifying their customers' hair, faces, hands and feet. In the more private recesses of the labyrinth, massage and sunbeds are also available.

FELICE MORETTI
Via Lazio 9, off Via Veneto ☎*484786. Map 6G7* 🅰🅱 🅲🅳 *Closed Sun; Mon.*
A very reputable hairdresser, much frequented by Romans.

SERGIO RUSSO
Piazza Mignanelli 25, off Piazza di Spagna ☎*6780457. Map 5G6.*
Another fashionable hairdresser, Sergio Russo offers top hair-styling at top prices. His clients include such elegant-stars as Audrey Hepburn and Claudia Cardinale, as well as Mrs. Henry Kissinger.

SERGIO VALENTE
Via Condotti 11 ☎*6791268. Map 5G6.*
The archetypal Roman beauty center, Sergio Valente's salon is reached through an imposing archway and up a grand flight of steps. Sergio is the top name in the business, and although hair-styling is the main activity, this rich women's playground includes a make-up studio and facilities for saunas, facials, waxing and massage. Additional delights are a movie-star room and a couple of sulking boxes for celebrities and common mortals who might wish to avoid the public eye. Sergio works regularly with Valentino and Fendi, and keeps an archive room to record his magazine work.

BOOKS
Rizzoli *(Galleria Colonna at Largo Chigi 15, map 5 H6)* is the largest bookstore in the whole of Italy. The biggest English-language bookstore is the **Lion Bookshop** *(Via del Babuino 181, map 5 G6)*. Also recommended for English and American books is the **American Book Co.** *(Via della Vite 57, map 5 G6)*. The place to buy, and sell, second-hand English-language paperbacks is the **Economy Book Center** *(Via Torino 136, map 6 G7)*. For a huge selection of beautiful art books, mostly at half price, go to **Libreria San Silvestro** *(Piazza San Silvestro 27, map 5 H6)*.

CLOTHES FOR WOMEN
Rome is an important center for *alta moda* (high fashion) and chic prêt-à-porter. A glance around the streets will show that the keyword of Italian women's fashion is elegance, and even if colors sometimes become adventurous, lines nearly always remain classic. You can find here the very best of Italian fashion, with outlets for Milanese and Florentine as well as local designers. French designers are also well represented: among the old brigade are **Givenchy** *(Via Borgognona 21, map 5 G6)*, **Courrèges** *(Via Bocca di Leone 84, map 5 G6)*, **Balenciaga** *(Via Bocca di Leone 83, map 5 G6)* and **Céline** *(Via Bocca di Leone 79, map 5 G6)*.

Expensive ready-to-wear is the Italians' forte, but they also excel at producing knitwear, and Rome is full of shops selling colorful woolen separates at moderate prices.

BENETTON

Via Condotti 59 ☎ *6797982. Map 5G6* 🔲
🔲 🔲 🔲

The most central of several branches, this shop sells classic young separates with the Benetton label, in wool and cotton. The clothes are well made and inexpensive, and there is an exciting choice of colors. Other shops selling Benetton are **Merceria** *(Via Frattina, map 5 G6)* and **Tagliacozzo** *(Via del Gambero, map 5 G6)*.

GIORGIO ARMANI

Via del Babuino 102 ☎ *6793777. Map 5G6*
🔲 🔲 🔲 🔲

The undisputed master of the suit for women, Armani has a flair for putting different textures, patterns and colors together, with sensational results. You won't find better Italian prêt-à-porter than this anywhere, and the shop is as delightful as the clothes. The staff are not in the least bit snooty.

GENTE

Via del Babuino 82 ☎ *3207671. Map 5G6*
🔲 🔲 🔲 🔲

Gente has exclusive rights to the couture collections of some of the best known Italian stylists, such as Dolce e Gabbana, Romeo Gigli and Moschino. Another branch at Via Cola di Rienzo 277 *(☎ 3211516, map 4 G4)* stocks these designers' prêt-à-porter collections.

FILIPPO   See MEN'S CLOTHES.

KENZO

Via del Babuino 124a ☎ *6797770. Map 5G6* 🔲 🔲 🔲 🔲

Admirers of Kenzo's color genius and wacky ideas will be delighted to find the full range of the Japanese stylist's collection here. Prices are the same as in Paris.

KRIZIA

Piazza di Spagna 77 ☎ *6793419. Map 5G6* 🔲 🔲 🔲 🔲

Designed in Milan by Mariuccia Mandella, Krizia knits have won an international reputation for stylish

sophistication. Selling separates as well, this shop will appeal to both the young and the not-so-young.

LINEA LUI/LEI/SPORT, PLAY JEANS

Via del Corso 49 ☎ *6786725. Map 5G5* 🔲
🔲 🔲 🔲

Four shops in one, this has good-value clothes for the young and young-at-heart, including a big selection of cheerful woolen separates.

MISSONI

Via del Babuino 96 ☎ *6797971. Map 5G6*
🔲 🔲 🔲 🔲

King and queen of the knitwear scene, Ottavio and Rosita Missoni continue to produce breathtakingly beautiful designs from their base at Varese, near Milan. Subtle color variations, geometric or flaring patterns and nubbly textures are the elements of the unmistakable Missoni style.

EMILIO PUCCI

Via Campania 59 ☎ *4758584. Map 6F7* 🔲
🔲 🔲

A longish walk away from the shops and lights of Via Veneto, a grand mansion contains the prêt-à-porter collection of this classic Florentine designer. Signed scarves and monogrammed ties are the specialties of the house, and Pucci designs all the silks out of which he makes his timeless blouses and dresses.

YVES ST LAURENT

Via Bocca di Leone 35 ☎ *6795577. Map 5G6* 🔲 🔲 🔲 🔲

St Laurent has seven shops in Italy, but this is the only one in Rome. There are no men's clothes (ties excepting) and no perfumes, but the women's prêt-à-porter collection is large, colorful and exciting. Sadly, St Laurent's prices are slightly higher here than they are in Paris.

LUISA SPAGNOLI

Via Frattina 116 ☎ *6795517. Map 5G6* 🔲
🔲 🔲 🔲

A highly respected doyenne among Italian knitwear designers, Luisa Spagnoli has, sadly, perhaps failed to keep pace with the times. The quality of the fine woolen knits is still superb, but styling and flair are noticeably absent.

STEFANEL
Via Frattina 31 ☎6792667. *Map* 5G6 🆎 💳 💳 📠
Vivacious woolen and cotton separates — pullovers, skirts *and* pants — in a multitude of bright colors are sold at this and other branches of the youthful chain. All are designed by Stefanel Beppino.

UNGARO
Via Bocca di Leone 24 ☎6789931. *Map* 5G6 🆎 💳 💳
Ungaro is probably the most Italian of the French designers. His classic silk dresses and wool suits are made in Italy, and actually cost less here than they do in Paris.

VALENTINO BOUTIQUE
Via Bocca di Leone 15 ☎6795862. *Map* 5G6 🆎 💳 💳 📠
Some people believe that Valentino has lost direction, but it could just be that by sometimes breaking all the rules he offends the Italian ideal of classic elegance. The undisputed giant of the Italian fashion scene, Valentino's haute couture, although often controversial, is still very respected, and his prêt-à-porter is always young and very original (*Via Gregoriana 24, map* 5 *G6*).

GIANNI VERSACE
Via Bocca di Leone 27 ☎6780521. *Map* 5G6 🆎 💳 💳 📠
This Milanese designer favors "unmatched" separates in plain, somber colors that work easily together. Prices are in the same range as **Giorgio Armani** or **Valentino** (see above for both).

CLOTHES FOR MEN
The Italian designer's preference for classic lines is perhaps nowhere better expressed than in men's clothing. Rome is full of grand tailors (most of them selling off-the-peg as well) and high-class men's retailers, and it has always been an important center for shirt-making.

BATTISTONI
Via Condotti 57-61a (through courtyard) ☎6786241. *Map* 5G6 🆎 💳 💳
For many years the most fashionable tailor in Rome, Battistoni started out 40 years ago as a small shirt-making operation. The transformation to society tailor was effected by the mid-1950s, and soon countless movie stars and members of royalty were having their suits and shirts made here. Now, Battistoni could be losing ground (and customers) to nearby **Cucci** (see below).

ENZO CECI
Via della Vite 52 ☎6798882. *Map* 5G6 🆎 💳 💳 📠
By far the most interesting of the many men's boutiques in Via della Vite, with good original and sporty fashions in great colors, all of them exclusively designed.

DAVIDE CENCI
Via Campo Marzio 1 ☎6784537. *Map* 4H5 🆎 💳 💳 📠
Dating from 1926, this shop has never stooped to follow the tumultuous changes in fashion. Davide Cenci has always preferred a classical and sober elegance for his sophisticated clientele.

CUCCI
Via Condotti 67 ☎6791882. *Map* 5G6 🆎 💳 💳 📠
A family firm like **Battistoni** (left), but the founding member was a tailor rather than a shirt-maker. Prices are as high as Battistoni's, but do not deter stars such as Alain Delon. Also a favorite of the late Salvador Dalí.

DEGLI EFFETTI
Piazza Capranica 75 ☎6791650. *Map* 4H5 🆎 💳 💳 📠

Romeo Gigli, Dolce e Gabbana, Jean Paul Gaultier, Katharine Hamnett, Comme des Garçons, Yamamoto: these are just some of the style gurus represented on the rails of this very trendy boutique, which opened in 1983. It has a smaller department for women.

FILIPPO BOUTIQUE
Via Condotti 6 ☎*6707906. Map 5G6* 🆎
💳 💳 🆅

Hairdresser extraordinaire (see BEAUTY CENTERS), Filippo creates the trendiest clothes in Rome. His ideas are young, exciting and bang up-to-the-minute. Clothes for women are included and prices are high.

MAX
Via Bocca di Leone 13 ☎*6783977. Map 5G6* 🆎 💳 💳 🆅

Shirt-making is still the most important part of Max Bertollini's business, but he now sells ready-made shirts (for men and women).

EDDY MONETTI
Via Condotti 63 ☎*6794117. Map 5G6* 🆎 💳 💳 🆅

The designs are not exclusive, but they make up one of the best and biggest collections of youngish, classic jackets, pants, pullovers and shirts.

SCHOSTAL
Via del Corso 158 ☎*6791240. Map 5G6.*
One of few good reasons to venture into the Corso, Schostal sells pure cotton and woolen socks at low prices.

TESTA
Via Frattina 104 ☎*6791296. Map 5G6* 🆎 💳 💳 🆅

For youngish men-about-town, here are classic suits and separates, with stylish touches to bring them out of the ordinary. Almost all the designs are exclusive, and prices are reasonable. There is another shop nearby *(Via Borgognona 13, map 5G6).*

78 UOMO
Piazza di Spagna 78 ☎*6792555. Map 5G6* 🆎 💳 💳 🆅

The one and only outlet for Missoni knits for men. The designs are unmistakable, the colors warm, soft and muted. The whole collection is irresistible.

VALENTINO UOMO
Via Mario de' Fiori 22 ☎*6783656. Map 5G6* 🆎 💳 💳 🆅

Valentino's suits are classic and understated, his belts and jewelry elegant and monogrammed. Prices are well within reach.

CLOTHES FOR CHILDREN
Like their parents, Italian children look extremely chic, and inordinate sums of *Lire* are spent on keeping them that way.

LA CICOGNA
Via Boccea ☎*6241641* 🆎 💳 💳 🆅
This is a reliable, reputable medium-priced shop selling children's and maternity clothes, nursery furniture, baby toys and shoes. La Cicogna has now opened several other branches in Rome.

SCIUNNACH
Via Piave 2c ☎*4819071. Map 6F8* 🆎 💳 🆅

This inexpensive shop specializes in good-value footwear for both children and women.

TABLÒ
Via della Croce 84 ☎*6794468; Piazza di Spagna 96* ☎*6781470. Map 5G6* 🆎 🆅
Well-dressed Roman children have their clothes bought at Tablò. The quality and styling here are superb, with a corresponding price-tag: you can pay enormous adult prices for the tiniest garments.

The shop in Via della Croce is for children of 9 years and upward, and that in Piazza di Spagna for those of 8 years and downward; there is another branch at 105, Via del Babuino *(map 5G6).*

DEPARTMENT STORES

The following department stores offer goods of a generally reasonable standard at moderate prices.

COIN
Piazzale Appio ☎ *7573241. Map* **10***J9* 🆎 💳 💳 💳
A modern, well-laid-out store with five floors of medium-quality clothing and household furnishings. By far the best of Rome's big stores, just s of the city walls.

LA RINASCENTE
Largo Chigi ☎ *6797691. Map* **5***H6* 🆎 💳 💳 💳
Clothing, perfumes, haberdashery and toys. For tourists with passports, there's a ten percent discount on perfumes, cosmetics and toiletries.

STANDA
Via Cola di Rienzo 173 ☎ *3243283. Map* **4***G4.*
A store worth investigating for its clothes and household goods — mostly of reasonable quality, at rock-bottom prices. There are branches all across the city.

UPIM
Via del Tritone 172 ☎ *6783336. Map* **5***H6* 💳
The most central of 18 branches, this store stocks cheap, unexciting clothes, household goods and toys.

FABRICS

For fabrics from the cheapest to the most exclusively fabulous, for clothes and curtains as well as tapestry and upholstery, here are the best addresses.

BISES
Via del Gesù 93 ☎ *6780941* 📠*622196. Map* **5***H5* 🆎 💳 💳
Rome's largest collection of furnishing and dress fabrics can be found in a beautiful 17thC palace, home of Cardinal Altieri before he became Pope Clement X. Under lofty painted and coffered ceilings, each huge chamber is devoted to just one type of material — silks, wools, velvets, and so on. This collection has to be seen to be believed.

CESARI
Via del Babuino 13-16 (and new showroom at 195) ☎ *3611441. Map* **5***G5* 🆎 💳 💳 💳
The setting may not be quite as grand as **Bises'** (above) but by any other standards this imposing house with its fluted Corinthian columns and molded ceilings would be impressive. Cesari is the top place for furnishing fabrics. For those, go along to **Via Aurelia, 137** (☎ *6381241* 📠*611319, map* **3***H2).* For **Cesari's linen store** (*Via Barberini, map* **6***G7),* see page 225.

POLIDORI
Via Condotti 21 ☎ *6784842. Map* **5***G6* 🆎 💳 💳 💳
Classic silk, cotton and wool dress materials, in the medium-expensive to very expensive price range. There is a branch for men's fabrics *(Via Borgognona 4b, map* **5***G6),* and also for men's fashions *(Polidori Uomo, Via Condotti 83, map* **5***G6).*

GLASS AND CHINA

The tradition of craftsmanship in glass and china goes back a long way in Italy, and beautiful handmade glasses and pottery are still to be found in Rome's shops.

RICHARD GINORI
Via Condotti 87 ☎6781013. *Map* **5**G6 [AE] [◆] [◐] [VISA]
Two floors laid out with traditional table settings in porcelain, china, glass and crystal.

MYRICAE
Via Frattina 36 ☎6795335. *Map* **5**G6 [AE] [◆] [◐] [VISA]
Regional pottery, painted trays, glass, colorful lampshades and other folk art, all extremely reasonably priced. Roman girls place their wedding lists at this shop for colorful, out-of-the-ordinary presents.

STILVETRO
Via Frattina 55 ☎6790258. *Map* **5**G6.
All-Italian china and glass, mostly from Tuscany, at rock-bottom prices. Most of it looks as cheap as it is, but some attractive rustic-style dinner services (plus cutlery) make real bargains.

C. TUPINI
Piazza San Lorenzo in Lucina 8
☎6871458. *Map* **5**G5.
Rome's most beautiful china store, lit by crystal chandeliers, is correspondingly expensive. Fine china and porcelain; also glass, silver and hand-painted ceramics.

GLOVES AND TIGHTS
Gloves and tights in a rainbow of colors, to suit any budget, are sold in shops all over the city. For a vast choice, there is no need to stray from the center of town.

CALZA E CALZE
Via della Croce 78 ☎6784281. *Map* **5**G6.
Selling tights and stockings like hot cakes, this inexpensive little shop has the best and brightest collection of all. A useful tip: try to call early to avoid the crush.

DI CORI
Piazza di Spagna 53 ☎6784439. *Map* **5**G6 [AE] [VISA]
It would be hard to fit any more stock into this tiny shop: brightly colored woolen and leather gloves line the walls

from floor to ceiling. Kid, pigskin, chamois and suede are all of the highest quality. Go next door if you are looking for scarves and belts.

AMEDEO PERRONE
Piazza di Spagna 92 ☎6783101. *Map* **5**G6 [AE] [◆] [◐] [VISA]
Gloves are the specialty here, in leather, cashmere and lambswool, and in a wide choice of colors. But there are also socks and tights, including colored tights for children aged 2-12 years, all at super-cheap prices.

JEWELRY AND SILVER
Have a look around: you will see that everyone in the city wears gold and silver, despite the snatchers. Rome, mostly thanks to Bulgari, is one of the jewelry capitals of the world.

BULGARI
Via Condotti 10 ☎6793876. *Map* **5**G6 [AE] [◆] [◐] [VISA]
Possibly the world's greatest jewelers, Bulgari discreetly guards the identities of its royal customers behind a grand

marble facade. As befits a princely clientele, the interior is palatial.

FORNARI
Via Condotti 80 ☎6794285. *Map* **5**G6 [AE] [◆] [◐] [VISA]

Specializing in gold jewelry, with some silver; traditionally where to go to if you can't afford **Bulgari**. A less rarefied atmosphere than some grander jewelers.

FUMIS
Piazza San Silvestro 14 ☎*6792510. Map 5H6* 🄰🄴 🄲

A medium-priced silver store, stocked entirely with Fumis' own designs. There is another branch (*Via del Gambero 4, map O 00*).

FÜRST
Via Vittorio Veneto 42 ☎*483992. Map 6G7* 🄲 🄲🄳 📠

After **Bulgari**, but a long way behind, are a number of high-class jewelers such as Fürst. Specialties are emeralds and rubies.

MASSONI
Largo Goldoni 48, w end of Via Condotti ☎*6790182. Map 5G6* 🄰🄴 🄲 🄲🄳 📠

Perhaps the grandest of the runners-up, this old-established family firm attracts its fair share of famous customers. Massoni believe in creating jewelry to the client's own ideas, which in the past has endeared them to such independent spirits as Ingrid Bergman and Ava Gardner.

LEATHER AND FUR
Italian leather is famous all over the world. The following list has shops at the upper and lower ends of the price scale.

PIER CARANTI
Piazza di Spagna 43 ☎*6791621. Map 5G6* 🄰🄴 🄲 🄲🄳 📠

This boutique sells classic bags, briefcases and belts at reasonable prices. You can also get an umbrella to go with your briefcase. There is another branch (*Via Frattina 77, map 5 G6*).

CERESA
Via del Tritone 118-122 ☎*4885516. Map 6G7* 🄰🄴 🄲 🄲🄳 📠

Clusters of fur pelts hanging on the walls identify the specialty here, and help you select the right quality and color before your order goes into the workshop upstairs. There is also a good collection of leather goods, particularly bags. Ceresa has been in the business longer than **Gucci** and can be relied on for top-quality, classic designs.

FENDI
Via Borgognona 39 ☎*6797642. Map 5G6* 🄰🄴 🄲🄳 📠

Looking at some of Karl Lagerfeld's models in the fabulous fur salon at Via

Borgognona 39, you can see why he has played such an important part in Fendi's success. In the same street at #36, Fendi's dark, printed-leather bags sell fast and well, even if the printing process succeeds in making them look like plastic. A boutique at #41 sells non-leather accessories such as canvas bags; another at #4e has shoes.

GUCCI
Via Condotti 8 and 76 ☎*6789340. Map 5G6* 🄰🄴 🄲 🄲🄳 📠

The twin GG stamp still attracts vast numbers of Italians and foreigners in search of soft leather and suede clothing, luggage, bags, shoes, belts and ties. For slightly younger styles, it's a good idea to try the well-stocked **Gucci Boutique** (*Via Borgognona 25, map 5 G6*).

MODI
Via Nazionale 237/8 ☎*4818280. Map 6H7* 🄰🄴 🄲 🄲🄳 📠

Inexpensive, with a good selection of bags, wallets, belts and gloves, all at factory prices.

LINENS AND LINGERIE
Although other parts of Italy are better known for their linen and lingerie, there are some Roman shops selling appliquéd and hand-embroidered table linen of fabulous beauty.

BELLINI
Piazza di Spagna 77 ☎6795956. *Map* **5**G6
🔲 🔲 🔲 🔲

Hand-embroidered and -appliquéd table linen, sheets and lingerie. Months, even years, of labor go into some of the more elaborate tablecloths; the same embroiderer is employed throughout to achieve a perfect finish.

CESARI
Via Barberini 1 ☎4881382. *Map* **6**G7 🔲
🔲 🔲 🔲

Rome's largest collection of fine linens, towels and lingerie. Affluent young brides order their trousseaux here, and such luminaries as Lauren Bacall and the Belgian Royal Family have their silk sheets hand-embroidered here to exclusive designs. Even the machine-embroidered linens are considered superb. Furnishing fabrics *(Via del Babuino 16, map 5 G6)* are available too — see FABRICS.

TINA
Via Bocca di Leone 9 ☎6784076. *Map* **5**G6 🔲 🔲 🔲 🔲

The best of the small boutiques selling lingerie and nightgowns, this shop offers pretty and exclusive designs at very reasonable prices.

SHOES
The most beautiful shoes in the world are made in Italy, and some of Italy's finest are found on and around the Via Condotti.

CAMPANILE SPATARELLA
Via Condotti 58 ☎6783041. *Map* **5**G6 🔲
🔲 🔲 🔲

The shoes may be the height of fashion, but they are fearfully expensive and service is not what you'd expect for such prices.

TANINO CRISCI
Via Borgognona 4m ☎6795461. *Map* **5**G6
🔲 🔲 🔲 🔲

This small, unassuming shop sells a limited range of sporty styles, produced in its factory at Casteggio near Pavia. Only moderately expensive and all hand-made, these shoes are probably superior in quality to any others sold in Rome.

FERRAGAMO
Via Condotti 66 ☎6781130. *Map* **5**G6 🔲
🔲 🔲 🔲

Top-quality classic shoes at top prices. Slightly more swayed by fashion trends than **Bruno Magli**, this Florence-based firm has women's shoes at Via Condotti 73/74.

FRAGIACOMO
Via Condotti 35 ☎6798780. *Map* **5**G6 🔲
🔲 🔲

One of the most conservative of the top shoe-makers, this Milanese designer produces elegant shoes at averagely expensive prices.

MAUD FRIZON
Via Borgognona 38 ☎6795370. *Map* **5**G6
🔲 🔲 🔲 🔲

Rome's most exciting shoe store. The colors are fun, the designs strikingly original. Maud Frizon lives and works in Paris, but her shoes are made in Italy. The styles seem aimed at a young market, but are sadly beyond the means of most young sophisticates. This is high fashion, for which you will pay super-high prices.

BRUNO MAGLI
Via del Gambero 1 ☎6793802. *Map* **5**G6
🔲 🔲 🔲 🔲

One of four Roman outlets for this Bologna shoe firm, selling sober, classic styles, at averagely high prices. Leather jackets are among the accessories.

GUIDO PASQUALI
Via Bocca di Leone 5 ☎6795023. *Map* **5**G6 🔲 🔲 🔲 🔲

A Milanese designer with a difference, Guido Pasquali creates young, fashion-conscious styles. As a bonus, he is not too expensive.

RAPHAEL SALATO
Piazza di Spagna 34 ☎*6795646. Map 5G6*
[AE] [◆] [◆] [VISA]

Intricately embroidered leather is a specialty of Raphael Salato, but the colors used are, disappointingly, on the dull side. Nevertheless, the quality is unimpeachable.

SANTINI
Via Frattina 120 ☎*6784114. Map 5G6* [AE]
[◆] [VISA]

A chic shop-front, with neon rainbow arches and a white-tiled window, displays one of the best young collections in town. The designs are original and inexpensive, and the colors distinctive.

STATIONERY
Two shops in which you can find all kinds of pens and pencils, and where paper is elevated into an art form, are listed below.

PINEIDER
Via Due Macelli 68 ☎*6795884. Map 5G6; Via della Fontanella Borghese 22* ☎*6878369.*
Map 5G5 [AE] [◆] [◆] [VISA]
Lots of internationally-known names get printed on Pineider's high-class stationery, but this firm is more famous for the quality of the artwork (you can have anything you like in the way of typefaces and symbols) than for the paper itself.

VERTECCHI
Via della Croce 38 ☎*6790100 and Via della Croce 70* ☎*6783110. Map 5G6* [AE] [◆] [◆] [VISA]
Useful and unpretentious, this is a good place for gifts as well as stationery. At Via della Croce 38 there are two floors of decorative candles, trays, gift wrappings, Christmas decorations, greeting cards, table-mats and kitchen gadgets. Across the street at #70 is an artists' paradise: a beautifully laid-out shop displaying walls of colored crayons, pens, pencils and paper, as well as more general stationery. The main stationery store is some way out of the city center (*Via Pietro da Cortona 12*).

STREET MARKETS
Romans buy their vegetables, fruit, flowers, meats and cheeses from one of the many street markets that are held daily all over the city. Rich people as well as poor shop in these markets, because this is where the best and freshest produce can be found. Stalls of cheap clothing are generally included among the food stands, but there are also whole markets devoted just to clothes and accessories.

The food and flower markets are the most entertaining as well as the most picturesque, and an early-morning wander through one of these is an essential part of any Roman vacation.

CAMPO DEI FIORI
Piazza Campo dei Fiori. Map 4I5. Open 6am-2pm. Closed Sun.
Rome's oldest market is held in a cobbled square in the heart of the medieval city and sells flowers, fruit and vegetables under makeshift awnings or giant parasols — all collapsible at the end of the morning. An old cast-iron pump marked *SPQR Acqua Vergine* cools wilting roses in the daytime heat, and in the ancient houses round the square are some good delicatessens.

MERCATO DEI FIORI
Via Trionfale/Via Paolo Sarpi. Map 3F2. Open 10am-1pm, Tues only.
Rome's only flower market takes place in a two-story covered hall some way out of the city center, in the suburb of

Prati. It is held daily, but is only open to the public on Tuesday. Upstairs, the air is heady with the scent of the flowers in season, and there is endless scope for bargaining. Downstairs, an exotica of giant house plants refreshes jaded spirits before the trip back to the city.

PIAZZA VITTORIO EMANUELE
Map 10I9. Open 7am-2pm. Closed Sun.
Stretching all the way round the edge of this huge garden square is the city's largest, most entertaining market. Clothes and leather goods are ranged along the s side and hold some fine bargains, but the food stalls on the N side are what make this market famous. The specialization is prodigious: one stall sells only calves' livers, another only fresh tuna, yet another nothing but lemons. This is the place for the most unusual cheeses, salad vegetables and shellfish, the rarest game birds, birds' eggs and fruits. Stallholders occupy themselves during slack moments by preparing their produce: trimming artichokes, plucking birds. Crowing cocks and scuttling crabs contribute to the lively atmosphere.

PORTA PORTESE
Ponte Sublicio. Map 8K5. Open 6.30am-2.30pm, Sun only.
This extremely popular clothes market skirts close to the Tiber in a narrow ribbon more than 1km ($\frac{1}{2}$ mile) long, from Ponte Sublicio in the N to Ponte Testaccio in the s. The clothes and accessories are cheap but of poor quality, and you would have to look elsewhere

for a real leather handbag. Romans throng here in vast numbers, and it is wise to arrive before 9am.

VIA ANDREA DORIA
Map 3F2. Open 8am-1pm. Closed Sun; Mon.
Ranged along almost the full length of Via Andrea Doria and spilling into the side streets to the s, this large and lively food market may not have all the specialties of **Piazza Vittorio Emanuele** (see left), but it wins on organization. The vegetable stands are laid out in effortlessly artistic arrangements, draped with strings of onions and chili peppers. The *salumerie* (delicatessen stalls) are packed with cheeses, bottled oils and *prosciutto*, framed by festoons of salami and sausages.

VIA SANNIO
Map 10J9. Open Mon-Fri 8am-1pm; Sat 8am-7pm. Closed Sun.
Just two stops on the Metropolitana from the larger market at **Piazza Vittorio Emanuele** (see left), Via Sannio is worth a visit if you are interested in secondhand clothes. Walk down the street past the beads and baubles until you reach a cobbled lane on your right. This is where the clothing stalls begin, but if you want secondhand clothes (in large numbers) you must walk to the open space at the end of the lane. The new clothing is of inferior quality to that at Piazza Vittorio Emanuele, and similar to (if not identical with) that at **Porta Portese** (left). (Some of these stallholders move their wares to Porta Portese on Sunday.)

TOY STORES
From the life-sized furry leopards in the tourist traps of Piazza Navona, to charming hand-made toys from northern Italy, to Pinocchios of all sizes, Rome has a vast choice of toys. For detailed information on gifts for the younger consumer, see ROME FOR CHILDREN on page 234.

Clothing sizes chart

LADIES
Suits and dresses

Australia	8	10	12	14	16	18	
France	34	36	38	40	42	44	
Germany	32	34	36	38	40	42	
Italy	38	40	42	44	46		
Japan	7	9	11	13			
UK	6	8	10	12	14	16	18
USA	4	6	8	10	12	14	16

Shoes

USA	6	$6\frac{1}{2}$	7	$7\frac{1}{2}$	8	$8\frac{1}{2}$
UK	$4\frac{1}{2}$	5	$5\frac{1}{2}$	6	$6\frac{1}{2}$	7
Europe	38	38	39	39	40	41

MEN
Shirts

USA, UK	14	$14\frac{1}{2}$	15	$15\frac{1}{2}$	16	$16\frac{1}{2}$	17
Europe, Japan Australia	36	37	38	39.5	41	42	43

Sweaters/T-shirts

Australia, USA, Germany	S		M		L		XL
UK	34		36-38		40		42-44
Italy	44		46-48		50		52
France	1		2-3		4		5
Japan			S-M		L		XL

Suits/Coats

UK, USA	36	38	40	42	44
Australia, Italy, France, Germany	46	48	50	52	54
Japan	S	M	L	XL	

Shoes

UK	7	$7\frac{1}{2}$	$8\frac{1}{2}$	$9\frac{1}{2}$	$10\frac{1}{2}$	11
USA	8	$8\frac{1}{2}$	$9\frac{1}{2}$	$10\frac{1}{2}$	$11\frac{1}{2}$	12
Europe	41	42	43	44	45	46

CHILDREN
Clothing

UK

Height (ins)	43	48	55	60	62	
Age	4-5	6-7	9-10	11	12	13

USA

Age	4	6	8	10	12	14

Europe

Height (cms)	125	135	150	155	160	165
Age	7	9	12	13	14	15

Recreation

Rome for children

Italians love children. They tend to spoil their own and, given the opportunity, are equally indulgent toward other people's. This attitude is perhaps most obvious in restaurants and cafés, where small children receive almost regal treatment. Parents who are happy to join in the general spirit of indulgence, or feel called upon to offer the occasional bribe, will find the best ice cream in the world a useful ally. (See REFRESHMENTS).

A mild climate, large parks and many traffic-free zones mean that children can spend much of the time playing out of doors. Bicycling and roller-skating are favorite pursuits, and there are plenty of safe open spaces for both (see PARKS AND ZOOS below). Most other activities also center on the parks and pedestrian piazzas, notably the **Villa Borghese** and **Piazza Navona**.

PARKS AND ZOOS

Villa Borghese *(N of center, map 5 F6)* is Rome's largest park, perfect for roller-skating and cycling. There are also mini-train rides, and pony and traps for the footsore. Boats can be rented at the **Giardino del Lago**. The small but well-kept zoo, **Giardino Zoologico**, is open from 8.30am to sunset, and feeding times are displayed near the entrance. Other attractions are a fairground and occasional puppet shows (see THEATER AND OTHER EVENTS below).

Several other parks in Rome offer the usual facilities — and some have more unusual entertainments. **Villa Ada** *(W of Via Salaria, map 12 B4-C4)* is ideal for energetic children, with two well-equipped playgrounds, a roller-skating rink, bicycling areas, ponds and wooded slopes. **Villa Celimontana** *(S of the Colosseum, map 9 J7-K7)* and **Villa Pamphili** *(on the Via Aurelia Antica, map 7 J3)* also have ponds and bicycle tracks. **Villa Glori** *(N of Villa Borghese, map 2 C5-6)* offers pony rides, and **Villa Balestra** *(NW of Villa Borghese, map 5 D5)* pony cart-rides. **Villa Sciarra** *(Trastevere, map 7 J4-K4)*, one of the smaller parks, has an aviary. A cannon is fired at noon from the **Gianicolo** park *(W bank of the Tiber, map 7 I3-J4)*, overlooking the city, and sometimes there are puppet shows.

The **Villaggio Olimpico** *(E of Corso di Francia, map 2 C5)* has a roller-skating rink and playground. Merry-go-rounds and a roller-skating rink are the main attractions of the gardens of the **Ministero degli Affari**

Esteri *(Piazzale della Farnesina, map 1 B3),* and the **Parco Oppio** *(N of the Colosseum, map 9 I7-10 I8)* also has a small fairground. But for a really impressive fairground, complete with big dipper and roller coaster, go to **Luna Park** *(Via delle Tre Fontane, EUR* ☎ *5925933, map 11 E3)* and use the boating lake and mini-golf course as well. **Piazza Navona** *(map 5 H5),* in the heart of the old city, is not strictly a park but is sealed off to traffic and makes an attractive play area.

There is a **safari park** near Fiumicino Airport *(Via Portuense, 35km/22 miles outside Rome* ☎ *6011188, open Wed-Mon 10.30am-1hr before sunset),* and a large **bird sanctuary** at Palo *(about same distance from city, run by the Worldwide Fund for Nature* ☎ *9911641, open Thurs-Sun 9.30am-sunset).*

MUSEUMS

There is an intriguing waxwork museum called **Museo della Cere** *(Piazza Santi Apostoli 67* ☎ *6796482, map 5 H6).* The **Museo Storico della Motorizzazione Militare** *(Viale dell' Esercito 86, near Via Laurentina* ☎ *5011885),* a museum of military vehicles, is about 20 minutes from the city center by car (☎ first to organize entry permits).

Children with rather more peaceful tastes might like to visit the **Museo degli Strumenti Musicali** *(Piazza Santa Croce in Gerusalemme 9* ☎ *7014796, map 10 J10),* a museum of musical instruments. The **Galleria Nazionale d'Arte Moderna** *(Viale delle Belle Arti 131* ☎ *802751, map 5 E6)* has a delightful garden dotted with modern works of art. The moving exhibits inside are equally fascinating. The **Museo Civico di Zoologia** *(Via Aldrovandi 18* ☎ *8073586, map 6 E7)* is a natural-history museum where visitors to the zoo are allowed free admittance.

THEATER AND OTHER EVENTS

Puppets are an Italian specialty. Shows take place at **Alla Ringhiera** *(Via dei Riari 81, Trastevere* ☎ *6568711, map 7 I4).* Irregular open-air shows are given in the **Villa Borghese** and in the **Gianicolo** park. A number of theaters, such as **Teatro Goldoni** *(Vicolo dei Soldati 3* ☎ *6561156, map 4 H5),* stage occasional children's productions. For current listings, look in *Il Messaggero* under "Attività per ragazzi."

OTHER IDEAS

An exciting way for a child to see Rome is from a horse-drawn carriage (see OTHER TRANSPORTATION, page 42). And in July and August you can take a river trip through central Rome organized by the **Amici del Tevere**: see *This Week in Rome* for details.

Many of the major historical sights such as the COLOSSEUM and CASTEL SANT' ANGELO make fascinating outings for children blessed with vivid imaginations and a stimulating guide. The city's many fountains are another big attraction: the TREVI FOUNTAIN is a special favorite with children, who delight in the tradition of throwing coins into the water to ensure that they will one day return to Rome.

If the children are running short of reading matter, buy them an Italian comic, such as *Topolino* (Mickey Mouse), published weekly.

Activities for children increase in the weeks leading up to Christmas, and decorations go up in **Piazza Navona**, **Via dei Coronari**, **Via Frattina** and **Via Condotti**. From mid-December until Epiphany (January 6), a market is held in **Piazza Navona**, with stalls selling Christmas cribs, figures and decorations, and toys and candies. The market ends with a carnival on the Eve of Epiphany. Next morning, Italian children traditionally receive presents from *La Befana,* a female version of Santa Claus.

For other annual festivals, see CALENDAR OF EVENTS on pages 56-58.

TOY STORES

Piazza Navona has a long association with children, culminating each year in the Christmas market (see above). But the year-round toy stores in the area are best avoided. Competition to attract tourists is fierce, and sizes and prices of the furry animals know no limits. Life-sized Alsatians and leopards may make ostentatious presents, but are less likely to please than some of the smaller toy animals found elsewhere.

At **Galleria San Carlo** *(Via del Corso 114* ☎ *6790571, map* **5** *G6),* furry animals on wheels double as rocking-horses, elephants and dogs. There are tiny bamboo rocking chairs for very small children and lace-draped bamboo cradles for very large dolls. Among the cuddly toys, woolly lambs steal the show.

Marina Menasci *(Via del Lavatore 87* ☎ *6781981, map* **5** *H6* 🔳 🔳 🔳 *),* close to the Trevi Fountain, is a friendly little shop that sells hand-made toys from northern Italy. Pinocchios of all sizes are the specialty, as they are at **Pinocchio** *(Via Sistina 135* ☎ *4743723, map* **5** *G6).*

Il Giocattolaio *(Via Parigi 7-9* ☎ *4880909, map* **6** *G8* 🔳 🔳 🔳 *),* close to Stazione Termini, boasts of having the largest choice of toys from the leading manufacturers of Italy and the rest of the world, and appears to make good the claim.

Sports

Rome can boast no less than three major sports centers, each of them within convenient reach of the city center: **Tre Fontane** (☎ *5926386 at EUR, about 15mins away on the Metropolitana, map 11 E3);* **Foro Italico** (☎ *36851, on the w bank of the Tiber, beyond Via Flaminia, map 1 B3);* and **Acqua Acetosa** (☎ *8070352, N of Villa Ada, map 11 B3).* EUR and the Foro Italico were both created by Mussolini. Additions were made to the Foro Italico before the 1960 Olympic Games.

Check availability for tourists with **CONI — Italian National Olympic Committee** *(Foro Italico* ☎ *36851, map 1 B3).*

AUTO RACING
Auto racing takes place at the **Valle Lunga** race-track *(Via Cassia, 34km/ 21 miles NW of Rome* ☎ *9041417, map 11 B3).* See local press for details.

BICYCLING
Reckless Roman drivers make bicycling hazardous, but many parks have areas where children can cycle in safety (see ROME FOR CHILDREN). Bicycles may be rented from **R. Collalti** *(Via del Pellegrino 82, map 4 H4)* — see OTHER TRANSPORTATION, page 42. There are racing-tracks for more serious cyclists at **Villa Celimontana** *(s of the Colosseum, map 9 K7)* and at **Villa Sciarra** *(Trastevere, map 7 K4).* For further information you should contact the **Federazione Ciclistica Italiana** *(Via Leopoldo Franchetti 2, 00194* ☎ *36851, map 1 C3).*

BOATING
Rowboats can be rented at the Giardino del Lago in the **Villa Borghese**. Farther away, there is the lake at **EUR**, and there are several sailing clubs at **Lake Bracciano** *(about 50km/30 miles N of Rome, map 13 C3),* offering sailing lessons and dinghies for rent. The same facilities are available on the coast at **Fregene** and **Lido di Roma** *(about 35km/21 miles and 30km/18 miles w of the city respectively, both map 13 D3).* International sailing championships are held at **Castel Gandolfo**, on **Lake Albano** *(25km/15 miles SE of Rome, map 14 D4).* For information, contact the **Federazione Italiana Canottaggio** *(Viale Tiziano 70, 00196* ☎ *36851, map 1 C4).*

BOWLING
There are two particularly good bowling alleys *(bocciodromi):*
Bowling Brunswick   Lungotevere Acqua Acetosa ☎ 8086147, map 11B3
Bowling Roma   Viale Regina Margherita 181 ☎ 8551184, map **6E8**

CAMPING
The most central camp site is **Roma Camping** *(Via Aurelia, SW of the Vatican* ☎ *6623018, map 3 H2).* For more information, contact:
Centro Nazionale Campeggiatori Stranieri   Casella Postale 649, Florence 50100

EPT (Ente Provinciale per il Turismo) Via Parigi 11, 00185 ☎4881851, map **6**G8

TCI (Touring Club Italiano) Via Ovidio 7a, 00187 ☎6874603, map **4**G4

FISHING

For river fishing you must buy a license from the police and join (for a small charge) the **Federazione Italiana della Pesca Sportiva** (*Piazza Emporio 16a, 00153* ☎ *5755253, map* ***8****K5*). Lakes outside Rome often display signs saying *Lago — Pesca Sportiva,* indicating that you may fish there for a fee.

GOLF

There are two 18-hole courses within the environs of Rome: the **Acqua Santa** (*Via Appia Nuova 716, 00178* ☎ *7843079*) and **Olgiata** (*Largo Olgiata 15, 00123* ☎ *3789141*). It is advisable to apply for guest membership in advance. Both courses are closed on Monday. There is also a 9-hole course, closed Wednesday, at **Fioranello a Santa Maria della Mole** (☎ *7138058*).

The "Open Internazionale" tournament is held in spring. For information, apply to the **Federazione Italiana Golf** (*Via Flaminia 388, 00196* ☎ *3231825, map ***5****E5*).

GREYHOUND RACING

Greyhound events are held at the **Cinodromo** (*Ponte Marconi, Via della Vasca Navale 6* ☎ *5566258*). Take a look in the local press for details.

HEALTH CLUBS

Most health clubs require long-term membership, but **Sporting Roma** (*Via Barberini 36* ☎ *483607, map ***6****G7*) and **The Health Club** (*Largo Somalia 60* ☎*8394488*) allow you to join for a month. The **Budokan** sports club offers all the facilities needed for a work-out at its two centers in Prati (*Via Stefano Porcari 6 and Via Properzio 4, map ***3****G3*) and welcomes temporary members. **Gregory Gym** (*Largo Galamini 18, off Via Gregorio VII* ☎*6380983, map ***3****I1*) offers body-building, gymnastics, solarium and yoga.

HORSE RACING

Flat races and steeplechases are held at the **Ippodromo delle Capanelle** (*Via Appia Nuova (12km/8 miles* SE *of Rome* ☎ *7188551, map ***12****D4*); and there are trotting races at the **Ippodromo di Tor di Valle** (*Via del Mare (9km/6 miles* SW *of Rome* ☎ *592683, map ***11****F2*). Look in the local press for details.

KARATE

A *dojo* is to be found in **Vicolo Moroni 2** (☎*5818473, map ***7****I4*), where classes are taken by 6th Dan Giancarlo Barbin. Gymnastics, judo and sauna can be had here too.

RIDING

Riding schools in the city are reluctant to accept short-stay visitors, but **The Riding Club** (*Via di Tor Carbone, near Via Appia Antica, 00178* ☎ *5423998, map 12 E4*) will take telephone reservations for single sessions. The major equestrian event is the international horse show, the "Concorso Ippico Internazionale," in Piazza Siena at the **Villa Borghese** in May. For information, write to the **Associazione Nazionale Turismo Equestre (ANTE)** (*Via A. Borelli 5* ☎ *4940969*).

SOCCER

Soccer is a popular spectator sport, and Rome is divided in its support of the Lazio and Roma teams, who play on alternate Sunday afternoons from September to May at the **Stadio Olimpico**. For information apply to the **Associazione Sportiva Lazio** (*Via Col di Lana 8, 00195* ☎ *3236605, map 1 E4*) or the **Associazione Sportiva Roma** (*Via Trigoria* ☎ *5060200*).

SWIMMING

The major outdoor pools in Rome are at the **Foro Italico** (*Stadio del Nuoto, Viale delle Olimpici, map 1 C3*) and **EUR** (*Viale dell'Oceano Pacifico, map 11 E3*), open June to September. An indoor pool at the Foro Italico (*Via N. Canevaro, map 1 C3*) is open from November to May (☎ *36851 for details*). The **Terme Acque Albule** at Bagni di Tivoli offers sulfur-water swimming pools for the health-conscious (*on the Via Tiburtina, 22km/13 miles NE of Rome* ☎ *529012*). The best beach is at **Fregene** (*map 13 D3*), less than one hour's drive w of the city.

TENNIS

The major event of the year is the "Campionati Internazionali d'Italia" held at the **Foro Italico** in May. For details, apply to the **Federazione Italiano Tennis** (*Via Tiziano 70* ☎ *3233804, map 2 E5*).

There are public courts at the following, for which reservations are necessary:

EUR   Viale dell' Artigianato 2 ☎5924693, map **11**E3
Foro Italico   ☎36851, map **1**B3
Tennis Belle Arti   Via Flaminia 158 ☎3200602, map **1**D3
Tre Fontane   Via delle Tre Fontane ☎5926386, map **11**E3

METROPOLITAN ROME

1 2
A
B

11

0   1   2   3 km
0   1   2 miles

Viterbo SS2   FLAM

La Giustiniana

CASSIA BIS

Volusia

CASSIA

Tomba di Nerone

Via Cassia Nuova

SS3

Ottavia

Tor di Q

Palmarola

Via Trionfale

Sant Onofrio

Olimpica

B

Torrevecchia

STADIO OLIMPICO

Via

Flaminio

C

Primavalle

Via della Pineta Sacchetti

Monte Mario 139

Via Flaminia

Pin

Villa Borgh

BOCCEA

Trionfale

Casalotti

Vittoria Prati

Grande Raccordo Anulare

Borgata Montespaccato

CITTÀ DEL VATICANO

S.PIETRO

S.ANGELO

del Corso

Aurelio

PANTHEON

Valcannuta

Via Aurelia SS1

C
Pisa, Grosseto Civitavecchia

PIAZ VENEZ

PALATI

Villa Doria Pamphili

Trastevere

D

AURELIA

Villini

Aventin

TE CA

Monteverde Nuovo

Via Pisana

Gianicolense

8SS

Viale G. Marconi

Garb

SAN PAOLO FUORI LE M

Corviale

LA PISANA

Ostiens

Via Cristofor

Portuense

D
E

Via Portuense

Bo
Lau

Magliana

MAGLIANA

Via Della Magliana

Civitavecchia, Fiumicino Aeroporto

SS201

IPPODROMO DI TOR DI VALLE

SS8

EUR

Via Laurentin

OSTIENSE

FIUME (TIBER)

Castelluccio

RUDERI DELLA BUFALORA

TEVERE

Mostacciano

E
F

Acilia

Via del Mare

CASTEL FUSANO

Grande

Rac

SS8

PONTINA

LAUR

Lido di Ostia

Vitinia

Via Cristoforo Colombo

Pomezia Latina SS148

Via Pontina

1 2
2 3

Key to area map symbols is located in HOW TO USE THIS BOOK

SIENA

SOUTH CENTRAL ITALY

13

Cortona

1 2

A

B

Massa Marittima

Roccastrada

Montepulciano

Castiglione di L.

Lago Trasimeno

PE

Pienza

Chianciano Terme

Città della Pieve

Ma

Castel d.Piano

1938

Abbadia S.Salvatore

U

GROSSETO

Ombrone

Acquapendente

Orvieto

B

Manciano

M. Volsini

Lago di Bolsena

Bolsena

Montefiascone

C

Capodimonte

Porto S.Stefano

Orbetello

Monte Argentario

Ansedonia

Port 'Ercole

Montalto di Castro

VITERBO

Tuscania

ne

Giglio Porto

I. del Giglio

L. di Vico

I bis

Ca

Tarquinia

M. Sab

Lago Braccia

Sutri

C

Civitavecchia

Bracciano

D

S. Marinella

S. Severa

Cervéte

Ladispoli

Fregene

Fiumicino

Lido di Ro (Ostia)

M A R E

(TYRRHENIAN SEA)

D

E

T I R R E N O

0 10 20 30 40 50 km

0   10   20   30 miles

E

F

240

1 2

2 3

Key to area map symbols is located in HOW TO USE THIS BOOK

Excursions

Environs of Rome

The rolling Roman *campagna,* or countryside, is almost as rich in historical associations as the city itself, and contains important monuments dating from late Antiquity to more recent times. It also offers extensive areas of outstanding natural beauty.

The Etruscans, who settled along the coast before the beginning of the Latin Era, have left fascinating tombs in the wide open plains and windswept plateaux around Cervéteri and Tarquinia — luxurious treasure-houses of this long-vanished civilization.

Temples, villas and other traces of the skill and splendor of Ancient Roman civilization can still be seen toward the coast at Ostia Antica and in the Castelli Romani (SE of Rome), as well as at Albano Laziale, Palestrina and Tivoli, where Adrian built his sumptuous villa. The Castelli can also boast a scattering of pleasant and interesting hillside towns, such as Castel Gandolfo, Frascati, Grottaferrata, Marino and Nemi, which are celebrated for their white wines and scenic views over crater-lakes and valleys. This is also the setting for a number of important Renaissance and Baroque *palazzi* of aristocratic Roman familes. To the NW of the city, on the way to Viterbo, the fairy-tale castle of the Orsini dominates another volcanic lake, Bracciano.

This chapter also includes EUR — Mussolini's regimented dream town and Rome's last monumental occupation of the countryside.

ALBANO LAZIALE
Map **14D4** ◀ 25km (15 miles) SE of Rome. By train, 40mins from Stazione Termini. By car, Via Appia Nuova (SS7). By bus, ACOTRAL from Anagnina (on Metropolitana Line A).
The chief attractions of the Castelli Romani — Albano and the other hill towns perched on the extinct volcanoes to the SE of Rome — are their white wines and welcome coolness in the heat of summer. It was probably for the very same reasons that the Emperor Domitian kept a vast estate here with a magnificent villa. Then, at the end of the 2ndC AD, Septimius Severus, wishing to instil a little respect in his Roman subjects, established a permanent legionary camp — the Castra Albana.

The nearby civilian settlement outgrew the camp and developed into a small town. In the Middle Ages this became an important bishopric. The modern town, largely rebuilt after World War II, reveals many traces of its varied history: an **amphitheater**, the gateway to the military camp and, most remarkably, a vast Roman **cistern**, still in use for the purpose of irrigation. The **Duomo**, much abused by history, still contains fragments of the 4thC basilica, but is of less interest than the church of **San Pietro**, founded in the 6thC over the ruins of the Roman baths.

Visitors to the town may eat in the restaurant of the **Miralago** hotel *(Via dei Cappuccini 12* ☎*9322253* ▥ ▱*)* or that of **Motel del Mare** *(Via Olivella 100/104* ☎*9322335* ▥*)*.

ANZIO   During the summer months, ferries and hydrofoils link this favorite Roman resort with the even more popular island of **Ponza**, both described in FARTHER AFIELD.

BRACCIANO
Map **13***C3* ◈ *42km (26 miles) NW of Rome. By train, 1hr from Stazione Termini. By car, Via Cassia (SS2) to Madonna di Bracciano, then 493. By bus, ACOTRAL from Via Lepanto (on Metropolitana Line A).*
The small town stands high over **Lake Bracciano**, an almost circular expanse of water that fills a volcanic crater in the Sabatini hills. A drive of 35km (22 miles) takes you right round the lake, passing the picturesque village of **Trevignano** and the popular resort of **Anguillara**. The shores, planted with pine and olive groves, make pleasant picnic spots and swimming areas. Bracciano itself is dominated by the **castle of the Orsini**, the former landlords of the town.

SIGHTS AND PLACES OF INTEREST

CASTELLO ORSINI 血 ★
Piazza Mazzini ☎*9024003* ▦ ✗ *compulsory. Open Tues-Sat 9am-noon, 3-6pm (Oct-Mar 3-4pm). Closed Sun, Mon.*
This magnificent example of a Renaissance private castle was completed about 1485. Its polygonal shape and five slender circular towers give it a certain austere grace, yet its battlemented walls were strong enough to withstand a determined assault carried out by the troops of Alexander VI, the Borgia pope.

Many of the rooms on show still boast their original frescoes and contain a wide assortment of family heirlooms of the Orsini and the Odescalchi (the present owners). These include some good Etruscan relics and a fascinating collection of arms and armor. (☎ to check that the castle is open — it is a popular movie set.)

Both reasonably priced are **Casina del Lago** *(Via Lungolago Argenti 1* ☎ *9024025* ▥ *closed Tues)* and **Selene** *(Via Claudia 115* ☎*9024040* ▥*)*.

CASTEL GANDOLFO
Map **14***D4* ◈ *25km (15 miles) SE of Rome. By train, 35mins from Stazione Termini. By car, Via Appia Nuova (SS7). By bus, ACOTRAL from Anagnina (on Metropolitana Line A).*
Superbly situated at 426m (1,400 feet), overlooking **Lake Albano**, the summer residence of the Pope enjoys a wonderful view of the wooded

slopes that plunge steeply down into the dark green waters of the volcanic crater. Castel Gandolfo is thought to be the site of the legendary Alba Longa, the most powerful city of the Latin League until it was superceded by the upstart Rome. The cheerful but far from prosperous little town shows no trace of its glorious prehistory, nor do the down-to-earth inhabitants pay particular attention to their most illustrious resident.

SIGHTS AND PLACES OF INTEREST

PALAZZO PAPALE 🏛
Piazza della Libertà.
Built in 1624 by Carlo Maderno on the orders of Urban VIII, the palace was radically altered and enlarged earlier this century by Pius XI. The original facade, however, was left untouched. During the summer and fall, when the Pope is in residence, Swiss Guards stand on duty outside its great central portal. General audiences are held in the modern hall of the **Villa Cybo** at 11am on Wednesday, but you must apply to the Vatican for tickets (see PAPAL AUDIENCES, page 45). At noon on Sunday the Pope gives an address in the courtyard of the palace, for which no permit is required.

🍴 🛏 The **Garden** hotel has a decent restaurant, **La Perla** (*Via Spiaggia al Lago 6* ☎ *9360064* 🆃🆇 *616244* 🅵🆇 *4817912* 🎢).

CERVÉTERI
Map **13**D3. *46km (28 miles) NW of Rome. By train, 1hr 10mins from Stazione Termini or 50mins from Roma Tiburtina to Cervéteri-Ladíspoli, then take local bus. By car, Via Aurelia (SS1) or Autostrada A12. By bus, ACOTRAL from Via Lepanto (on Metropolitana Line A).*
The chief interest of Cervéteri lies not in the remains of the medieval town, but in the fact that, as Caere, it was one of the wealthiest and most powerful cities of the Etruscan Federation. Etruscan cities are known to have been well planned, with fine temples and public amenities, but hardly anything remains of them, mainly because the houses were built of wood. Archeological discoveries in the 18th and 19thC opened up a marvelous lost Etruscan world, for this quite extraordinary civilization built necropolises of stone, with paved streets between long rows of *tu-muli*.

6thC terracotta **sarcophagus** from Cervéteri, on view at the Villa Giulia museum.

Just 2km (1 mile) N of Cervéteri, in the open country known as the **Banditaccia**, lies one of the finest of these cities of the dead.

SIGHTS AND PLACES OF INTEREST

NECROPOLI DELLA BANDITACCIA 🏛 ★
☎9950003 ▨ 𝄞 ➡ Open Tues-Sun, 9am-1hr before sunset. Closed Mon.
Do not be disappointed by your first sight of the tombs, which resemble beehives
thatched with grass. All the ornamentation was reserved for the inside, where the
sarcophagi of the Etruscan nobility were surrounded with worldly goods — food,
drink, jewelry and weapons — while the walls were painted to remind them of the
pleasures of this life, with scenes of banquets, dancing, fishing, swimming and all
manner of sporting activities. Only a few of the finest tombs are lit and, as
tomb-robbing is still a flourishing profession, all their portable relics have been
removed to museums.

Many of the tombs are constructed as exact replicas of houses. The **Tomb of
the Seats and Shields** has no fewer than seven chambers. The seats after which
it is named are carved from the living rock, complete with footrests. Originally they
would have supported effigies of the deceased husband and wife.

Unfortunately the most fascinating of all the tombs, the **Tomb of the Reliefs**,
is now closed to the public, but special permission to visit it can be obtained in
Rome from the VILLA GIULIA. One of its painted stucco reliefs depicts beautifully
detailed scenes of animal life, and the central pillars are decorated with an inventory
of Etruscan household equipment, including knives, spoons, ladles and axes.

A tour can take 2-4 hours, depending on how many of the major tombs are
open, so it is wise to bring some refreshment with you. The spirits of the Etruscan
dead will certainly not object: they would be more likely to take it as a mark of
respect.

EUR
Map 11E3 ✿ 6km (4 miles) s of Rome. By car, Via Cristoforo Colombo (Porta
Ardeatina). By Metropolitana, Line B. By bus, 93 from Stazione Termini or 97
from Piazza Sonnino (Trastevere).
The initials stand for Esposizione Universale Romana, a grandiose project sponsored by Mussolini as a permanent exhibition to the glory of
Rome, as renewed by the cleansing power of Fascism. Its intended
opening in 1942 was prevented by the war, and work did not begin
again in earnest until 1952. The large modern buildings are laid out on
an expansive plan, and even today the wide spaces are practically
empty of traffic and pedestrians. The structure that will most interest
students of modern architecture is the **Palazzo dello Sport**, built for
the·1960 Olympics. The dome, with a span of 100m (330 feet), is the
work of the great engineer, Pier Luigi Nervi.

For children (with a lot of money in their pockets) there is a permanent
fairground, **Luna Park**, to the left as you enter EUR along Via Cristoforo
Colombo. The central area above the artificial lake consists almost
entirely of ministries and museums.

SIGHTS AND PLACES OF INTEREST

MUSEO DELLE ARTI E TRADIZIONI POPOLARI
Piazza Marconi 8 ☎5926148 ▨ Open Tues-Sat 9am-2pm; Sun 9am-1pm. Closed Mon.
A vast collection of artifacts illustrating every aspect of Italian life at the turn of the
century. Particularly interesting are the sections on agriculture and traditional
costumes.

MUSEO DELLA CIVILTÀ ROMANA ★

Piazzale Giovanni Agnelli 10 ☎*5926135* ▨ *Open Tues, Thurs 9am-2pm, 5-8pm; Wed, Fri, Sat 9am-2pm; Sun 9am-1pm. Closed Mon.*

The museum was a gift from FIAT to the city of Rome and houses a large collection of plaster-casts of famous monuments and statues, including the entire series of reliefs from **Trajan's Column**.

MUSEO PREISTORICO ED ETNOGRAFICO LUIGI PIGORINI

Viale Lincoln 1 ☎*5910702* ▨ *Open Tues-Fri 9am-2pm; Sat 9am-6pm; Sun 9am-1pm. Closed Mon.*

One of the most comprehensive collections of its kind in the world, the Museo Preistorico charts the development of the Stone, Bronze and Iron Ages, with particular reference to Italy and the Aegean.

═ EUR's eating places tend to be expensive and ostentatious. Less pretentious than some is **Shangri-La** *(Viale Algeria 141* ☎*5918861* ▥ ▨ ▣ ▨ *).*

FRASCATI

*Map **14D4** ◀€ 22km (14 miles) SE of Rome. By train, 30mins from Stazione Termini. By car, Via Tuscolana (SS215). By bus, ACOTRAL from Anagnina (on Metropolitana Line A).*

A sizeable town of 22,000 inhabitants, Frascati is the best-known of the Castelli Romani, famous for its white wines and its villas. It suffered heavy damage during bombing in World War II, when the Germans made the town their headquarters in the defense of Rome. Several buildings of note, including the cathedral of **San Pietro**, were rebuilt after the war. Frascati is an ideal place for a day's outing from the city, with splendid views across the Roman *campagna*. In the sweeping panorama from the town's main square, **Piazza Marconi**, you will see the gardens of the **Villa Torlonia** (now a public park) and the magnificent avenue of clipped trees that sweeps up to the entrance of the **Villa Aldobrandini**. There are several other equally fine estates, but these are the only ones you are allowed to visit.

SIGHTS AND PLACES OF INTEREST

VILLA ALDOBRANDINI ▥

Via Cardinale Massaia ▨ *Tickets must be obtained from the Azienda di Soggiorno (local tourist office), Piazza G. Marconi* ☎*9420331. Open Mon-Sat 9am-1pm. Closed Sun.*

The villa is closed to the public, but from the terrace there is a glorious view of the whole city of Rome, stretching away to the NW. The building was begun at the end of the 16thC by Giacomo della Porta, but is not as spectacular as the park, which has dense groves of ilex, ornamental gardens, statues, grottoes and fountains.

═ Both popular are **Cacciani** *(Via Diaz 13* ☎*9420378* ▥ ▭ ▤ ▥ ▨ *)* and **Spartaco** *(Viale Letizia Bonaparte 1* ☎*9420431* ▥ ▭ ▤ ▥ ▨ ▣ *).*

GROTTAFERRATA

*Map **14D4**. 21km (13 miles) SE of Rome. By car, Via Tuscolana (SS215), then 511. By bus, ACOTRAL from Anagnina (on Metropolitana Line A).*

The great attraction of Grottaferrata, which would otherwise be the most peaceful of the Castelli Romani, is its famous abbey. This looks more like a moated castle than a monastery, but the real reason for its celebrity is the fact that the liturgy of its Basilian monks is Greek. Since its foundation in 1004, the Abbey has been a center of Greek scholarship, but it was only 100 years ago that the pope again allowed the use of a completely Byzantine rite.

The services, those in Holy Week in particular, are noted for their color and spectacle.

SIGHTS AND PLACES OF INTEREST

GROTTAFERRATA ABBEY ▥ ✝

Corso del Popolo ☎ *945309* ⊡ ✗ *compulsory. Visitors should make a donation. Open 9am-12.30pm, 4.15-7pm.*

On crossing the bridge, you should ring the bell. One of the monks will come to show you around the monastery, with its **library** of rare Greek texts and **museum** of ecclesiastical treasures. Giuliano della Rovere, before he became Pope Julius II, was Abbot of Grottaferrata. The warlike cardinal was responsible for much of the fortification, and the fine portico of the monastery by Sangallo bears his crest.

Returning to the main courtyard of the abbey, you go left to visit the church of **Santa Maria** with its magnificent 12thC campanile. Most of the interior is Baroque, and in the **Chapel of San Nilo**, dedicated to the founder of the abbey, there is a series of **frescoes** (★) by Domenichino.

━ᴈ The wine of Grottaferrata is highly regarded by connoisseurs of the Castelli vineyards and may be enjoyed under the pine trees of **Al Fico** *(Via Anagnina 134* ☎ *9459214* ▥ ▭ ➤ 🛋 AE ⊙ *).*

Alternatively, you can eat at **Taverna dello Spuntino** *(Via Cicerone 20* ☎ *9459336* ▤ ✿ ▥ *)* or **La Cavola d'Oro** *(Via Anagnina 35* ☎ *9459955* ➤ 🛋 AE VISA ▥ *).*

LIDO DI ROMA (Ostia)

Map **13**D3. *30km (18 miles)* sw *of Rome. By train, 30mins from Porta San Paolo. By car, Via del Mare (SS8) or Via Cristoforo Colombo. By Metropolitana, from Termini (see* OSTIA ANTICA*). By bus, ACOTRAL from Via Giolitti.*

The nearest and most accessible resort to the city, Ostia — or Lido di Roma, as it is now more commonly called — becomes very overcrowded in summer. Private enterprise run riot has covered all the beaches with restaurants, bars, changing huts and video games. On Sundays, massive traffic jams tail far back along the roads to Rome. Unfortunately it is healthier to remain ashore and inhale the gasoline fumes than to dip into the Mediterranean, since pollution there is even higher.

Along the coast to the E, however, at **Castel Fusano**, there are beautiful pine woods and the sea is much cleaner. Many of the beaches there are private, but fortunately, by law, the 10m (11 yards) of sand next to the sea itself is public property.

━ᴈ Wiser Romans drive to Ostia not to swim but to eat the seafood. Mussels, crayfish, *fritto misto di mare* and *spaghetti alle vongole* are on offer at nearly every restaurant. Two recommended ones are **Ferrantelli** *(Via Claudio 7* ☎ *5625751* ▥ ▤ ▭ AE *)* and **La Nuova Capricciosa** *(Via Rutilio Namanziano* ☎ *5696250* ▥ ▭ AE *).*

MARINO

*Map **14D4** ◀€ 22km (14 miles) SE of Rome. By train, 30mins from Stazione Termini. By car, Via Appia Nuova (SS7), then Via dei Laghi (217). By bus, ACOTRAL from Cinecittà (on Metropolitana Line A).*

The vineyards of Marino produce excellent white wine, considerably stronger than you might expect from the Castelli Romani. On the first Sunday in October it literally flows in the streets at the annual *Sagra dell' Uva* (Festival of the Grape). The town is a favorite spot for outings from Rome, yet comparatively unspoiled. The beautiful road that climbs from the town in the direction of NEMI reaches over 600m (2,000 feet) and gives a glorious view across **Lake Albano** to the hills beyond.

🍴 Many of the simple *osterie* serve only wine but, if asked, are only too pleased to let you eat your own food. Try some of the cold pork on sale at roadside stalls, where the pigs are roasted whole and sliced to order. For a more substantial meal to accompany your wine, try **Antonio al Vigneto** *(Via dei Laghi* ☎ *9387034* ▥ ▭ 🍴 🚗 AE ♦ ⊙ VISA *).*

NEMI

*Map **14D4** ◀€ 34km (20 miles) SE of Rome. By car, Via Appia Nuova (SS7), then Via dei Laghi (217). By bus, ACOTRAL from Cinecittà (on Metropolitana Line A).*

The village of Nemi balances high above the road along an escarpment that falls away abruptly to **Lake Nemi** below. The lake itself is the loveliest of all the crater-lakes around Rome, its still waters reflecting the colors of the changing seasons on the surrounding wooded hills. These are famous for their wild strawberries, but the strawberries consumed in the village in their millions in early summer are, alas, all cultivated.

The name of the lake and village derives from *Nemus Dianae* (the Grove of Diana), which has been identified with the site of a temple overlooking the lake's NE shore. The primitive cult of the goddess, with its homicidal rite of succession to the priesthood, was the starting point of Frazer's great anthropological treatise *The Golden Bough*.

Throughout Roman times the lake was known as the Mirror of Diana, and festivals in her honor reached such a scale that Caligula built two huge ships to navigate its restricted waters. These, not surprisingly, sank and lay beneath the lake for nearly 1,900 years. They were eventually raised in 1932, but were then tragically burned in World War II.

🍴 During the strawberry festival in June, you have little hope of finding somewhere to eat. At other times of the year, try **Lo Specchio di Diana** *(Corso Vittorio Emanuele 13* ☎ *9378016* ▥ ▭ 🚗 *)*, with its terrace overlooking the lake.

OSTIA ANTICA

*Map **13D3**. 25km (15 miles) SW of Rome. By train, 30mins from Porta San Paolo. By car, Via del Mare (SS8). By Metropolitana, from Termini, only three trains per day depart, at 8.03am, 9.03am and 10.03am, returning at 1.14pm, 5.24pm and 6.24pm. By bus, ACOTRAL from Via Giolitti.*

The ruins of Ostia provide a fascinating insight into daily urban life in Roman times. After the 2ndC AD, the prosperity of Ostia, until then the main port of Rome, began a steady decline. From the time of Constantine, Rome's other port (Portus Romae, on the other side of the Tiber) handled more and more of the city's shipping. The Barbarian invasions and endemic malaria finally killed off the town completely, and its ruins were buried in the sand that has so magically preserved it. As at POMPEII (see FARTHER AFIELD), you have the sensation that the clock has been turned back nearly 2,000 years. In summer, a visit in the late afternoon is preferable, as there is little shade among the ruins.

SIGHTS AND PLACES OF INTEREST

SCAVI DI OSTIA ANTICA 🏛

☎5650022 🎫 ➥ *Open Tues-Sun 9am-1hr before sunset. Closed Mon.*

You enter the excavations at the Porta Romana, then follow the long main street, the Decumanus Maximus. The first large public building you will come to is the expertly restored **Theater** (★). From here you overlook the **Piazzale delle Corporazioni**, where the important traders and shippers had their offices, many paved with beautiful mosaics indicating the nature of their business. The chief commodity was corn, but they also imported such luxuries as ivory (which is illustrated by an elephant).

Farther along the Decumanus Maximus you reach the **Capitolium** (★), high above steps that are now brick but were once faced with rich marble. Sited at the end of the **Forum**, it was a temple dedicated to Jupiter and Minerva, begun during the reign of Hadrian (AD117-138).

Of particular interest at Ostia today are the remains (★) of the **insulae** (apartment blocks), often four or five stories high. Similar blocks are known to have existed in contemporary Rome, but there not one has survived. They were robustly built of brick, decently lit, well supplied with running water, and had sanitation on every floor. Most of the population lived in apartments, for only rich merchants could afford to build themselves villas. The larger *insulae* had integrated rows of shops, as did the enormous **horrea** (warehouse). The well-preserved **laundry** and **wine shop** should also be visited.

Two splendid private houses that must be seen are the **House of Cupid and Psyche** (★), w of the Capitolium, and the **House of the Dioscuri** (★), at the sw end of the town. The former has a fine **nymphaeum** (loggia), while in the latter there are mosaics of Castor and Pollux and of Venus, as well as a complete sequence of baths.

🍴 Most tourists end up eating under the trellis of **Allo Sbarco di Enea** *(Via dei Romagnoli 675* ☎*5650034* 🎟 ⌷ 🚗 ➥*)* or at **Monumento** *(Piazza Umberto I, 8* ☎*5650021* 🔲 🖌*).*

PALESTRINA

*Map **14**D4* ◄ *38km (23 miles)* SE *of Rome. By car, Via Casilina (SS6) then 155. By bus, ACOTRAL from Anagnina Metropolitana station.*

Many people today are familiar with Palestrina as the birthplace of the great 16thC composer, who took his name from the town. The reasons for its fame in Classical times date back to prehistory. By the 7thC BC, Praeneste, as it was then called, was a thriving community and an important religious center for the Etruscans. Subsequently the Romans also went there to consult its celebrated oracle, and in the 2ndC BC they built the enormous and prestigious **Temple of Fortune**. In a major feat of engineering, great terraces were projected from the hillside, supported on huge arches. Only after the bomb damage of World War II did archeologists realize the full extent of the temple, most of which is concealed by the medieval town.

The heart of the town is **Piazza Regina Margherita**, flanked by the **cathedral** and the weathered facade at the **Sala Absidata**, an impressive assortment of ancient stones and columns. Nobody is certain to what use the Romans put it. Only traces of the original Romanesque exterior of the cathedral remain, while the interior is pleasant, if unoriginal, Baroque. The crypt, however, reveals massive Roman foundation stones, probably those of the Sanctuary of Juno.

Even on the hottest summer's day, you will want to make the steep climb up the terraces to where the **Palazzo Colonna Barberini** follows the original lines of the Rotunda of the Temple of Fortune. From the fourth terrace the view out across the valley between the Alban Hills and the Monti Lepini still excites the awe that made Praeneste one of the most revered shrines of Classical Italy. The interior of the palace has been redesigned to house the **Archeological Museum**.

SIGHTS AND PLACES OF INTEREST

MUSEO NAZIONALE ARCHEOLOGICO PRENESTINO ☆
Piazza della Cortina ☎ *9558100* ✉ *Open Tues-Sat 9am-1.30pm; Sun 9am-noon. Closed Mon.*

Although many of the more valuable finds at this site have been transferred to the VILLA GIULIA in Rome, the museum's collection gives a fascinating picture of the early history of Praeneste. Its prize exhibit is the Roman mosaic of *The Nile in Flood,* which once decorated the floor of the Sala Absidata.

▬ If you are suffering from the heat and a surfeit of Antiquity, the modern **Hotel Stella** has a very reasonable air-conditioned restaurant, the **Ristorante da Coccia** *(Piazzale della Liberazione 3* ☎ *9558172* ▯ ▯ ▯ ▯ ▯ ▯ *).*

ROCCA DI PAPA
Map **14D4** ◀◀ *27km (16 miles)* SE *of Rome. By car, Via Tuscolana (SS215), then 511 to Grottaferrata, then 218. By bus, ACOTRAL from Anagnina (on Metropolitana Line A).*

The town, so-named in the 12thC after a castle built here by the popes, stands at over 680m (2,200 feet) and is the highest of all the Castelli Romani. The lower part is modern, but the medieval quarter at the top is still a picturesque maze of crooked stairways and narrow alleys. The countryside around is excellent for walking, which, at this altitude, is agreeable even in midsummer.

Above the town soars the summit of **Monte Cavo** (949m/3,113 feet), which is visible from the eastern heights of Rome itself. The ascent can be made by road (6km/4 miles) or on foot along a mule track. This follows part of the ancient **Via Triumphalis** or Via Sacra, up which victorious Roman generals carried their spoils to the **Temple of Jupiter Latialis**.

No trace remains of the temple, once the rallying point of the entire Latin League. Its place has been taken by a hotel and a television mast. From the summit there are magnificent panoramic views across the Castelli, the lakes of Albano and Nemi and the entire *campagna* as far as the coast. To the E you can even see the snow-capped peaks of the Apennines, while to the s you can follow the coastline beyond the island of Ponza to the promontory of Circeo.

➤ If you take the road to Lake Albano, 4km (2½ miles) sw of Rocca di Papa, you will find a very pleasant restaurant in **Le Mimose** *(Via dei Laghi ☎ 949195 ▥ ▭ ⬤ ▧)*. Alternatively, in Rocca di Papa itself, with a fine view across the countryside, there's **Angolleto** *(Via del Tufo 32 ☎ 949020 ▥ ⬤ ⬤)*.

TARQUINIA
Map 13C3 ⬅ 96km (58 miles) NW of Rome. By train, 1hr 10mins from Stazione Termini. By car, Autostrada A12 to junction with SS1 (12km/7½ miles s of Tarquinia). By bus, ACOTRAL from Via Lepanto (on Metropolitana Line A).

Unlike nearby CERVÉTERI, Tarquinia is today a town of some substance with many fine medieval and Renaissance buildings. The pleasure of walking around the medieval streets and the view across gently rolling plains toward the sea would be reasons enough for a day excursion from Rome. But, of course, Tarquinia's real attraction lies in its great **Etruscan necropolis**.

Tarquinii was one of the three major cities of Etruria, the others being Vulci and Caere. It had a population of over 100,000 and formed the commercial and artistic center of the entire civilization. The finds here have been even more spectacular than at Cervéteri, but the fabulous vases, silverware and jewelry are now scattered throughout the world in museums and private collections. Many fine pieces may be seen in Rome at the VILLA GIULIA and in the VATICAN MUSEUMS.

The Necropolis stands on a high, windy plateau called Monterozzi, 4km (2½ miles) to the E of the town. You can drive straight up to the tombs, but in the morning it is better to go to the **museum** in Tarquinia, which organizes guided tours at regular intervals.

SIGHTS AND PLACES OF INTEREST

MUSEO NAZIONALE TARQUINIESE
Palazzo Vitelleschi ☎ (0766) 856036 ▨ Open Tues-Sat 9am-2pm; Sun 9am-1pm. Closed Mon.

The museum is housed in the beautiful 15thC Palazzo Vitelleschi. The **courtyard**, with its fine Gothic arcade, is used to display some of the larger exhibits. Its best-known treasure is the superb pair of **winged horses** (★) placed high on a wall, at which height they once decorated the front of an Etruscan temple. There are also many splendid sarcophagi, on which the effigies of the deceased recline, reflecting their former indulgence in their noticeably generous paunches.

In one room, several tombs have been reconstructed to house precious frescoes under controlled conditions. The dancers and musicians of the **Tomb of the Triclinium** (★) are the work of an exceptional artist, as are the athletes of the **Tomb of the Olympic Games** (★).

NECROPOLI DI MONTEROZZI 🏛 ★

✗ *compulsory (guided tours also start from the museum — see above). Open Tues-Sun 9am-7pm. Closed Mon* 🔲

Many tombs are still undiscovered or unexplored, but over the last 25 years the excavations have accelerated enormously, thanks to such modern inventions as aerial photography and the probe camera, which does away with the need to investigate each burial chamber. More than a thousand new tombs were discovered between 1958 and 1959. In a tour of about 1½ hours, you will be shown only five or six of the more famous ones. These should certainly include the **Tomb of the Augurs** (★), with its frescoes of a funeral and the attendant games. On the far wall, professional mourners strike their foreheads in attitudes of grief, while on the right, in complete contrast to this solemnity, two naked wrestlers strive vigorously to grab hold of each other. You should also see the **Tomb of the Leopards** (★), the walls of which depict a variety of scenes from a banquet, a subject close to the Etruscan heart. You will notice that all the men are colored reddish-brown, while the women are always white with blonde hair.

▬ An excellent meal, if not an Etruscan banquet, can be had at **Solengo**, the restaurant of the modern **Hotel Tarconte** *(Via Tuscia 19* ☎ *(0766) 856585* 🔲 *612172*▥⬜ 🖵 🍴 🔲 🔲 *)*; there is also **Il Bersagliere** *(Via Benedetto Croce 2* ☎ *856047*▥⬜ 🍴 🔲 ⬛ 🔧 *)*.

TIVOLI

Map **14**D4 ⬿ *38km (23 miles)* E *of Rome. By train, 40mins from Stazione Termini. By car, Via Tiburtina (SS5): Villa Adriana lies to the right, 6km (3½ miles) before you reach the town. By bus, ACOTRAL from Via Gaeta: inquire which buses go nearest to Villa Adriana.*

Modern Tivoli is an attractive, lively town of some 45,000 inhabitants. It stands on the Aniene, a tributary of the Tiber, overlooking Rome from the slopes of the Sabine Hills. In order to prevent flooding, the river has been diverted through a tunnel, from which it emerges in a spectacular cascade. This is enclosed in the park of Villa Gregoriana.

In Classical times called Tibur, it was here that wealthy Romans built their magnificent summer villas. The most splendid of these, **Hadrian's Villa**, now competes for the considerable tourist trade with the **Villa d'Este**, world-renowned for its terraced gardens and fountains.

SIGHTS AND PLACES OF INTEREST

VILLA ADRIANA 🏛 ★

Bivio Villa Adriana, 6km (3½ miles) SW *of Tivoli* 🔲 *Open Tues-Sun 9am-1hr before sunset. Closed Mon.*

Begun in AD125 and completed ten years later, this was the largest and most sumptuous villa in the Roman Empire. Hadrian's own enjoyment of it was brief, as he was forced by illness to seek a healthier climate farther S. The Emperor was himself an accomplished architect and on his constant journeys around his dominions was inspired to reproduce his favorite buildings in the grounds of his villa. From Athens came the **Poikile**, the massive colonnade through which one enters the villa, while the **Serapeum** and **Canal of Canopus**, with its delightful caryatids, were based on the Temple of Serapis complex near Alexandria.

The charming circular building that stands surrounded by a moat is the misnamed **Maritime Theater** and was probably a summer-house where Hadrian withdrew to indulge in his favorite relaxations: poetry, music and the study of architecture. Today in the huge grounds, where lizards bask on scattered fragments of masonry, there are plenty of secluded spots to read poetry or simply to have a picnic on the grass.

Villa d'Este ★

Viale delle Cento Fontane 🚆 *Open Tues-Sun 9am-1hr before sunset; May-Sept also open 9-11.30pm with gardens floodlit. Closed Mon.*

The villa itself has reopened to the public after extensive restoration. It was built on the site of a Benedictine convent for Cardinal Ippolito d'Este II in the mid-16thC. Its fountains immediately became one of the wonders of Italy. Montaigne was here in 1580, and was much amused by the **Owl Fountain**, as was John Evelyn, the diarist, in the following century. This no longer emits screeches and birdsong, nor does the **Organ Fountain** produce music, for in the 18thC all the fountains fell into a sad state of decay. Fortunately, in recent years the Italian State has done all it can to maintain the unique display of hydraulic wizardry. From the bottom of the garden, make your way up past the ornamental pools to where three magnificent jets of water soar like silver cypresses to the level of the balustrade above, or stroll along the secluded pathway of the **Terrace of the Hundred Fountains**.

Villa Gregoriana

Largo Sant' Angelo 🚆 *Open 9am-1hr before sunset.*

Besides the *Grande Cascata,* the product of the engineering works ordered in the last century by the public-spirited Gregory XVI, this park has smaller cascades, grottoes and a fine belvedere.

🍴 Tivoli abounds in restaurants, many offering panoramic views of Rome. Popular, but reasonably good value, is the **Sibilla** *(Via della Sibilla 50* 📞 *(0774) 20281 💷 🍴).*

Farther afield

A general exodus from the city gets underway during the hot summer months, as residents and tourists take to the cool of the hills and beaches in vast numbers. On the following pages, you can take your pick from simple, one-day excursions around Rome (s to **Anzio** or N to **Viterbo** and **Orvieto**) to more ambitious sorties into the Neapolitan region (to **Pompeii and Herculaneum** or to the island of **Capri**), which will almost certainly involve an overnight stop. All the inland destinations make good winter breaks, too.

ANZIO

*Map **14**E4. 62km (39 miles) s of Rome. Population: 23,000. By train, 1hr 20mins from Stazione Termini. By car, SS148 to junction at Aprilia, then 207. By bus, ACOTRAL from Anagnina (on Metropolitana Line A)* **i** *AAST, Riviera Zanardelli 115* **☎** *9848135.*

The town of Anzio suffered extensive damage in World War II during the course of a combined Anglo-American landing, and much of the town has been rebuilt. However, the older parts close to the port have retained some character, and the port itself is lively, especially in the evenings. Judging by the amount of fresh fish and other seafood sold from harbor stalls, the local fishing industry is booming. (It is now rare to see fish being sold elsewhere in Italy: generally it is packed in ice and transported to the big cities.) The harbor has numerous fishing boats and a separate basin for yachts.

Anzio is a favorite Roman vacation resort. The Emperor Nero built a villa here, now known as **Nero's Villa** (★). You can see the ruins of this along the coast, not far from the lighthouse. It is an important archeological site and is soon to be excavated. The town also has the large Carmelite church of **Santa Teresa** — a Neo-Romanesque building dating from 1927 — and the beautifully maintained **British Military Cemetery**.

The coast running NW from Anzio has sandy beaches and several small resorts, the most important of which is **Lavinio-Lido di Enea**, where there are a number of hotels and *pensioni*. There is good swimming all along this coast, and a large campground at **Lido dei Pini**, 5km (3 miles) NW of Lavinio. On the other side of Anzio, and running E, is the twin town of **Nettuno**, with long sandy beaches and, inland, the huge **American Military Cemetery**.

In summer, ferries and hydrofoils leave Anzio daily for **Ponza** *(June 15-Sept 15)*. The chief attraction of this rugged, almost treeless island is the wonderful clarity of the sea, so different from the polluted waters along the mainland coast. Ponza is therefore a favorite place for swimming, snorkeling and subaqua fishing. For a day trip from Anzio, take the hydrofoil (1 hour 10 minutes) rather than the ferry (2 hours 30 minutes), to give more time to explore the island.

☙ **Dei Cesari** *(Via Ardeatina* **☎** *9844353 ▥□)* has sea views and a swimming pool and is open all year; **Lido Garda** *(Piazza Caboto 8* **☎** *9845389 ▥□)* is open from April to October.

◫ **Flora** *(Via Flora 9* ☎ *9846001* ▥ ▤ ᴀᴇ ◘ ◙ ✔ *)*; **Al Turcotto** *(Riviera Mallozzi 44* ☎ *9846340* ▥ ➡ ◖).

VITERBO

Map 13C3. 81km (50 miles) NW of Rome. Population: 57,000. By train, 2hrs from Stazione San Pietro. By car, Via Cassia (SS2). By bus, 1hr 30mins by ACOTRAL from Via Lepanto (on Metropolitana Line A) **i** *EPT, Piazzale dei Caduti 16* ☎ *(0761) 226161.*

Originally an Etruscan town, Viterbo was colonized by the Romans in 310BC. By the early Middle Ages it had become an important city and an episcopal see. A number of popes sought refuge here during the recurring conflict between the papacy and the Holy Roman Emperors, and in 1257 Alexander IV was the first of several pontiffs to make Viterbo his official city of residence.

SIGHTS AND PLACES OF INTEREST

The strong flavor of the Middle Ages is obvious the moment you pass through one of the graceful gateways in the well-preserved medieval walls — an impression reinforced within the quarter of **San Pellegrino**, with its solid-stone, small-windowed buildings and low, dark archways.

Viterbo is unusually rich in buildings of outstanding architectural interest. Perhaps the most famous is the 13thC **Papal Palace** (★), a fine example of Gothic civil architecture. Beside the palace is the **Cathedral of San Lorenzo**, its Baroque facade masking an essentially Romanesque structure, largely rebuilt after damage in World War II. The splendid Gothic campanile in striped white and gray stone shows the Sienese influence, and the interior is notable for its delicately carved nave capitals and fine marble floor.

Viterbo has many other lovely churches. **Santa Maria Nuova** (★) in the San Pellegrino quarter dates from the 12thC and has graceful cloisters and an external pulpit from which St Thomas Aquinas once preached. It too was heavily restored following bomb damage. **Santa Maria in Gradi** has beautiful 13thC cloisters. **San Sisto**, built in the 11thC and enlarged in the 12th and 13thC, has a magnificent campanile. The early 13thC **San Francesco**, also rebuilt after World War II, contains two fine monuments: the **Tomb of Clement IV** (died 1268) by Pietro di Oderisio and the **Tomb of Adrian V** (died 1276), attributed to Arnolfo di Cambio.

Piazza San Lorenzo (★) is an imposing square, flanked by the cathedral and Papal Palace. It occupies the site of the former Etruscan acropolis. But the real heart of the town is **Piazza del Plebiscito**, overlooked by the 13thC **Palazzo del Podestà** (with 15thC tower) and 15thC **Palazzo Comunale**. The **Municipal Museum** (▦ *open Tues-Sun 8.30am-1.30pm, 3.30-6pm, closed Mon)* is housed in the former Convent of Santa Maria della Verità and contains Etruscan objects, and a number of fine paintings including works by del Piombo and Salvator Rosa.

◈ **Balletti Park** *(at San Martino al Cimino, 6km/4 miles outside Viterbo* ☎ *(0761) 379777* ⌧ *623059* ▥ ᴀᴇ ◘ ▨ *)*; **Leon d'Oro** *(Via della Cava 36* ☎ *(0761) 344444* ▥ ᴀᴇ ◘ ◙ ▨ *)*; **Mini Palace** *(Via Santa Maria della Grotticella 2* ☎ *(0761) 239742* ⌧ *(0761) 341930* ▥ ᴀᴇ ◘ ◙ ▨ ✔ *)*.

◫ **Aquilanti** *(at La Quercia, 3km/2 miles outside Viterbo* ☎ *(0761) 341701* ▥ ▤ ᴀᴇ ▨ *)*; **12L** *(Via Carioli 24* ☎ *(0761) 235921* ▥ ᴀᴇ *)*; for excellent peasant cuisine, try **Il Richiastro** *(Via della Marrocca 18* ☎ *(0761) 223609* ▢ ❧ *)*.

ORVIETO

Map 13B3. 100km (62 miles) N of Rome. Population: 23,000. By train, 1hr 20mins from Stazione Termini. By car, Autostrada A1 ℹ AAST, Corso Cavour 36 ☎(0763) 35562.

The town of Orvieto sits proudly on a broad plinth of tufa rock, commanding magnificent views across the surrounding Umbrian countryside. It is equally famous for its cathedral and its white wine, the one a brilliant array of multicolored mosaics, the other golden and deliciously smooth. You can savor the delights of both at once by sitting outside a wine bar in **Piazza del Duomo** opposite the cathedral facade.

Originally an Etruscan town, Orvieto became a Roman colony and later, in the Middle Ages, enjoyed mixed fortunes. Its loyalty to the papacy never faltered, and it was rewarded with the motto *Fortis et fidelis* (Strong and faithful) by Adrian IV. The overwhelming impression of the town, with its winding, narrow streets, ancient houses and venerable churches, is still medieval. Orvieto is noted for its ceramics, and each Saturday there is a pottery market in **Piazza del Popolo**.

SIGHTS AND PLACES OF INTEREST

CATHEDRAL ▥ ✝ ★

This marvelous blend of Romanesque and Gothic styles is one of the finest cathedrals in the whole of Italy. The sumptuous facade (★), with its exquisite mosaics and complementary low-reliefs, is mainly the work of the Sienese architect Lorenzo Maitani, although it was completed after his death in 1330 by Andrea Pisano. The nave and aisles are in alternating courses of black and white stone.

In the N transept, the **Corporal Chapel** houses a finely-wrought **tabernacle** (★) richly studded with precious stones and containing the relics of the Miracle of Bolsena — the phenomenon that inspired Urban IV to build this cathedral. The beautifully carved and inlaid **choir stalls** and the **stained-glass window** behind them are also 14thC. In the S transept, in the **Chapel of San Brizio**, are frescoes of *The Apocalypse* (★) begun by Fra Angelico and continued by Luca Signorelli.

OTHER SIGHTS

Although the cathedral dominates the town architecturally, there are other buildings that are well worth seeing. The **Papal Palace** (★) is a severe yet handsome structure to the right of the cathedral, dating from the time of **Boniface VIII** (1294-1303). The **Great Hall** on the first floor houses the **Cathedral Museum** (▨ *open Tues-Sun 9am-noon, 2-4pm (summer 6pm); closed Mon)*. Also notable are the **Palazzo del Popolo**, begun in the 11thC, modified in 1280 and recently restored, and **San Bernardino**, a charming Baroque monastic church.

☙ **La Badia** *(at La Badia, 5km/3 miles outside Orvieto ☎(0763) 90359 ▥ ▬ ▤ 🆗 ▥ ▥ ✍)* is beautifully situated in a 12thC monastery; **Maitani** *(Via Maitani 5 ☎(0763) 42001 ▥ 564021 ▥ ▤ 🆗 ▥ ▥ ✍)* is close to the cathedral, with quiet rooms.

≡ **Maurizio** *(Via del Duomo 78 ☎41114 ✍)*, closed Tuesday and January. **Dell' Ancora** *(Via di Piazza del Popolo 7/11 ☎42766 ▤ ▤ 🆗 ▥ ▥)*.

POMPEII AND HERCULANEUM

See map on page 260. Pompeii, 237km (147 miles) SE of Rome. Population 23,000. Herculaneum (modern name Ercolano), 224km (140 miles) SE of Rome.

Population 58,000. By train, from Stazione Termini to Napoli Centrale, then 5mins' walk to Circumvesuviana station for local train to Ercolano or Pompeii Scavi (allow 3-3½hrs for total journey). By car, Autostrada A2 to Naples, then S18, S70. By tourist bus, inquire at CIT, Piazza della Repubblica 68 ☎47941. Both sites ☒ ✗ Open Tues-Sun 9am-1hr before sunset; closed Mon i Pompeii: AAST, Via Sacra 1 ☎(081) 8631041 i Herculaneum: EPT, Via Partenope 10a, Naples ☎(081) 418988.

POMPEII

The eruption of Vesuvius in AD79, which submerged Pompeii, Herculaneum and Stabiae, was a tragedy for the 2,000 inhabitants who died and the thousands more who lost their homes, but a boon for 20thC archeologists. It created an almost perfect time capsule, sealing in for many centuries an important cross-section of ancient civilization. Before the catastrophe, Pompeii was an old-established city with a polyglot population of about 25,000 that reflected successive waves of colonization: Oscan, Greek, Samnite and Roman. By 80BC it was a favorite resort of affluent Romans — Cicero, for example, had a villa here. Although the ruins were discovered in the 16thC and excavations of a kind began in 1763, systematic excavation did not get under way until 1911. Since then about three-fifths of the site has been revealed.

As you stroll through the narrow lanes of the city now, and walk in and out of the buildings, it is not hard to imagine yourself in the 1stC AD. The walls are covered in *graffiti,* ranging from erotic drawings to political slogans: a local election was taking place when the eruption occurred.

The rich Pompeiians lived in style, as you can tell from the grander houses with their spacious rooms, elegant courtyards and abundant frescoes. The **House of the Faun** (✮) and **House of the Vettii** (✮) — in the residential area N of the **Forum** — are among the most magnificent examples. The bronze statuette of the *Faun* in the former is a copy of the original, now in the National Archeological Museum in Naples. The House of the Vettii belonged to a couple of rich Roman merchants; it has some of the finest ancient frescoes in existence, depicting mythological scenes with nymphs and *putti.* Other particularly luxurious residences are the **House of Menander** (to the E of the Forum), which takes its name from the painting of the poet Menander, and the **Villa of the Mysteries** (✮), a suburban residence to the W of the main town, which contains paintings of secret Dionysiac rites. The **House of Pansa** (to the N of the Forum) is a large, symmetrically-planned building that included rented apartments.

The Dionysos cult was only one of many that flourished in the city. The **Temple of Isis**, to the E of the Forum, testifies to the strong following that the Egyptian goddess had here. More important still (and both forming part of the Forum) are the **Temple of Jupiter** and **Temple of Apollo** (✮), the latter with a superb colonnade and dramatic backdrop of Vesuvius. Other public buildings include the **amphitheater**, in the E of the city, begun c.80BC and the first in Italy to be built of stone; the **odeon** (✮), just E of the **Temple of Isis**, a small covered theater dating from the same period; and the **basilica** (✮), in the Forum, the largest building in Pompeii, where legal matters were hammered out, judgments pronounced and commercial transactions made. The most up-to-date building in the city at the time of the eruption was the **Stabian Baths** (★), E of the Forum, with spacious rooms, elaborate bathing facilities and sophisticated heating arrangements.

HERCULANEUM (Ercolano)

Lying 27km (17 miles) to the NE of Pompeii, Herculaneum was a much smaller town, with only 5,000 inhabitants. Unlike Pompeii, it had virtually no commerce and its industry was restricted to fishing. The volcanic mud that flowed through every building and street in Herculaneum was different from that which buried Pompeii; it settled eventually to a depth of 12m (40 feet) and set rock-hard, sealing and preserving everything with which it came into contact.

The absence of the hail of pumice and hot ash that rained down on Pompeii, smashing and burning its buildings, meant that many of the inhabitants of Herculaneum were able to get away in time, and that complete houses, with their woodwork, household goods and furniture, were preserved.

Although Herculaneum was a relatively unimportant town compared with Pompeii, several of the houses that have been excavated were in the luxury class, their owners perhaps being prosperous Romans seeking to pass their retirement years in the peace of a small seaside town. The most desirable residential area was in the SW, on the edge of the promontory overlooking the ocean, where terraces made the most of the sea view. Here you will find the **House of the Stags** (★), famous for its sculpted stags and drunken figure of Hercules as well as its beautiful frescoes, and to the W of this, the equally fine **House of the Mosaic Atrium** (★).

Farther to the N, the **House of the Wooden Trellis** is named after the building technique used in its construction. Next to this, the **House of the Wooden Partition** (★) is marvelously preserved, one of the most complete examples of a private residence in either town. The partition itself, now in fragments, is a screen separating the atrium from the living room. To the N of this house are the **baths**, an elaborate complex incorporating a gymnasium and assorted men's and women's baths, and to the E of them, the small but delightful **House of the Charred Furniture**. The few crafts shops that have been discovered were solely for the manufacture of luxury goods. The artisans who worked in them lived in apartment blocks clustered around the **Palestra** to the E.

✎ For those planning to stay overnight, Naples is convenient for both sites, 26km (16 miles) from Pompeii and 9km (6 miles) from Herculaneum. The **Excelsior** (*Via Partenope 48* ☎ *(081) 417111* ☒ *710043* ☒ *(081) 411743* ▥ ▤ ✦ ❑ ⌂ 🜨 ⊙ ⊙ ▦ ✿) is in the luxury class; the **Palace** (*Piazza Garibaldi 9* ☎ *(081) 264575* ☒ *720262* ▥ ▥ ⊙ ⊙ ▦ ✿) has first-class amenities.

🚅 **La Sacrestia** (*Via Orazio 116* ☎ *664186* ▥ ▥ ⊙ ⊙ ▦ ✿), elegance with a terrace; **La Cantinella** (*Via Cuma 42* ☎ *405375* ▥ ▥ ⊙ ⊙ ▦ ✿), specializing in seafood; **Giuseppone a Mare** (*Via Ferdinando Russo 13* ☎ *7696002* ▥ ▥ ⊙ ▦).

CAPRI

*See map on page 260. 200km (125 miles) s of Rome. Population: 8,000. By
train, 2hrs 30mins from Stazione Termini to Napoli Centrale, then taxi or bus to
Mole Beverello for ferry or hydrofoil to the island. By car, Autostrada A2 to
Naples, then ferry or hydrofoil from Mole Beverello (tourist cars are not allowed
on the island). By tourist bus, inquire at CIT, Piazza della Repubblica 68 ☎47941
i AAST, Piazzetta Ignazio Cerio 11 ☎(081) 370424.*

The population of Capri fluctuates perhaps more than that of any other
island in the world. In summer, apart from the temporary residents on
vacation, there is the daily invasion of tourists from the mainland. In
winter, life reverts to the dreamy pace that was so characteristic of
Capri over the centuries until 20thC tourism jolted it from its slumbers.

From **Marina Grande**, the main harbor, take the funicular up to the
town of **Capri**, where you can enjoy a memorable view across the **Bay
of Naples** from **Piazza Umberto I**, famous meeting place of movie and
opera stars. On the NE tip of the island is a remarkable relic of ancient
Roman times, the ruined **Palace of Tiberius** (★). It is perched on a
dizzying cliff-top from which the Emperor is said to have thrown his
enemies. The longish walk from the town of Capri is rewarded by
spectacular views. On the s edge of the town is the **Certosa di San
Giacomo**, a 14thC Carthusian monastery now largely in ruins. Another
atmospheric place is the **Parco Augusto** (★), with its dramatic series of
belvederes and a fine view to the s. From here, a road leads to the **Marina
Piccola** (Small Harbor). Between here and the SE tip of the island are
many places where you can swim from the rocks in crystal-clear water.

Anacapri is another charming town, perched high up on a rocky
plateau, its flat-roofed buildings distinctly Moorish in style. The 18thC
church of **San Michele** (★) is remarkable for its majolica pavement
depicting the *Garden of Eden*. Nearby is the romantic **Villa San Michele**
(★), with a beautiful garden and a rich collection of Classical sculpture.
From Anacapri you can walk or take a chair lift up to **Monte Solaro**,
which has amazing views across the entire island and toward **Ischia**.

Natural features include the famous **Grotta Azzurra** or **Blue Grotto**.
Visitors are taken from Marina Grande by motorboat and transferred to
rowboats to enter the grotto. The silver-blue color of the water is caused
by refraction of light entering the grotto from an opening beneath the
surface. Equally beautiful are the three limestone rock pinnacles known
as the **Faraglioni** that soar almost vertically out of the sea, and the **Arco
Naturale**, an arch of rock carved by wind erosion, just off the E shore.

Walking is by far the best way of getting about the island, but
horse-drawn carriages and buses operate, the latter linking Capri and
Anacapri, and Marina Grande and Marina Piccola.

🕿 **Quisisana** (*Via Camerelle 2, Capri* ☎(081) 8370788 ⊠ 710520 ⊠(081)
8376080 ▥ ▦ ◻ ◲ ⊞ ◉ ▣ ▨ ✻) is ultraluxurious, with swimming pool
and good views; **La Vega** (*Via Occhio Marino 10, Capri* ☎(081) 8370481
⊠ 710531 ▥ ⊞ ◉ ▣ ▨).

▬55 **Da Gemma** (*Via Madre Serafina 6, Capri* ☎(081) 8370461 ▥ ⊞ ◉
▣ ▨); **La Pigna** (*Via Lo Palazzo 30, Capri* ☎(081) 8370280 ▥ ⊞ ◉ ▣ ▨).

Travelling is the ruin of all happiness! There's no looking
at a building here after seeing Italy.
(*Cecilia*, Fanny Burney)

Words and phrases

A guide to Italian

This glossary covers the basic language needs of the traveler: for essential vocabulary and simple conversation, finding accommodations, visiting the bank, shopping and using public transportation or a car. There is also a special menu decoder, explaining all the most common descriptions of food terms.

REFERENCE WORDS

Monday	*lunedì*	Friday	*venerdì*
Tuesday	*martedì*	Saturday	*sabato*
Wednesday	*mercoledì*	Sunday	*domenica*
Thursday	*giovedì*		

January	*gennaio*	July	*luglio*
February	*febbraio*	August	*agosto*
March	*marzo*	September	*settembre*
April	*aprile*	October	*ottobre*
May	*maggio*	November	*novembre*
June	*giugno*	December	*dicembre*

1	*uno*	12	*dodici*	30	*trenta*
2	*due*	13	*tredici*	40	*quaranta*
3	*tre*	14	*quattordici*	50	*cincuanta*
4	*quattro*	15	*quindici*	60	*sessanta*
5	*cinque*	16	*sedici*	70	*settanta*
6	*sei*	17	*diciassette*	80	*ottanta*
7	*sette*	18	*diciotto*	90	*novanta*
8	*otto*	19	*diciannove*	100	*cento*
9	*nove*	20	*venti*	200	*duecento*
10	*dieci*	21	*ventuno*	1,000	*mille*
11	*undici*	22	*ventidue*	2,000	*duemila*

1992/93/94   *millenovecento novantadue/tre/quattro*

First	*primo, -a*	Fourth	*quarto, -a*
Second	*secondo, -a*	One o'clock	*l'una*
Third	*terzo, -a*	Six o'clock	*le sei*

| Quarter-past.... | ....*e un quarto* | Quarter to.... | ....*meno un* |
| Half-past.... | ....*e mezzo* | | *quarto* |

Mr	*signor(e)*	Ladies	*signore, donne*
Mrs	*signora*	Gents	*signori, uomini*
Miss	*signorina*		

BASIC COMMUNICATION

Yes   *sì*

No   *no*

Please   *per favore/per piacere*

Thank you   *grazie*

I'm very sorry   *mi dispiace molto/mi scusi*

Excuse me   *senta!* (to attract attention), *permesso!* (on bus, train, etc.), *mi scusi*

Not at all/you're welcome   *prego*

Hello   *ciao* (familiar), *pronto* (on telephone)

Good morning   *buon giorno*

Good afternoon   *buona sera*

Good evening   *buona sera*

Good night   *buona notte*

Goodbye   *ciao* (familiar), *addio* (final or familiar), *arrivederci*

Morning   *mattino*

Afternoon   *pomeriggio*

Evening   *sera*

Night   *notte* (f)

Yesterday   *ieri*

Today   *oggi*

Tomorrow   *domani*

Next week   *la settimana prossima*

Last week   *la settimana scorsa*

....days ago   ....*giorni fa*

Month   *mese* (m)

Year   *anno*

Here   *qui*

There   *lì*

Big   *grande*

Small   *piccolo, -a*

Hot   *caldo, -a*

Cold   *freddo, -a*

Good   *buono, -a*

Bad   *cattivo, -a*

Beautiful   *bello, -a*

Well   *bene*

Badly   *male*

With   *con*

And   *e, ed*

But   *ma*

Very   *molto*

All   *tutto, -a*

Open   *aperto*

Closed   *chiuso*

Entrance   *entrata*

Exit   *uscita*

Free   *libero*

On the left   *a sinistra*

On the right   *a destra*

Straight ahead   *diritto*

Near   *vicino*

Far   *lontano*

Up   *su*

Down   *giù*

Early   *presto*

Late   *tardi*

Quickly   *presto*

Pleased to meet you.   *Molto lieto/piacere.*

How are you?   *Come sta?*

Very well, thank you.   *Benissimo, grazie.*

Do you speak English?   *Parla inglese?*

I don't understand.   *Non capisco.*

I don't know.   *Non lo so.*

Please explain.   *Può spiegare per favore.*

Please speak more slowly.   *Parli più lentamente per favore.*

My name is....   *Mi chiamo....*

I am American/English. *Sono americano/inglese, -a.*
Where is/are....? *Dov'e/dove si trova/dove sono....?*
Is there a....? *C'è un, una....?*
What? *Cosa?*
When? *Quando?*
How much? *Quanto?*
That's too much. *È troppo caro.*
Expensive *caro*

Cheap *a buon mercato*
I would like.... *Vorrei....*
Do you have....? *Avete....?*
Just a minute. *Un momento.*
That's fine/OK. *Va bene/ benissimo/OK*
What time is it? *Che ore sono?*
I don't feel well. *Non mi sento bene/sto male.*

ACCOMMODATIONS

Making a reservation by letter

Dear Sir/Madam, *Egregio Signore/Signora,*
I would like to reserve one double room *Vorrei prenotare una camera doppia* (with bathroom) *(con bagno)* — a twin-bedded room *una camera con due letti* — and one single room (with shower) *e una camera singola (con doccia)* for 7 nights from August 12 *per 7 notti dal 12 agosto.*
    We would like bed and breakfast/half board/full board *Vorremmo una camera con colazione/mezza pensione/ pensione completa* and would prefer rooms with a sea view. *e possibilmente camere con vista sul mare.*
    Please send me details of your terms with the confirmation. *Sarei lieto di ricevere dettagli del prezzo e la conferma.*
    Yours sincerely, *Cordi ali saluti,*

Arriving at the hotel

I have a reservation. My name is....
Ho già prenotato. Sono il signor/la signora....
A quiet room with bath/shower/WC/wash basin
Una camera tranquilla con bagno/doccia/WC/lavandino
....overlooking the sea/park/street/the back.
....con vista sul mare/sul parco/sulla strada/sul retro
Does the price include breakfast/tax/service?
E'tutto compreso/colazione/tasse/servizio?
This room is too large/small/cold/hot/noisy.
Questa camera è troppo grande/piccola/fredda/calda/rumorosa.
That's too expensive. Have you anything cheaper?
Costa troppo. Avete qualcosa meno caro?

Floor/story *piano*
Dining room/restaurant *sala da pranzo/ristorante* (m)
Manager *direttore, -trice*
Porter *portiere*

Have you got a room? *Avete una camera?*
What time is breakfast/dinner? *A che ora è la prima colazione/la
cena?*
Is there a laundry service? *C'e il servizio lavanderia?*
What time does the hotel close? *A che ora chiude l'albergo?*
Will I need a key? *Avrò bisogno della chiave?*
Is there a night porter? *C'è un portiere di notte?*
I'll be leaving tomorrow morning. *Parto domani mattina.*
Please give me a call at.... *Mi può chiamare alle....*
Come in! *Avanti!*

SHOPPING (LA SPESA)

Where is the nearest/a good....? *Dov'è il più vicino/la più vicina....?
Dov'è un buon/una buona....?*
Can you help me/show me....? *Mi può aiutare/Può mostrarmi....?*
I'm just looking. *Sto soltanto guardando.*
Do you accept credit cards/travelers checks? *Accettate carte di
credito/travelers checks?*
Can you deliver to....? *Può consegnare a....?*
I'll take it. *Lo prendo.*
I'll leave it. *Lo lascio.*
Can I have it tax-free for export? *Posso averlo senza tasse per
l'esportazione?*
This is faulty. Can I have a replacement/refund? *C'è difetto. Me lo
potrebbe cambiare/rimborsare?*
I don't want to spend more than.... *Non voglio spendere più di....*
Can I have a stamp for....? *Vorrei un francobollo per....*

Shops

Antique store *negozio di antiquariato*	Greengrocer *ortolano, erbivendolo, fruttivendolo*
Art gallery *galleria d'arte*	Grocer *drogheria*
Bakery *panificio, forno*	Haberdasher *merciaio*
Bank *banca*	Hairdresser *parrucchiere, -a*
Beauty parlor *istituto di bellezza*	Jeweler *gioielleria*
Bookstore *libreria*	Market *mercato*
Butcher *macelleria*	Newsstand *giornalaio, edicola* (kiosk)
Cake shop *pasticceria*	Optician *ottico*
Clothes store *negozio di abbigliamento, di confezioni*	Perfumery *profumeria*
	Pharmacy/drugstore *farmacia*
Dairy *latteria*	Photographic store *negozio fotografico*
Delicatessen *salumeria, pizzicheria*	Post office *ufficio postale*
Fish store *pescheria*	Shoe store *negozio di calzature*
Florist *fioraio*	Stationers *cartoleria*
	Supermarket *supermercato*

Tailor *sarto*

Tobacconist *tabaccheria* (also sells stamps)

Tourist office *ente del turismo*

Toy store *negozio di giocattoli*

Travel agent *agenzia di viaggio*

At the bank

I would like to change some dollars/pounds/travelers checks
Vorrei cambiare dei dollari/delle sterline/dei travelers checks

What is the exchange rate?
Com'è il cambio?

Can you cash a personal check?
Può cambiare un assegno?

Can I obtain cash with this charge/credit card?
Posso avere soldi in contanti con questa carta di credito?

Do you need to see my passport?
Ha bisogno del mio passaporto?

From the pharmacy

Antiseptic cream *crema antisettica*

Aspirin *aspirina*

Bandages *fasciature*

Band-Aid, sticking plaster *cerotto*

Cotton (wool) *cotone idrofilo* (m)

Diarrhea/upset stomach pills *pillole anti-coliche*

Indigestion tablets *pillole per l'indigestione*

Insect repellant *insettifugo*

Laxative *lassativo*

Sanitary napkins *assorbenti igienici*

Shampoo *shampoo*

Shaving cream *crema da barba*

Soap *sapone* (m)

Sunburn cream *crema antisolare*

Sunglasses *occhiali da sole*

Suntan cream/oil *crema/olio solare*

Tampons *tamponi*

Tissues *fazzoletti di carta*

Toothbrush *spazzolino da denti*

Toothpaste *dentifricio*

Travel sickness pills *pillole contro il mal di viaggio*

Clothing

Bra *reggiseno*

Coat *cappotto*

Dress *vestito*

Jacket *giacca*

Pullover *maglione* (m)

Shirt *camicia*

Shoes *scarpe*

Skirt *gonna*

Stockings/tights *calze/collants*

Swimsuit *costume da bagno* (m)

Trousers *pantaloni*

Underpants *mutande*

Miscellanous goods

Film *pellicola*

Letter *lettera*

Money order *vaglia*

Postcard *cartolina*

Stamp *francobollo*

Telegram *telegramma* (m)

DRIVING

Service station   *stazione di rifornimento* (f), *distributore* (m)
Fill it up.   *Faccia il pieno, per favore.*
Give me.... lire worth.   *Mi dia.... lire.*
I would like.... liters of gasoline.   *Vorrei.... litri di benzina.*
Can you check the....?   *Può controllare....?*
There is something wrong with the....   *C'e un difetto nel/nella....*

Accelerator *acceleratore* (m)	Gear box *la scatola del cambio*
Axle *l'asse* (m)	Lights *fanali, fari, luci*
Battery *batteria*	Oil *olio*
Brakes *freni*	Spares *i pezzi di ricambio*
Exhaust *lo scarico, scappamento*	Spark plugs *le candele*
Fan belt *la cinghia del ventilatore*	Tires *gomme*
	Water *acqua*
	Windshield *parabrezza* (m)

My car won't start.   *La mia macchina non s'accende.*
My car has broken down/had a flat tire.   *La macchina è guasta/la gomma è forata.*
The engine is overheating.   *Il motore si scalda.*
How long will it take to repair?   *Quanto tempo ci vorrà per la riparazione?*
I need it as soon as possible.   *Ne ho bisogno il più presto possibile.*

Car rental

Where can I rent a car?   *Dove posso noleggiare una macchina?*
Is full/comprehensive insurance included?   *E'completamente assicurata?*
Is it insured for another driver?   *E'assicurata per un altro guidatore?*
Does the price include mileage?   *Il kilometraggio è compreso?*
Unlimited mileage   *kilometraggio illimitato*
Deposit   *deposito*
By what time must I return it?   *A che ora devo consegnarla?*
Can I return it to another depot?   *Posso riportarla ad un altro deposito?*
Is the gas tank full?   *E'il serbatoio pieno?*

Road signs

Accendere le luci in galleria
lights on in tunnel
Autostrada   4-lane highway, motorway
Caduta di massi   falling stones
Casello   toll gate
Dare la precedenza   yield, give way

Divieto di accesso, senso vietato
no entry
Divieto di parcheggio   no parking
Divieto di sorpasso   no passing
Divieto di sosta   no stopping
Lavori in corso   road repairs ahead

Passaggio a livello level crossing
Pedaggio toll road
Raccordo anulare beltway, ring road
Rallentare slow down

Senso unico one-way street
Tangenziale bypass
Tenersi in corsia keep in lane
Uscita (autocarri) exit (for trucks)

OTHER METHODS OF TRANSPORTATION

Aircraft *aeroplano*
Airport *aeroporto*
Bus *autobus* (m)
Bus stop *fermata*
Coach *corriera*
Ferry/boat *traghetto*
Ferry port *porto*
Hovercraft *aliscafo*
Station *stazione* (f)
Train *treno*

ticket *biglietto*
Ticket office *biglietteria*
One-way, single *andata*
Round trip, return *andata e ritorno*
Half fare *metà prezzo*
First/second/economy *prima classe/seconda classe/turistico*
Sleeper/couchette *cuccetta*

When is the next.... for....? *Quando parte il prossimo.... per....?*
What time does it arrive? *A che ora arriva?*
What time does the last.... for.... leave? *Quando parte l'ultimo.... per....?*
Which track (platform)/quay/gate? *Quale binario/molo/uscita?*
Is this the.... for....? *E'questo il.... per....?*
Is it direct? Where does it stop? *E'diretto? Dove si ferma?*
Do I need to change anywhere? *Devo cambiare?*
Please tell me where to get off. *Mi può dire dove devo scendere.*
Take me to.... *Mi vuol portare a....*
Is there a dining car? *C'è un vagone ristorante?*

FOOD AND DRINK

Have you a table for....? *Avete un tavolo per....?*
I want to reserve a table for.... at.... *Vorrei prenotare un tavolo per.... alle....*
A quiet table. *Un tavolo tranquillo.*
A table near the window. *Un tavolo vicino alla finestra.*
Could we have another table? *Potremmo spostarci?*
I did not order this. *Non ho ordinato questo.*
Breakfast/lunch/dinner *prima colazione/pranzo/cena*
Bring me another.... please. *Un altro.... per favore.*
The bill please. *Il conto per favore.*
Is service included? *Il servizio è incluso?*

Hot *caldo*
Cold *freddo*
Glass *bicchiere* (m)
Bottle *bottiglia*

Half-bottle *mezza bottiglia*
Beer/lager (draft) *birra (alla spina)*
Fruit juice *succo di frutta*

267

Mineral water   *acqua minerale*
Orangeade/lemonade
   aranciata/ limonata
Carbonated/noncarbonated
   gassata/non gassata
Flask/carafe   *fiasco/caraffa*
Red wine   *vino rosso, vino nero*
White wine   *vino bianco*
Rosé wine   *vino rosé*
Vintage   *di annata*
Dry   *secco*
Sweet   *dolce, amabile*
Salt   *sale* (m)
Pepper   *pepe* (m)
Oil   *olio*

Vinegar   *aceto*
Mustard   *senape* (f)
Bread   *pane* (m)
Butter   *burro*
Cheese   *formaggio*
Milk   *latte* (m)
Coffee   *caffè* (m)
Tea   *tè* (m)
Chocolate   *cioccolato*
Sugar   *zucchero*
Steak   *bistecca*
   well done   *ben cotto*
   medium   *medio*
   rare   *al sangue*

Menu decoder

Abbacchio   baby lamb
Acciughe   anchovies
Acqua cotta   thick bread and
   vegetable soup with egg
Affettati   sliced cold meats
Affumicato   smoked
Aglio   garlic
Agnello   lamb
Agnolotti   pasta envelopes
Agro   sour
Albicocche   apricots
Amaro   bitter
Ananas   pineapple
Anatra/anitra   duck
Anguilla   eel
Animelle   sweetbreads
Antipasto   hors d'oeuvre
Aragosta   langouste,
   lobster
Arancia   orange
Aringa   herring
Arrosto   roast meat
Arselle   baby clams
Asparagi   asparagus
Baccalà   dried salt cod
Basilico   basil
Bianchetti   whitebait
Bianco   plain, boiled
Bietola   Swiss chard
Biscottini di Prato   small, hard
   almond biscuits

Bistecca alla fiorentina   grilled
   T-bone steak
Bollito misto   boiled meats
Brace (alla)   charcoal grilled
Braciola   chop
Branzino   sea bass
Bresaola   dried salt beef
Brodetto   fish soup
Brodo   consommé
Bruschetta   garlic bread
Burrida   fish stew
Burro (al)   (cooked in) butter
Cacciagione   game
Cacciucco   fish stew
Calamaretti   baby squid
Calamari   squid
Calzone   half-moon-shaped
   pizza
Cannelloni   stuffed pasta tubes
Capitone   large conger eel
Cappelletti   stuffed pasta hats
Cappe sante   scallops
Capretto   kid
Carciofi alla giudia   artichokes
   fried in oil and lemon
Carne   meat
Carote   carrots
Carpa   carp
Carpaccio   raw lean beef fillet
Carrello (al)   from the trolley
Casa (della)   of the restaurant

Cassalingo, -a   homemade
Castagnaccio   chestnut cake
Castagne   chestnuts
Castrato   mutton
Cavolfiore   cauliflower
Cavolini di Bruxelles   sprouts
Cavolo   cabbage
Ceci   chick peas
Cenci   fried pastry twists
Cervella   brains
Cervo   venison
Cetriolo   cucumber
Cicoria   chicory
Ciliege   cherries
Cima   cold stuffed veal
Cinghiale   wild boar
Cipolle   onions
Cocomero   watermelon
Coda di bue   oxtail
Coniglio   rabbit
Contorno   vegetable side-dish
Controfiletto   sirloin steak
Coppa   cooked pressed neck of
   pork or an ice cream sundae
Cosciotto di agnello   leg of lamb
Costata di bue   entrecôte steak
Costolette   cutlèts
Cotto   cooked
Cozze   mussels
Crema   custard, cream soup
Crespolini   savory pancakes
Crostacei   shellfish
Crostini   small savory toasts
Crudo   raw
Diavola (alla)   in a spicy sauce
Dolci   desserts, sweets
Espresso   small black coffee
Fagiano   pheasant
Fagioli all'uccelletto   beans
   with tomatoes and garlic
Fagiolini   French beans
Faraona   guinea fowl
Farcito   stuffed
Fatto in casa   homemade
Fave   broad beans
Fegatini   chicken livers
Fegato   liver
Ferri (ai)   grilled
Fesa di vitello   leg of veal

Fettina   slice
Fettuccine   thin flat pasta
Fettunta   garlic bread
Fichi   figs
Filetto   fillet
Finocchio   fennel
Finocchiona   fennel-flavored
   salami
Focaccia   dimpled savory bread
Formaggio   cheese
Forno (al)   cooked in the oven
Fragole   strawberries
Fresco   fresh
Frittata   omelet
Frittelle   fritters
Fritto   fried
Frutta   fruit
Frutti di mare   shellfish
Funghi   mushrooms
Gamberetti   shrimps
Gamberi   big prawns
Gelato   ice cream
Giorno (del)   of the day
Girarrosto (al)   spit-roasted
Girello   topside of beef
Gnocchi   small pasta dumplings
Grana   Parmesan cheese
Granchio   crab
Granita   water ice
Graticola (alla)   grilled
Griglia (alla)   grilled
Indivia   endive
Insalata   salad
Involtini   skewered veal and
   ham
Lamponi   raspberries
Lampreda   lamprey
Lasagne   baked flat pasta
Lenticchie   lentils
Lepre   hare
Lesso   boiled (meat)
Limone   lemon
Lingua di bue   ox tongue
Lombata, -ina   loin, loin chop
Lonza   cured fillet of pork
Luccio   pike
Lumache   snails
Macedonia di frutta   fruit salad
Magro   lean

Maiale   pork
Mandorle   almonds
Manzo   beef
Marmellata   jam
Medaglioni   rounds of meat
Mela   apple
Melagrana   pomegranate
Melanzane   eggplant, aubergine
Melone   melon
Merluzzo   cod
Miele   honey
Minestra   soup
Minestrone   vegetable soup
Misto   mixed
Mostarda   pickle
Muscolo alla fiorentina   beef casserole with beans
Naturale (al)   plain
Nocciole   hazelnuts
Noci   nuts
Nodino di vitello   veal chop
Nostrale, nostrano   local
Oca   goose
Ombrina   black umber
Orata   gilt-head bream
Osso buco   veal knuckle
Ostriche   oysters
Paglia e fieno   green and white tagliatelle
Paillard   thin grilled steak
Palombo   dogfish
Panforte di Siena   hard cake with honey, fruit and almonds
Panino imbottito   roll
Panna   cream
Panzanella   salad of soaked bread and fresh vegetables
Pappa al pomodoro   thick tomato and bread soup
Pappardelle   long flat pasta
Parmigiano-Reggiano   Parmesan
Passato   purée
Pasta e fagioli   bean and pasta soup
Pasticcio   layered pasta pie
Pasto   meal
Patate   potatoes

Pecorino   hard ewes' milk cheese
Penne all'arrabbiata   short pasta tubes with a fiery sauce
Peperoni   sweet peppers
Pera   pear
Pernice   partridge
Pesca   peach
Pesce   fish
Pesce persico   perch
Pesce spada   swordfish
Pesciolini   small fry
Pesto   green basil sauce
Petto di pollo   chicken breast
Pezzo   piece
Piacere   according to taste
Piatto del giorno   today's dish
Piccante   spicy, piquant
Piccata   thin escalope
Piccione   pigeon
Pinzimonio   oily vegetable dip
Piselli   peas
Polenta   maize porridge
Pollame   poultry
Pollo   chicken
Polpette   meatballs
Polpettone   meatloaf
Polpo   octopus
Pomodoro   tomato
Pompelmo   grapefruit
Porchetta   roast sucking pig
Primizie   spring vegetables
Prosciutto   ham
Prugne   plums
Quaglie   quails
Radicchio   red bitter lettuce
Ragù   meat and tomato sauce
Rane   frogs
Ravanelli   radishes
Ravioli   stuffed pasta squares
Razza   skate
Ribollita   thick vegetable soup
Ricciarelli   almond biscuits
Ricotta   cheese — similar to cottage cheese
Rigatoni   ridged pasta tubes
Ripieno   stuffed
Risi e bisi   pea and rice soup
Riso   rice

Risotto   savory rice dish
Rognoni   kidneys
Rombo maggiore   turbot
Rosmarino   rosemary
Rospo   angler fish
Salsa (verde)   (green) sauce
Salsiccia   sausage
Saltimbocca alla romana   veal
  escalopes with ham and sage
Salvia   sage
Sarde   sardines
Scaloppine   escalopes
Scelta (a)   of your choice
Schiacciata alla fiorentina
vanilla sponge cake
Scottadito   grilled lamb cutlets
Selvaggina   game, venison
Semifreddo   frozen dessert
Semplice   plain
Seppie   cuttlefish
Sgombro   mackerel
Sogliola   sole
Sottaceti   pickled vegetables
Spaghetti all'amatriciana
  spaghetti with bacon and
  tomatoes
    alla bolognese   with *ragù*
    alla carbonara   with bacon
    and eggs
    alla napoletana   with
    tomato
Spezzatino   meat stew
Spiedini   skewers, kebabs
Spiedo (allo)   on the spit
Spigola   sea bass
Spinaci   spinach
Squadro   anglerfish, monkfish
Stagionato   hung, well-aged
Stagione (di)   in season
Stoccafisso   stockfish

Stracciatella   clear egg soup
Stracotto   beef in red wine
Stufato   braised, stew(ed)
Sugo   sauce
Supplì   rice croquettes
Susina   plum
Tacchino   turkey
Tagliatelle   thin flat pasta
Tartufi   truffles
Tegame (al)   fried or baked
Telline   cockles
Timballo   savory pasta pie
Tinca   tench
Tonno   tuna
Tordi   thrushes
Torta   flan, tart
Tortellini   small stuffed pasta
Tost   toasted sandwich
Totano   squid
Tramezzino   sandwich
Trancia   slice
Trenette   flat, thinnish pasta
Trifolato   fried in garlic
Triglia   red mullet
Trippa   tripe
Trota   trout
Uccelletti   grilled beef on
  skewers
Umido (in)   stewed
Uova   eggs
Uva   grapes
Verdure   green vegetables
Vitello   veal
Vongole   clams
Zabaglione   egg yolks and
  Marsala whip
Zuccotto   ice cream liqueur
  cake
Zuppa   soup
Zuppa inglese   trifle

271

Index

Page numbers in **bold** type indicate main entries. *Italic* page numbers refer to illustrations, plans and maps. See also the LIST OF STREET NAMES on page 289.

List of street names

All streets mentioned in this book that fall within the area covered by our maps are listed below. Map numbers are printed in **bold** type. Some smaller streets are not named on the maps, but the map reference given below will help you locate the correct neighborhood.

ITALY

N

AUSTRIA

SWITZERLAND

FRANCE

Dolomiti

Cortina

SLOVENIA

Alpi

LOMBARDIA

VENETO

Vicenza

CROATIA

Torino

Milano

Verona

Trieste

PIEMONTE

Po

Padova

Venezia

Genova

Modena

Bologna

A

MONACO

Pisa

Arno

SAN MARINO

Pesaro

MARE ADRIATICO

Livorno

Firenze

Ancona

(ADRIATIC SEA)

MARE LIGURE

(LIGURIAN SEA)

Siena

Elba

TOSCANA

Perugia

Appennini

Corsica

UMBRIA

Pescara

LAZIO

ABRUZZO

ROMA

Foggia

Bari

CAMPANIA

Napoli

PUGLIA

Brindisi

MARE TIRRENO

Capri

Taranto

Alghero

(TYRRHENIAN SEA)

SARDEGNA

Cagliari

Cosenza

CALABRIA

Messina

Palermo

Reggio di Calabria

Etna

SICILIA

Catania

Siracusa

0   50 100 150km

0   50   100miles

CONVERSION FORMULAE

To convert	Multiply by
Inches to Centimeters	2.540
Centimeters to Inches	0.39370
Feet to Meters	0.3048
Meters to feet	3.2808
Yards to Meters	0.9144
Meters to Yards	1.09361
Miles to Kilometers	1.60934
Kilometers to Miles	0.621371
Sq Meters to Sq Feet	10.7638
Sq Feet to Sq Meters	0.092903
Sq Yards to Sq Meters	0.83612
Sq Meters to Sq Yards	1.19599
Sq Miles to Sq Kilometers	2.5899
Sq Kilometers to Sq Miles	0.386103
Acres to Hectares	0.40468
Hectares to Acres	2.47105
Gallons to Liters	4.545
Liters to Gallons	0.22
Ounces to Grams	28.3495
Grams to Ounces	0.03528
Pounds to Grams	453.592
Grams to Pounds	0.00220
Pounds to Kilograms	0.4536
Kilograms to Pounds	2.2046
Tons (UK) to Kilograms	1016.05
Kilograms to Tons (UK)	0.0009842
Tons (US) to Kilograms	746.483
Kilograms to Tons (US)	0.0013396

Quick conversions

Kilometers to Miles	Divide by 8, multiply by 5
Miles to Kilometers	Divide by 5, multiply by 8
1 meter =	Approximately 3 feet 3 inches
2 centimeters =	Approximately 1 inch
1 pound (weight) =	475 grams (nearly $\frac{1}{2}$ kilogram)
Celsius to Fahrenheit	Divide by 5, multiply by 9, add 32
Fahrenheit to Celsius	Subtract 32, divide by 9, multiply by 5

ROME Metropolitana

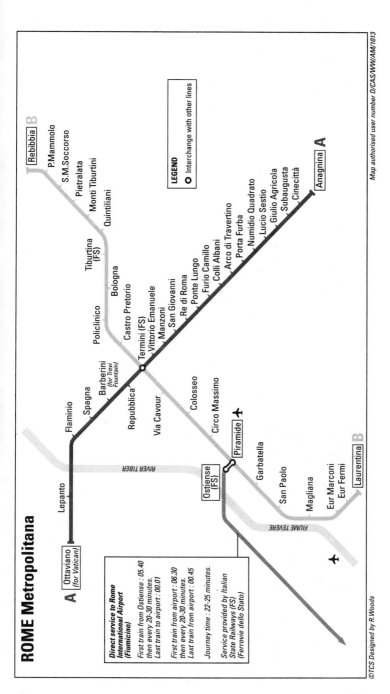

A Ottaviano (for Vatican)

Lepanto
Flaminio
Spagna
Barberini (for Trevi Fountain)
Repubblica
Via Cavour
Colosseo
Circo Massimo

Rebibbia **B**
P.Mammolo
S.M.Soccorso
Pietralata
Monti Tiburtini
Quintiliani

Tiburtina (FS)
Bologna
Policlinico
Castro Pretorio
Termini (FS)
Vittorio Emanuele
Manzoni
San Giovanni
Re di Roma
Ponte Lungo
Furio Camillo
Colli Albani
Arco di Travertino
Porta Furba
Numidio Quadrato
Lucio Sestio
Giulio Agricola
Subaugusta
Cinecittà

A Anagnina

LEGEND
○ Interchange with other lines

RIVER TIBER
FIUME TEVERE

Piramide ✈

Ostiense (FS)

Garbatella
San Paolo
Magliana
Eur Marconi
Eur Fermi

Laurentina **B**

✈

Direct service to Rome International Airport (Fiumicino)

First train from Ostiense : 05.40 then every 20-30 minutes.
Last train to airport : 00.01

First train from airport : 06.30 then every 20-30 minutes.
Last train from airport : 00.45

Journey time : 22-25 minutes.

Service provided by Italian State Railways (FS) (Ferrovie dello Stato)

Map authorised user number D/CAS/WW/AM/1013

©TCS Designed by R.Woods

295

What the papers said:

• "The expertly edited American Express series has the knack of pin-pointing precisely the details you need to know, and doing it concisely and intelligently." (*The Washington Post*)

• "*(Venice)* ... the best guide book I have ever used." (*The Standard* — London)

• "Amid the welter of guides to individual countries, American Express stands out...." (*Time*)

• "Possibly the best ... guides on the market, they come close to the oft-claimed 'all you need to know' comprehensiveness, with much original experience, research and opinions." (*Sunday Telegraph* — London)

• "The most useful general guide was *American Express New York* by Herbert Bailey Livesey. It also has the best street and subway maps." (*Daily Telegraph* — London)

• "...in the flood of travel guides, the *American Express* guides come closest to the needs of traveling managers with little time." (*Die Zeit* — Germany)

What the experts said:

• "We only used one guide book, Sheila Hale's *Amex Venice*, for which she and the editors deserve a Nobel Prize." (Eric Newby, London)

• "Congratulations to you and your staff for putting out the best guide book of *any* size *(Barcelona & Madrid)*. I'm recommending it to everyone." (Barnaby Conrad, Santa Barbara, California)

• "If you're only buying one guide book, we recommend American Express...." (*Which?* — Britain's leading consumer magazine)

What readers from all over the world have said:

• "The book *(Hong Kong, Singapore & Bangkok)* was written in such a personal way that I feel as if you were actually writing this book for me." (L.Z., Orange, Conn., USA)

• "Your book *(Florence and Tuscany)* proved a wonderful companion for us in the past fortnight. It went with us everywhere...." (E.H., Kingston-on-Thames, Surrey, England)

• "I feel as if you have been a silent friend shadowing my time in Tuscany." (T.G., Washington, DC, USA)

• "We followed your book *(Los Angeles & San Francisco)* to the letter. It proved to be wonderful, indispensable, a joy...." (C.C., London, England)

• "We could never have had the wonderful time that we did without your guide to *Paris*. The compactness was very convenient, your maps were all we needed, but it was your restaurant guide that truly made our stay special.... We have learned first-hand: *American Express — don't leave home without it.*" (A. R., Virginia Beach, Va., USA)

• "Much of our enjoyment came from the way your book *(Venice)* sent us off scurrying around the interesting streets and off to the right places at the right times". (Lord H., London, England)

• "It *(Paris)* was my constant companion and totally dependable...." (V. N., Johannesburg, South Africa)

• "I could go on and on about how useful the book *(Amsterdam)* was — the trouble was that it was almost getting to be a case of not venturing out without it...." (J.C.W., Manchester, England)

• "We have heartily recommended these books to all our friends who have plans to travel abroad." (A.S. and J.C., New York, USA)

• "Despite many previous visits to Italy, I wish I had had your guide *(Florence and Tuscany)* ages ago. I love the author's crisp, literate writing and her devotion to her subject." (M. B-K., Denver, Colorado, USA)

• "We never made a restaurant reservation without checking your book *(Venice)*. The recommendations were excellent, and the historical and artistic text got us through the sights beautifully." (L.S., Boston, Ma., USA)

• "We became almost a club as we found people sitting at tables all around, consulting their little blue books!" (F.C., Glasgow, Scotland)

• "This guide *(Paris)* we warmly recommend to all the many international visitors we work with." (M.L., Paris, France)

• "It's not often I would write such a letter, but it's one of the best guide books we have ever used *(Rome)* — we can't fault it!" (S.H., Berkhamsted, Herts, England)

American Express Travel Guides

spanning the globe....

EUROPE
Amsterdam, Rotterdam
  & The Hague
Athens and the
  Classical Sites ‡
Barcelona & Madrid ‡
Berlin ‡
Brussels #
Dublin and Cork #
Florence and Tuscany
London #
Moscow & St Petersburg *
Paris #
Prague *
Provence and the
  Côte d'Azur *
Rome
Venice ‡
Vienna & Budapest

NORTH AMERICA
Boston and New
  England *
Los Angeles & San
  Diego #
Mexico ‡
New York #
San Francisco and
  the Wine Regions
Toronto, Montréal and
  Québec City ‡
Washington, DC

THE PACIFIC
Cities of Australia
Hong Kong & Taiwan
Singapore &
  Bangkok ‡
Tokyo #

*   Paperbacks in preparation   #   Paperbacks appearing January 1993
‡   Hardback pocket guides (in paperback 1993)

Clarity and quality of information, combined with outstanding maps — the ultimate in travelers' guides

Buying an AmEx guide has never been easier....

The *American Express Travel Guides* are now available by mail order direct from the publisher, for customers resident in the UK and Eire. Payment can be made by credit card or cheque/P.O. Simply complete the form below, and send it, together with your remittance.

New paperback series (£6.99)   # Available from January 1993

- [ ] Amsterdam, Rotterdam
  & The Hague
  1 85732 918 X
- [ ] Brussels #
  1 85732 966 X
- [ ] Cities of Australia
  1 85732 921 X
- [ ] Dublin & Cork #
  1 85732 967 8
- [ ] Florence and Tuscany
  1 85732 922 8
- [ ] Hong Kong & Taiwan
  0 85533 955 1
- [ ] London #
  1 85732 968 6
- [ ] Los Angeles & San Diego #
  1 85732 919 8

- [ ] New York #
  1 85732 971 6
- [ ] Paris #
  1 85732 969 4
- [ ] Rome
  1 85732 923 6
- [ ] San Francisco and
  the Wine Regions
  1 85732 920 1
- [ ] Tokyo #
  1 85732 970 8
- [ ] Vienna & Budapest
  1 85732 962 7
- [ ] Washington, DC
  1 85732 924 4

Hardback pocket guides (£7.99)

- [ ] Athens and the Classical Sites
  0 85533 954 3
- [ ] Barcelona & Madrid
  0 85533 951 9
- [ ] Berlin
  0 85533 952 7
- [ ] Mexico
  0 85533 872 5

- [ ] Singapore & Bangkok
  0 85533 956 X
- [ ] Toronto, Montréal
  & Québec City
  0 85533 866 0
- [ ] Venice
  0 85533 871 7

While every effort is made to keep prices low, it is sometimes necessary to increase them at short notice. American Express Travel Guides reserves the right to amend prices from those previously advertised.

Please send the titles ticked above.   **ROM**

Number of titles @ £6.99 [ ]   Value: £

Number of titles @ £7.99 [ ]   Value: £
Add £1.50 for postage and packing   £   1.50

Total value of order: £
I enclose a cheque or postal order [ ] payable to Reed Book Services Ltd, or please charge my credit card account:

[ ] Barclaycard/Visa   [ ] Access/MasterCard   [ ] American Express

Card number [ ]

Signature _____   Expiry date _____

Name _____

Address _____

_____ Postcode _____

Send this order to American Express Travel Guides, Cash Sales Dept,
Reed Book Services Ltd, PO Box 5, Rushden, Northants NN10 9YX.